Exploring
1 CORINTHIANS

Exploring
1 CORINTHIANS

An Expository Commentary

JOHN PHILLIPS

kregel
PUBLICATIONS

Grand Rapids, MI 49501

Exploring 1 Corinthians: An Expository Commentary

© 2002 by John Phillips

Published in 2002 by Kregel Publications, a division of Kregel, Inc., 2450 Oak Industrial Dr. NE, Grand Rapids, MI 49505.

Scripture quotations are from the King James Version of the Holy Bible.

Library of Congress Cataloging-in-Publication Data
Phillips, John.
    Exploring 1 Corinthians: an expository commentary / by John Phillips.
        p.   cm.
    1. Bible N.T. Corinthians, 1st—Commentaries. I. Title: Exploring first Corinthians. II. Title.
BS2675.53 .P45 2002   227'.207—dc21   2001050843

ISBN 978-0-8254-3495-2

Printed in the United States of America

19 20 21 22 23 24 / 11 10 9 8

Summary Outline

Preface

"Then I saw in my dream that when they were got out of the wilderness, they [Christian and Faithful] presently saw a town before them, and the name of that town is Vanity; and at the town there is a fair kept, called Vanity Fair. It is kept all the year long. It beareth the name of Vanity Fair because the town where it is kept is lighter than vanity, and also because all that is sold, or that cometh thither, is vanity. . . .

"At this fair are all such merchandise sold as houses, lands, trades, places, honors, preferments, titles, countries, kingdoms, lusts, pleasures, and delights of all sorts, as whores, bawds, wives, husbands, children, masters, servants, lives, blood, bodies, souls, silver, gold, pearls, precious stones, and what not.

"And, moreover, at this fair there are at all times to be seen jugglings, cheats, games, plays, fools, apes, knaves and rogues, and that of every kind.

"Here are to be seen, too, and that for nothing, thefts, murders, adulteries, false swearers, and that of a blood-red color. . . ." Thus John Bunyan introduces us to a notorious place, Vanity Fair.

As Christian and Faithful made their way through this Fair all the people about them were moved to mockery. Their clothing was different for they were robed with such raiment as this world does not offer. Their speech was different for they spoke the language of Canaan. What astonished and annoyed people most, however, was their indifference to the wares that were for sale.

"They cared not so much as to look upon them," Bunyan says, "and if they called upon them to buy, they would put their fingers in their ears and cry, 'Turn away mine eyes from beholding vanity,' and look upwards, signifying that their trade and traffic were in heaven."

Little wonder, indeed, that Faithful met martyrdom in Vanity Fair. Bunyan introduces us to the jury which unanimously condemned him to death. There were Mr. Highmind, Mr. Liar, Mr. Cruelty, Mr. Hate-light, Mr. Implacable, Mr. Blindman, Mr. No-good, Mr. Malice, Mr. Love-lust, Mr. Enmity, and Mr. Heady. Christian, himself, barely escaped from Vanity Fair with his life.

We have no trouble identifying Vanity Fair. In Paul's day, it was Corinth. Paul was actually in Corinth when he wrote Romans 1:19–32. The sins listed there were everyday sins on the streets of Corinth, displayed as much in broadest daylight as at darkest midnight. It was no small thing to be a Christian at Corinth, to spurn its ways and its wares, to live there unspotted from the world.

Christianity is in no peril from the Corinths and Vanity Fairs of this world, however, just so long as it stays true to its call. Christians are safe, even in Corinth, so long as they recall that their home is in heaven and that they have become citizens of another world. Christianity was designed to enable us to make our way through this world, on our way to the world to come. It is not the water outside a ship that sinks it. A ship is designed for deep waters. It is the water that gets in that imperils a ship.

That was what imperiled the Christians at Corinth. The world had come into the church. What Paul had to say about *that* is the subject matter of his Corinthian letters.

PART 1

Introduction

1 Corinthians 1:1–9

A.	Paul sends his greetings (1:1–3)
	1.	The signature (1:1)
		a.	Paul's commission (1:1a–b)
			(1)	His status is declared (1:1a)
			(2)	His status was derived (1:1b)
		b.	Paul's companion (1:1c)

Picture yourself in the church at Corinth on the day Paul's letter arrived. In those days there were a number of gathering places for the Christians in Corinth, and of these some were in the homes of prominent believers. It was probably well known that some, who met at Chloe's house, had been to Ephesus to see Paul. Chloe herself seems to have made no secret about it. The Corinthian believers could well imagine the kinds of things Paul would be told. His informants would tell him about the squabbling, the rivalries, the immorality, the lawsuits, and the abuse of grace and gifts. Doubtless some thought Paul would drop everything and rush over to Corinth, especially since he had written to the Corinthian churches once already. An apostolic visit was nothing to take lightly, for an apostle had remarkable powers. He could smite with blindness, even death. Others thought that Paul would simply write another letter for, after all, he was not that brilliant a speaker. His letters, by contrast, were weighty and eloquent.

All debate was settled when the letter arrived. Probably some convenient, central gathering place was chosen so that one and all could come. Perhaps the house of Justus was chosen (Acts 18:7) or some large room where believers from all over the city could congregate.

We can see them come. There were the rich, the noble, and the influential. There was Aquila, for example, who seems to have been in a fair way of business, possibly with branches at Rome and Ephesus, and his wife Priscilla, possibly a Roman lady of high rank. There was not only Titus Justus, Crispus, and Sosthenes, former rulers of the synagogue, there was Erastus, the treasurer of the city. There were others, too, whose names became household words in the family of God— Stephanus, Gaius, Chloe, Tertius, Fortunatus, Achaicus, and Quartus. Then, too, there were the leading men in the various factions, some not on speaking terms with others. There were the gifted believers, too, as well as the great men, some prominent for having the much coveted "charismatic" gifts. And, of course, there were the rank and file of the congregation, many still slaves, some freedmen, along with the boys and girls and young people.

It must have been quite a gathering! As we join the throng, we can pick up snatches of conversation and catch the thrill as the hubbub dies away when one of the leading Christians stands up with the great letter in his hand. For us, Paul's Corinthian letters are simply "epistles," documents to be studied and analyzed, subjected to clause analysis and etymological scrutiny. For the great throng that day what was seen in the moderator's hand was a *letter*, addressed to them, written in their Greek mother tongue, a long letter, one they were anxious and eager to hear read. We can not only imagine how they listened to every word, we can join them, sit with them, ponder each and every phrase of this letter as though we, too, were hearing it, reading it, for the very first time.

Paul begins by sending *his greetings* (1 Cor. 1:1–3). "Paul!" There was *the signature* (1:1). We append our signatures to the end of our letters and documents, but in Paul's day the signature appeared first. It seems a sensible thing to do! This signature appears on thirteen of the books that comprise our New Testament, and probably belongs on a fourteenth. What a treasury of truth is introduced by that name!

By far the majority of people in that audience knew about Paul, for he was already famous. People either loved or loathed him, admired or despised him, imitated him fondly or ridiculed him passionately, but they could not ignore him. He had turned the world upside down. He was at once a Roman citizen, a Greek cosmopolitan, and a trained Jewish rabbi. He had a greater mind than Einstein, Shakespeare, or Beethoven, and a surer grasp of strategy than Caesar or Alexander. Moreover, he was as brave as a lion. All the forces of his giant intellect, his white-hot emotions, and his determined will combined to make him what he was—Paul!

He had long since jettisoned his Hebrew name of Saul, along with all the baggage of the rabbinical Judaism in which he had been nurtured and trained. His first known Gentile convert had been Sergius Paulus, proconsul of Rome over the island of Cyprus (Acts 13:4–12). It had not escaped the apostle that his own name, too, was Paul. He put that name to the fore. From now on he would identify himself with the Gentiles, with whom his future lay, rather than emphasize his Hebrew name, "Saul," which spoke so loudly of the past.

Paul! It was a name to conjure with, a name that spoke volumes. It was a name known in Jerusalem, Antioch, and Galatia, in Macedonia and Athens, in Corinth, and in Ephesus. It was a name to head a dozen New Testament books. It is a name that puts in the shade all the other names we associate with the church, save that of Jesus only.

The people recognized the name. To many it raised the memory of an earnest man who had sat down beside them one day and led them to Christ.

Having signed the letter, Paul at once reminds his readers of *his commission* (1 Cor. 1:1a–b). Since he was about to "lay down the law," it was important that one and all be reminded just who he was. So without hesitation his status is *declared.* He was "an apostle of Jesus Christ through the will of God." That was far more important than being an ambassador or viceroy by the will of Caesar. The title appears as a challenge. Let anyone in the church take issue with it if they dare! His credentials were every bit as good as those of Peter or John, and probably a great deal better than those of James, the presiding elder of the Jerusalem church.

Paul uses his title in every letter except the very personal one written to Philemon, which dealt with a very delicate subject, and the two letters he wrote to the Thessalonians, which were the earliest of his letters. Probably the Judaizers had not yet begun that organized and universal attack upon his apostleship when he wrote to the Thessalonians, so there was no need for him to assert his authority.

His status was *derived,* not from human hands but directly from the pierced hands of the risen and ascended Lord. He was God's chosen apostle to the Gentile world. This apostleship gave him unique authority over the Gentile churches, even those, such as the Roman and Colossian churches, which he himself had not founded.

If there was a thrill in that title, there was a threat in it, too. Let the listeners to that letter beware. This was not the word of a prophet, an evangelist, a pastor, or a teacher, however gifted and inspired; this was the word of an apostle—and an apostle "by the will of God" no less. An apostle could deal in death as well as life.

There are no apostles left now. They died out with the church's first generation. God made only about a dozen of them and the nursery no longer exists where such men can be bred. Besides, the need for them no longer exists. They were a dying breed even as Paul penned the word. Paul had no wish to exert his apostolic authority and power. He had no desire to deal out death, dismissal, or disease. He would rather use his apostleship to reveal, revive, and restore, but let no one underestimate him. He was "an apostle by the will of God," and neither Moses nor Elijah possessed greater powers than he. He had a whole arsenal of weapons if it came to outright war. There was, however, as he would tell his beloved Corinthians later on, "a more excellent way."

Then, too, Paul, unweariedly the most courteous of men, reminds his readers of *his companion* (1:1c). Sosthenes was probably Paul's secretary. The name evokes memories.

When Paul first went to Corinth he took the local synagogue by storm. Crispus, "the chief ruler of the synagogue," succumbed at once to the logic of the gospel, and so did a host of others (Acts 18:8). Then the synagogue authorities rallied, Paul was thrown out, and Crispus was replaced by a new ethnarch, a man named Sosthenes (18:17). It is hard to resist the temptation. Surely Paul's penman was the synagogue Sosthenes. It is not at all impossible that Sosthenes became a believer. Perhaps his former colleague Crispus had a hand in it. Who knows? If so, then the name *Sosthenes* here, in Paul's letter, would give rise to many a knowing nod in the congregation. The name, perhaps, would carry some weight with the Cephas faction in the church. In any case, he must have been well known in Corinth. Paul refers to him as "our brother"—some commentators change that to "the brother," as though he were, indeed, some well-known member of the family of faith.

> 2. The saints (1:2)
>   a. The local church (1:2a–c)
>   (1) The place (1:2a)
>   (2) The people (1:2b–c)
>   (a) They were sanctified (1:2b)
>   (b) They were saints (1:2c)
>   b. The larger church (1:2d–f)
>   (1) Universal in its breadth (1:2d)
>   (2) United in its bonds (1:2e–f)
>   (a) A common conversion (1:2e)
>   (b) A common commitment (1:2f)
> 3. The salutation (1:3)
>   a. As to its substance (1:3a)
>   b. As to its source (1:3b)

Paul now describes *the saints* (1 Cor. 1:2). He addresses, first, *the local church* and draws immediate attention to *the place* (1:2a). He speaks of the church at Corinth. Mark those words—the church! at Corinth! Between the two there was a great gulf fixed. The Corinth known to Paul had been founded by Julius Caesar; the church had been founded by Jesus Christ. The great word at Corinth was commerce; the great word in the church was Calvary. Corinth was noted for its filth; the church was noted for its faith. Corinth was a place for business; the church was a place for believers. The great commodity at Corinth was pleasure; the great commodity in the church was purity. Corinth was a product of the world; the church was a product of the Word.

It is likely that Paul originally arrived at Corinth by sea. He doubtless knew its history. The Roman general Mummius had destroyed it because it had played a key role in the Achaian league and its revolt against Rome. He had sold its people into slavery and seized all their land. Corinth had been allowed to lie in ruins for a hundred years. Then Julius Caesar recognized its strategic location and rebuilt it. It became the seat of the Roman province of Achaia and was soon one of the great centers of commerce in the Roman world.

The city itself was built on the north side of the Acrocorinthus, which rises 1,900 feet above the plain. It had two ports, one facing west, the other east. Lechaeum, in the Corinthian Bay, was a scant mile and a half from the city. Cenchrea, in the Saronic Bay, was about nine miles away. Since navigation around the peninsula was dangerous, much of the commerce was simply carried across the Isthmus.

The Corinthians set a fast pace. Every two years they hosted the Isthmian Games. Their city was a bustling center of business and many possessed great wealth. The temple of Aphrodite, with its famous cult statue and its thousand consecrated prostitutes, drew thousands of people to Corinth and did a thriving business. Corinth was notorious around the world for its immorality and drunkenness. It was a Greek Sodom. Paul's graphic description of paganism (Rom. 1:21–32) was dictated from this city.

It was famous, too, for its bronze foundries. The Corinthian smiths jealously guarded a secret formula for mixing copper, gold, and silver. Indeed, Corinthian bronze was world famous. The smelting ovens, deep in caverns dug out of the rocks, were like a scene from Dante's *Inferno*. The wretched slaves who stoked the ovens never saw the light of day. They existed as subterranean, human moles from childhood. The heat they had to endure was unbearable and the fumes they breathed poisonous. Their exposed flesh was pitted and scarred from the constant shower of metallic sparks to which they were exposed. Life was short and cheap and those who died were simply thrown into the furnace.

Men, women, and children lived to do the will of this Moloch. The use of the whip was frequent. Slaves were allowed to mate because this produced a supply of free labor. The last ounce of energy was squeezed out of the wretched slaves.

Anyone who became blind or incapacitated was simply thrown aside to starve to death or grovel on the garbage heaps. Many a wretched mother watched a loved child so discarded by callous masters only interested in making a profit.

The man who presided over Corinth during much of the time Paul was in the city was Junius Aeneus Gallio. He was the son of a learned father and the brother of the great philosopher Seneca, a Stoic and the tutor of Nero. Gallio had a reputation for culture and refinement and was of an amiable disposition. The religious affairs of the Jews bored him.

It was into this cosmopolitan city of some 600,000 inhabitants that Paul had come. He walked its streets, rubbing shoulders with Jews and peddlers, merchants and seamen, retired soldiers and shopkeepers, slaves, harlots, jugglers, and purveyors of vice. He took them all to his heart and set about winning as many as he could to Christ.

Paul turns his attention to *the people* who made up what Paul calls "the ecclesia of God," the company of "called-out" ones. They were "*sanctified* in Christ Jesus" and they were "called to be *saints.*" The two words are akin (*hagiazō,* "to be hallowed, or holy," and *hagios,* "holy, or separated ones"). In His prayer for His own the Lord Jesus pleaded with His Father: "*Sanctify [hagiazō]* them through thy truth." He added, "And for their sakes I sanctify *[hagiazō]* myself (John 17:17, 19). Thus the Corinthian Christians stood in stark contrast with the unregenerate crowds who walked the streets of Corinth. In a pornographic and perverted society, which approved the worst forms of decadence and depravity as some kind of "an alternative lifestyle," Christians were to live as Jesus lived. So far as their standing was concerned, they were "in Christ" (a favorite Pauline expression) and perfect. Their actual state was much different, which is what this Corinthian letter is all about.

The local church, whether at Corinth, Colossae, Cleveland, or Cologne, is only part of *the larger church* (1 Cor. 1:2d–f). This church is the church *universal in its breadth.* It is rooted in eternity and spread out through all time and space (1:2d). Most of its members are already in heaven. This larger church is the subject of his epistle to the Ephesians. Paul keeps it in mind, here, even though he is writing to a local church. For while he specifically addresses the church at *Corinth,* his letter is also for "all that in every place call upon the name of Jesus Christ." This letter, then, is as much for us, who dwell in lands of which Paul never dreamed and at a time as far from his age as was that of Abraham, as it was for those dear Christians in nearby Corinth in A.D. 55.

This larger church is also *united in its bonds* (1:2e–f). We all share *a common conversion* for we all call upon the name of Jesus Christ. Later on Paul wrote to the Romans from this very city of Corinth to say that "whosoever shall call upon the name of the Lord shall be saved" (Rom. 10:13). And we all share *a common commitment.* No sooner does Paul write down that saving Name than he reminds us, one and all, that it is also a sovereign name. He is "Jesus Christ our Lord, both theirs and ours." The Corinthians had lost sight of the lordship of Christ—hence all their sins, squabbles, and shortcomings.

Now comes *the salutation* (1:3). As to *its substance* it was both brief and benevolent, combining the two characteristic greetings of Paul's day. We greet someone with a "Good morning," and part with an equivalent "Goodbye." The Greeks said "Grace!" *(charis)* and the Jews said "Peace!" *(shalom).* East and west meet and become one in the bonds of Christ. The middle wall of partition between Jew and Gentile is broken down when they become Christians. God makes of both "one new man" (Eph. 2:15). Paul has not yet begun to deal with the discords and divisions that rent the Corinthian church—but his cheery opening greeting confronts one and all with the divine ideal.

As to its *source,* the salutation of grace and peace comes from "God our Father, and the Lord Jesus Christ." The deity of the Lord Jesus is taken for granted. As the Father's coequal, He shares in bestowing the blessing on His own. In the first nine verses of this chapter, which make up the general introduction to the letter, the name *Jesus Christ* occurs nine times. Paul nails the Corinthians down to that name, pointedly ignoring all other names. The Corinthians were marching off in all directions, waving as banners the names of Paul, Apollos, and Peter. Paul brings them back again and again to the one and only Name.

It was a thrilling name. When Paul first invaded Corinth with the good news of the gospel, the Lord Jesus had been crucified, buried, raised, and ascended into heaven only about seventeen years before! Multitudes were still alive who had vivid recollections of the man, and His miracles, His messages, and His ministry. His name was still very much alive in the world.

    B. Paul states his gratitude (1:4–9)
        1. For their grace (1:4)
            a. He was personally thankful for it (1:4a)
            b. He was perpetually thankful for it (1:4b)
            c. He was pastorally thankful for it (1:4c)
            d. He was perceptively thankful for it (1:4d)
        2. For their gifts (1:5–8)

    a. This was a talented church (1:5)

      (1) They had a gift of utterance (1:5a)

      (2) They had a gift of understanding (1:5b)

    b. This was a testifying church (1:6)

    c. This was a triumphant church (1:7a)

    d. This was a trusting church (1:7b–8)

      (1) The Lord's coming expected (1:7b)

      (2) The Lord's confirmation expected (1:8)

  3. For their God (1:9)

    a. His faithfulness (1:9a)

    b. His fellowship (1:9b)

Now Paul states *his gratitude* (1 Cor. 1:4–9). It was typical of Paul that he could always find something for which to be thankful. It is one of the keys to the victorious life. Judah, in the Old Testament, was the praising man (that's what his name signifies), so no wonder he was the prevailing man. The Lord Jesus could "give thanks" for the bread which spoke of His body broken, and for the cup which spoke of His blood poured forth. He could give thanks over and over again in that Upper Room high-priestly prayer of His. Paul had taken on color and character from his Master. He was always thankful.

He was thankful for the Corinthians and *for their grace* (1:4). Paul had been in Corinth for two or three months before he had been joined by his colleagues Silas and Timothy. Silas brought good news from Berea and Timothy glad tidings from Thessalonica. Some of the things Timothy had to tell, however, caused Paul to ply his pen and send the Thessalonians a letter. One of the things he said to them was this: "In everything give thanks, for this is the will of God in Christ concerning you" (1 Thess. 5:18). It was a principle by which Paul lived. No matter how dark the day, or how dire the circumstances, Paul could always be thankful for something.

So far as the Corinthians were concerned, he was thankful, to begin with, for the grace of God into which they had been brought. *Grace,* in the New Testament, means unmerited favor—getting something we don't deserve. The word occurs 155 times and Paul uses it some 110 times, more than all the other New Testament writers put together.

Paul stands in the vanguard of a vast host of saints who, down the ages, have come to appreciate the astounding grace of a thrice-holy God offered to rebel sinners ruined by the Fall. John Bunyan carried the banner in his day and his

Pilgrim's Progress and other writings bear tribute to his understanding of the grace of God. John Newton, who sank so low as a sinner and who soared so high as a saint, was another. His hymn, "Amazing Grace," is his tribute to the grace of God. That grace had found him, literally, the slave of a slave and had set him among princes. Paul's story was even greater. He never tired of eulogizing the grace of God, whether experienced by himself or evidenced in the lives of others.

Many of Paul's Corinthian converts had been saved from lives of depravity, for Corinth was the home of vice. The city was always full of drunken sailors who reveled and rioted in its streets. Cenchrea, only a mile or so down the highway, was home port to some of them. Soldiers on leave flocked to Corinth's taverns and bawdy houses. The gambling dens did a roaring trade. A man could not walk a city block in the seamier sections of the city without being propositioned by a pimp or a prostitute, or else accosted by some horrifying painted pervert who had Sodom itself for sale.

Then, too, there was the world famous temple of Venus Pandemos, home of a vile Phoenician sex cult, which did a roaring trade night and day. Sin was for sale on a massive scale in that temple. Its priests wholesaled lust and vice, in the name of religion, to those who were willing to buy.

Visitors to Corinth who had satiated their lusts and seen all the sights, poured into the marketplace, where a fresh crop of shysters lay in wait. Every kind of thievery was practiced on the unwary. Jews and Greeks alike marketed their wares. The pawnshops did a thriving business. Pickpockets slipped in and out of the crowds. Entertainers attracted their share of the ever-changing throngs. Down the back alleys muggings were commonplace.

Paul had been there. He had seen it. He had seen other sinful cities. Antioch and Ephesus were bad enough, but Corinth outclassed them all. It was from this background of wantonness and vice that many of Paul's converts had come. Even the better class Corinthians had been so inoculated by the lifestyle of their city that they thought little or nothing of its sins. A considerable number of Paul's converts were Jews who looked with horror on the licentiousness of the Corinthians, but many of Paul's converts had been raw pagans who had taken Corinth's corruption for granted. All had alike come into the good of God's grace, a grace extended to them, as Paul notes, by Jesus Christ. God's goodness reaches out to all men regardless of color, class, or creed. His grace is to be found in Jesus.

"The law was given by Moses," John said, "grace and truth came by Jesus Christ" (John 1:17). It is in the Lord Jesus that God's infinite, inimitable grace has been personified, made visible, tangible, and audible, and made available to all. If we want to see God's grace in action we must look away to Jesus. In the person of the Lord Jesus, God's grace is first shown to us, and then shared with us. Paul was thankful that so many Corinthians had come into the good of that grace.

He was equally thankful *for their gifts* (1:5–8), for there can be no doubt that the Corinthian church was *a talented church* (1:5). The word Paul uses here for *gift* is akin to the word for *grace, (charisma).* It actually means "a gift of grace, a free gift," and it occurs seventeen times in the New Testament, always in reference to God's gifts. A whole section of this letter will later be devoted to the abuse of the "charisma" by the "charismatics" of Corinth.

Here Paul notes just two of the gifts, "utterance" and "knowledge." The word for utterance is *logos,* which can be rendered "eloquence" or "discourse." It denotes a saying or a word as the expression of thought. It can refer to things spoken or written. The Corinthians placed an exaggerated importance on utterance and eloquence and they were especially infatuated by the gift of tongues.

"Knowledge" was also high on their list of desirable gifts. The word Paul uses is derived from the word *gnosis,* from which the gnostics derived their name. Like most Greeks, the Corinthians cherished an inflated love for things of the mind and for intellectual attainment. The Corinthian believers had trouble understanding the fact that mere natural cleverness and intellectualism are valueless as a means of spiritual life.

At this point in his epistle Paul simply gives the Corinthians credit for their gifts, for this was, indeed, a gifted church. Apart from the unique gift of an apostle, the Corinthians had all the gifts and they were proud of them and made great display of them. Moreover, they abused their gifts. Paul simply says, here, that he is grateful that they have such spiritual gifts, especially the gifts of utterance and understanding.

The Corinthian church, moreover, was *a testifying church* (1:6). The world could look at the church in Corinth and mark the difference between Christians and pagans. The church was bearing testimony to Christ. Moreover, there was a divine confirmation of the message they proclaimed. The word for *confirmed* is *bebaioō,* used in Greek commercial law to signify a guarantee of title. The effects being wrought in changed lives validated the message. Doubtless the fact that the sign gifts were still in force also helped to confirm its truth. Genuine healings, miracles, and tongues would be a strong argument in favor of the Corinthians' testimony to Christ. Paul could well have wished, however, that people would be drawn to Christ by the holy lives of the believers and by their evident love, rather than by a display of the gifts.

The Corinthian church was also *a triumphant church.* Paul acknowledged that, indeed, the Corinthians came behind in no gift (1:7a).

The Corinthian church was also *a trusting church* (1:7b–8), for the believers were "waiting for the coming" of the Lord Jesus Christ. The word for *waiting* is *apekdechomai.* It implies that the saints at Corinth were eagerly expecting the coming again of Christ. After all, it had been only a couple of decades since the Lord's ascension. From Corinth Paul had already written his two Thessalonian epistles, both weighted down with truth concerning the second coming of Christ. We can be sure that once Paul had these great second-coming truths hammered out in his mind and confirmed to him by divine revelation, he would preach them everywhere. We can be sure he taught the Corinthians not only Old Testament eschatology but also the truths we now find in the Gospels, in Thessalonians, and elsewhere in the New Testament.

Since truth concerning the second coming of Christ is sanctifying truth (1 John 3:3), Paul evidently took heart from the fact that his fractious followers at Corinth were occupied with the truth of the second coming of Christ. Indeed, they were eagerly expecting His coming.

Not only was the Lord's coming expected, His confirmation was expected (1 Cor. 1:8). The Lord Jesus Christ (Paul again uses the full title indicating His deity, His humanity, and His ministry) would confirm them (the same verb *bebaioō*) unto the end (*telos,* "the very end") that they might be blameless in the day of our Lord Jesus Christ. What a day that will be!

The expression "the day of our Lord Jesus Christ" parallels similar expressions, such as "the day of Christ" (Phil. 1:10; 2:16), "the day of Jesus Christ" (1:6), and "the day of the Lord Jesus" (1 Cor. 5:5; 2 Cor. 1:14). This day is not to be confused with "the day of the Lord" (essentially an Old Testament expression), the day when the Lord will step back into the arena of human affairs in power and glory to overthrow Gentile misrule (Isa. 13:9–11; 34:8; Dan. 2:34, 44; Obad. 15), to rescue the Jews, and to establish His kingdom on earth (Ps. 2:6).

All four of the parallel expressions above refer to the time of the Rapture (1 Thess. 4:14–5:11) and to the *Parousia,* when we shall gather with the Lord in the air. During this period, while end time events are coming to their climax on earth, the saints will appear before the judgment seat of Christ—about which Paul will soon have much more to say to the Corinthians. The great goal is to be "blameless" *(anegklētos),* "unreprovable" in that day. The aim is to so live that we shall not be called to account at this assize, to have nothing which, as a result of investigation, can be laid to our charge. The word implies more than acquittal. It infers the very absence of even a charge or accusation. That is the kind of life Paul recommends to his Corinthian converts, the kind of life, indeed, the Lord wants to confirm in all His people now and to applaud in His people then.

Paul, then, was grateful for their grace and for their gifts. He was also grateful *for their God* (1 Cor. 1:9). He mentions *His faithfulness.* "God is faithful," he exclaims (1:9a). We may let Him down but He will never let us down. Any failure will be on our side, not His. He is utterly dependable. His power to secure us is as great as His power to save us. Sooner could the sun cease to shine and the stars be blotted out and the earth cease to rotate than God could be untrue to His own character. He is faithful.

Paul mentions also *His fellowship.* The church has been "called unto the fellowship of his Son Jesus Christ our Lord" (1:9b). Called! In his letter to the Romans, Paul would later trace the whole sequence—foreknown, predestinated, called, justified, and glorified (Rom. 8:30). By putting all the verbs in the past tense he affirms that believers are as sure of heaven as though they were already there!

We read words such as "called into the fellowship of his Son" almost glibly and thoughtlessly. Yet it is an astounding statement. He loves us! He actually likes us! He wants to be with us, now and for all eternity. He wants to share all He has with us! The word *fellowship (koinonia)* suggests partnership, communion, having things in common. He has been down here. He was born into this world. He has been a babe and a boy, a teenager and a man. He has lived in a human home, been to school, worked at a carpenter's bench, been a traveling preacher. He knows all about us and about life on this lonely planet in space. He has laughed and cried. He has been tempted and tried. He has known applause and abuse. He has even tasted death. He shares our humanity. Now He wants to continue His fellowship with those who respond to His call. He will tread life's pathways with us. He will talk to us and commune with us. With *us.* When He could have chosen rather the fellowship of angels! We are invited to walk arm-in-arm with the Creator of the universe. No wonder Paul gives thanks. What more could we say than "Thank you, Lord!"

At this point we can almost see Paul put down his pen and pause. So much for the introduction! That was the easy part. He takes his pen again. Now for the hard part!

PART 2

Divisions in the Church
1 Corinthians 1:10–4:21

A. The source of their sectarianism (1:10–2:16)
    1. The folly of their clannishness (1:10–17)
        a. How Paul revealed their divisions (1:10–12)
            (1) An appeal (1:10)
                (a) An invocation (1:10a)
                (b) An invitation (1:10b–d)
                    To put aside
                      i. Their divisive orations (1:10b)
                    ii. Their divisive organizations (1:10c)
                    iii. Their divisive opinions (1:10d)
            (2) An appraisal (1:11–12)
                (a) The source of Paul's information (1:11)
                (b) The substance of Paul's information (1:12)
                    i. The personality cults (1:12a–c)
                      a. Those for the educated Paul (1:12a)
                      b. Those for the eloquent Apollos (1:12b)
                      c. Those for the eminent Cephas (1:12c)
                  ii. The presumptuous cult (1:12d)

The problem at Corinth was one of blatant sectarianism, budding denominationalism. Paul intends to expose *the source* (1 Cor. 1:10–2:16) and *the spirit* (3:1–4:21) of their divisions. He is going to expose both the folly of *their clannishness* (1:10–17) and the folly of *their cleverness* (1:18–2:16). He is going to *reveal* their divisions (1:10–12) and *repudiate* their divisions (10:13–17).

The incipient denominationalism at Corinth was organized around party names, such as Paul, Apollos, and Cephas. Today we have Lutherans and Wesleyans, Baptists and Brethren, Methodists and Presbyterians. The names have changed; the results are the same. Some have sought to find a cure in ecumenicalism, a joining of forces at the expense of doctrinal integrity and moral principle. Others have sought oneness in a common so-called charismatic experience and have paid the same high price. Paul tried to nip this "denominational" thing in the bud, and failed. It is hardly likely we today are going to cure it, root and branch, now that it has grown into a mighty tree. At least we can acknowledge all those "of like precious faith," who truly belong to Christ, who hold sound doctrine, and who live above reproach.

Divisions are always ready to raise their heads. I was raised in a church that had no pastor and felt no need for one. It had no organization or church machinery and felt no need for such. The pastoring was carried on by the elders. The preaching was done by the local believers themselves, with occasional help from visiting evangelists, missionaries, and teachers. The church was directed from the pew rather than from the pulpit. We had a wide variety of Bible teaching, some of it mediocre, some of it brilliant, all of it sound.

There were two factions in this church. On the one side were those who called loudly for "separation"—by which they really meant isolation. This faction regarded the entire organized church, as represented by the denominations (good, bad, and indifferent alike) as "ecclesiastical Babylon."

In the same church there was a faction of very open-minded brethren who found it hard to tolerate the "shibboleths" of the exclusive group. The more tolerant brethren had fellowship with believers across a wide denominational spectrum. They would heartily endorse transdenominational evangelistic efforts. They would willingly invite ordained clergymen to their pulpit, so long as they were sound in faith and doctrine. They irritated the more narrow brethren as much as they irritated them. They announced and supported various religious events, of a sound nature, in the city. They sponsored special evangelistic meetings in which other fundamental churches were invited to join.

Between the two extremes was the main body of believers. These had no party loyalty to either side. They just enjoyed the Word of God and the worship at the Lord's table and longed for a quiet and peaceable church life. In spite of it all, this church was growing and prosperous. It ran a Sunday school of over a thousand members—a very large Sunday school indeed in those days. But the squabbles continued.

In the end, division was inevitable. The more open-minded brethren pulled out and started a new church in another part of town where they were free to do as they pleased, and the more narrow group gained control of what was left behind and applied their legalistic principles at will. In the meantime the new church experimented with innovations and tried several interesting evangelistic experiments with more or less success.

Perhaps it would have been best, after all, if the church had stayed together, if the two sides had reached out to each other in love, if differences could have been resolved, or at least allowed to continue in an atmosphere of mutual love, understanding, and respect. Each side had strengths and weaknesses. It is a pity love did not dictate the "more excellent way" (1 Cor. 12:31). After all, there was no heresy and no moral sin dividing the two groups—toleration does not extend to that. The cure for that is rebuke and excommunication.

The church at Corinth was as divided as the church I was raised in. Paul now deals with those divisions. He *reveals their divisions* (1:10–12). He begins with *an appeal* (1:10) and introduces the appeal with *an invocation:* "Now I beseech you, brethren, by the name of our Lord Jesus Christ. . . ."

"Brethren!" Whatever differences they might have, they were all members of the same family. This lovely title occurs in Scripture for the first time under similar conditions. Abraham, filled with the vision of that "city which hath foundations," had become a pilgrim and a stranger on the earth and his nephew Lot had joined him. They arrived in the promised land of Canaan and here difficulties arose. Abraham and Lot had too many flocks and herds for the available pasturage. Before long, squabbles broke out between their herdsmen. Worse, those squabbles took place in full view of the unsaved Canaanites and Perizzites.

Lot was all for having his own way, but spiritually minded Abraham had higher and nobler ideas. "Let there be no strife, I pray thee, between me and thee," he said, "for we be brethren" (Gen. 13:8). That was the crux of the whole matter. Abraham took the humble place and resigned his own indisputable rights and soon discovered he had lost nothing. Lot took advantage of his uncle's generosity and eventually discovered that he had lost everything. Abraham was right! The things which united them, as brethren, were far more important than the things which divided them.

So Paul invoked the title *brethren!* He also invoked the one thing all believers have in common—the name of "our Lord Jesus Christ." He uses the expression again and again. He is *our* Lord Jesus Christ. No matter whether it was Paul, Apollos, or Cephas, Chloe or Stephanus, Erastus or Quartus, believers then or believers now, rich believers or poor, educated believers or illiterate, members of the nobility or believers of peasant stock, all have one thing in common—an attachment to *our* Lord Jesus Christ.

The word *beseech* is *parakaleō*, which means "to call aside." When people are squabbling, taking sides, giving way to emotion, the best thing to do is to call the contenders aside.

It was thus Paul and Barnabas sought to defuse the explosive issue that arose in the early church: must Gentiles become Jews in order to become Christians? The Jewish legalists passionately asserted they must. Paul adamantly said "No!" Such a requirement would make Christianity a Jewish sect and effectively abort wholesale Gentile conversion.

Paul and Barnabas went to Jerusalem to see if matters could not be talked out and settled amicably. The Jewish church in Jerusalem imagined itself to be some sort of mother church. Paul did not recognize that, but he did realize that this thorny issue would have to be settled in Jerusalem or nowhere. When he and Barnabas arrived in Jerusalem they did not throw the matter onto the floor of the church for open debate. The issues involved were too critical for that; emotions on both sides would soon generate more heat than light. Instead they called aside "the apostles and elders" (Acts 15:2, 4, 6) and met with them in private session. The smaller the circle, the easier it usually is to reach a proper conclusion. It was only after general agreement had been reached that the matter was aired before the rank and file of the church.

Similarly, Paul here calls the contestants aside, as it were. He beseeches them, urging upon them a common brotherhood and a common belief.

He follows up his appeal with *an invitation* (1:10b–d). He puts his finger on three divisive elements in the Corinthian church. Some of their *orations* were divisive: "I beseech you . . . that ye all speak the same thing," he said. So long as they were arguing and contradicting each other there could be no peace. Paul is not asking for uniformity of utterance but for agreement on important truths.

Some of their *organizations* were divisive: "I beseech you . . . that there be no divisions among you," he added. The word *schisma* denotes a cleft or a rent. Sharp differences between brethren have a way of becoming institutionalized into opposing factions. Groups organize to better defend and propagate the cause.

Some of their *opinions* were divisive: "I beseech you . . . that ye be perfectly joined together in the same mind and in the same judgment." Evidently sharp differences of opinion had arisen, although, as yet, the Corinthian church was still one corporate body. There was need for damage control. The expression "perfectly joined together" reflects the verb *katartizo,* a word used of mending nets (Matt. 4:21).

Paul's appeal is now followed by *an appraisal* (1 Cor. 1:11–12). Now he comes to cases. There were serious divisions at Corinth. He knew all about them. He states first *the source of his information* (1:11). He had been told "by them which are of the house of Chloe" about the "contentions" among them.

We have no idea who Chloe was, although it is conjectured she was a wealthy woman who had a number of servants, some of whom were Christians. The fact that Paul does not hesitate to use her name indicates her willingness to be known as the source of Paul's information. She was not just telling tales. She and her friends were genuinely concerned about what was going on. She considered that if anyone had the authority to speak to the issues it was Paul. Human nature being what it is, we can be sure that there were some in the church at Corinth who reacted angrily to the disclosure that Chloe had appealed to Paul. No matter! We owe Chloe a debt of gratitude. It was her concern which prompted this letter without which, indeed, the whole church, in all ages, would have been greatly impoverished. It has been suggested that Stephanus, Fortunatus, and Achaicus were the ones who actually conveyed Chloe's news to Paul. It has also been suggested that they were also Chloe's slaves or freedmen.

There were four factions in the Corinthian church. Three of them comprised *personality cults.* Some of these were *partisans of Paul.* Paul was *the educated man.* He had deliberately refrained from any kind of intellectualism in his gospel preaching at Corinth, but he could not deny himself. He had a mind for the universe. No one ever had a greater mind than Paul's. It was bound to show. Word of his brilliant address on Mars Hill in Athens may have followed him to Corinth. Nor would the fact that he was a trained rabbi and had been tutored by the illustrious Gamaliel be lost on the Jewish believers. Nor would Paul be able to hide his brilliance in the various discourses and discussions that accompanied his preaching of the cross of Christ. Such intellectualism would appeal to many in this great Greek city. Besides, he was the founder of the church, a fact that would carry considerable weight with many. Paul was far from flattered to learn that his name was being used to attract a following.

There were others who claimed to be *partisans of Apollos,* a Jewish convert from Alexandria in Egypt. The city of Alexandria had a large Jewish population. It was in Alexandria that the Hebrew Scriptures had been translated into Greek. It is likely that Apollos had been influenced, in his interpretive style, by the famous Jew Philo, who sought to reconcile Platonic philosophy with the Hebrew Scriptures. Philo resorted to extremes of allegorical interpretation of the Scriptures. Apollos may have been somewhat influenced by this renowned Alexandrian.

In any case, he showed up in Ephesus in A.D. 52, shortly after Paul had left the city. When he spoke in the local synagogue, Aquila and Priscilla were impressed by his style. He was *the eloquent man.* They were equally impressed by the gaps in his knowledge of Christ. Indeed, they took him home with them and privately taught him the way of God more perfectly (Acts 18:24–28).

It is likely that visitors from Corinth heard Apollos preach at Ephesus and invited him to come over to their city and preach to them. The Ephesian believers warmly endorsed this venture. Apollos went and was enthusiastically received at Corinth. Many were impressed by his oratory. Doubtless, too, his allegories intrigued them. They were captured by the man and by his culture, polish, and style. He soon had a following.

Then there were those who claimed to be *partisans of Cephas* (Simon Peter). If Paul was the educated man, and Apollos the eloquent man, Peter was *the eminent man.* He stood tall among the apostles. His discipleship, his leading role at Pentecost and at Caesarea, his leading position in the Jerusalem church were all matters of common knowledge. He would be in great demand as one who had known the Lord Jesus personally and intimately. The use of his Aramaic name, Cephas, suggests that the Cephas party at Corinth was made up of Judaizers who capitalized on the magic of Peter's name and fame. This faction actively disliked Paul and constantly challenged his apostleship and his authority. The rise and influence of this party in the Corinthian church seems to have been centered in one particular unnamed individual (2 Cor. 2:7).

Jewish Christianity had its headquarters in Jerusalem, a city that continued to cast its Judaistic shadow over the church until it was destroyed in A.D. 70. Paul was never much liked there. Nor did he have much patience with the legalistic brand of Christianity it advocated. The provisos appended by James to the emancipation agreement for Gentiles adopted by the Jerusalem church at the end of the Jerusalem Council (Acts 15:19–20, 29) must have irritated Paul, although he let them stand. He went along with them because they did not undermine anything essential and because they might help improve relations between Jews and Gentiles in the church. However, he does not seem to have regarded them as having any lasting weight. The emissaries of Judaistic Christianity in Corinth, by contrast, would gleefully insist on these and many other such rules and regulations. They soon attracted a following, especially, perhaps, among Paul's Jewish converts.

Doubtless this particular faction especially alarmed Paul. He had experience already, both in Antioch and in Galatia, of the wholesale damage Judaistic teaching could do once it gained a place in a predominantly Gentile church. This Judaizing faction in the Corinthian church, with or without authorization, was, it seems, invoking the names of Peter and James (the Lord's brother) to add weight to its claims. If this was so, and if it was indeed being countenanced by either of these two men, it would constitute a breach of the Council agreement. The Gentile churches, it had been agreed, were to be left alone. Insofar as anyone wanted to proclaim a Judaistic message, he must confine his activities to Jerusalem and Judea and not seek to undermine Paul's Gentile churches.

Far worse, to Paul's mind, than the personality cults was the *presumptive cult.*

This group rallied around the cry "I of Christ!" We do not know who was behind this party. Some think it was headed by a man devoted to James. He may even have been drawn from the ranks of the Lord's earthly relatives (1 Cor. 9:5). He may have been someone from Palestine who had seen Christ in the flesh and who traded on that. In any case, this particular group was especially obnoxious to Paul. To think that anyone would actually use the name of Christ Himself to promote a partisan cause!

Paul could see where all this would end if someone did not put a stop to it. Soon there would be the Apollos Free Church, and the Church of St. Cephas of Jerusalem, and the Pauline Apostolic Church, and the Corinthian Church of Christ. Paul set out to nip this kind of thing in the bud.

> b. How Paul repudiated their divisions (1:13–17)
> > (1) Ridiculing them (1:13)
> > > (a) Focus on God's Son: an impossible conclusion (1:13a)
> > > (b) Focus on God's Servant: an impossible contention (1:13b–c)
> > > He takes them back to
> > > > i. The cross of Christ (1:13b)
> > > > ii. Their confession of Christ (1:13c)
> > (2) Rebuking them (1:14–16)
> > In terms of whom he had baptized, there were:
> > > (a) A remarkable few (1:14)
> > > (b) A remaining fear (1:15)
> > > (c.) A remembered fact (1:16)
> > (3) Redirecting them (1:17)
> > > (a) The great obligation (1:17a)
> > > (b) The great objective (1:17b–c)
> > > > i. The way of it (1:17b)
> > > > ii. The "why" of it (1:17c)

We have seen how Paul *revealed* the Corinthians' divisions (1 Cor. 1:10–12), now we see how Paul *repudiated* their divisions (1:13–17). He begins by *ridiculing* them (1:13). He puts *the focus on God's Son.* "Is Christ divided?" he asks.

What a ridiculous idea! The Godhead is absolute in its oneness. There are three distinct Persons but only one God. Each is coexistent, coeternal, and coequal with the others. There are not three gods (which we would express as 1 + 1 + 1 = 3) but one God (which we express as 1 x 1 x 1 = 1). The Lord Jesus constantly taught the eternal and essential oneness within the Godhead. He said to the Jews, "I and my Father are one." They understood Him to be making Himself equal with God and attempted to stone Him (John 10:30–33). When Philip said, "Shew us the Father," Jesus replied, "He that hath seen me hath seen the Father" (John 14:8–9). Jesus was "the express image" of the Father's own Person (Heb. 1:1–3). In the Upper Room He prayed that His people might share that mysterious and marvelous oneness (John 17:21–23).

In this unique oneness the Holy Spirit shared. The Lord Jesus was conceived by the Holy Spirit (Matt. 1:20). He was "full of the Holy Ghost" (Luke 4:1). In Him, indeed, dwelt "all the fulness of the Godhead bodily" (Col. 1:19; 2:9). It was "through the eternal Spirit" that the Lord Jesus "offered himself without spot unto God" (Heb. 9:14). It was the Holy Spirit who raised Him from the dead (Rom. 8:11). The coming of the Holy Spirit at Pentecost was a joint decision of all three members of the Godhead (John 15:26).

No wonder Paul indignantly asked, "Is Christ divided?" What folly to try to make Christ party to a movement to split and divide the church. This was *an impossible conclusion.*

He puts *the focus on God's Servant* (1 Cor. 1:13b–c) and shows, moreover, that theirs was *an impossible contention.* "Was Paul crucified for you?" he demanded. "Were ye baptized in the name of Paul?" He took them back to the *cross* of Christ and to their public *confession* of Christ. Far from being crucified for them, Paul had been, in those early days, the avowed enemy of the cross of Christ, and had carried his campaign of persecution to distant cities. The notion that he, Paul, had been crucified for them was patently ridiculous! But that is just what would have been necessary if Paul were to accept the role of church party leader bestowed on him by his admirers.

Equally satirical was the question "Were ye baptized in the name of Paul?" There is only one name that matters. Maybe Paul had been present at the sitting of the Sanhedrin that investigated Peter and John in Jerusalem. The two issues being considered were Peter's recent healing of a lame man and his subsequent preaching in the name of Jesus. Peter had boldly faced down the whole council. "There is none other name under heaven given among men, whereby we must be saved," he declared (Acts 4:12).

There was only one name. It certainly wasn't Peter's or Paul's or that of Apollos. Believers were to be baptized upon their confession of faith in the name of the One who had saved them.

Then Paul continues by *rebuking* them (1 Cor. 1:14–16). He breathes an almost audible sigh of relief that, in actual fact, he had baptized so few of them. For the most part, he had left the actual baptizing of converts to others.

He could recall baptizing Crispus and Gaius. Crispus had been a notable convert, the ruler of the synagogue when Paul first preached Christ there (Acts 18:8). Gaius was likely the man in whose home Paul was living when he wrote his letter to the Romans. He describes him as "Gaius mine host, and of the whole church" (Rom. 16:23). Evidently he was a most hospitable believer.

When the synagogue in Corinth closed its doors to Paul he moved next door to continue his evangelistic efforts in the house of a man named Justus (Acts 18:7). Evidently he was an early convert. His full name is thought to have been Gaius Titius Justus, and he is believed by some to be the same Gaius referred to both here and in Paul's Roman epistle. If so, it is little wonder Paul baptized him.

As an afterthought, Paul adds the name of Stephanus to the list of those he had personally baptized. Paul later describes this man's household as "the firstfruits of Achaia" (Rom. 16:5). No wonder, then, that Paul baptized him. Beyond these few names Paul could not recall baptizing any others at Corinth. Now he was glad he had exercised this restraint—"lest any should say that I had baptized in mine own name," he adds.

Finally, we see him *redirecting* them (1 Cor. 1:17). Baptism was important and Paul has no intention of depreciating it. However, there were things more important than baptism: "For Christ sent me not to baptize, but to preach the gospel," Paul declared. That puts the lie to the teaching that baptism is essential to salvation. Baptism is simply the outward expression of an inward experience. In baptism a person is publicly identified with Christ in His death, burial, and resurrection.

A preacher friend of mine entered into a discussion with the man sitting alongside him on a plane. The man was a minister of a church that teaches a person cannot be saved unless baptized. He warmly defended his view. Finally my friend said to him, "Suppose the pilot of this plane were to announce that we should fasten our seat belts because the plane was about to crash. What message would you have for these people? For myself, I would tell them: 'Whosoever shall call upon the name of the Lord shall be saved.' Or I would direct them to John 3:16.

"But you believe people cannot be saved unless they are baptized. What would you tell these people?" The man admitted to be at a loss. The great thing is to tell people how to be saved. Baptism neither confers salvation nor confirms salvation. It is the first step of a saved person in a life of obedience. Were it any more than that Paul would have baptized everyone just to make sure.

The great *obligation* is not to baptize, whether infants or adults, so as to secure their salvation. The great *objective* is to "preach the gospel," to tell people that "God so loved the world that he gave his only begotten Son, that whosoever believeth in him should not perish, but have everlasting life" (John 3:16).

Paul states *the way* of it, and *the why* of it. "Not with wisdom of words," he says. The salvation message is simplicity itself. Paul said to the Philippian jailer, "Believe on the Lord Jesus Christ and thou shalt be saved." That's all a sinner needs to know. A saint needs to know much more than that. A child of God can spend a lifetime exploring the mysteries of regeneration and redemption, justification and sanctification, election and identification. The sinner does not need to know all that. He simply needs to know his need of a Savior and God's provision of that Savior in Christ.

How often we confuse things "with wisdom of words"! Paul explains why we should keep the message simple—"Lest the cross of Christ should be made of none effect." Extreme Calvinism, for instance, when preached to the unsaved, makes the cross of Christ of none effect. The message that comes across is that only the elect can be saved. The reaction then is "If I'm one of the elect, I'll be saved; if I'm not one of the elect I'll be lost. There's nothing I can do about it one way or the other." Probably such issues should be kept out of gospel preaching, however much they may be aired and discussed at other times. Those who preach that a person can be saved and lost and saved again and lost again also make the cross of Christ of none effect. In the end, that preaching makes salvation depend on our own works and faithfulness rather than on Christ's finished work and unchanging faithfulness.

Thus Paul deals with the folly of the clannishness of the Corinthians and some of the confusion it caused. He turns now to

> 2. The folly of their cleverness (1:18–2:16)
> The Cross exposes
> a. The incompleteness of man's viewpoint (1:18–2:8)
> Man cannot understand
> (1) The way of the Cross (1:18–31)
> (a) It is contrary to man's ideas (1:18–24)
> i. The fact declared (1:18)
> *a.* It is repudiated by the sinner as ridiculous (1:18a)

      b. It is recognized by the saint as real (1:18b)

  ii. The fact debated (1:19–20)

      a. A quotation (1:19)

      b. A question (1:20)

        1. Regarding the wisdom of the world (1:20a–c)

          (i)   Where are its sages? (1:20a)

          (ii)   Where are its scribes? (1:20b)

          (iii) Where are its skeptics? (1:20c)

        2. Regarding the wisdom of the Word (1:20d)

  iii. The fact demonstrated (1:21–24)

      a. In the arena of public exposure (1:21–22)

        1. The world's religions exposed (1:21)

          (i)   Categorically, by means of their terrible blindness (1:21a)

          (ii)   Conversely, by means of our transforming belief (1:21b)

        2. The world's rationalism exposed (1:22)

          (i)   The Hebrews want to be convinced miraculously (1:22a)

          (ii)   The heathen want to be convinced mentally (1:22b)

      b. In the arena of personal experience (1:23–24)

        1. Negative reactions to the gospel (1:23)

          (i)   To the Hebrew the preaching of the cross is scandalous (1:23a)

          (ii)   To the heathen the preaching of the cross is senseless (1:23b)

        2. Noble reactions to the gospel (1:24)

          (i)   The call heard (1:24a)

          (ii)   The call heeded (1:24b–c)

              (a) The gospel's transforming power (1:24b)

              (b) The gospel's transcendent wisdom (1:24c)

Like the Athenians, the Corinthians were Greek and, as such, they considered themselves to be very clever. Greek culture was unsurpassed in the ancient world.

The great names of poetry and oratory, of art and science, of philosophy and learning were Greek names. We think of men like Homer and Herodotus, Sophocles and Socrates, Plato, Plutarch and Pericles, Aristotle and Archimedes, Anaxagoras and Alexander, Euclid and Euripides. They are men we associate with Greece. There is no doubt the Greeks were clever. The problem was that this Greek penchant for cleverness had invaded the Corinthian church.

Paul's answer to *their clannishness* was the cross. Paul's answer to *their cleverness* was the cross (1 Cor. 1:18–2:16). He begins by showing the incompleteness of man's *viewpoint* (1:18–2:8) and then shows the incompleteness of man's *vision* (2:9–16). As to man's incomplete viewpoint, man cannot understand *the way of the cross* (1:18–31), nor can he understand *the wisdom of the cross* (2:1–8). The way of the cross is contrary to man's *ideas* (1:18–24) and it is contrary to man's *ideals* (1:25–31).

The fact that the way of the cross is contrary to man's ideas is first of all *declared* (1:18). The preaching of the cross is foolishness, Paul says, to those that perish. By contrast it proves itself to be the power of God to us who are saved. The word for *foolishness* here is *moria*. This word for foolishness appears in the New Testament only in this epistle. It refers to things regarded as stupid, or silly. The clever people of this world regard the message of salvation, through the preaching of the cross, as nonsense.

In Paul's day there was even greater stigma attached to such a message, for the cross was a gallows, the equivalent to an electric chair. Slaves, the lowest type of criminals, rebels, and enemies, were executed by crucifixion. The utmost shame and horror were attached to such a death. To preach the cross was ridiculous.

The Greeks peopled Mount Olympus with gods made in the image and likeness of men. Their gods lusted and warred at will. They abducted desirable women and played havoc with the world. After all, what was the point of being a god or goddess if you could not have your own way and indulge your passions unopposed? The idea of a god becoming a man was not so strange. But that he should be born in a reeking cow barn, be raised in poverty and obscurity, go about doing good with no thought of reward, meekly accept insults and false accusations, and, finally, submit to the unspeakable ignominy and torment of death by crucifixion, well, that was nonsense.

It still is to many! Modern man has not changed his mind about that. Our educational institutions preach humanism, not holiness; they eulogize cleverness, not Calvary. Faced with the horrendous ills of society, modern man looks to science, technology, and engineering. He looks to sociology, psychology, and philosophy; to education, business, and politics; to government programs and the occult. It never occurs to him that God's answer is the Cross! The Cross changes people, and changed people transform society. Those who embrace the message of the Cross find it works! It releases the very power of God into human lives. It makes crooked men straight, profligate people pure, drunken men sober, weak people strong.

The fact that the way of the Cross is contrary to man's ideas is not only declared, it is *debated* (1:19–20). Paul introduces *a quotation* (1:19) from Isaiah 29:14. In Isaiah's background was the dreaded might of Assyria, a superpower that had embarked on a course of expansion. Little Judah lay directly in its path. Isaiah urged the people to trust God. The king's counselors and wise men advised an alliance with Egypt (30:1–3), a policy Isaiah denounced. The king went along with the politicians so the prophet declared God's Word: "I will destroy the wisdom of the wise, and will bring to nothing the understanding of the prudent."

Sennacherib's army rolled south and Egypt soon proved to be a broken reed. Most of Judah was overrun by the Assyrians and Jerusalem itself was besieged. God simply turned the counsel of the clever politicians into foolishness and brought Judah to its knees and Jerusalem to the point where it had no place to go but to God.

Paul applies this incident here to the gospel. It is not until we come to an end of ourselves, of our own ideas, our own cleverness, our own efforts, and our own self-will and see our own folly and futility that we can experience the mighty power of God to save.

Now Paul asks *a question* (1 Cor. 1:20), a whole series of questions, in fact. Three of them relate to *the wisdom of the world.* He challenges the world to produce its scholars, its scribes, and its skeptics. "Where are they?" he demands. Paul, himself one of the greatest intellectuals of all time, was willing to take on anyone. He knew the mighty, life-transforming power of the gospel. He had grasped the mighty, divine logic of Calvary. Calvary is rooted and grounded in the omniscience of God. When God the Father, God the Son, and God the Holy Spirit decided in a dateless, timeless past that they would act in creation, they knew that, in time, the "mystery of iniquity" would raise its head in the universe. When that happened they would have to act in redemption. The same omniscient genius, which underlies every law of nature, which planned the paths and orbits of the galaxies and the inner mysteries of the atom, has planned the process of salvation. The logic behind the Cross is infinite, infallible, and indisputable. Paul was willing to pit that logic against all the scholarship, sophistication, and skepticism of the world.

The fourth question refers to *the wisdom of the Word.* "Hath not God made foolish the wisdom of this world?" Paul demands. Human reason is exposed as folly when it is set alongside divine revelation. Human philosophy wanders far and wide in the realm of thought but its conclusions are often conceited and confusing, contradictory and incomplete. Nowhere is this more evident than in man's religious philosophy. The wisdom of the world says that salvation has to be earned. This is the basic, unifying concept of Islam, Hinduism, Buddhism, the cults of Christendom, and all false religion. Religion calls for feasts and fasts, pilgrimages and penances, sacrifice and suffering, rules and rituals. The whole emphasis is on works. God makes this seeming wisdom to be utter folly by making His "so great salvation" available as a free gift to be accepted by faith, man's wisdom says "Do!" God's Word says "Done!"

So, then, Paul dares the world to bring on its wise men. The Jews had their scribes. Paul, who had lived in Jerusalem, knew what they had to offer. They paraded as exalted beings and looked down scornfully on the ignorant people of the land. Paul was not impressed by them. They mistook their wordy hair-splitting for profound wisdom. Paul had demolished their religious notions in synagogues all the way from Antioch to Corinth. The Greeks had their clever dialecticians. Paul had taken their measure on Mars Hill.

D. L. Moody, too, took the measure of the clever disputers of his day. Unlike Paul, who was a scholar, Moody was just an uneducated shoe salesman. Notwithstanding his humble status in life, this Spirit-filled man dared to challenge the atheists, agnostics, and free-thinkers of London. He convened a meeting just for them and they came by the hundreds. Moody had more sense than to engage the battle on the level of the intellect. He went after their hearts. He told stories out of his own experience of the deathbeds of believers and the deathbeds of agnostics. He kept up this running broadside at their most vulnerable point until, at last, some five hundred men stood to their feet to accept Christ. To all their clever arguments he brought to bear one single word from God: "Their rock is not as our Rock, even our enemies themselves being judges" (Deut. 32:31). The Word of God, in the anointed hands of this untutored evangelist, "made foolish the wisdom of this world."

The fact that the way of the Cross is contrary to man's ideas, having been declared and debated, it is now *demonstrated* (1 Cor. 1:21–24). Paul demonstrates the truth of this in two arenas: in the arena of *public exposure* (1:21–22) and in the arena of *personal experience* (1:23–24). First, the world's *religions* are exposed (1:21). Paul contrasts *their terrible blindness* with *our transforming belief.*

It is one of the demonstrations of God's wisdom that "the world by wisdom knew not God." God makes no concession to human intellectual pride. One reason for this lies in man's fallen nature.

When God created the animal kingdom He gave each creature a controlling principle we call instinct. Each creature is locked into a behavior pattern. A bee, for example, does what it does because it is what it is. It does not need to be taught to behave as it does. It instinctively does what it is designed to do.

By contrast, when God made man He did something quite different from that. Man is not a highly developed animal. He belongs to a distinctly different order of creation. Man has a body and a soul, just like an animal. He has intellect, emotions, and will, as well as a variety of senses and a functioning body. But God did not lock him into an instinctive behavior pattern, thus guaranteeing his good behavior. He did not create puppets, He created people, able to think and feel and decide. To control his behavior, God gave man a human spirit to be the home of His Holy Spirit. The Holy Spirit indwelling man's human spirit and cooperating with man's spirit was to control the intellect, emotions, will, senses, and functions of man. Man, in other words, was made to be inhabited by God and to know and love and obey God.

Then sin came in. When sin came in the Holy Spirit went out, leaving man's spirit empty and void. Man in sin has no governing principle. He relies on his senses, or on his intellect, his emotions, his conscience, and his will. But he is lost. He is blind to spiritual truth, feels deeply about the wrong or lesser things, makes the wrong decisions, goes by his senses, abuses his body, and stifles the conscience that now haunts the empty human spirit. Indeed, man is so totally lost in his sin that he cannot even know God apart from God's revelation of Himself in His Word and the Holy Spirit's illumination of that Word in his soul.

The Holy Spirit through "the foolishness of preaching" saves those who believe. The Holy Spirit brings the Word of God to bear upon the mind of man, revealing to him truth he can know no other way. He stirs his emotions, quickens his conscience, and imparts "conviction of sin." The last citadel to fall is the human will. When that is conquered, the awakened soul turns to Christ, accepts Him by faith, is cleansed by the blood of Christ, and his human spirit is again indwelt by the Holy Spirit. He has been "born again." The unregenerate mind is so wholly alienated from God that the unsaved man considers all such preaching as foolishness.

The world's religions, in which man displays his thinking about God, are all prime exhibits of man's natural spiritual blindness. We do not need to go beyond the confines of Christendom to see this illustrated. Think, for instance, of the sheer folly of Mormonism. People are taught that a doubtful character by the name of Joseph Smith found some golden plates inscribed in Egyptian hieroglyphics. An angel supplied him with some magic glasses by the aid of which he was able to translate the plates into pseudo King James English and thus produce the Book of Mormon. Adherents to Mormonism gloss over the sensuality of Joseph Smith and Brigham Young and the unblushing polygamy that still clings to some members of their cult. Mormons are taught they can become gods and so are brought into bondage to Satan's oldest lie: "Ye shall be as gods" (Gen. 3:5).

Equally incredible, yet just as fervently believed, are the lies and delusions of Christian Science, the untruths of the Jehovah's Witnesses, the distortions of liberal theology, the dark deceptions of spiritism, the New Age, and the occult. Beyond the boundaries of Christendom is the gross polytheism, immorality, and satanism of Hinduism, the fierce religion of Islam, the idolatry of Buddhism, and the rationalism of humanism. The world's religions stand exposed.

Not only are the world's religions exposed but the world's *rationalism* is exposed (1 Cor. 1:22). Both Jews and Gentiles are weighed in the balance and found wanting." "The Jews require a sign," Paul says. That is to say, they want to be convinced *miraculously.* Signs indeed! For three and a half years, the Son of God walked the length and breadth of their land. He healed their sick and raised their dead. He cleansed their lepers and liberated their demoniacs. He walked upon the waves and stilled the storm. He fed their hungry multitudes and transformed ruined lives. Yet they demanded a sign! "Give us a sign from heaven," they said. When He was born He put a new star in the sky and when He died He put out the sun. Still they insisted they wanted a sign. He took them back to Jonah and then on to His own resurrection. After Pentecost, the church was born doing signs and wonders and the Jews ignored these and persecuted the church as vehemently as they had persecuted the Christ. Signs indeed! The demand for more and more signs and their refusal to believe the astounding signs they had already been given was proof enough of their rationalism, as deep and dark as that of Cain.

"The Greeks seek after wisdom," Paul continued. They wanted to be convinced *mentally.* It was an endless search. In Athens, Paul was surrounded by Stoics and Epicureans. He soon discovered that they really did not want the truth. They wanted to hear "some new thing." As he stood before them, anointed by the Spirit of God, with ultimate truth to proclaim, they called him a "babbler." The word they used was *spermologos,* "seed picker," a derisive term used of birds and applied to men who retailed scraps of information they picked up from others (Acts 17:18). They listened to him with some degree of patience until he came to the greatest truth ever preached on this planet—the resurrection of Christ. Some prevaricated, others mocked openly. To Epicureans and Stoics alike, representing, as they did, opposite extremes of human philosophy, the proclamation of the resurrection of a dead man was a madman's dream.

Having proved in the arena of public exposure the fact that the way of the Cross is contrary to man's ideas, Paul now demonstrates it in the arena of *personal experience* (1 Cor. 1:23–24). He contrasts two kinds of reaction to the gospel. First, he gives two examples of *negative reactions* to the gospel (1:23). To the *Hebrew,* the preaching of "Christ crucified" was *scandalous* (a "stumbling block," *skandalon*). It outraged them. Instead of the signs of the kingdom promised by the Old Testament prophets, Jesus, while claiming to be the Messiah and the Son of God, actually allowed Himself to be crucified. He had died under the very curse of the Mosaic Law (Deut. 21:23). They ignored or actively denied His resurrection, inventing a phony theory to explain the empty tomb. From that day to this many Jews have reviled Jesus. Their craving for signs will reassert itself after the rapture of the church, making many of them an easy prey to the deceiving miracles of the Antichrist and the False Prophet.

To the *heathen,* the preaching of the Cross was *senseless.* How could anyone accept as lord and savior someone who did not have enough common sense to avoid the disgrace of death by crucifixion? If *He* could not save Himself, how could He save anyone else! What folly to enthrone such a Man as the epitome of wisdom!

Paul turns from such blindness and unbelief, and from such negative reactions to the gospel, to cite *noble reactions* to the gospel (1 Cor. 1:24). When the gospel call is both heard and heeded, evidence is at once seen of its *transforming power.* To those who are called, both Jews and Greeks, Christ is seen to be "the power of God." The word for *power* is *dunamis.* It suggests untrammeled, unequaled power. It is surely significant that, while listing the mighty miracles that accompanied the death of the Lord Jesus on the cross (the darkening of the sun, the rending of the temple veil, the quaking earth and rending rocks, and the opening of countless graves), Matthew also records the conversion of the Roman centurion (Matt. 27:45, 50–54). It took the same mighty power to change that man's heart as it did to accomplish the other wonders.

When the gospel call is heard and heeded, evidence is seen also of its *transcendent wisdom.* Both Jews and Greeks discover in Christ the wisdom of God. In him "are hid all the treasures of wisdom," Paul told the Colossians (2:3). When He lived on earth the Lord was constantly opening that treasure chest to give men glimpses of the extraordinary wisdom that was His. Men said in astonishment, "How knoweth this man letters, having never learned?" (John 7:15). The word *letters* is the plural of the Greek word *gramma,* a word which, by extension, referred to literature in general and the Talmudic writings in particular. Those sent to arrest Him returned empty-handed. Their explanation was "Never man spake like this man" (John 7:46). He Himself declared that He was greater than Solomon, whose wisdom was proverbial (Matt. 12:42).

The world in which we live has little or no use for the wisdom of the Lord Jesus. In the United States, the Bible has been banned from public school classrooms. Educators direct their students to Marx and to Machiavelli, to Dewey and to Darwin, to the gurus and to Gibbon, but they will not point them to Christ. Once a man is saved, however, he soon sees through this world's philosophers. He tastes of the wisdom of Christ and is spoiled for the philosophies of the world.

(b) It is contrary to man's ideals (1:25–31)

    i. An explosive statement (1:25)

        a. Regarding foolishness (1:25a)

        b. Regarding feebleness (1:25b)

    ii. An explanatory statement (1:26–29)

        a. Who God calls when He does (1:26–28)

            1. Illumination (1:26)

            He does not call many

            (i)   Sophisticated people (1:26a)

            (ii) Self-sufficient people (1:26b)

            (iii) Society people (1:26c)

            2. Illustration (1:27–28)

            He does call

            (i)   The foolish, to confound the gifted ones of this world (1:27a)

            (ii) The feeble, to confound the great ones of this world (1:27b)

            (iii) The failures, to confound the grand ones of this world (1:28)

                (a) Those with no family or friends (1:28a)

                (b) Those with no fame or fortune (1:28b)

        (c) Those with no face or form
            (1:28c)
     b. Why God calls who He does (1:29)
  iii. An expository statement (1:30–31)
     a. Our relation to Him (1:30a)
     b. Our resources in Him (1:30b–c)
        He is made unto us:
        1. Wisdom, to transform our minds (1:30b)
        2. Righteousness, to transform our morals (1:30c)
        3. Sanctification, to transform our motives (1:30d)
        4. Redemption, to transform our members (1:30e)
     c. Our rejoicing through Him (1:31)
        1. His book (1:31a)
        2. Our boast (1:31b)

Paul is still discussing the folly of the Corinthians' cleverness. Because of *the incompleteness of man's viewpoint* (1 Cor. 1:18–2:8) man cannot understand the *way of the Cross* (1:18–31). Paul has just demonstrated the fact that it is *contrary to man's ideas* (1:18–24). He now shows it to be equally *contrary to man's ideals* (1:25–31). He makes three statements. The first is *an explosive statement* (1:25). He says that the reason why people cannot comprehend the logic of Calvary is because the foolishness of God is wiser than men; and the weakness of God is stronger than men. Truly an extraordinary statement.

The prophet Isaiah had said much the same thing to the unbelieving people of his day: "For my thoughts are not your thoughts, neither are your ways my ways, saith the Lord. For as the heavens are higher than the earth, so are my ways higher than your ways, and my thoughts than your thoughts" (Isa. 55:8–9). The thought emphasized is not only the contrast between God's thoughts and ours but also the vastness that separates the two. The ways of man are as far removed from the ways of God as impotence is removed from omnipotence and the thoughts of God are as far removed from the thoughts of man as ignorance is removed from omniscience. The great gulf fixed is infinite; the distance that separates the creature from the Creator is immeasurable.

This explains why people can study the marvels and mysteries of the universe, the incredible complexity of the human body, for instance, and explain it in terms of mechanistic evolution—when everything about the physical universe, from the smallest atom to the greatest galaxy, declares the existence of an omniscient mind, and therefore of an omniscient and omnipotent Person. When the astronomers thought their way back to the beginning of time, they boldly postulated the Big Bang and confidently asserted what the universe was like at that moment and a second or so afterward. But Einstein and the others shrank from going back one step beyond the Big Bang to the split second before that beginning. That would have brought them face to face with God, and the last thing they wanted to do was prove the theologians to have been right after all.[1]

If this is so in terms of science and philosophy it is even more so in terms of man's religion. Man says "Do!" God says "Done!" Man says "Toil!" God says "Trust!" Man says "Behave!" God says "Believe!" Man says "Achieve!" God says "Accept!" Cain, who founded the world's first false religion, said, "I'll bring the fruits of my own good works." His brother Abel said, "I'll sacrifice a lamb without blemish." Cain's religion emphasized beauty; Abel's faith emphasized blood. Cain only compounded the curse; Abel simply claimed the Cross. Cain's religion produced a murderer; Abel's faith produced a martyr. Cain's religion looks fine to man and Abel's faith seems folly to man. Cain's religion illustrates man's thoughts and man's ways. Abel's offering illustrates God's thoughts and God's ways. God is neither foolish nor weak—He only seems so to self-inflated, ego-centered, Christ-rejecting men. Paul, of course, is being somewhat sarcastic. As though God, eternal, uncreated, and self-existing, omnipotent, omniscient, and omnipresent, could ever be foolish or weak!

The wisdom of God has devised a means of salvation for lost people. It fully accommodates the competing claims of His own holiness on the one hand and His love on the other hand. It is a means of salvation that both levels man's pride and compensates for his moral and spiritual blindness, impotence, and death. The power of God carried that salvation through to completion by means of incarnation, atonement, resurrection, and regeneration.

Next comes *an explanatory statement* (1 Cor. 1:26–29). Paul begins with *illumination* (1:26). God has His own infallible ways of leveling man's pride. By and large it is not the high and mighty who respond to the gospel call, but the weak and poor, the common people, those who live daily with the struggles and harsh realities of life. The wise and wealthy of this world usually have too great a stake

---

1. See Robert Jastrow, *God and the Astronomers* (New York: W. W. Norton, 1992).

in this world to want to pay the price of confessing Christ in the face of this world's scorn and rage.

The Countess of Huntingdon (in an often-told story) said that she thanked God for the letter *m* in the word *many*. If God had said "not any" instead of "not many," it would have excluded her. There are some of wealth and power and influence who get saved. The infant church had its Joseph of Arimathea, its Nicodemus, its Sergius Paulus, and its Dionysius the Areopagite. The church at Corinth had its Erastus (Rom. 16:23). The rank and file of the church, however, in its early days and throughout its history, has been made up of slaves, freedmen, and artisans. The Sanhedrin sneered at the apostles because they counted them as "unlearned and ignorant men" (Acts 4:13). Down through the ages God has delighted to use this world's nobodies. The ranks of the church are full of them—nobodies on earth, but notables in heaven.

And well Satan knows their power! When Screwtape, a senior devil, wrote to Wormwood, a junior devil, to instruct him more fully in the fiendish art of temptation, he drew his pupil's attention to this fact.[2] It seems Wormwood's particular charge had just become a Christian. Although he deplored the fact, Screwtape did not despair. He pointed out the possibilities, indeed, of the local church. He reminded Wormwood that it comprised just that collection of acquaintances the new convert had hitherto been careful to avoid. There was, for instance, the local grocer. He would come sidling up, with an oily expression on his face, the moment Wormwood's patient set foot inside the door of the local church. He would usher him unctuously to a seat and offer him an incomprehensible prayer book. Screwtape urged Wormwood to make the most of the fact that there were numbers of such people in the local church. They had squeaky boots and ill-fitting clothes and spoke poor English. Perhaps the new convert could be persuaded to dwell on such trivia and remain ignorant of the fact that some of these very people were known to the hosts of hell as mighty warriors in God's camp.

Not many *sophisticated* people, it seems, are called, "not many wise men after the flesh." Not many Sir Isaac Newtons. And not many *self-sufficient* people. "Not many mighty." Not many General Gordons of Khartoum fame. And not many *society* people. "Not many noble." Not many with blue blood in their vein. Not many Queen Victorias or Count Zinzendorfs.

Paul turns from illumination to *illustration* (1 Cor. 1:27–28). God has chosen

---

2. See C. S. Lewis, *The Screwtape Letters* (New York: Macmillan, 1961).

"the foolish things of the world to confound the wise." The cleverest counselor David had was Ahithophel. He was so clever that, at the height of his influence, his words seemed to be the very oracle of God. He was, however, a vengeful man, and it was to indulge his spite that he made common cause with Absalom. When David heard that his former counselor was now whispering in Absalom's ear, he paused in his headlong flight to ask God to "turn the counsel of Ahithophel into foolishness" (2 Sam. 15:31). God used a fool to accomplish His answer to that prayer. The fool was Absalom himself, who heeded the advice of Hushai, a man secretly on David's side, rather than the advice of Ahithophel (17:1–14). As a result, Ahithophel, David's Judas, a man who raged against "the Lord's anointed," ended his life by committing suicide on a homemade gallows in Giloh.

God has chosen "the weak things of the world to confound the things which are mighty." When Pharaoh decided to exterminate the Hebrew slaves by murdering each newborn male, he had the might of Egypt behind him. His Hebrew captives had nobody. In the providence of God a Hebrew couple, Amram and Jochabed, had a baby boy born to them. In defiance of the king's command, they hid the child in a small ark of bulrushes. The royal princess of Egypt found the ark, opened it, and saw the attractive babe within. At that very moment "the babe wept" (Exod. 2:6). That was all God needed to thwart the king's decree and guarantee the eventual emancipation of Israel and the humiliation of Egypt— just a tear on the cheek of a babe!

God has chosen the base things." The word for "base" is *agenēs*, which literally means "without family or descent." He has chosen those with *no family or friends,* no illustrious lineage, no powerful kinsmen. He has chosen "things which are despised." The word here is *exoutheneō,* literally things "counted as nothing." He has chosen those with *no fame or fortune.* He has chosen "things which are not to bring to nought things that are." The word *not* here is the Greek subjective negative, signifying things that men regard as nothing, not existing, nonentities. God has chosen things with *no face or form.*

The book of Judges is full of examples of this kind of thing. God used a left-handed man (3:21), He used an ox-goad (3:31), and He used a feeble woman (4:4). He used a nail (4:21), a piece of millstone (9:53), a pitcher and trumpet (7:20), and the jawbone of an ass (15:16). He used David with a sling and a stone to overthrow Goliath (1 Sam. 17:49). He used a little maid to teach haughty Naaman a lesson (2 Kings 5:1–3) and a dose of insomnia to humble all the proud plans of Haman (Esther 6:1). He used raindrops to immobilize the nine hundred chariots of Sisera (Judg. 4:3; 5:4) and snowflakes to stop both the armies of

Napoleon and Hitler. And so it has been throughout history. Martin Luther was a miner's son, John Calvin a cooper's son, Ulrich Zwingli a shepherd's son, Philip Melanchthon an armorer's son, and John Knox a plain burgess's son. Moody was an uneducated shoe salesman; William Carey was a cobbler.

So, having explained *who God calls when He does,* Paul goes on to explain *why God calls who He does* (1 Cor. 1:29). The explanation for God's use of nobodies is very simple. It is "that no flesh should glory in His presence." God reduced Gideon's army from some 32,000 men to a mere 300 soldiers so that Gideon would never be able to boast of having won the war with Midian. After the overthrow of mighty Jericho, Joshua was filled with self-confidence and readily listened to the carnal advice he was given. "The men went up and viewed Ai," we are told, the next city in the line of advance. "And they returned to Joshua and said unto him, Let not all the people go up; but let about two or three thousand men go up and smite Ai, and make not all the people labour thither; for they are but few" (Josh. 7:2–3). It proved to be a disaster. Not only was there sin in the camp that cut off the divine power, but, in the euphoria after the fall of Jericho, Joshua was too sure of himself. He trusted in the arm of the flesh—and was thoroughly humiliated in consequence.

God will not allow us to glory in the flesh. Indeed, the morrow after a great victory is always a perilous time. Peter had great confidence in the flesh when he boasted he could never deny the Lord. Little did he know the terrible sifting he would have to experience before God could destroy this self-glorying and use him on the day of Pentecost.

Having recorded an explosive statement and an explanatory statement, Paul now records *an expository statement* (1 Cor. 1:30–31), relating everything to the Lord Jesus Christ. First, he relates our *relationship* to Him: "But of him are ye in Christ Jesus." We derive all we have and are from Him. We are "ensphered" in Christ. The spiritual resources of the believer are written off by the world as "nonentities." They are, however, in every sense of the statement "the things that *are.*" A man born blind can have no idea what a sunset looks like, or a rainbow, or the soaring splendor of a thundercloud. We can tell him that the rainbow displays the seven colors of the spectrum, but he cannot conceive the reds, the blues, and the greens we so much admire. He has no concept of color, no faculty to see it. We can tell him how a western sunset turns the evening sky to blood and flame. He knows what blood and flame feel like but he does not know what they look like. Similarly, the unregenerate man is blind to the glories of Christ as seen by those who are "in" Him. Our relationship to Him is what makes the difference. Once we, too, were blind. Now we can see. What once to us were nonentities have now become glorious realities.

Next, Paul relates our *resources* in Christ. He is "made unto us wisdom, and righteousness, and sanctification, and redemption." These four words are the key words of this epistle. Often the Holy Spirit will hang the key to a book by the front door, so to speak. A key verse will be found near the beginning of the book, that unlocks the basic teaching of that book. These four words, here, divide the truth of 1 Corinthians—wisdom (chaps. 1–3), righteousness (chaps. 4–6), sanctification (chaps. 7–14), and redemption (chaps. 15–16).

The Lord Jesus is made unto us *wisdom—to transform our minds.* In Him "are hid all the treasures of wisdom" (Col. 2:3). The fabled wisdom of Solomon pales before the unerring wisdom of the Lord Jesus. His was omniscient wisdom. As Man, His wisdom was based upon His total mastery of the Scriptures and His unreserved commitment to their inerrancy. We recall the day the Jewish authorities pitted their best brains against Him and handed Him three loaded questions, one after another. The Herodians sought to trap Him with a racial issue—should the Jews pay taxes to the Romans? The Sadducees tried to trap Him with a rationalistic issue—how could there be such a thing as resurrection when anyone could think of reasons why such belief was patently ridiculous? The Pharisees tried to trap Him with a rabbinical issue—which was the great commandment of the law?[3] The Lord Jesus deftly sidestepped the traps, answered their questions, and then, with a penetrating question of His own, dealing with a relevant issue, put them to silence (Matt. 22). Such was *His* wisdom. Such can be ours in Christ. Instead of relying on our own mental agility, we can draw on the infinite resources of true wisdom made available to us in Him.

He is made unto us *righteousness—to transform our morals.* The world's standards of right and wrong are relative, cultural, and accommodating. The world calls wrong right and right wrong. God's standards are absolute, universal, and inflexible, and are based on His own absolute holiness. In the Sermon on the Mount, the Lord Jesus took the law of Moses, passed it through the prism of His own mind, broke it into the pristine colors of the rainbow, and lifted it to the highest heaven. Where the law dealt basically with sins, He dealt with sin; where the law went after the fruits, He went straight to the root; where the law dealt with wrongful deeds, He dealt with wrong desires. Then, having lifted the law far beyond the reach of the

---

3. The scribes divided the law into 613 commandments—248 affirmative commands (the total number of parts in the body!) and 365 negative commands (one for each day of the year!). The total represented the number of letters in the Decalogue.

best and most earnest and zealous of men, He lived it out Himself in immaculate perfection all the days of His life. Our righteousness, by comparison, is like the disease-ridden shirt of a leper. His righteousness won the undiluted commendation of His Father in heaven. The genius of the gospel lies in the fact that He clothes us in His righteousness when we come to Him for salvation.

The Lord Jesus is made unto us *sanctification—to transform our motives.* The word for sanctification is *hagiosmos,* literally "holiness." It means to be set apart for God. It stands for the kind of life that belongs to those who are thus separated. Righteousness has to do with our standing; sanctification has to do with our state. Righteousness meets the demands of the law; sanctification meets the demands of the Lord. Righteousness is imputed to us by Christ when we put our faith in Him; sanctification is implemented in us by the indwelling Holy Spirit. Righteousness has to do with what we are by our natural birth—sinners; sanctification has to do with what we have become through our new birth—saints. As a sinner I am motivated to live a sinful life; as a saint I am motivated to live a sanctified life. That life is ours in Christ.

The Lord Jesus is made unto us *redemption—to transform our members.* While we have redeemed souls, we do not yet have our redemption bodies. Our present bodies remain susceptible to disease, death, and decay and, all too often, are the instrument for carrying out our sinful desires, just as they are the instrument for carrying out the purposes of God. It will not be until the Resurrection and the accompanying Rapture that we shall receive our redemption bodies. We will then, each one of us, have a body "like unto his glorious body" (Phil. 3:21), a body capable of feats of which we can only dream today. Paul devotes the best part of a whole chapter to this subject later on in this letter (1 Cor. 15).

Paul now turns to our *rejoicing* in Christ (1 Cor. 1:31). He draws our attention to *His book* and to *our boast:* "That, according as it is written, He that glorieth, let him glory in the Lord." This is a summary quotation from Jeremiah 9:23–24. The Corinthians were glorying in men by eulogizing Peter, Apollos, and Paul. The apostle tells them to get back to their Bibles and learn to glory only in the Lord. If the Corinthians had been half so well acquainted with the Bible as they were with other things, Paul never would have had to write as he did. Jeremiah had long since declared, "Thus saith the LORD, Let not the wise man glory in his wisdom, neither let the mighty man glory in his might, let not the rich man glory in his riches. But let him that glorieth glory in this, that he understandeth and knoweth me, that I am the LORD."

Man cannot understand some aspects of the Cross.

> (2) The wisdom of the Cross (2:1–8)
> > (a) The effectual preaching of the Cross (2:1–3)
> > > i. What Paul determined (2:1–2)
> > > > a. To avoid when preaching the gospel (2:1)
> > > > > 1. Advantages of elocution (2:1a)
> > > > > 2. Advantages of education (2:1b)
> > > > b. To avow when preaching the gospel (2:2)
> > > > > 1. Only the Christ (2:2a)
> > > > > 2. Only the Cross (2:2b)
> > > ii. What Paul displayed (2:3–4)
> > > > a. A conspicuous denial of all human persuasiveness (2:3–4a)
> > > > > 1. His undisguised weakness (2:3)
> > > > > 2. His unadorned words (2:4a)
> > > > b. A convincing demonstration of a higher power (2:4b)
> > > iii. What Paul desired (2:5)
> > > > a. What he wanted excluded (2:5a)
> > > > b. What he wanted exhibited (2:5b)
> > (b) The eternal provision of the Cross (2:6–8)
> > > i. Those who are inspired by true wisdom (2:6–7)
> > > > a. Its sphere (2:6)
> > > > b. Its source (2:7a)
> > > > c. Its secret (2:7b)
> > > > d. Its scope (2:7c)
> > > ii. Those who are insensitive to true wisdom (2:8)
> > > > a. The princes are noted (2:8a)
> > > > b. The proof is noted (2:8b)

Paul is still exposing *the folly of their cleverness* (1 Cor. 1:18–2:16), especially man's inability to comprehend the Cross. The Cross, indeed, exposes the incompleteness *of man's viewpoint* (1:18–2:8). Man cannot understand, Paul says, *the way of the Cross* (1:18–31). Paul now enlarges on his theme. Man cannot understand, either, *the wisdom of the Cross* (2:1–8).

He begins this new section by describing *the effectual preaching of the Cross* (2:1–5). We note, first, *what Paul* determined (2:1–2). He tells *what he determined to avoid* when preaching the gospel (2:1). He tells his Corinthian converts that when he first came to their city it was not with excellency of speech or wisdom, "declaring unto you the testimony of God." In other words, he deliberately avoided the natural advantages of elocution and education. That Paul was an accomplished speaker is evident from his sermons and speeches recorded in the book of Acts. He knew all the tricks of the trade. He knew how to divide or move an audience. The Corinthians, however, applauded the eloquence of Apollos and categorized Paul's speech as "contemptible" (2 Cor. 10:10), not knowing that Paul had deliberately crucified his own great persuasive abilities before he even began the evangelization of their city.

Human eloquence can move people to action. Vast audiences came to hear Hitler. He had an almost hypnotic effect on them. They would cheer and chant. He could move them to tears or rage. He gave them hope and purpose. Shakespeare could do the same thing with words. In Mark Anthony's great speech at the burial of Caesar, Shakespeare shows how a clever orator can so play upon the mind and heart and will of an audience as to turn it from indifference to furious rage. Any preacher with a touch of native eloquence and some knowledge of his audience can move it to applause. Paul determined to avoid such means of getting "decisions" out of the people of Corinth. If he was to be criticized for his studied avoidance of rhetoric, cleverness, and passion, well, that was another cross he was prepared to bear.

Next, he tells us *what he determined to avow* when preaching the gospel (1 Cor. 2:2). "For I determined not to know any thing among you," he says, "save Jesus Christ, and him crucified." Paul had arrived in Corinth from Athens. On Mars Hill he had delivered an oration worthy of the highest applause. It was a masterpiece of reasoning. He appealed to the Athenians' religious concerns and cleverly made use of an image dedicated "to the unknown God" he had seen somewhere in his tour of the town. He appealed to their own poets, showing them that he, as an educated man, knew of Aratus and Cleanthes. He held up their idolatry to the test of reason. But it was all a magnificent failure. He had tried to use the world's weapons and they had misfired. The Athenian philosophers listened to him courteously enough, until he mentioned the Lord's resurrection, then they laughed him out of court. True, he had made one or two converts, but he founded no church.

All the way from Athens to Corinth Paul thought things through. At Corinth he would resist all temptation to display his education and erudition. He would preach nothing but Christ and the Cross. A more unpromising message, humanly speaking, could scarcely be imagined. The Athenians had mocked when he mentioned the Resurrection. Very well! He would defy human wisdom. He would preach Calvary. He would preach the Cross. He would hold up before the Corinthians a man, dying on a Roman cross, suffering for the sin of the world under the curse of God. That was what Paul determined. That cast all upon God.

We are told also *what Paul displayed* (2:3–4). He displayed *a conspicuous denial of all human persuasiveness.* "I was with you in weakness, and in fear, and in much trembling" (2:3). There was *undisguised weakness.* Paul lived with physical infirmity. He was in constant need of the ministrations of a physician. He arrived in Corinth after horrendous experiences in Macedonia. He had been badly beaten and imprisoned at Philippi. At Thessalonica his preaching had resulted in a citywide uproar. At Berea the Jews, who had incited riot at Thessalonica, showed up to stir up the Bereans against him. While walking the streets of Athens, friendless and alone, anxious for the infant Macedonian churches, he was "stirred" by the crass idolatry of the world's intellectual capital—the word used is *paroxunomai,* a medical word meaning "to be moved to anger" (Acts 17:16). The meager results from his preaching at Athens seem to have depressed him. He shrank from the formidable task of evangelizing the most notoriously sinful city of his day. Indeed, even though his initial success at Corinth was considerable, God, who is exceedingly sparing in the matter of words and visitations, spoke personally and directly to Paul, giving him encouragement and assurance.

Not only was there undisguised weakness, there were *unadorned words:* "And my speech and my preaching was not with enticing words of man's wisdom . . ." (1 Cor. 2:4a). Paul had made up his mind—he would not fight Greek philosophy and intellectualism with its own weapons. He had discovered at Athens how blunt and ineffective the world's weapons were when wielded in spiritual war. It did not pay to try to bring about conviction of sin, repentance, and faith in Christ by using clever arguments, by quoting worldly philosophers, and by appealing to the intellect. No, indeed! He would rely solely upon the Word of God, the message of the Cross, and the power of the Holy Spirit of God

Along with this conspicuous denial of all human persuasiveness, there went *a convincing demonstration of a higher power.* His speech and his preaching was "in demonstration of the Spirit and of power" (2:4b). The word *demonstration* here is *apodeixis,* meaning "to point out." It was not that Paul avoided all argument and reasoning in his preaching. It was that he relied only on "demonstrating," on pointing out facts as made clear by God's Word and Calvary. He left the results up to the Holy Spirit who responded with power. After all, it is the Holy Spirit alone who can convict people who are by nature dead and blind to spiritual truth, to the nature of sin, to the need for righteousness and to the nearness of judgment (John 16:8–11).

We are, however, reminded not only of what Paul determined and displayed. We are reminded of *what Paul desired* (1 Cor. 2:5). He wanted something *excluded* from his preaching—"that your faith should not stand in the wisdom of men." After all, if someone is persuaded to make a profession of faith as a result of some person's clever arguments, then that person will likely abandon his profession of faith if some other person presents a clever enough argument. Many a young person from a Christian home, brought up under the sound of the gospel in a Bible-believing church, has gone off to college, or to a liberal seminary, and has had his faith systematically destroyed by clever professors. Such a person's faith was superficial, the intellectual or emotional response to inadequate preaching. At Corinth Paul took great care to make sure that his converts understood the significance of the Cross and that their faith in Christ was firmly anchored to the Word of God. One "thus saith the Lord" will silence any amount of scoffing and skepticism brought against the gospel by those who have great learning, personal charm, and glib tongues.

Paul also wanted something *exhibited* by his converts: "That your faith should . . . stand in . . . the power of God." No clever arguments, no amount of high-sounding nonsense is going to shake the belief of someone who has experienced the life-transforming, soul-thrilling, heartwarming power of God in his life.

Having discussed, then, the effectual preaching of the Cross (2:1–5), Paul now turns to *the eternal provision of the Cross* (2:6–8). He describes two kinds of persons. First, there are *those who are inspired by true wisdom* (2:6–7). He underlines, first, *the sphere* of true wisdom (2:6). He says, "Howbeit we speak wisdom among them that are perfect." The "perfect" here are those who are spiritually mature. Within the circle of those genuinely saved, and therefore enabled by the Holy Spirit to understand spiritual truth, there are always new Christians, carnal Christians, and mature Christians. At Corinth, some of the immature believers had been carried away by the eloquence and sophistication of Apollos. They thought Paul's content and style to be rather elementary. Those who had genuine spiritual discernment, however, would soon appreciate Paul's message, motives, and method, and understand the true wisdom of his low-key and almost mundane approach.

Sometimes the most profound truths can be presented in a deceptively simple way. The formula $E = MC^2$ is unsophisticated enough to look at. However, behind that equation lies the brain and brilliance of Einstein, and it unlocks one of the most profound mysteries of the universe. The ordinary man in the street, untrained in advanced physics, can have but the most elementary understanding of its hidden depths. The man who says, "I cannot see anything in mathematics" is saying something very significant—about himself! Just because he cannot see anything in mathematics doesn't mean that there is nothing there to see. Other men spend their whole lives studying it. Those who were unable to see the amazing depths beneath the surface of Paul's supposedly elementary teaching were simply revealing their own spiritual ignorance. Some of the keenest minds for the past two thousand years have explored the depths of Paul's teaching—and we still have not touched bottom.

Then, too, there is *the source* of true wisdom (1 Cor. 2:7a). "But," says Paul, "we speak the wisdom of God." The wisdom of God, in contrast with the wisdom of men! In the book of Job, especially, we see the wisdom of men set in plain contrast with the wisdom of God. Job's friends sought to convince the suffering patriarch that the horrifying and unprecedented sufferings that had overtaken him were punishment for his sins—and what enormous sins they must be to merit such overwhelming punishment! Eliphaz was the man with the exotic experience. He talked about dreams and visions and spirits. Bildad was the man with the clever clichés. He had a pet proverb or a pat answer for everything. Zophar was the man with the made-up mind. He thought he had a monopoly on God. Eliphaz suggested Job was a sinner, Bildad supposed Job was a sinner, Zophar said Job was a sinner. One and all they agreed that Job's sufferings were a divine visitation on him for some sin in his life.

Job vehemently denied the accusations, although he had no explanation for his sufferings. In his final speech, he justified himself at great length, using the personal pronouns *I, me,* and *my* no less than 195 times! He came close to accusing God of injustice and, on one occasion, challenged God to treat him with the same compassion and concern with which he had treated others. As for Job's wife, she recommended that he curse God and commit suicide. Even Elihu, sometimes called "the mediator," spoke wrathfully both to Job and his other friends. Words! Words! Words! And all wrong! Not one of the people involved in the great debate had sufficient information to make a proper judgment. They did not have either the first two chapters or the last chapter. They did not know why the disasters had come nor how or when they would end. All were arguing from incomplete data. Such is man's wisdom.

Then God spoke, sweeping aside all the wordy arguments of Job and his accusers: "Who is this that darkeneth counsel by words without knowledge?" He demanded (Job 38:2). He asked Job a whole series of questions about the material universe, none of which Job could answer. The point was that if Job could not explain God's ways in the material universe, how could he hope to explain His ways in the much more complex and mysterious moral universe? Job confessed that he had spoken far too much (40:2–5) and that he had spoken of "things too wonderful for me" (42:1–6). Indeed, he repented of his rash words, as well he might, for if we cannot understand God's ways in the material and moral realms, still less, apart from the Holy Spirit, can we understand God's ways in the spiritual realm. Paul could speak only "the wisdom of God" because he was inspired and instructed by the Spirit of God (Eph. 1:17).

Next, Paul speaks of *the secret* of true wisdom (1 Cor. 2:7b). "We speak the wisdom of God in a mystery that God ordained before the world." The English word "mystery" is derived from the Greek word *mysterion,* which denotes a sacred secret. Throughout the Old Testament age, God, at different times and in different ways, made His mind known to men (Heb. 1:1–2). He also kept some things secret, to be revealed in the New Testament. There are a number of such "mysteries," or secrets, revealed in the New Testament which were concealed from God's people in prior ages.[4]

Nearly all of the "mystery" truths of the New Testament were revealed to Paul. All the dark and tragic story of sin in the universe was known to God before the rustle of an angel's wing disturbed the silence of eternity. The whole plan of redemption was conceived in the mind of God long ages before Lucifer raised the standard of rebellion in heaven. For some mysterious reason, which satisfies the omniscient wisdom of God, our planet was chosen as the arena where all the issues of sin would be settled to God's entire and eternal satisfaction. Paul was in on most of these secrets.

Then, too, Paul speaks of *the scope* of true wisdom (1 Cor. 2:7c). It is "unto our glory." We know and can understand that God does all things for His own glory— indeed, this is the basic premise of all true Bible hermeneutics. But that God

---

4. These include the mysteries of the kingdom of heaven (Matt. 13:3–50), the mystery of Israel's blindness during this present age (Rom. 11:25), the mystery of the Rapture (1 Cor. 15:51–52), the mystery of the church as the body of Christ (Eph. 3:11; Rom. 16:25; Eph. 6:19; Col. 4:3), the mystery of the church as the bride of Christ (Eph. 5:28–32), the mystery of the indwelling Christ (Gal. 2:20; Col. 1:26–27), the mystery of the incarnate Christ embodying the fullness of the Godhead (Col. 2:2, 9; 1 Cor. 2:7), the mystery of the process by means of which godliness is restored to men (1 Tim. 3:16), the mystery of iniquity (2 Thess. 2:7; Matt. 13:33), the mystery of the seven stars (Rev. 1:20), and the mystery of Babylon (Rev. 1:20).

should have planned things and permitted things and pursued things "unto *our* glory" is a thought beyond all thought. We would never have dared to think it had God not said so Himself. That guilty, daring rebels of Adam's ruined race should not only be redeemed at infinite cost but be constituted children of God, joint-heirs with Jesus Christ, and be raised up to sit with Him in heavenly places, far above principalities and powers, and held up to an admiring universe as trophies of God's grace is wisdom beyond anything we ourselves could have thought or conceived. The thought ought to inspire us!

In concluding this discussion of the wisdom of the Cross, for it is all because of Calvary, Paul mentions *those who are insensitive to true wisdom* (2:8). The wisdom of God was displayed at Bethlehem when the second Person of the Godhead was incarnated in human flesh. He came to live on earth as a man among men while retaining and demonstrating His absolute Godhead, although veiling His glory. He did all this in order to become the great Mediator between God and men. The princes of this world were ignorant of all this. Caiaphas and his clique in the Sanhedrin categorically denied the evidence of the life, teaching, and miracles of Jesus. They regarded Him as a mere man and a trouble-making and blaspheming one at that. They conspired to get rid of Him. Herod concluded that because Jesus refused to perform a miracle to satisfy his curiosity, the man was a fraud and he mocked Him openly. Pilate was troubled by the Lord's silences, answers, and behavior and was inclined to half believe that Jesus was more than mere man. Certainly he had never met anyone like Him. However, when it came to a crunch, he signed His death warrant and had Him scourged and condemned Him to the cruel death of the cross.

"None of the princes of this world" knew the wisdom of God in Christ, "for had they known it they would not have crucified the Lord of glory." As they were nailing Him to the tree, Jesus prayed for those who were carrying out the infamous sentence. He said, "Father, forgive them, for they know not what they do" (Luke 23:34). Nothing but the restraining hand of God held back twelve legions of angels from pouring over the battlements of heaven and ushering in Armageddon then and there.

It was not until after Pentecost that Peter and the other disciples really began to understand something of the wisdom of the Cross. Peter charged the Jewish people and their leaders with their appalling guilt. However, he saw, at last, a higher wisdom at work. He said, "Ye men of Israel, hear these words; Jesus of Nazareth, a man approved of God among you by miracles and wonders and signs, which God did by him in the midst of you, as ye yourselves also know: Him, being delivered by the determinate counsel and foreknowledge of God, ye have taken, and by wicked hands have crucified and slain: whom God hath raised up, having loosed the pains of death; because it was not possible that he should be holden of it" (Acts 2:22–24).

    b. The incompleteness of man's vision (2:9–16)
        (1) Before God's secrets can be revealed, the inspiration of God is necessary (2:9–11)
          (a) Realization (2:9)
              i. We are naturally ignorant of divine things (2:9a–c)
                  a. The head is unenlightened (2:9a–b)
                      1. Because the eye is incapacitated (2:9a)
                      2. Because the ear is incapacitated (2:9b)
                  b. The heart is unenlightened (2:9c)
              ii. We are notably ignorant of divine things (2:9d)
          (b) Revelation (2:10–11)
              i. Our spiritual comprehension (2:10)
                  a. The source of divine revelation (2:10a)
                  b. The scope of divine revelation (2:10b)
              ii. His simple comparison (2:11)
                  a. What the human spirit knows (2:11a)
                  b. What the Holy Spirit knows (2:11b)
        (2) Before God's secrets can be received, the illumination of God is necessary (2:12–16)
          (a) A new conception (2:12–13)
               i. The person of the Holy Spirit received (2:12)
                  a. A new enablement (2:12a)
                  b. A new enlightenment (2:12b)
               ii. The perception of the Holy Spirit realized (2:13)
                  a. Comprehending the Holy Spirit (2:13a)
                  b. Comparing the Holy Scriptures (2:13b)
          (b) A natural condition (2:14)
               i. Man's natural spiritual blindness (2:14a)
              ii. Man's natural spiritual bondage (2:14b)
          (c) A notable consideration (2:15–16)
            A new ability to
              i. Apprehend what we have in the Scriptures (2:15–16a)
              ii. Appropriate what we have in the Scriptures (2:16b)

Paul has been discussing *the incompleteness of man's viewpoint* (1 Cor. 1:18–2:8) as manifested in his inability to comprehend either the way of the Cross or the wisdom of the Cross. He turns now to *the incompleteness of man's vision* (2:9–16). Sin has so blinded man to spiritual and eternal truth that only God, acting in sovereign, saving grace, can open his blind eyes and quicken his dead spirit.

Paul begins this segment of his epistle by showing that *before God's secrets can be revealed, the inspiration of God is necessary* (2:9–11). First, there has to be *realization* (2:9). We must recognize that we are *naturally ignorant of divine things* (2:9). Both the head and the heart of the unregenerate person are involved. Man's spiritual blindness is total. "Eye hath not seen, nor ear heard, neither hath entered into the heart of man, the things which God hath prepared for them that love him." Paul introduces this statement by referring his readers back to the Old Testament. The quotation as it stands, however, is not found there. There seems here to be an echo of Isaiah 64:4 or 52:15 and 65:17. Paul evidently and primarily wants to draw a distinction between things that can be discovered by a process of human reasoning and things that can be known only as a result of divine revelation.

Man has truly extraordinary intellectual powers. He has explored the secrets of the atom and learned much about the marvels and mysteries of space. He has split the atom, explored the genetic structure of living things, and put men on the moon. There seems nothing man cannot do when it comes to science, technology, and engineering. However, God is not to be discovered by gazing into a microscope or a telescope. We can see His fingerprints everywhere in creation, but we can never know Him, His mind, His heart, His will, apart from divine revelation. The great truths revealed in the Bible never could have been thought out by the mind of man.

We are not only naturally ignorant of divine things, we are *notably ignorant of divine things* as well. For the things of which we are so lamentably ignorant are the very things, indeed, He has "prepared for them that love him."

While the passage undoubtedly refers to man's natural ignorance of divine things, many have seen in it also a reference to our inability to conceive the wonders of the world to come. We cannot even begin to imagine what God has in store for us in eternity. When I was a young boy my father was a businessman in South Wales. Occasionally his business took him to London. If he was to be gone for several days, he would say to us youngsters, "If you're good, when I come back, I'll bring you something!" Of course we always wanted to know what it was going to be. My father had one pet phrase that took care of the matter. He used to say, "You'll have to wait and see!"

We should so much like to know what we are going to be doing in eternity. For the most part, however, God simply says: "You'll have to wait and see!" Even those whose eyes and ears and hearts have been opened, through the new birth, to comprehend spiritual things cannot take in the wonders of that other world— any more than the disciples could comprehend many of the things the Lord talked about prior to Calvary and Pentecost. We can, however, be sure of one thing. We have a God of omniscient genius, a God of omnipotent power. He will never run out of ideas for making heaven an exciting place to be.

Then, too, there is *revelation* (2:10–11). Paul emphasizes first, here, *our spiritual comprehension* (2:10). As to *the source* of what has been revealed, he tells us that "God hath revealed them unto us by his Spirit." Unto us, not the rulers and reasoners of this world. He has revealed to *us* the great truths set before us in the Bible. He has given grand and glorious glimpses of those things "eye hath not seen nor ear heard." Indeed, it is in the Bible, and in the Bible alone, that we have any reliable information on what life and death is all about and what lies beyond the grave for saint and sinner alike. The Holy Spirit has told us all that we need to know. He tells us about creation, about the fall of man, about salvation, sanctification, and service, and about the life to come. The philosophies and theories of men about these things amount to so many wild guesses. Many Eastern religions are based on the theory of reincarnation, the notion that we live over and over again, that what we do in this life determines what we will be in our next life, whether we will come back as a conqueror or a cockroach. Atheists, often arguing from the ills and injustices of life, as life is perceived by them, declare that there is no God at all. The old Viking seafarers went roaring into battle, confident that if they died in war they would feast in the halls of Valhalla. Muslims believe much the same, only their heaven is even more sensuous than the Vikings'. The great goal of Buddhism is extinction. The ways and means men have conceived for achieving the unachievable are as many and as varied as the goals themselves—prayers and penances, rules and rituals, feasts and fasts, sufferings and sacrifices, flames and flagellations. The common note in all of them is salvation by works, by human merit, by our own effort.

Such is human reasoning. The Bible simply says, "For by grace are ye saved through faith; and that not of yourselves: it is the gift of God: not of works, lest any man should boast" (Eph. 2:8–9).

As to *the scope* of what has been revealed, Paul tells us that "the Spirit searcheth all things, yea, the deep things of God." The word for *searcheth* is *eraunaō*. It is used of God, and of the Lord Jesus, searching men's hearts (Rom. 8:27; Rev.

2:23). It is used of the Old Testament prophets diligently searching their own divinely inspired writings concerning truth revealed to them about Christ (1 Peter 1:11). Similarly, the Lord told the Jews to "search the Scriptures" (John 5:39). The Gnostics seized on this expression "the deep things of God" as justification for their heresies, which is perhaps why we are warned of "the depths [deep things] of Satan" (Rev. 2:24).

There are, indeed, unfathomable depths in the Word of God. As David exclaimed in reference to God's omniscience, "such knowledge is too wonderful for me" (Ps. 139:6). So Paul exclaimed, "O the depth of the riches both of the wisdom and knowledge of God! How unsearchable are his judgments, and his ways past finding out," as he thought of the wonder of God's past, present, and promised dealings with the nation of Israel (Rom. 11:33).

It is the Spirit of God who opens to us the deep things of God. He "searcheth" them. The idea is not that He investigates them with a view to acquiring knowledge, for He is the Author of all revealed truth. He penetrates the depths of Scripture and makes those depths clear to those who reverently, patiently, and humbly explore their Bibles. Devout students of the Scriptures are ceaselessly amazed as they come across a new mine of truth here, a new vast vista there, things in the Bible they never saw before. The Bible is, after all, the Word of God and is as infinite and as eternal as the One who has breathed it into being.

Having discussed our spiritual comprehension, Paul gives us *a simple comparison* (1 Cor. 2:11). He compares what the *human spirit* knows with what the *Holy Spirit* knows. A man's innermost thoughts can be known only by the spirit of the man himself. Just so, God's can be known only to God Himself. We reveal our innermost thoughts when we put them into words. Just so, God makes known His thoughts by His Word. The Spirit of God imparts them to us by a process of divine revelation and divine inspiration. The end result of this process is the book we call the Bible.

So then, before God's secrets can be revealed, the inspiration of God is necessary (2:9–11). Now, Paul adds, *before God's secrets can be received, the illumination of God is necessary* (2:12–16). First, there is *a new conception* to be considered (2:12–13). We *receive the Person of the Holy Spirit* (2:12). Paul says, "Now we have received, not the spirit of the world, but the spirit which is of God; that we may know the things that are freely given to us of God." The Holy Spirit enlightens us as we meditate upon God's Word and shows us what we have in Christ. We cannot understand the Bible apart from diligent study, using sound principles of interpretation, and waiting upon God to cast light upon the sacred page. Of course, we can also learn from what others have taught, being careful, however, to test their concepts and conclusions by the Word of God.

This is what the Bereans did. The Holy Spirit says of them that they "were more noble than those in Thessalonica, in that they received the word with all readiness of mind and searched the scriptures daily, whether those things were so" (Acts 17:11). Daniel did the same. "I, Daniel," he says, "understood by books the number of the years whereof the word of the LORD came to Jeremiah the prophet, that he would accomplish seventy years in the desolations of Jerusalem" (Dan. 9:2). It dawned upon Daniel that the Babylonian captivity was about to end, had to end indeed, because God had long since set its bounds. This sudden illumination of the Scriptures set Daniel to praying and, as a result, he was given even more information about things by the Holy Spirit. The seventy years had about run their course, but now he must think in terms of a new prophetic calendar, a period of seventy times seven of years (9:24–27).

So, then, we receive the Spirit of God who illumines for us the Word of God. Those who have "the spirit of the world" will never plumb the depths of the Word of God. Once we receive the Person of the Holy Spirit we can begin to *realize the perception of the Holy Spirit* (1 Cor. 2:13). "We speak," Paul says, referring to the things that are freely given to us of God, "not in the words which man's wisdom teacheth, but which the Holy Ghost teacheth; comparing spiritual things with spiritual." We dig and delve into the Word of God, comparing one Scripture with another. We share spiritual treasure we have discovered with spiritually minded people. Great intellectual attainments are not a prerequisite for understanding spiritual things. Such things can become a liability and certainly do become so when, in the name of scholarship, the Bible is criticized and dissected and reduced to the level of just another religious book.

Take, for instance, the great spiritual truths hidden in the heart of the Pentateuch. Only a person taught of the Spirit of God, comparing Scripture with Scripture, could have first unlocked the amazing typology of the tabernacle, the offerings, the Aaronic priesthood, the wilderness wanderings, and the annual feasts. To the spiritually unenlightened the early chapters of Leviticus are a wilderness. To those who have the key they are among the most amazing chapters in the Bible. Bible names and Bible numbers likewise yield stores of wealth to those who realize their importance. It takes a lifetime to explore just a small part of it all. Mere human cleverness is no help in understanding the great truths of God's Word.

This new conception, this new ability to see and comprehend the hidden depths of God's Word, is contrasted with *our natural condition* (2:14). "The natural man receiveth not the things of the Spirit of God . . . neither can he know them, because they are spiritually discerned." I remember on one occasion taking a neighbor of mine to hear a gifted preacher. The man spoke with great clarity and power on the text, "Ye must be born again." I reveled in the message. I thought to myself, "This must be making an impression on my neighbor." The preacher showed so clearly the spiritual blindness of the devout and religious Nicodemus and how the Lord astounded him with a demand for a brand-new birth. He explained just how a person becomes a child of God. He took us back to Moses and the serpent on the pole, and then took us on to Calvary. To me it was so crystal clear. My neighbor sat stolidly through it all. He maintained a dignified silence on the way home. The next morning we shared a ride downtown. I ventured to ask him what he thought of the message. He hadn't understood a word of it, although he was an educated, clever, and successful man. He said, "My wife is a descendant of John Wesley." And that was that. Somewhere in the family background there was a remote link to somebody religious. He was content with that. The concept of the new birth had gone right over his head!

The Ethiopian eunuch was much the same. He had obtained a copy of Isaiah's prophecy and had read nearly all of it. He had come, indeed, to the magnificent fifty-third chapter that speaks so clearly of Calvary. When Philip asked the man if he understood what he was reading, he admitted his blindness, the spiritual blindness of the natural man. "How can I, except some man should guide me?" he said. Philip, spiritually enlightened, "began at the same scripture and preached unto him Jesus" (Acts 8:26–35).

Paul's discussion of the illumination necessary before God's secrets can be received concludes with *a notable consideration* (1 Cor. 2:15–16). "But he that is spiritual judgeth all things, yet he himself is judged of no man. For who hath known the mind of the Lord, that he may instruct him? But we have the mind of Christ." The spiritual man has spiritual discernment. He judges all things. The word is *anakrinō,* meaning that he discerns all things. The "all things" here are the things of God. Nor is he much concerned when he is judged. Paul was able to shrug off as worthless the criticism he was receiving at Corinth (4:3–4). Paul was not adverse to self-judgment, to constructive criticism, or to community discipline. However, he argued, the believer is answerable only to God. Moreover, those who do not have the Spirit cannot even evaluate the values of the spiritual man.

Paul illustrates his point with a quotation from Isaiah 40:13. Who can know the mind of God? Who can instruct Him? Nobody! The natural man is equally incompetent to judge the spiritual man and his spiritual values. The spiritual man actually has "the mind of Christ." He has the very thoughts of Christ! It is the Holy Spirit who imparts the mind of Christ to the believer.

    B.   The spirit of their sectarianism (3:1–4:21)
        1. It was a carnal spirit (3:1–17)
           a. The fact of their carnality (3:1–4)
              (1) Their carnality decried (3:1–3)
                  (a) The childish level of their beliefs (3:1–2)
                      i. Paul found them as babes (3:1)
                      ii. Paul fed them as babes (3:2)
                  (b) The childish level of their behavior (3:3)
                      i. In their sectarian wars (3:3a)
                      ii. In their spiritual walk (3:3b)
               (2) Their carnality described (3:4)
           b. The folly of their carnality (3:5–8)
              (1) The question of reality (3:5)
                  (a) The men involved (3:5a)
                  (b) The ministry involved (3:5b)
              (2) The question of results (3:6–7)
                  (a) An appeal (3:6)
                      i. The human partners (3:6a)
                      ii. The heavenly partner (3:6b)
                  (b) An application (3:7)
                      i. Who are involved (3:7a)
                      ii. What is involved (3:7b)
              (3) The question of rewards (3:8)
                  (a) Perfect accord in the body (3:8a)
                  (b) Personal acclaim at the Bema (3:8b)

Paul has been speaking to the Corinthians about *the source of their sectarianism* (1 Cor. 1:10–2:16), exposing the folly of *their clannishness* (1:10–17) and of *their cleverness* (1:18–2:16). He now turns instead to *the spirit of their sectarianism* (3:1–4:21). It was, first of all, *a carnal spirit* (3:1–17). Paul will show *the fact* (3:1–4), *the folly* (3:5–8), and *the fruits* (3:9–17) of their sectarianism.

Beginning with the fact of their carnality, *their carnality is decried* (3:1–3).

Paul underlines, first, *the childish level of their beliefs* (3:1–2). He *found* them to be babes: "And I, brethren, could not speak unto you as unto spiritual, but as unto carnal, even as unto babes in Christ" (3:1). In his letter to Rome, written from this very city of Corinth, Paul outlines for us the characteristics of three men. First there is *the spiritual man* (Rom. 7:1–6), the person who knows the truth of being "married to another, even to him who is raised from the dead," and who, consequently, is producing "fruit unto God." Free from the law, the spiritual person lives for the Lord. This is the kind of person every believer should be. He is indwelt and filled with the Holy Spirit who Himself makes Christ real to him just as the servant, in the matchless Old Testament type, sought to make Isaac real to Rebekah (Gen. 24:65).

Then there is *the natural man* (Rom. 7:7–13). The picture here is of a person in his unregenerate state doing his best to keep the commandments of God and miserably failing. Indeed, the law, far from being an instrument of salvation, proves to be a means of condemnation. Nobody tried harder than Saul of Tarsus to merit salvation by the works of the law. No one understood better than he the inner gnawing of conviction of sin, failure, and judgment to come (Phil. 2:3–11).

In concluding this great treatise on the nature of man, Paul talks about *the carnal man* (Rom. 7:14–23). The carnal man is a saved man, indwelt by the Holy Spirit, who nevertheless tries to live the Christian life on the same principle that the unsaved man tries to merit eternal life. He tries to live the Christian life in the energy of the flesh—and fails. The failure is dismal and complete. The carnal man is thoroughly wretched. The Holy Spirit indwelling him will not let him enjoy worldliness and sensuality; the old nature within him will not let him enjoy his new life in Christ.[5]

Paul holds the Corinthian believers accountable for their carnality. He could not even speak to them on a high spiritual plane. He could only talk to them as babes. Babes are attractive enough so long as they grow up, but a babe who remains a babe for twenty years is a tragedy. Babes are self-centered. They are dependent on others for all their needs. They have short attention spans. They go for things that glitter, and they have no sense of values. They are illiterate and ignorant of much they need to know. Their own wants are predominant. They are ruled by their appetites and move fitfully from one thing to another. They are unable to feed themselves, or to protect themselves, or to defend themselves. They cannot see beyond their own little world. They enjoy being the center of

---

5. See John Phillips, *Exploring Romans* (Grand Rapids: Kregel, 2002).

attention and soon learn how to get their share of it. They have no thought for the needs and concerns of others. They are demanding. They get themselves in the most frightful messes and seem blissfully unaware of it. They demand a great deal of care. But, in time, they grow up. The trouble with the Corinthians was that they did not grow up. Paul found them to be still babes.

Consequently, he had to *feed* them as babes: "I have fed you with milk, and not with meat: for hitherto ye were not able to bear it, neither yet now are ye able" (1 Cor. 3:2). It was not for lack of teaching. Paul had remained in Corinth for a year and a half (Acts 18:11) "teaching the word of God among them." He labored there as an evangelist, as a pastor, and as a teacher. Imagine having the apostle Paul as your teacher! He soon took the measure of his beloved Corinthians, however. Doctrine did not interest them; what they wanted were the gifts—the spectacular sign gifts. No wonder Paul tells them bluntly that clever and capable as they no doubt were, they were childish (1 Cor. 13:11). There was so much he wanted to teach them—all the great truths we find in Philippians, Ephesians, Colossians, Thessalonians, and Hebrews. He would have liked to have taken them through the Old Testament explaining the types, highlighting prophecy, showing them Christ. They, however, were restless under the most prosaic and elementary teaching. As for a full course of doctrine—soteriology, pneumatology, anthropology, angelology, ecclesiology, theology, eschatology, and the like—they were nowhere ready for that. He had to feed them as babes—just a few simple truths about salvation, baptism, the ordinances, resurrection, giving, and personal accountability—that was about all they were able to handle.

He underlines, too, *the childish level of their behavior* (3:3). He mentions envy, strife, and divisions. "Are ye not carnal, and walk as men?" he demands. The word for *carnal* is *sarkikos*, "men of the flesh," sensual, under the control of their animal appetites, governed by their human nature and not by the Holy Spirit. The word for *envying* is *zēlos*—jealousy. W. E. Vine says that the distinction between envy and jealousy lies in this—that envy wants to deprive another of what he has, jealousy desires the same sort of thing for itself.[6] At Corinth, this attitude of jealousy was particularly noticeable in connection with the sign gifts. The word for *strife* is *eris*, contention as an expression, indeed, of enmity. There were all kinds of quarreling, rivalry, and wrangling going on in this church. It was in the same spiritual state as Israel in the wilderness when they spent their time murmuring and arguing and contending with Moses and Aaron. Paul could very

---

6. W. E. Vine, *Vine's Expository Dictionary of New Testament Words* (London: Oliphants, 1952).

well have written Hebrews 3:7–4:11 to this church. It certainly stood in need of that teaching.

So, then, their carnality is *decried* (1 Cor. 3:1–3). Now it is *described*: "For while one saith, I am of Paul; and another, I am of Apollos; are ye not carnal?" (3:4). That was the proof that there was jealousy and strife at work in the Corinthian church. It was also proof that they were unspiritual. We have grown up with denominationalism and more or less accept it as normal and necessary. Paul had a horror of it and of the spirit that produced it. The Lord prayed that all His people might be one in the same bond of oneness He and His Father enjoyed (John 17:21–23). It has been part of Satan's master strategy against the church to divide it. Yet within the mystical body of Christ there is a oneness that the Father sees, which we occasionally glimpse, and which will be displayed to the universe in eternity. Satan cannot destroy that.

In one of the grand old worship hymns we sang when I was a boy, one stanza went thus:

> We would remember we are one
> With every saint that loves Thy Name;
> United to Thee on the throne,
> Our life, our hope, our Lord the same.

Having, then, discussed *the fact* of their carnality, Paul turns to *the folly of their carnality* (1 Cor. 3:5–8). He confronts the Corinthians, first, with *the question of reality*: "Who then," he demands, "is Paul, and who is Apollos, but ministers by whom ye believed, even as the Lord gave to every man?" Who were these men, even Paul himself? Just servants of the Lord! The Corinthians preferred one above the other. Paul says God simply used them as His instruments to bring about their conversion. They had different gifts but the same grace (Rom. 12:6). What would heaven be like, indeed, if this Corinthian contentiousness were to be carried over to there? Here would be one set of believers boosting D. L. Moody, another group singing the praises of Martin Luther, another bragging about John Calvin or John Wesley or General William Booth! The very idea is ludicrous! Paul urges the Corinthians to face the facts. Men, even the most illustrious of men, are only men even though they brought a great deal of background, variety, and gift with them into the ministry.

Paul, for instance, came from a Pharisaical background. He was a trained rabbi, a pupil of the illustrious Gamaliel. He grew up among the Hellenist Jews of

Tarsus, the chief city of Cilicia. He prized the invaluable asset of being a Roman citizen. He was not only thoroughly at home in rabbinical law but well versed in Greek philosophy. He had been a rabid persecutor of the church and became the foremost missionary, theologian, and spokesman of the church.

Apollos, by contrast, grew up in Alexandria, which had a large Jewish community. The Jews of Alexandria enjoyed a considerable amount of self-government. Some even held influential posts in the city administration. Philo's brother, Alexander, was not only chief customs officer, he was fabulously wealthy. Philo himself was a patriotic Jew. He was also an eager student of Greek philosophy, especially that of Plato, the Stoics, and the Neo-Pythagoreans. His goal was to interpret the Old Testament in the light of Greek philosophy. He developed a system of hermeneutics based on an allegorical interpretation of the Scriptures, pressed to the point of absurdity. He was, nevertheless, one of the most influential Jews of his day. Apollos was an Alexandrian and would have found it difficult to escape the influence of Philo. Apollos, well versed in the Old Testament Scriptures, probably the Septuagint version, pointed people to Christ, even though his understanding of the gospel was defective at first. It is very likely that Apollos favored Philo's allegorical hermeneutics. In any case, his style, so unlike Paul's, appealed to many.

Even so, Paul and Apollos, great and gifted as they were, were only servants whom God had been pleased to use as instruments in His hand to bring numbers of the Corinthians to Christ. That was the reality. Both the *men* involved and the *ministry* involved were of God.

Paul turns now to *the question of results* (1 Cor. 3:6–7). First we have *his appeal* (3:6). He says, "I have planted, Apollos watered [the *human* partners in the work of winning souls]; but God gave the increase [the heavenly Partner]." We do not know what Paul may have thought about Alexandrian Christianity, which certainly seems to have been somewhat defective, or what he may have thought of Apollos's tendency to over-allegorize the Old Testament Scriptures. He never cuts him down. They were workers together in the great task of winning people to Christ. One did this, one did that. Paul and Apollos were on the same side.

When John on one occasion said to the Lord Jesus, "Master, we saw one casting out devils in thy name, and he followeth not us: and we forbad him, because he followeth not us." Jesus replied, "Forbid him not: for there is no man which shall do a miracle in my name, that can lightly speak evil of me. For he that is not against us is on our part" (Mark 9:38–40).

So Paul saw Apollos as a partner, not as a rival. On all the really important issues they were one. There was plenty of work for everyone. Not all are gifted to plow and plant. Not all have the patience and concern to water. In any case, neither one could accomplish anything without God, who alone can give the harvest.

Now comes his *application* (1 Cor. 3:7). "So then," he says, "neither is he that planteth anything, neither he that watereth; but God that giveth the increase." The seed was sown, a very simple operation indeed. The farmer made a make-shift bag out of the folds of his garment, filled it with seed, and walked up and down his field throwing the seed far and wide upon the ground. The seed was watered. Again, the operation was simple in the extreme. The water ran down channels. As the farmer wanted to direct it here or there he dammed one channel by moving some earth with his foot and opened another the same way. Nothing could be simpler than sowing or watering. Anyone could do it. It took little or no skill. Besides, in the whole process of working for a harvest, that was about all anyone could do.

Then came the hard part, the mysterious part, the impossible part. That dry seed germinated! There was life there! Tiny roots went down into the moist soil. Tiny green shoots showed tentatively above the ground. A miracle had taken place which had no explanation apart from God. There was life and growth. Shoots became stems. The stems produced another wonder, fragrant, colored, and beautiful flowers. The bees came. The pollen was transferred from plant to plant. Fruit appeared. The miracle happens so often we take it for granted. We call it "nature." It is God! God at work, giving the increase. Only God knows how to turn a seed into fruit.

Paul planted the seed, the Word of God (Matt. 13:19). Apollos came along and did what he could. Paul and Apollos alike were nothing. Anybody could do what they did. It calls for no great skill to pass on a verse of Scripture or to encourage someone to heed God's Word. But by what mysterious process does the seed germinate in a human heart? "Being born again," says Peter, "not of corruptible seed, but of incorruptible, by the word of God, which liveth and abideth for ever . . . and this is the word which by the gospel is preached unto you" (1 Peter 1:23, 25). But how does it happen? When talking to Nicodemus about the same mystery, only using a different illustration, Jesus bluntly said, "Thou . . . canst not tell" (John 3:8). Nicodemus may have been a learned doctor of the law but he did not have the slightest idea how spiritual life is germinated in a human soul. Nor do we.

Paul recognized that the whole mysterious process of conviction, conversion,

and consecration, with all its ramifications of election, justification, sanctification, atonement, redemption, reconciliation, regeneration, and glorification, was
one vast mystery which had no explanation apart from God. All is of God. God
gives the increase. "How does blood cleanse sin?" an unbeliever demanded of a
Christian. "How does water quench thirst?" responded the Christian. "I don't
know," said the unbeliever, "but I know that it does." Just so! We don't know how
blood cleanses sin but we know that it does because God says that it does (1 John
1:7). We don't know how the planting and watering of the gospel seed results in
people being born again but we know that it does. All the glory belongs to God
who gives the increase.

Paul follows all this up by raising *the question of rewards* (1 Cor. 3:8). He calls
for *perfect accord in the body:* "Now he that planteth and he that watereth are
one." It is not a question of rivalry. We all have different gifts and abilities and
different tasks. The Holy Spirit is "the Lord of the harvest" (Matt. 9:37–38).
There are few enough willing to labor; we cannot afford to spend time fighting
among ourselves, raiding other men's fields, pushing for recognition and position. We are to be one when it comes to evangelizing a lost world.

Paul speaks also of *personal acclaim at the Bema,* the judgment seat of Christ:
"Every man shall receive his own reward according to his own labour." The emphasis is on the words "his own." We may, perhaps, derive inspiration from some other
man's ministry but we are not to lionize anyone. The important thing is to get on
with the work entrusted to us. The promised reward is a powerful incentive. There
are some who decry the idea of working for reward. It seems to them to be an
inferior motive. "We should work for the Lord because we love Him," they say.
"We should work to win souls out of compassion for them." All well and true.
However, the offer of reward as an incentive for service is one often encountered in
Scripture. Indeed, right here, Paul goes on to expand his own teaching on the
subject. He himself never lost sight of his promised crown (2 Tim. 4:6–8). The
Lord Jesus Himself held out the prospect of rewards (Matt. 5:10–12). However, we
are not going to be rewarded because of what someone else has done. We shall have
plenty to do if we pay attention to the work the Lord has entrusted to us. We are
neither to covet nor criticize another person's field. We need to cultivate our own.

    c. The fruits of their carnality (3:9–17)
       (1) The promised judgment of their labors by the Savior (3:9–15)
          (a) Two pictures suggested (3:9)
             i. Working in the harvest (3:9a)

          ii. Working on a house (3:9b)

      (b) Two potentials stated (3:10–15)

          i. The work is trusted to us (3:10–12)

             a. The finished work (3:10–11)

                1. The diligent servant and the foundation of the building (3:10)

                   (i) The appropriate grace he received (3:10a)

                   (ii) The apostolic gift he received (3:10b)

                2. The divine Son and the foundation of the building (3:11)

             b. The further work (3:12)

                1. Building with the choicest of materials (3:12a)

                2. Building with the cheapest of materials (3:12b)

          ii. The work is tested by Him (3:13–15)

             a. A day of revelation (3:13)

                1. The date has been set (3:13a)

                2. The day will be sobering (3:13b)

             b. A day of reward (3:14)

             c. A day of regrets (3:15)

                1. What cannot be changed (3:15a)

                2. What cannot be challenged (3:15b)

  (2) The present judgment of their lives by the Spirit (3:16–17)

      (a) The temple defined (3:16)

          i. The sanctuary of God (3:16a)

          ii. The Spirit of God (3:16b)

      (b) The temple defiled (3:17a)

      (c) The temple destroyed (3:17b–c)

          i. The awesome reason (3:17b)

          ii. The awesome realization (3:17c)

Paul has been discussing the carnality of the Corinthians, especially as manifested by their sectarian spirit, an utterly carnal spirit, in which this one or that one was promoted and applauded and the other one decried and put down. He has shown *the fact* of their carnality (1 Cor. 3:1–4) and *the folly* of their carnality

(3:5–8). He now turns to *the fruits of their carnality* (3:9–17). He develops the theme against the background of the judgment seat of Christ. He deals first with *the promised judgment of their labors by the Savior* (3:9–15) and then with *the present judgment of their lives by the Spirit* (3:16–17).

Nothing is more certain from Scripture than the fact of "judgment to come" (John 16:8, 11). Much confusion has arisen because of a general failure to distinguish between the various judgments revealed in the Bible. There is the judgment of *sin.* This took place on the cross when "Christ died for our sins according to the Scriptures" (1 Cor. 15:3). Those who trust Christ will never have to face the penal and eternal consequences of their sin (Rom. 8:1).

There is the judgment of *society.* God sovereignly intervenes in the affairs of men at times and executes summary judgment as He did in the days of Noah, in the overthrow of Sodom, and the fall of Jerusalem in the days of Nebuchadnezzar and again under the Romans. The judgment of society and the Gentile nations will climax in the great assize held at Jerusalem in the Valley of Jehoshaphat at the end of the battle of Armageddon and just prior to the establishment of the millennial kingdom (Joel 3:2; Matt. 25:31–46).

There is the judgment of *sinners.* This will take place at the great white throne, after the millennium and just prior to the creation of a new heaven and a new earth (Rev. 20:11–21:1). Those who stand at this judgment are lost eternally.

There is the judgment of *saints.* God's people are judged in two capacities. We are judged as *sons* (Heb. 12:5–11). This judgment results in chastisement down here. It is parental and remedial and can be avoided (1 Cor. 11:31). We are also to be judged as *servants* (Rom. 14:10; 2 Cor. 5:10) when our lives will be reviewed and our works assessed. Both rebukes and rewards will be dispensed at this judgment, which takes place at the judgment seat of Christ. It is this judgment Paul has in mind here in 1 Corinthians 3:9–15.

Before he begins to detail the promised judgment of their labors by the Lord, *Paul suggests two pictures* (3:9). This verse is transitional, bridging the gap between the previous verses and the ones which follow. The first picture is that of a man *working in the harvest:* "For we are labourers together with God: ye are God's husbandry." This ties on to the previous illustration of planting and watering. It is an agricultural illustration. What grace and condescension on God's part, what a privilege and responsibility on our part—to be "God's fellow workers" in this world! He could have evangelized the world by means of a miracle. He could have sent twelve legions of angels to be His messengers to men. He chose not to do so, but rather to make use of us. He oversees the work and directs us where He will in the mission field. He supplies the things we need. But He uses us. He has "given to us the ministry of reconciliation; to wit, that God was in Christ, reconciling the world unto himself, not imputing their trespasses unto them; and hath committed unto us the word of reconciliation" (2 Cor. 5:18–20). Doubtless, the work would have been done much more efficiently and expeditiously by angels, but such was neither God's will nor God's way. He reaches lost people by means of saved people. In the words of an old hymn,

> "Glory!" is what the angels sing,
> And I expect to help them make the courts of heaven ring.
> But when I sing redemption's story, they will fold their wings,
> For angels never felt the joys that my salvation brings.

By using us as His fellow workers, He not only lifts us to great heights of glory and honor, He also trains and disciplines us in the process and prepares us for spheres of service in the millennial and eternal ages to come. And more! He gives us the opportunity to earn rewards!

Slightly changing the illustration, the Holy Spirit adds, "Ye are God's husbandry." We are, so to speak, not only the farmer, but also the field! The word for *husbandry* is *georgiōn*. It suggests a field under God's cultivation.

Then Paul abruptly changes the whole picture. "Ye are God's building," he says. The apostle switches to an architectural illustration and shows us a man *working on a house*. The concept of the believer as a dwelling place for God, and the church being "an habitation of God through the Spirit" is one Paul often used (1 Cor. 6:19–20; Eph. 2:22). This illustration prepares the way for the discussion which follows, in which this whole idea of working in partnership with God on a building is developed against the background of the judgment seat of Christ.

In the light of this great and inescapable coming assize, *Paul states two potentials* (1 Cor. 3:10–15). First of all, while the work is *trusted to us* (3:10–12), it is to be *tested by Him* (3:13–15). We must never lose sight of that. We look, initially, at *the finished work* (3:10–11). We are given two views of the foundation of this building, for that part of the work has been finished to God's entire satisfaction. We are invited by Paul himself, God's *diligent servant* (3:10), to inspect the part played in laying the foundation. He emphasizes the *appropriate* grace he received in order to do what had to be done: "According to the grace of God which is given unto me . . . I have laid the foundation" (3:10a). This is one of Paul's favorite expressions (15:10; Rom. 15:15; Gal. 2:9; Eph. 3:2). Paul could never get over the amazing grace of God which sought him out and saved him and entrusted him with his extraordinary ministry (1 Tim. 1:12). The grace here, however, seems to have to do with the special grace needed to found a local church, such as the church at Corinth.

Paul emphasizes also *the apostolic gift* he received: "As a wise masterbuilder, I have laid the foundation, and another buildeth thereon. But let every man take heed how he buildeth thereon" (1 Cor. 3:10b). The word for master builder is *architekton,* from which we derive our word "architect." It occurs only here in the New Testament. The Greek word carried the idea not only of a designer but also of a principal builder, so Paul describes himself as a "wise" *master builder.* The word *wise* here means "skillful" and was doubtless aimed at those of Paul's critics who thought he was anything but wise. Paul knew how clearly he had been guided by the Holy Spirit in the policies he had adopted at Corinth.

We learn from Ephesians that the church is "built upon the foundation of the apostles and prophets" (2:20). The two gifts of apostle and prophet were essential for guiding and guarding the church in its early stages and until such time as the New Testament was complete.

The warning "But let every man take heed how he buildeth thereon" seems to have specific overtones. It was Paul's settled policy not to build on another man's foundation (Rom. 15:20). We can understand, therefore, why he kept a sharp watch on what others wanted to build on to his churches. Religious leaders from Jerusalem and Judea had already tried to build legalism and Judaism onto the churches he had founded in Galatia. Some think that Paul had the Cephas party in mind here and that the reference to "every man" (literally "another man") is a reference to the leader of the legalizers in the church at Corinth, or even a barely veiled reference to Peter himself.

We are invited to look, moreover, at the part played by God's *divine Son* in laying the foundation of the church : "For other foundation can no man lay than that is laid, which is Jesus Christ" (1 Cor. 3:11). The Peter enthusiasts, especially, should have been aware that the Lord had called Peter a mere pebble *(petros)* and declared Himself the great foundation rock *(petra)* on which the church was to be built (Matt. 16:18). The reference there, as here, primarily is to the universal church although, of course, the foundation on which every local church rests is also Christ. Moreover, the great doctrines of the New Testament are inseparable from Christ, "the church's one foundation." It is a serious matter to tamper with truth.

Paul now turns from *the finished work,* the work on the foundation, to *the further work* in which we are all invited to participate. He contrasts building with *choice materials* with building with *cheap materials:* "Now if any man build upon this foundation, gold, silver, precious stones, wood, hay, stubble" (1 Cor. 3:12). The precious metals and stones set forth the glories of Christ. In the gold we have a reference to the glory of *His Person*, for throughout Scripture gold is frequently used as a symbol of deity. The Lord Jesus is God over all, "blessed for evermore" (2 Cor. 11:31). In the tabernacle the acacia wood was overlaid with gold (Exod. 25:11), a reference to both the humanity (acacia wood) and the deity (gold) of Christ. In the silver we have a reference to *His passion.* We are reminded by the silver of our redemption (Exod. 30:12–16; 1 Peter 1:18) and of the infinite cost of Calvary which no amount of silver could ever portray. In the precious stones we have a reference to *His position*, now seated in heaven at the right hand of God. "To whom coming, as unto a living stone," Peter says, "disallowed [rejected] of men, but chosen of God and precious" (1 Peter 2:4). When John saw the One who sat upon the throne in glory he could only describe Him as being "like a jasper and a sardine stone" (Rev. 4:3). Precious stones of all kinds adorn the foundations of the celestial city (21:14–20), the very streets are paved with gold, and the city itself is ablaze with the glory of God, "and her light," John says, "was like unto a stone most precious" (21:11, 21).

It is our responsibility to set forth the glories of Christ. The Holy Spirit is here supremely to speak of Him (John 16:13). We are to speak to men of His Person, who He really is, the uncreated, self-existing, second Person of the Godhead, who stepped out of eternity into time so that He might become man and show us in His Person what God is really like.

We are to speak also of His passion. "For Christ also hath once suffered for sins, the just for the unjust, that he might bring us to God, being put to death in the flesh, but quickened by the Spirit" (1 Peter 3:18). We are to take people to Calvary and tell them that in Him "we have redemption through his blood, the forgiveness of sins" (Eph. 1:7). We are to take people to Calvary and expound to them the mystery of Christ's cross.

Moreover, we are to speak of His position, for "God also hath highly exalted him, and given him a name which is above every name: that at the name of Jesus every knee should bow . . . and that every tongue should confess that Jesus Christ is Lord" (Phil. 2:9–11). We are to remind people of where He now is. He is seated on His Father's throne in heaven (Heb. 1:3), there to function as our Great High Priest and Advocate (7:24–28), while waiting for the day when He can come again in glory and in power. Such is the gold, the silver, and the precious stones.

By contrast, wood, hay, and stubble are worthless things. They represent things added to the church that do not belong to it. How much has been imported from the world and incorporated into the church by men! How much, considered important, is nothing more than the product of human reasoning and carnal religious energy! At Corinth, Paul doubtless had in mind "the wisdom of men," things men thought it important to add to the church but really had no part in vital Christianity. In his letter to the Colossians, for example, Paul attacks intellectualism (2:8–10), ritualism (2:11–13), legalism (2:14–17), mysticism (2:18–19), and asceticism (2:20–22)—all the paraphernalia, indeed, of man-made religion and all foreign to New Testament Christianity, yet all considered by some as important features of the church.

The work trusted to us (1 Cor. 3:10–12) will be *tested by Him* (3:13–15). Paul reminds us of the day when we will stand at the judgment seat of Christ. It will be *a day of revelation* (3:13). He says, "Every man's work shall be made manifest: for the day shall declare it, because it shall be revealed by fire; and the fire shall try every man's work of what sort it is." The truth is that, while God gives us unmerited salvation, He never gives us unmerited rewards. Rewards have to be earned. We should remember, moreover, that this is to be a judgment seat, not a mercy seat. We can thank God that there *is* a mercy seat and it is available to any child of God at any time (Heb. 4:16; 10:13–22). As long as we are still down here we can seek cleansing and forgiveness for our sins and shortcomings, make restitution for wrongs done, and yield ourselves to the Holy Spirit for restoration. Sin can be confessed and cleansed and put away down here. However, at the judgment seat of Christ, our lives will pass in review and it will be too late to put things right. As a result, there will be rebukes as well as rewards.

The word for *declare* is *dēloō,* which means "to make plain," or "to signify." How many issues there are that will be made plain enough at the judgment seat of Christ! We can think of such things as unconfessed sin, wrong influence, ruined lives, wasted time and talents, squandered opportunities, neglect of spiritual things, ignorance or indifference in regard to God's Word and God's will, prayerlessness, worldliness, and carnality. All such things will be reviewed in the presence of the Lord who bought us with His own blood. How ashamed we shall be of all such things!

"Revealed by fire," Paul says, for "our God is a consuming fire" (Heb. 12:29). The reference is doubtless to God's burning holiness. Paul reminds us here of the seriousness of this judgment seat. It is no light matter for us to have to stand before it. In a parallel reference to it in 2 Corinthians 5:10–11, he links it contextually to "the terror of the Lord." What is at issue at the judgment seat of Christ is not our *position* in the family—God has sovereignly decided that and it has been eternally secured for us by the precious blood of Christ. In his famous passage on eternal security Paul begins with "no condemnation" and ends with "no separation" (Rom. 8:1, 35–39). What is at issue is our *performance* in the family. For performance in the family determines position in the kingdom. Our rank and responsibilities in the millennial kingdom hinge upon what we have done with our lives since we accepted Christ. There are numerous proofs of this in the Bible—the Lord's parable of the negligent servant being a case in point (Matt. 25:14–30). The parable of the pounds teaches similar truth (Luke 19:11–27).

It will not only be a day of revelation, it will also be *a day of reward:* "If any man's work abide which he hath built thereon, he shall receive a reward" (1 Cor. 3:14). The nature of the reward is not eternal life, since that is a gift (Rom. 6:23). It is rather a place of dignity and honor in the millennial kingdom. The Lord is coming back to earth, to the scene of His sufferings, to the world where He was tried and tortured, mocked and murdered, cursed and crucified. But He is coming back in power and great glory (Matt. 24:30–31). Every eye will see Him, "and they also which pierced him" (Rev. 1:7). He is going to reign like David and put down all His enemies. Then He is going to reign like Solomon in such magnificence, wisdom, and power as the world has never seen. His global empire will embrace every nook and cranny of the planet and will last for a thousand years. From the dazzling splendor of His capital to earth's remotest bounds, His greatness and glory will be known. He will bestow upon those, whose works endure the fiery test of the judgment seat, positions of enormous power and prestige during this kingdom age. This is what is at stake.

When I was in my middle teens, I graduated from high school in Britain and went to work for Barclay's Bank. I was given a written examination and an interview. Then I was told that I was hired "on probation." That sounded very impressive to me. It sounded less so when my father explained to me that for the next three months I should be on trial! The bank officials would be watching my behavior, evaluating my performance, studying my character. I was on probation, on trial.

The Lord could have taken us home to heaven the moment we were saved, for our standing in Christ assures us of that. The dying thief went from Calvary to Paradise (Luke 23:39–43). Instead, He has left us here to "work out our salvation with fear and trembling" (Phil. 2:12–13). We are on probation. We are being given time and opportunity to make full use of the spiritual gifts that have been entrusted to us—not to see if we qualify for heaven, for that is never in question, but to see if we qualify for a position of honor in the millennial kingdom.[7] There is one encouraging truth connected with this otherwise forbidding prospect of standing at the judgment seat of Christ. "Then shall every man have praise of God," Paul says (1 Cor. 4:5). The Lord will always praise and reward what He can.[8]

Moreover, this will be *a day of regrets* (1 Cor. 3:15). There are some things which *cannot be changed:* "If any man's work shall be burned he shall suffer loss." It will be too late at the judgment seat of Christ to say, "I'm sorry! I wish I hadn't done that. I wish I hadn't said that. I wish I had taken more seriously living the Christian life." It was too late for Achan to make confession once he had been found out (Josh. 7:16–26). It was too late for Ananias and Sapphira to confess once they had been exposed (Acts 5:1–10). It was too late for Reuben to confess his sin once he was called before the judgment seat of Jacob (Gen. 49), a remarkable type, indeed, of the judgment seat of Christ.[9] Now is the time to confess our sins and seek cleansing, to make what restitution we can and to begin to seriously cultivate the ministry of the Holy Spirit in our lives. By the time we get to the judgment seat of Christ it will be too late.

Christians as a whole have seriously neglected or willfully diluted the whole concept of this assize. We treat the judgment seat of Christ as though it were a Sunday school picnic. Paul evidently sees the occasion as terrifying enough to append a final word of assurance. He concludes with *what cannot be challenged:* "but he himself shall be saved: yet so as by fire." The ship is lost, the sailor is saved. The work is burned, the believer is not. But oh! what loss.

When I was a boy, we used to sing a hymn that seems to have gone out of style now, but the words are poignant. The hymn enshrines the last words of a dying believer who, like so many, had a saved soul and a lost life:

> Must I go and empty-handed,
> Must I meet my Savior so?
> Not one soul with which to greet Him,
> Must I empty-handed go?

---

7. For a further discussion of this, see John Phillips, *Exploring the Psalms, vol. 1* (Grand Rapids: Kregel, 2002), Psalm 24.
8. See His words to the seven churches (Rev. 2–3).
9. See John Phillips, *Exploring Genesis* (Grand Rapids: Kregel, 2001).

Years ago, at the Moody Bible Institute annual Founder's Week Conference, I heard Allen Redpath tell of his call to full-time Christian service. He was a successful businessman at the time and, at first, he resisted the call of God. However, six words kept ringing through his soul: "A saved soul, a lost life! A saved soul, a lost life!" He could not get away from these words—nor can we.

Having thus dealt, in some considerable detail, with the promised judgment of their labor by the Savior (1 Cor. 3:9–15), Paul turns to *the present judgment of their lives by the Spirit* (3:16–17). Naturally so! In view of the judgment seat of Christ it is imperative that we get our lives in order now and not wait until it is too late. Everything hinges here upon the sobering yet splendid fact that our bodies are now the temple of the Holy Spirit. First we have *the temple defined:* "Know ye not that ye are the temple of God, and that the Spirit of God dwelleth in you?" (3:16). "Know ye not?" Much of our failure to live the Christian life stems from ignorance. Paul uses the expression here and in 5:6; 6:2, 9, 15; 9:13–24; Romans 6:16 and 11:2. The challenge is directed to matters that were acknowledged by the Corinthians, or which, at least, should have been obvious to them.

It is an awesome truth that the body of the believer is the Holy Spirit's temple. When Solomon finished building his magnificent temple in Jerusalem, he dedicated it with one of the truly magnificent prayers of the Bible. There it stood on Mount Moriah, all polished stone and gleaming gold. No expense had been spared. Armies of men had toiled for seven years to produce what was, indeed, one of the unsung wonders of the world. As part of the dedication, Solomon sacrificed thousands of oxen and sheep. Then he threw a nationwide, week-long feast for all his people. It is his prayer, however, which draws our attention. He said, "Will God in very deed dwell with men on earth? behold, heaven and the heaven of heavens cannot contain thee; how much less this house which I have built!" (2 Chron. 6:18).

The Jews of Paul's day were inordinately proud of their temple, even though it was really Herod's temple, a temple which then replaced the long-since departed temple of Solomon. During his trial Stephen virtually guaranteed a death sentence for himself when he bluntly declared, "Solomon built him [God] an house. Howbeit the most High dwelleth not in temples made with hands" (Acts 7:48).

Although God has no need of temples made of marble and gold, He condescends to live in the body of the believer! Indeed, this is the only way the Christ-life can become real in our experience. It is the indwelling Spirit of God who enables us to live the life of the Son of God. As the Son of God lived, and now lives forever, in a human body, so the Holy Spirit now lives in the believer's body. He, the third Person of the Godhead, omniscient, omnipotent, and omnipresent, holy and righteous, loving and wise, now lives in me! It is a thought beyond all thought!

But, horror of horrors! Paul envisions *the temple defiled:* "If any man defile the temple of God . . ." (1 Cor. 3:17a). The word for *defile* is *phtheirō,* meaning "to mar." Throughout the course of their history, the Jews persistently defiled their temple. King Ahaz, for instance, after a meeting with the king of Assyria in Damascus, became infatuated by a pagan altar in that city. He had a pattern made of it and sent it to Jerusalem with orders that a replica should be made. When he returned to Jerusalem he put his new altar where the brazen altar was supposed to stand and unceremoniously pushed God's altar to one side (2 Kings 16:10–14). Manasseh did much the same (21:4), but went even further, dedicating the altars he installed in the temple courts to "all the hosts of heaven" (21:5). No wonder God sent Nebuchadnezzar to pull that temple down!

It is all too easy for us to defile our bodies, thus grieving the Holy Spirit who dwells within. We can defile ourselves by the books we read, or by the movies we watch, or by the habits we indulge, or by the lusts we express, or by the thoughts we entertain. The Spirit of God, who is known supremely in the New Testament as the Holy Spirit, grieves over these things.

But Paul moves on. We now have *the temple destroyed:* "If any man defile the temple of God, him shall God destroy, for the temple of God is holy, which temple ye are" (1 Cor. 3:17b). The word for *destroy* is the same as the word for "defile" *(phtheirō).* The two verbs are brought vividly together: "God will ruin the ruiner of His temple."

At the beginning of His public ministry the Lord Jesus cleansed the temple in Jerusalem of the merchandisers and moneychangers who had turned its courts into a den of thieves (John 2:13–17). He did the same thing at the close of His ministry (Matt. 21:12–13). The leaders of the Sanhedrin, who had a vested interest in the moneymaking and thievery which went on in the temple, and who found these activities to be very lucrative, were enraged. The Lord's actions only goaded them on to plot His murder. Accordingly, the Lord decreed that He would pull their temple down (24:1–2). And so He did. Better no temple at all than a defiled temple.

So let us beware! The Holy Spirit is very patient with us, but He is not to be trifled with. There comes a time when, after repeated warnings, He pulls down the bodily temple of the offender.

This teaching here, regarding the temple, is not to be confined to the temple of the believer's body. The truth applies equally to the local church. Persistent defiling of a local gathering of believers, by the introduction of false teaching, by acceptance of immoral behavior, or by adoption of the world's methods, grieves and hinders the Holy Spirit. These things weaken the church and can lead to the total demise of its testimony. "Repent . . . or else!" Jesus said to the church at Ephesus (Rev. 2:5). Remember, Ephesus was Paul's *climax* church just as it was John's *crisis* church. "I will remove thy candlestick," the Lord threatened. And so He did!

Where today are all the churches that once made Asia Minor (modern Turkey) the brightest spot on earth for gospel testimony? Their toleration of idolatry, of false doctrine, and of immorality led to their demise. The Lord allowed Islam to come in and sweep them all away.

2. It was a contentious spirit (3:18–4:21)
   a. Their prejudices revealed (3:18–23)
     (1) Away with all deception (3:18–20)
       (a) The folly of self-deception (3:18)
         i. Recognizing it (3:18a)
         ii. Rectifying it (3:18b)
       (b) The futility of self-deception (3:19–20)
         i. God sees through crafty people (3:19)
         ii. God sees through clever people (3:20)
     (2) Away with all distinctions (3:21–23)
       (a) What is expected of us (3:21a)
       (b) What is explained to us (3:21b–23)
         i. Our possessions (3:21b–22)
          a. No matter who (3:21b–22a)
          b. No matter where (3:22b)
          c. No matter what (3:22c)
          d. No matter when (3:22d)
         ii. Our position (3:23)

Paul is still discussing the sectarian spirit so prevalent in the Corinthian church. It was *a carnal spirit,* as we have just seen (1 Cor. 3:1–17), and would be shown to be such at the judgment seat of Christ. It was also *a contentious spirit,* as Paul now shows (3:18–4:21). The searching light of the judgment seat of Christ will be cast upon all such unseemly behavior. Paul reveals *their prejudices* (3:18–22), *their presumptions* (4:1–5), and *their pride* (4:6–21). He begins by demanding that they *do away with all deception* (3:18–20) and shows them *the folly* of their self-deception (3:18). "Let no man deceive himself," he says. "If any man among you seemeth to be wise in this world, let him become a fool that he may be wise."

The first thing to do is to *recognize* one's self-deception, by no means an easy thing to do. The best way, if not the only way, is to read the Word of God with an open mind and a teachable spirit, so that the Holy Spirit Himself can reveal our self-deceptions to us. After all, He is the One who "searcheth the hearts (Rom. 8:27).

The other day I was walking out of the motel where I was staying, on the way to the lobby to meet the pastor of the church to which I was going. There happened to be a full-length mirror on the door of the motel and I caught a glimpse of myself. I was fully dressed, all ready to step into the pulpit—or so I thought. My suit was spotless, my shirt all buttoned up to the collar, my hair was in place and tidy. I had my Bible and my notebook. I was ready for action. Then I saw myself in the mirror. I had forgotten to put on a tie! Nothing is more incomplete, to my mind, than a business suit and a dress shirt, and no tie! I thought I was completely attired. I was self-deceived. The mirror showed me that fact in a moment. One look was all it took. Having recognized the true state of affairs, it was the work of a few moments to *rectify* it.

It is James who reminds us that the Bible is like that mirror (James 1:23–25). It shows us what we are like, blemishes and all. It also tells us how to put right those things that are wrong. In the Old Testament, before they were sent into the sanctuary to minister, the priests had to pay a visit to the brazen laver. The laver was made of brass (bronze) and its base was made "of the looking-glasses of the women" (Exod. 38:8). The laver itself contained water (another symbol of the Word of God) for the various ablutions of the priests. As they approached the laver, the mirrors would *reveal* their defilement and the water would *remove* their defilement. The Word of God has this double action.

Self-deception dies hard. Paul recommends that when we see what fools we have been in our self-deception, we go to the other extreme and become fools indeed, in the eyes of the world, by wholeheartedly embracing the true wisdom of God's Word. When the five young men were martyred by the Auca Indians in Ecuador, many following the wisdom of the world said, "To what purpose this waste?", echoing the carnal sentiment of the Lord's disciples as influenced by Judas (Matt. 26:8; John 12:4–5). The martyrs, bright young men, college-trained, with all of life before them and with promising careers beckoning them, turned their backs on all that to devote themselves, instead, to the evangelization of a remote and barbarous Indian tribe. Their reward was an early and a violent death at the hands of the people they sought to reach. Jim Elliot, one of the young martyrs, had his own answer to those who branded him a fool for burying himself in an equatorial jungle for the cause of Christ. "He is no fool," he said, "who gives what he cannot keep to gain that which he cannot lose." Paul would have endorsed the sentiment.

Next, Paul reveals the *futility* of self-deception (1 Cor. 3:19–20). In the first place, God sees through the *crafty* man: "For the wisdom of this world is foolishness with God. For it is written, He taketh the wise in their own craftiness" (3:19). The quotation is from the book of Job (5:13)—incidentally, the only time the book of Job is quoted in the New Testament. The remark occurs in the first speech of Eliphaz, in which he suggests Job must have been a very great sinner, indeed, otherwise he would not have been overtaken by such a series of overwhelming and horrendous calamities—a contention Job vigorously denied.

The word for *taketh* here is *drassomai,* signifying "to grasp with the hand." It occurs only here. The word for *craftiness* is *panourgia,* a word always used in a bad sense in the New Testament. It suggests unscrupulous conduct. When the Lord Jesus instantly saw through the machinations of His enemies, when they asked Him if it was lawful for a Jew to pay taxes imposed by Rome, Luke says, "He perceived their craftiness *[panourgia],*" and asked them why they were tempting Him (Luke 20:23).

The classic Old Testament example of God taking "the wise" in their own craftiness is found in the story of Jacob and Laban. Jacob was full of guile. His craftiness, practiced on his twin brother Esau, came home to roost when Esau threatened to murder him. As a result, Jacob had to flee to Padan-Aram. There he fell into the hands of his Uncle Laban, who was just as crafty as Jacob, only older and much more experienced. God used Laban to discipline Jacob. He took him in his own craftiness. In the end Jacob triumphed over Laban, not as a result of the craftiness which he, too, practiced in his dealings with his wily uncle, but simply because God chose to bless and protect him—something Jacob himself eventually acknowledged (Gen. 31:36–42). In the end, too, Laban lost his daughters, his grandchildren, and the wealth of Jacob along with Jacob's invaluable service, all because of his craftiness.

Paul wanted to remind the crafty ones at Corinth, who were seeking to build a following at his expense, that they had God to reckon with and that God could see through all their little schemes.

Moreover, God sees through the *clever* man: "And again, The Lord knoweth the thoughts of the wise, that they are vain" (1 Cor. 3:20). The quotation is from Psalm 94:11: "He that planted the ear, shall he not hear? He that formed the eye, shall he not see?" demands the psalmist (94:9) in leading up to the statement Paul quotes.

Paul says that the thoughts of this world's clever people are "vain" in God's sight. The word *mataios* means "void of result." It is sometimes used of idolatry (Acts 14:15). One suspects that the Cephas party at Corinth was indulging in craftiness and that the Apollos party was promoting cleverness. God could see through both. Neither party had God's blessing. What they were trying to accomplish would come to nothing and would be judged at the judgment seat of Christ.

They had their "thoughts" *(dialogismoi),* of course, that is to say their "reasonings." They could pile up all kinds of clever arguments. The word is used by the Lord in His parable of the wicked husbandmen who plotted together to murder the son of the owner of the vineyard and seize the property for themselves (Luke 20:14). He used the word, too, to describe the logic of the rich fool who planned to build bigger and better barns, not knowing that his time had run out (Luke 12:17). Paul evidently thought that the sectarian schemes of the Corinthians were equally vain.

"Away with all deception!" exclaims Paul, and *away with all distinctions* (1 Cor. 3:21–23) as well! He tells us *what is expected of us:* "Therefore let no man glory in men" (3:21a). Men, after all, are only men. We need to get back to the Word of God and not be overly concerned with men who, even when greatly used of God, are still only men, frail, prone to error, able to fall. Flaws can be found in all of them. Abraham was a great man who earned the title "friend of God," but he failed when he went down to Egypt and again when he went to Philistia (Gen. 12:10–20; 20:1–18). Moses was a great man but he failed when he smote the rock the second time (Num. 20:1–13). David was a great man but he failed when he seduced Bathsheba and again when he numbered Israel (2 Sam. 11:1–27; 24:1–15). Calvin was a great man but he was not averse to burning his enemies at the stake. Luther was a great man but he never did see clearly the error of Rome's doctrine of transubstantiation. Spurgeon was a great man but he disagreed with John Nelson Darby, a far greater scholar than he was and a man with a grasp of truth far beyond Spurgeon's. We all have feet of clay. It is best not to glory in man.

We note, also, *what is explained to us* (1 Cor. 3:21b–23). Paul begins with *our possessions* in Christ. And what magnificent possessions they are! "All are yours!" he says. We have no need to look anywhere else once we have looked to Christ. Look at the things which are ours!

No matter who! "Paul? Apollos? Cephas? All are yours," Paul says. There were those who liked Paul because of his *strengths.* While the other apostles were content to huddle at home, Paul went out to evangelize the western world. He "wrote the book" on foreign missions, just as he wrote a major part of the New Testament. In him were combined the Talmudic Jew, the Greek scholar, and the Roman citizen. "Why, man, he doth bestride the world like a Colossus," said Julius Caesar's envious enemies. Paul had ten times the genius of Caesar. The gravitational force of his Spirit-filled, Christ-centered, God-enthroned personality drew countless people into orbit around him. He towered above his contemporaries like Gulliver in Lilliput and his shadow lies over the past 2,000 years of history. Paul!

There were those who liked Apollos because of his *style.* They listened spellbound when he spoke. He had the eloquence of an archangel, it seemed. He was a golden-tongued orator. He could preach people right out of their seats and have them shouting and applauding with a standing ovation.

There were those who liked Cephas because of his *stand.* He stood for the old paths. He was wedded to the faith of the fathers. "After all," his admirers would say, "the Lord did not give the keys of the kingdom to Paul or Apollos, He gave them to Peter. He was the one who preached at Pentecost and he was the one who came to Cornelius. Besides, he was one of the Lord's very earliest disciples. Who can know the mind of the Lord better than Peter?"

"True! True! True!" Paul would say. "But we are *all* yours! It's not a case of this one, that one, or the other one. All are yours."

No matter where! The world is ours. It was not a case of Jerusalem being more important than Rome. The cities Paul evangelized were no more important than the cities Peter evangelized. Alexandria was not more important than Corinth. The whole world was theirs. The world is ours.

Look, for instance, at David Livingstone. Time and time again he had faced death. On some thirty occasions fever had laid him low. Savage tribes had threatened him, evil tongues had slandered his marriage, his left arm hung useless, crushed by a lion. Yet he stood, a grand old man, before the student body of the Glasgow University and voiced his unwavering resolve: "I'm going back!" he said. Cheer after cheer rang through the great hall. David Livingstone was a man who knew that the world was his.

No matter what! Life and death are ours. *Life!* Only the believer knows how to live. In Genesis 4 and 5, the Holy Spirit draws a contrast between the descendants of Cain and the descendants of Seth. To picture Cain's kind of people He takes us into the market and shows us great cities, filled with the fruits of science, art, and industry. To show us Seth's kind of people the Holy Spirit, by contrast, takes us into the morgue. All down the chapter we hear the tolling of the bell. "He died!" He says, "and he died!" Cain's people lived for this world; Seth's people lived for the world to come. But death was not the end for them. It simply opened the gates of glory to let them in. But something else is recorded of the godly, too. The Holy Spirit says of each of them that *"he lived"!* Doubtless Cain's crowd thought they were living, with their music and dancing, with their great cities, their flowering civilization, their commerce, and their many inventions. The Holy Spirit did not think so. Doubtless, too, the Cainites looked with disdain on the Sethites and their quiet, separated, godly lives. Prayer meetings! Preaching! Fellowship picnics! Call that living? The Holy Spirit did. That is to say, He said that they *lived!*

Life is ours! Only the believer has the secret to life. Jesus said, "I am come that they might have life, and that they might have it more abundantly" (John 10:10). No one has any control over the advantages or handicaps under which he is launched upon the sea of life. One person is born a beggar, another a billionaire. One person is born as handsome as a god, another as ugly as a goblin. One person is born with genius, another hopelessly retarded. No matter! When we are born again we receive the gift of life!

When Fanny Crosby was six weeks old she caught a common cold. The doctor prescribed a hot mustard poultice and, as a result, little Fanny Crosby was blinded for life. When she was five, sympathetic friends and neighbors pooled their money and sent her to an eminent New York specialist. Sadly he shook his head. Nothing could be done. "Poor little blind girl," he said.

Fanny Crosby came to know Jesus and He turned tragedy into triumph. Fanny Crosby learned to live and became a blessing and a benediction to millions. She was hymn-writer to the church of her day. The great revivals under D. L. Moody and Ira Sankey were borne along on the wings of Fanny Crosby's hymns. She wrote as her testimony,

> All the way my Savior leads me;
> What have I to ask beside?
> Can I doubt His tender mercy,
> Who thro' life has been my Guide?

> Heav'nly peace, divinest comfort,
> Here by faith in Him to dwell!
> For I know, whate'er befall me,
> Jesus doeth all things well.

Death! Christians are the only ones who really know how to die. Some worldly people have shown us how to die bravely. Some have died with bravado. The believer knows how to die blessedly!

Few deaths have been more starkly dreadful than that of England's famed Queen Elizabeth. Her path to the throne was perilous, but once firmly there she reigned supreme in the hearts of her subjects. "Good Queen Bess" they called her. When Philip of Spain sent an armada to fasten Spain's and Rome's dread yoke upon England, Elizabeth defied him. She paraded her soldiers and sailors. "I have the body of a weak woman," she told them, "but I have the heart of a king, and a king of England, too! I think foul scorn that Parma or Spain or any prince of Europe should dare invade the borders of my realm." Then she sent her small ships out to sink the great galleons of Spain, and sink them they did!

She made England great. Her court was crowded with men of genius. A galaxy of poets and playwrights orbited her throne. Her sea dogs roamed the world's oceans, plundering Spanish treasure ships and raiding Spain's colonies. She decried popery and set England on the road to empire.

But Elizabeth did not know how to die. She chased her doctors from her room. She was afraid to go to bed lest she die in her sleep. She piled cushions on the floor and stubbornly refused to move. She fought death inch by inch as she had once fought Spain. Even as the dread moment arrived she cried, "All my possessions for a moment of time!"

We come back to David Livingstone. There he is, back in Africa, on his knees. He is up among the bogs and marshes of Chitambo's village, all alone except for his native helpers. He has walked as long as he can, ridden as long as he can, been carried as long as he can bear it. Now he is at an utter end of his strength. His feet are too ulcerated to bear contact with the ground and his body is so emaciated it frightens him to look at it. Internal hemorrhage is draining away what is left of his strength. A drizzling rain is falling outside his tent and in his fever he babbles of the fountains and the sources of the Nile.

The black boys, almost as worn out as their master, fall asleep. At length one of them wakes up. A bleak, gray dawn is breaking. He creeps into the master's tent. The white man is not in bed—he is on his knees beside it, stiff and cold.

Their great master is dead! There was no other white man within hundreds upon hundreds of miles. No woman's hand was there to close his eyes. No friend was there to fortify him at the end. He died alone. No! Not alone. For into his tent that night there came his dearest Friend. "Dr. Livingstone, I presume!" He said, and took him Home.

No matter when! Things present, things to come! Our present circumstances are His gift to us. He has thought it all out. He is too loving to be unkind and too wise to make any mistakes. He knows just what we need. He knows all about us. Whether "things present" include facing an irritable boss, an unsaved son, a financial crisis, a serious illness, He has it all under His control. When Peter tried walking on the waves at the bidding of Jesus, he made a few successful steps, then began to sink. Terrified, he called out to Jesus. He never forgot the experience. He learned that things which were over his head were already under the Master's feet. So, come what may, we can know that He knows and that He knows how to "temper the wind to the shorn lamb."

Things to come! In this life and in the life to come, all are ours. We can face "things to come" not just with courage but with confidence. Martin Luther was given until tomorrow. There sat the Emperor Charles, sovereign of half the world. There sat the peers and princes of Germany and the bishops, archbishops, and cardinals of Rome. There stood the miner's son in his drab monk's frock and hood. One man against five thousand. They had put the question. Alexander of Treeves, the pope's nuncio, chosen for his eloquence, had flicked a contemptuous finger at Luther's books and writings. "There are enough errors in these," he sneered, "to burn a hundred heretics. Two questions, Luther. Did you write them? If so, are you prepared to retract them?"

Luther agreed to the patently obvious fact that he had written them. As for the second question, whether he would recant, he asked for time. "You have until tomorrow," he was told.

Tomorrow! Things to come! What thoughts flooded his mind—the shame of recanting! The possibility of being tortured and burned at the stake! Things to come! He spent the night in prayer "O God! O God! O God! Stand by my side for the sake of Thy well-beloved, Jesus Christ, who is my defense, my shield, my strong tower."

The morrow came. Once again the lone monk stood before the glare and glitter of Europe's most brilliant court. Again he faced the question: "Do you recant?" Seizing opportunity by the forelock, like Paul before Felix and before Agrippa, Martin Luther began to speak. "I have written against the Papacy," he said, "and the doctrines of the Papists . . . their false doctrines, their scandalous lives, their evil ways are known to all mankind."

He was silenced at once. "Will you, or won't you recant?" His foes would brook no more delay. "I cannot and I will not recant." The words came out boldly and clearly. He looked around at the vast assembly, gazed on all who were mighty in power in this world, on all that was venerable with antiquity. "Here I take my stand," he said at last. "I cannot do otherwise. So help me God."

No matter who! No matter where! No matter what! No matter when! *All* are ours. Those are our possessions. And here is *our position:* "And ye are Christ's, and Christ is God's" (1 Cor. 3:23b). What more could be said than that! Here we have total, absolute, and eternal security. Here we have an end to all mere party loyalties. We all belong to Christ and He belongs to God.

Some years ago, a friend of mine went through some very deep waters indeed. His wife was dying of cancer and in great pain in a hospital. He loved his wife very dearly and the daily sight of her terrible sufferings wracked his own soul. I went to see him. The so-called charismatics had been at him. They had told him that if he had enough faith, his wife would be healed. Of all the cruel distortions of divine truth to add to the anguish of a broken man! His wife was still dying in a torment of pain. It was his fault! He didn't have enough faith! So they said.

When I arrived at the hospital my friend was distractedly walking the corridors, weeping, pleading with God to help his unbelief. We went down together to the hospital restaurant and ordered some coffee.

"My dear friend," I said, "Your beloved is going to die! Face it! She's going to die—and it is not your fault! It is God's will. It has nothing to do with your faith." I read him these verses from 1 Corinthians 3:21–23. I emphasized the word *death*. "All things are yours; whether Paul, or Apollos, or Cephas, or the world, or life, or *death,* or things present, or things to come, *all are yours;* and ye are Christ's, and Christ is God's."

"One of the things God has given us is death," I continued. "It is God's *gift.* It may not be what you are asking Him for. It may not be what you want. Nevertheless, He Himself says it is His gift to us. Right now, death is God's gift to your beloved and it is God's gift to you. Death will bring an immediate end to her pain. Any moment now she will close her eyes on earth for the last time. She will open them again to look straight into the face of Jesus. Death is God's gift to her. Death will open the gates of glory for her. Death is also God's gift to you, for the Holy Spirit will come to you in a new way, as the Comforter. He will comfort you. He will heal this wracking torment and pain. He will help you to get on with your life. You are His, and He is

God's." My friend dried his eyes and the ghost of a smile appeared on his face. He said, "Thank you," and went forward to face "things to come," healed, at least, of the hurt of thinking himself to blame for his beloved one's death.

      b. Their presumptions revealed (4:1–5)
          (1) What is required of the servants of God (4:1–2)
             (a) Paul and his service (4:1)
             (b) Paul and his stewardship (4:2)
          (2) What is required of the saints of God (4:3–5)
             (a) The question of present judgment (4:3a)
             (b) The question of personal judgment (4:3b–4)
                i. Paul's refusal (4:3b)
                ii. Paul's reason (4:4)
                   a. Our limitations (4:4a)
                   b. Our Lord (4:4b)
             (c) The question of prospective judgment (4:5)
                i. Be patient (4:5a)
                ii. Be prepared (4:5b–c)
                   a. The coming probe we can expect (4:5b)
                   b. The coming praise we can expect (4:5c)

Paul continues with his discussion of the contentious spirit that motivated the divisions in the Corinthian church. He has dealt decisively with *their prejudices* in preferring this one or that one over the other one. Now he turns to *their presumptions* (1 Cor. 4:1–5). They thought they had a right to judge Paul, Apollos, and Cephas. "Nonsense!" says Paul. Judgment is God's prerogative and it will be amply displayed at the judgment seat of Christ.

He begins this segment by showing *what is required of God's servants* (4:1–2). He points first to his own *service* (4:1). He says, "Let a man so account of us, as the ministers of Christ, and stewards of the mysteries of God." The word for *minister* is *hupēretēs,* literally meaning "an under-rower" in a boat and it denotes someone in a subordinate capacity. Thus Paul, the greatest of all apostles, the greatest of all teachers, the greatest of all missionaries, the greatest of all pastors, describes himself as "an under-rower." He was a man under authority. Let the Corinthians boast of their favorite preachers. He wanted no part in it. He, like all the others, was just one of those who belonged to Christ.

Doubtless Paul had often seen the great seagoing galleys which enabled Rome to rule the seas. They were a beautiful sight. Their long, lean lines were full of grace and menace. Their banks of oars, tier above tier of them, moved rhythmically back and forth, up and down, like the wings of some great bird. He had seen the galley slaves in long lines, chained to their seats, wedded to their oars. He had seen the overseers with their whips ready to enforce discipline and keep the rowers up to the mark. He had seen the slave master who gave the orders which called for a faster pace or for one side to hold water while the other side pulled, enabling the great ship to turn like a door on a hinge. He had heard the steady, endless beat of the drum which governed the number of strokes per minute and which guaranteed that all oars would be pulled together in perfect harmony and time.

That was how he saw his service. He was not the slave driver, swaggering up and down the tiers, whip in hand, driving the galley-slaves to their ceaseless toil. He was not the slave master, sitting at ease, giving his orders. He was not the man who beat the drum. He was just "an under-rower." For that matter, so was the golden-tongued Apollos and the Galilean Cephas. Paul endeavored to pull his oar to the Master's command in harmony, cooperation, and fellowship with all those who served. If there was any judging to be done, let him be judged by this.

Then Paul points to his *stewardship:* "Moreover it is required in stewards, that a man be found faithful" (1 Cor. 4:2). The word for *steward* is *oikonomos,* someone who managed the affairs of his master's household. The primary responsibility of a steward is to be faithful. We all have been entrusted with something by the Lord and we shall be held accountable at the judgment seat of Christ for what we have done with it.

When I was a young man I joined the Bank of Montreal in London and went to Canada. I well remember what would happen on the day when the examiners came. The day would be like any other day. The bank would open to the general public at 10 A.M. and close for the day at 3 P.M. There was always a sudden lightening of the atmosphere once the last customer was out of the door. Coats came off, ties were loosened, voices rose above the sepulchral whisper of the business hours. Coffee and cakes appeared. The tellers began balancing the day's transactions. The foreign exchange items were processed. The manager dictated his letters in peace, free from interruptions. Everyone hoped that all the books would be balanced expeditiously so that we might get out in reasonable time.

Then, all unexpectedly, there would come a knock at the door. Some customer, perhaps, who had forgotten his checkbook, or a messenger, maybe, from one of the other banks, with an overlooked item of exchange. Someone would go to the door—and there they were, the bank auditors, as many as half a dozen of them. The chief examiner would go directly to the manager's office. The rest would swoop down on the tellers' cages and demand the keys to the vault. The audit had begun. Every penny in the bank was counted. Every item of collateral and security was checked. For the next few weeks there was always one or two of these men around, poking and prying into every transaction since the last audit. Every book and every entry was examined. Nor did the audit end until the chief examiner was satisfied. We were stewards of other people's money and securities. It was required of us that we be faithful.

Paul had a high sense of accountability. He was, himself, a steward of the mysteries of God. There were numerous divine mysteries, secrets, which had been revealed to him and for which he was responsible, but three of them were key. They are expounded by him in Romans, Ephesians, and Thessalonians. In *Romans,* Paul expounded *the mystery of Christ's cross.* The truth of salvation through the shed blood of Christ is the theme of this letter, a saving truth for sinners (1 Cor. 3:23–26) and a sanctifying truth for saints (6:4–11). The Corinthian church had departed from the truth and were reproved for their *practical* failure to live as those who had passed through death to resurrection ground. The Galatian church also had departed from the truth and were corrected for their *doctrinal* failure.

In *Ephesians,* Paul expounded *the mystery of Christ's church.* It was no mystery that God intended to save Gentiles, a truth often taught in the Old Testament. The mystery was that Jew and Gentile alike would be made members of the one, mystical body of Christ and an object of wonder and admiration to the heavenly hosts. The Philippian church was reproved for its *practical* failure to uphold this truth because of its failure to exhibit "the mind of Christ." The Colossian church needed correction for *doctrinal* departure, for "not holding the Head" (2:19), and for tolerating various cultic errors.

In *Thessalonians,* Paul expounded *the mystery of Christ's coming.* The believer is not only "dead and risen with Christ" as in Romans, and not only "seated in heavenly places in Christ" as in Ephesians, but he is to be "caught up [to the sky] to meet the Lord in the air" and thus to be "ever with the Lord." The believer is led from the depths of degradation (in Romans) to the heights of glory (in Thessalonians). No church epistles follow Thessalonians because the consummation is reached.

So, then, Paul invites the Corinthian church to evaluate him, if evaluate him they must, along these lines—his service and his stewardship.

Having shown the Corinthians what is required of a servant of God, he goes on to show them *what is required of God's saints* (1 Cor. 4:3–5). There is, for instance, the question of *present judgment:* "But with me it is a very small thing that I should be judged of you" (4:3a). Paul was not too concerned about what they thought of him. He does not say that he has no concern at all about their opinion, just that it counted for very little. The word for *judged* here is *anarkrithō.* It literally means "to be examined." Technically it means a preliminary examination in preparation for a trial. Paul did not consider himself on trial. He was not answerable to the Corinthians. Clever though they were, carnal as they were, it was a matter of indifference to Paul what they thought about him. We spend far too much time wondering, even worrying, what people think about us. So long as we have a clear conscience before God it should not concern us overmuch one way or the other. Some of God's choicest saints have been bitterly criticized and wrongly accused by those not fit to tie their shoes. Job spent far too much time defending himself before his critics. Paul had no intention of doing any such thing.

There is also the question of *personal judgment* (1 Cor. 4:3b–4). We have, for instance, Paul's *refusal:* "Yea, I judge not mine own self" (4:3b). "I do not examine myself," he says. Some people are given to morbid self-introspection. That is one of the Devil's favorite tricks, to get us perpetually taken up with our faults and failings, our sins and shortcomings, so that we are permanently disabled from any real usefulness in the Lord's work. Some believers become so taken up with themselves that they miss altogether God's will for their lives.

The classic Old Testament example is old Barzillai. He had rendered David a great service at the time the king was in full flight from Absalom (2 Sam. 17:27–29). When David came back to the throne, he wanted to reward the courageous tribesman. He had great plans for him. He wanted him to come to Jerusalem, take his place at the king's table, and become one of his counselors, doubtless to replace the scoundrel Ahithophel, who had so treacherously betrayed him. Barzillai was full of excuses. "I'm too old," he said, "I have no skill in counseling. I have no appetite for delicacies of the king's table and no ability to enjoy music. I do not have the gifts or the graces to comfortably fill the position the king has in mind. I would only be a burden to the king. I'll be very happy to escort the king over Jordan but that's about as far as I feel able to go. In any case, I have my plans made, I want to die here among my own people and be buried alongside my parents. Why don't you take someone else? I've a young man here who would be delighted to become one of the king's courtiers" (19:31–38). Barzillai talked himself out of a kingdom and a crown. We must beware lest we do the same.

Then, too, we have Paul's *reason* for refusing to engage in constant introspection and perpetual hand-wringing: "For I know nothing by myself; yet am I not hereby justified: but he that judgeth me is the Lord." Paul does not wish to convey the idea that he was altogether free of self-reproach. After all, he was human. He once called Israel's high priest a "whited wall," and roundly rebuked him, only to apologize a moment later (Acts 23:3–5). Paul, here, is simply recognizing his own limitations. Our consciences are treacherous indicators of ultimate moral and spiritual values. They can excuse or accuse us quite wrongfully at times. All human judgment is fallible, and especially self-judgment. We might, for instance, be quite ignorant of some fault in ourselves, but that does not justify us before God. The heart is very prone to self-deceit (Jer. 17:9–10). If Paul did not know how to properly evaluate his own behavior, how much less could the critical Corinthians evaluate it? The only competent Judge is the Lord.

Which brings Paul to the question of *prospective judgment* (1 Cor. 4:5). Paul tells us to *be patient:* "Therefore judge nothing before the time, until the Lord come" (4:5a). Censoriousness is a very common fault (Rom. 14:4, 10, 13). Indeed, censoriousness itself will be judged by the Lord when He comes. Job's friends were censorious. One and all they concluded that Job must have been a very great sinner, an accusation quite contrary to the fact (Job 1:8). Indeed, in the end, the Lord said to Eliphaz the Temanite, "My wrath is kindled against thee and against thy two friends: for ye have not spoken of me the thing that is right, as my servant Job hath. Therefore take unto you now seven bullocks and seven rams, and go to my servant Job, and offer up for yourselves a burnt offering; and my servant Job shall pray for you; for him I will accept: lest I deal with you after your folly, in that ye have not spoken of me the thing that is right, as my servant Job hath" (42:7–8). Paul's advice is that we refrain from judgment.

Paul tells us to *be prepared* (1 Cor. 4:5b–c) for we can expect to be *probed:* "The Lord . . . will bring to light the hidden things of darkness" (4:5b). Our guilty secrets are well known to the Lord. We may conceal them from man but we cannot conceal them from Him.

None of the disciples suspected Judas. He was, after all, the only Judean in that little Galilean band of the Lord's disciples. He was their treasurer. He had earned a reputation of having compassion for the poor. When he criticized Mary's gift of expensive ointment, the other disciples followed his lead. When the Lord announced in the Upper Room that one of those present would betray Him, Judas said, "Is it I?" along with the others and not one of them suspected him. When the Lord said to him, "What thou doest, do quickly," the disciples thought

Judas was being sent on a legitimate errand—so thoroughly did he cover up the hidden things of darkness in his soul. But he did not deceive Jesus. The Lord knew all about him. "Have not I chosen you twelve," He said, "and one of you is a devil." When John pointedly asked Jesus, in the Upper Room, who the betrayer was, Jesus gave him a sign and then pointed directly to Judas. Judas was able to play-act the part of a disciple so well that he deceived the very elect, but Jesus read his heart and thoughts. He can as easily read ours. We shall be probed. We do not need to judge others of the Lord's servants. We have enough to do to keep our own record clean.

But we can take heart, too, for we can expect to be *praised:* "And then shall every man have praise of God" (4:5c). After all, there is something of Christ in every Christian. Those who have nothing of Christ about them at all will not be at the judgment seat of Christ, but at the great white throne with all those who know not the Lord.

    c. Their pride revealed (4:6–21)
        (1) How Paul regards their pride (4:6)
            (a) The model (4:6a)
            (b) The moral (4:6b)
        (2) How Paul ridicules their pride (4:7–8)
            (a) Their gift and its source (4:7)
                i. Who?
                ii. What?
                iii. Why?
            (b) Their glory and its stupidity (4:8)
                i. How full they are—of their own importance (4:8a)
                ii. How foolish they are—in their own importance (4:8b–c)
                    a. Their mistake as to the truth (4:8b)
                    b. Their mistake as to the time (4:8c)
        (3) How Paul repudiates their pride (4:9–17)
            (a) The dignity of an apostle (4:9–10)
                i. The grim facts (4:9)
                ii. The great farce (4:10)
            (b) The distinctives of an apostle (4:11–17)
                i. Material considerations (4:11–12a)
                ii. Moral considerations (4:12b–13)

Paul has dealt with the *prejudices* and with the *presumptions* of the Corinthians. Now he turns his attention to *their pride* (1 Cor. 4:6–21). We see how he *regarded* it (4:6), how he *ridiculed* it (4:7–8), how he *repudiated* it (4:9–17), and how he *rebuked* it (4:18–21).

We note at once the obvious disfavor with which he regarded the pride the Corinthians had in their sectarian spirit. We note first *the model* (4:6a): "And these things, brethren, I have in a figure transferred to myself and to Apollos for your sakes, that ye might learn in us not to think of men above that which is written." In other words, he had deliberately used himself and Apollos as an illustration. The expression *I have in a figure transferred* renders the one word *metaschēmatizō*. The word is used in 1 Corinthians 11:13 of false teachers masquerading as apostles of Christ and of Satan disguising himself as an angel of light. Here Paul used the word to make a masked allusion to those who were actually responsible for the divisions in the Corinthian church. Instead of using their names, he used his own name and the name of his dear friend and colleague, Apollos. He set himself and Apollos forth as denominational rivals in whom the divisions at Corinth centered. In actual fact, as everyone at Corinth surely knew, the most cordial and friendly relations existed between them. He deliberately omitted the name of Cephas from the illustration since there had been tension between them at one time (Gal. 2:11–15). He did not want to say anything, directly or indirectly, by way of intimation or by way of illustration, which some might seize upon as a criticism of Peter.

Now Paul turned to *the moral.* First, he urged the Corinthians to learn from the friendship between him and Apollos not to think of men "above what is written." This phrase is taken to be some kind of a proverb or popular expression in the Corinthian church. The rendering "Keep to the Book!" has been suggested. Perhaps the tendency in the Corinthian church to go beyond what God's Word authorized had produced this popular catch phrase. In any case it is good advice.

Paul then applied this popular expression—"that no one of you be puffed up for one against another" (1 Cor. 4:6b). To choose sectarian sides was certainly to exceed the bounds of Scripture (John 17:20–21), for the Lord Himself had prayed for the unity of believers.

The word for *puffed up* is *physioomai.* It comes from the Greek work for a bellows. It means "to be inflated," and is often used by Paul in this letter to denote attitudes that express human pride (1 Cor. 4:18, 19; 5:2; 8:1; 13:4). The Lord hates pride. In the Corinthian church there were those who were blowing themselves up like bullfrogs, seeking to draw off partisans to their particular views. Paul decried all of them.

Next we are told how Paul *ridiculed* their pride (4:7–8). First, he speaks of *their gift and its source* (4:7). "Who?" he demands, "What?" "Why?" "For who maketh you to differ from another? and what hast thou that thou didst not receive? now if thou didst receive it, why dost thou glory, as if thou hadst not received it?" Every natural talent, gift, and ability we possess we have received from God. He made us. He gave us our physique, our looks, our intelligence, our abilities. Every spiritual gift we have is ours by the grace of God and useful only under the control and direction of the Spirit of God. Although the Lord may permit us to achieve some measure of success, even fame, in the development, exercise, and use of our gifts, the glory all belongs to Him.

This is true in the secular realm as well as in the spiritual. A person can, perhaps, take a measure of satisfaction in something he has created or accomplished. Michelangelo might well have been satisfied by his Pieta, his most important work as a youth and the one which established his reputation as a sculptor. The simple, solemn quality of the work has drawn the admiration of millions. Sir Christopher Wren could be excused for admiring his masterpiece, St. Paul's Cathedral. Charles Dickens could be excused for admiring his *Tale of Two Cities.* Einstein could surely be justly proud of having discovered the equation $E = MC^2$. Henry Ford could be proud of having created a commercial empire, and in so doing changing the face of the world. George Frederic Handel might well be gratified with his famous *Messiah* for his thrilling "Hallelujah Chorus" shows him to be a master of choral effects, particularly in dividing a chorus into two groups singing different themes. Indeed, to this day audiences invariably stand to pay tribute when the "Hallelujah Chorus" is sung.

Even so, the genius which enables people to accomplish such things is given to them by God, so all praise belongs to Him. Can a person be proud, for instance, of possessing a van Gogh, especially if it were given to him?

In his great classic, *White Fang,* Jack London describes the wolf dog's extraordinary fighting powers, much of which was the result of long experience, cunning, courage, and coordination. "The parts of him," says London, "were better adjusted than those of the average dog. When his eyes conveyed to his brain the moving image of an action, his brain, without conscious effort, knew the space that limited the action and the time required for its completion. Thus he could avoid the leap of another dog, or the drive of its fangs, and at the same moment could seize the infinitesimal fraction of time in which to deliver his own attack. Body and brain, his was a more perfected mechanism. Not that he was to be praised for it. Nature had been more generous to him than to the average animal, that was all."

When it comes to spiritual things, all is of God. Well might the hymn writer say,

> Naught have I gotten but what I received,
> Grace hath bestowed it since I believed;
> Boasting excluded, pride I abase,
> I'm only a sinner, saved by grace.

Next, Paul speaks of *their glory and its stupidity* (1 Cor. 4:8): "Now ye are full, now ye are rich, ye have reigned as kings without us, and I would to God ye did reign, that we also might reign with you." Paul pours on the sarcasm. "Ye are full!" Paul exclaims. "Full?" The word is *korennumi,* "satiated"! The word is used in connection with Paul's voyage to Rome and the impending shipwreck of the storm-tossed vessel on the island of Malta. Paul had already told the passengers and crew that no lives would be lost because God had promised him that. Now he urged his shipmates to eat. In their toil and terror it had been two weeks since they had last had a decent meal. They heeded his advice. Then, we read, "when they had eaten enough *[korennumi]* they lightened the ship" (Acts 27:38). This is the word Paul uses to describe the bloated self-importance of the Corinthians. They were replete. They were fully satisfied with themselves, satiated with their good opinion of themselves, smugly complacent.

Paul pricked their bubble. Kings indeed! Reigning indeed! Some throne! They had attracted some adherents! Congratulations! Too bad it was all a grand delusion! How wonderful to be a big frog in a little puddle! What a pity they had not already passed the great and fiery test of the judgment seat of Christ! How sad that the millennial age had not really dawned! Too bad they were not already reigning from thrones set for them in the Celestial City! Too bad, indeed! For in that case he, too, would be wearing a crown, swaying a scepter, and judging angels. What a pity he had missed the Rapture! Let him be the first to congratulate them for having made it ahead of him! They were like the Laodiceans of whom the Lord said, "Thou sayest, I am rich, and increased with goods, and have need of nothing; and knowest not that thou art wretched, and miserable, and poor, and blind, and naked" (Rev. 3:17).

Next we see how Paul *repudiated* their pride (1 Cor. 4:9–17). He contrasts their self-importance with both the dignity and the distinctives of an apostle such as he.

He begins with *the dignity of an apostle* (4:9–10). He reminds them of *the grim facts* (4:4). It was time they came down to earth: "For I think that God hath set forth us the apostles last, as it were appointed to death: for we are a spectacle unto the world, and to angels, and to men." If it came to rank within the church there was no higher rank and no greater gift than that of an apostle. It implied a special and inimitable personal relationship with the Lord (9:1), and it carried with it enormous authority and power. If the apostles weren't reigning, nobody was reigning. Far from reigning, the apostles were the special targets of the world's hate. The apostles themselves looked upon themselves as "last," that is, as the lowliest servants of all. Far from reigning, they were men under the sentence of death. James had already been martyred. Peter had barely escaped (Acts 12:1–11). Indeed, the apostles were "a spectacle"—the word used is *theatron,* from which we derive our word "theater." The apostles were like condemned criminals in the amphitheater, those exhibited last of all to fight with wild beasts. The eyes of those on earth and in heaven were fastened on them. Far from being the crowned royalties of heaven, as yet the apostles themselves were no better than a public spectacle. Those were the grim facts. Death stalked every one of them. Cruel deaths awaited them. It was not until Nero's executioner was already sharpening his ax that Paul could write confidently about his crown (2 Tim. 4:6–8).

Paul contrasts the grim facts with *the great farce:* "We are fools for Christ's sake, but ye are wise in Christ; we are weak, but ye are strong; ye are honourable, but we are despised" (1 Cor. 4:10). More sarcasm!

I remember when I first introduced George Verwer to a group of Christian businessmen. Those present were mostly men of influence and wealth. Many of them were elders and deacons in their churches. They commanded respect and wielded authority. In some cases it was their success in business which secured them a commanding voice in the decisions of the church. They came to the luncheon, polished, well-dressed, self-assured. Many of them were my personal friends. They came in and sat down, addressed themselves to the meal, and engaged in polite conversation. None of them spared more than a passing glance for the stranger among them, quiet, thin almost to the point of being gaunt, poorly dressed, my friend George.

I had first met him soon after I joined the staff of the Moody Bible Institute, when he was a student in his senior year. He had already made a tremendous impact on faculty, staff, and the student body. He would go on to launch Operation Mobilization, a missionary organization designed to reach the world's unsaved masses with the gospel. Student though he was, he had already started ministries in Mexico and Spain. He had already been thrown out of the Soviet Union and was pioneering crusades in India. Every vacation he mobilized hundreds of students in all-out door-to-door evangelism in major European cities. He was a mover and motivator of men. His vision was for closed countries, for the big cities, for the seaports of the world. His faith was childlike and phenomenal. His text was "nothing shall be impossible unto you." His ambition was to have an ocean-going gospel ship, able to reach the islands of the sea and the seaports of the world, a ship that could be a powerful base from which cities could be blitzed with the gospel. Eventually God gave him two, the *Logos* and the *Doulos*. The story of those ships has become a legend.

Well, there sat George, inconspicuous and ignored. And there sat a group of men who had the reputation of being people of note in the Christian life of that southern town. Judging by the conversation, the bonhomie, and the easy way these men exerted their influence, an observer would have concluded that these were the wise, the strong, and the honorable. I knew and liked these men. Most of them were quite sincere in their belief that their presence and influence were indispensable in their respective churches. An observer would have concluded that George was a misfit in this gathering.

The time came for me to introduce my guest. Several looked around, wondering who it would be. Few associated him with the unassuming stranger. Until he spoke! Within a minute there was a dead silence in that room. The longer George spoke, the more intense it became, until the room was charged with Holy Spirit power. For nearly an hour he held those men entranced. The world of the lost in all their poverty, anguish, superstition, hopelessness, and despair came into that room. The vast vision of one lone, single-minded, Spirit-driven man held everyone spellbound. The daring faith of a George Muller! The missionary passion of a William Carey! The evangelistic fervor of a D. L. Moody! The devastating courage and honesty of a John Knox! The single-mindedness of a David Livingstone! The authority and power of a General Booth! That was what filled that room. Within ten minutes an observer would have known who was the wise man and who were the "fools," who was strong and who were weak, who was the honorable man and who, by comparison, were of no account, who was really an ambassador for Christ and who were really simply playing church. I have never forgotten it. And so it was, exactly, when it came to the clever, contentious, and conceited Corinthians and the battered and berated apostle Paul.

Paul talks next about *the distinctives of an apostle* (1 Cor. 4:11–17). He talks first along the line of *material considerations* (4:11–12a): "Even unto this present hour we both hunger and thirst, and are naked, and are buffeted, and have no certain dwellingplace; and labour, working with our own hands." So much for reigning as kings! Paul's trail to Corinth had led through Antioch, Iconium, Lystra, and Derbe, through Philippi, Thessalonica, Berea, and Athens. He had been imprisoned, stoned, whipped, and flogged all along the way. He had been mocked and maligned. He had been treated with utter contempt. He supported himself by plying his needle at the dreary and unpleasant task of tent making. This has often been the lot of pioneer missionaries in foreign lands, as well as workers in homelands hostile to the gospel. John Knox labored at the oar of a French galley, Adoniram Judson suffered unbelievable hardships and persecution in Burma, Paton faced horrors unimaginable in the cannibal islands of the New Hebrides.

Not only did the apostles have to face adverse material conditions, there were also adverse *moral considerations* to be remembered (4:12b–13). The scorn, the spite, the slanders of this world all had to be faced: "Being reviled, we bless; being persecuted, we suffer it: being defamed, we entreat: we are made as the filth and offscouring of all things unto this day." The apostles' method of responding to abuse would be regarded as cowardly and with contempt by the world. The Jerusalem mob much preferred the bold and colorful robber chieftain, Barabbas the freedom-fighter, to the meek and lowly Jesus. This gentle way of meeting persecution and abuse does not appeal to the flesh, but it was the Savior's way. Paul and his colleagues accepted meekly the world's estimate of them as the filth and offscouring of the world. So much for the conceited ideas of the Corinthian faction leaders! They had no concept whatever of the mind of Christ.

Paul now turns from the moral and material considerations of apostleship to *ministerial considerations* (4:14–17). He mentions, first, his *message* (4:14–16). He begins with *his approach:* "I write not these things to shame you, but as my beloved sons I warn you" (4:14). Paul really did not desire to embarrass his Corinthian converts. After all, they were his beloved children in the faith. True, he had been sarcastic, but only because the irony of the situation was so obvious to any thinking person, he wanted to save them from real shame. He had to warn them, however, as later he would warn the Ephesian elders (Acts 20:29–31). Pride is the usual forerunner of a fall (Prov. 16:18). It was essential the Corinthians be warned to where their quarrelsome behavior was leading them.

We note *his application:* "For though ye have ten thousand instructors in Christ, ye have not many fathers: for in Christ Jesus I have begotten you through the gospel" (1 Cor. 4:15). The one who led them to Christ should surely speak with more spiritual authority than anyone else. There are "ten thousand instructors in Christ" for every true evangelist. Not all these instructors have the same love and concern that the soul-winner has for the spiritual well-being of those he has led to Christ. Some have a doctrinal ax to grind. Some have an eye on a big pulpit somewhere. Some are interested mostly in the size of the honorarium. Neither Apollos nor Cephas, or those who promoted their distinctives, could possibly have the same concern for the Corinthians that Paul had.

The word for *instructor* here is *paidagōgos.* In Paul's day there were often a multitude of slaves in a household. Some of them acted as nannies to the smaller children. Some were selected to be *pedagogues* to the growing boys in the family. The word itself literally means "a child-leader." The connotation leans more on the side of the pastoral role the slave played than on the teaching role he had. This slave "kept them in ward." That is, he was responsible to take the boys to and from school, to supervise their homework, and to teach them their manners. He usually commanded their respect. Paul knew that any number of people could be found to function in such a capacity in the local church. There was no comparison, however, between the function and authority of a pedagogue and that of a parent. A father commanded love and obedience far beyond that which a mere servant could command. Incidentally, the only other place where Paul uses this actual word is in Galatians 3:24–25, where he describes the role of the Mosaic Law in bringing people to Christ. The Corinthians could doubtless find countless pedagogues. They would have only one spiritual father.

Hence *his appeal:* "Wherefore I beseech you, be ye followers of me" (1 Cor. 4:16). Paul was a superlative example of what a believer should be. He combined the gifts of evangelist, pastor, and teacher. His motives, his morals, and his manner of life were all impeccable. He spoke with authority and often wrote under the direct inspiration of the Holy Spirit. He spared himself no effort or suffering in the cause of Christ. If their newfound leaders set themselves up against him, it would be the mark of plain common sense to follow Paul rather than them. That was his message.

Now he refers to his *messenger* (4:17). He was going to send Timothy to see them. The usual assumption is that Timothy, indeed, had already left (Acts 19:22). Timothy was one of Paul's closest associates. He is linked with Paul in the introduction to half a dozen new Testament epistles (2 Cor. 1:1; 1 Thess. 1:1–2; 2 Thess. 1:1; Philem. 1). Paul valued this young convert of his very highly. He was an appropriate messenger, for he stood in the same spiritual relationship to Paul as did the Corinthians.

Paul waxed eloquent over Timothy. He mentions here his *competence.* Paul calls him "my beloved son, and faithful in the Lord" (1 Cor. 4:17), emphasizing both his relationship and his reliability. Paul had every confidence in him. When he first arrived in Corinth, Timothy had not been with him because he had been dispatched by Paul to minister to the young converts recently left behind in Macedonia. Doubtless the Corinthians knew of this. It was, in any case, an appropriate example of Paul's willingness to trust his young colleague with difficult, even dangerous undertakings.

He mentions also his *commission.* He was coming to Corinth as Paul's personal envoy to remind them of Paul's own conduct and consistency: "who shall bring you into remembrance my ways which be in Christ, as I teach everywhere in every church." The very sight of Timothy would be enough to remind the contentious Corinthians of Paul himself. They knew perfectly well the absolute integrity with which Paul had conducted himself when among them. His personal life was above question or reproach. His teaching was authoritative, scriptural, and inspired. Timothy would remind them of that. Paul was a master tactician. He did not send the youthful Timothy to lord it over them. They might well have resented and resisted him in that case. They certainly would not want, some of them, to have their soaring ambitions and prideful exercise of gift clipped by a mere youth. Paul had more sense than to send Timothy to impose with a heavy hand apostolic authority on the church. No, indeed! Timothy would be a go-between. He would pose no threat to the Corinthians. He would simply remind them of what the great apostle was really like and explain to them that Paul's teaching was the same everywhere. He himself had been with Paul for years and had seen him in action in various churches. He would have a fund of stories, incidents, and anecdotes to illustrate Paul's point.

We have seen how Paul regarded, ridiculed, and repudiated their pride. Now we see *how he rebuked their pride* (1 Cor. 4:18–20) and how he brings this division of his letter to a close. We note *Paul's purpose:* "Now some are puffed up, as though I would not come to you," he says (4:18), adding "but I will come" (4:19a). If they thought Paul was afraid to confront them in person and that he was hiding behind Timothy, they were very much mistaken. The man who had not been afraid to confront Peter to the face (Gal. 2:11–14), and who had not hesitated to confront the entire Jerusalem church, including the formidable James and the entire apostolic company (Gal. 2:1–10), was not the kind of man to be intimidated by some puffed-up, petty popes at Corinth. Let them not underestimate him or misunderstand his purpose in sending Timothy. He was simply doing his best to resolve the crisis at Corinth without a face-to-face confrontation.

We note also *Paul's power* (1 Cor. 4:19–20). He issues a word of *warning:* "But I will come to you shortly, if the Lord will, and will know, not the speech of them which are puffed up, but the power" (4:19). Paul, in fact, was about to start for Macedonia on his way to visit them (16:5). On thinking things over, however, he decided it would be best to postpone his visit. He evidently feared that he would have resorted to some very drastic action were he to come at that time (2 Cor. 1:15–16, 23). When he had left Corinth, after his evangelistic efforts in the city had been crowned with such spectacular success, he had promised he would return (Acts 18:21). His critics at Corinth were crowing over his failure to keep his promise. "I will . . . if the Lord will," he says, reminding them that he was very much under the control of the Holy Spirit in the matter of his movements as in everything else.

However, come he would, when the Lord opened the door. Then there would be a showdown indeed. Words? Anyone can prate words. He was going to demand that the wordy troublemakers back their words with deeds. Did they have Holy Ghost power? He intended to find out. Well he knew that all their noisy pretensions were just so much talk.

He gives them a word of *wisdom:* "For the kingdom of God is not in word, but in power" (1 Cor. 4:20). That is the acid test of a teacher. He is to be tested, not by his eloquence or his party line, but by results. The only way into the kingdom of God is by means of the new birth (John 3:3, 5), for it is by means of the gospel that people are brought into the good of the new birth. Paul told the Romans that he was "not ashamed of the gospel of Christ: for it is the power of God unto salvation to every one that believeth; to the Jew first, and also to the Greek" (Rom. 1:16). Moreover, once in the kingdom of God, a person would evidence it by "righteousness, and peace, and joy in the Holy Ghost" (Rom. 14:17). This is the kind of power for which he would be looking when he came, the power that transformed people's lives.

Finally we note *Paul's patience:* "What will ye? shall I come unto you with a rod, or in love, and in the spirit of meekness?" (1 Cor. 4:21). A lesser man than Paul, armed as he was with apostolic powers, might well have dropped everything, made a swift trip to Corinth, faced the troublemakers, hurled a few fearful thunderbolts, left death and terror behind him, and returned to his interrupted labors. He had the power, but divine patience held back his hand. He had no wish to bury the Ananiases and Sapphiras of Corinth as Peter had done at Jerusalem (Acts 5:1–13), although Peter's action had certainly put the fear of God into the Jerusalem church. That was not what Paul was after. He had no wish to smite his foes with blindness, as he once had done to Elymas the sorcerer (Acts 13:4–12), although such summary judgment produced faith in the heart of a very important man. No, indeed! Paul had a higher purpose. He wanted love to win, the kind of love he will talk about later (1 Cor. 13).

PART 3

Discipline in the Church
1 Corinthians 5:1–6:20

A. Matters of a moral nature (5:1–13)
  1. The charge (5:1–5)
    a. Accusation (5:1–2)
      (1) The sin of the culprit (5:1)
        (a) Its fleshly nature (5:1a)
        (b) Its flagrant nature (5:1b)
      (2) The sin of the Corinthians (5:2)
        (a) Their inflation (5:2a)
        (b) Their insensitivity (5:2b)
        (c) Their inaction (5:2c)
    b. Adjudication (5:3–5)
      (1) Paul's indignation (5:3)
      (2) Paul's injunction (5:4–5)
        (a) The source of his authority (5:4)
        (b) The force of his authority (5:5)
          i. Excommunication (5:5a)
          ii. Expectation (5:5b)
  2. The challenge (5:6–13)
    a. The leaven (5:6–8)
      (1) A disclaimer (5:6a)
      (2) A declaration (5:6b)
      (3) A demand (5:7–8)
        (a) The reason for discipline (5:7)
        (b) The results of discipline (5:8)
    b. The letters (5:9–13)
      (1) The past letter (5:9–10)
        (a) Its content (5:9)
        (b) Its context (5:10)
      (2) The present letter (5:11–13)
        (a) The expansion of the rule (5:11)
        (b) The explanation of the rule (5:12–13a)
        (c) The execution of the rule (5:13b)

H aving dealt with *divisions in the church* (1 Cor. 1:10–4:21), Paul turns to *discipline in the church* (5:1–6:20). The abruptness of the change in subject suggests that the report of gross immorality being tolerated in the Corinthian church had only just reached him. His righteous indignation at the flagrant nature of the immorality is exacerbated by the fact that he was left to find out about it by rumor and common report. There were two critical issues which now engaged his attention and which called for judgment. The first was an issue of a *moral* nature (5:1–13), the second was one of a *material* nature (6:1–20). The moral issue was the more pressing. In fact, he has barely finished with the material issue before he is back to the moral issue (6:12–20).

He begins with *the charge* (5:1–5), first of all spelling out *the accusation* (5:1–2). There were two sins here—that of *the culprit* (5:1) and that of *the Corinthians* (5:2). The sin of the guilty person was one of a *fleshly* nature: "It is reported commonly that there is fornication among you," he says. The word *commonly* here is *holōs,* meaning "actually." There was no need for Paul to name his informants. The matter was on everybody's tongue. Paul, however, was astounded that such behavior could be tolerated for a moment. Evidently some in the church, particularly the brother being indicted, thought that liberty meant license, that being emancipated from the ceremonial law meant freedom from the moral law. The natural heart, even of a Christian, is deceitful and desperately wicked. Satan, moreover, is adept at persuading us that wrong is right, that immorality can be condoned and indulged as an expression of our liberty. The word for *fornication* is *porneia,* and is used for all kinds of illicit sexual intercourse, including adultery.

The sin of the guilty person was not only of a fleshly nature, it was also of a *flagrant* nature: "And such fornication as is not so much as named among the Gentiles, that one should have his father's wife" (1 Cor. 5:1b). Both the Greeks and the Romans were notoriously unscrupulous when it came to carnal indulgence, but both deplored this degree of vice. Euripides, in *Hippolytus,* tells a story, indeed, of such a crime, one which had as its setting the neighborhood of Corinth, and records that the feelings of the pagans were shocked by it. Cicero, in his *Pro Cluentio,* denounces a marriage between in-laws as "incredible" and practically unheard of. Even pagan societies, while often tolerant of all kinds of promiscuity, drew the line at incest.

The verb *hath* here suggests that the incestuous relationship was intended to be of a continuing nature. The Law of God legislated against such close liaisons (Lev. 18:17; Deut. 27:20). It is inferred by some that the man's father was still alive (2 Cor. 7:12), a fact which would make the sin more glaring than ever. It is also supposed, since the woman herself is not mentioned, that she must have been a pagan and, hence, outside the jurisdiction of church discipline (7:13). The expression *his father's wife* is taken to be the man's stepmother, who could, of course, have been much of an age, or even younger, than the offender. Or, perhaps, the circumlocution is intended to emphasize the outrageous nature of the sin.

Paul turns next to the sin of *the Corinthians*, which was almost as bad as that of the culprit. Paul indicts them on three counts. They were guilty of *inflation:* "Ye are puffed up," he says. They were guilty of *insensitivity:* "and have not rather mourned," he adds. They were guilty of *inaction*. They had done absolutely nothing to see "that he that hath done this deed might be taken away from among you" (1 Cor. 5:2). The word *ye* is emphatic. The very people who should have been most concerned about this situation were the most complacent. Worse than that, they were "puffed up" over it as though the guilty person were some kind of a hero. They were proud of themselves for being so broad-minded. The man, in their opinion, had demonstrated complete emancipation from both Jewish law and Gentile custom. It has been suggested that perhaps some embryonic form of antinomianism, such as later existed among some of the Gnostic sects, had already put forth its deadly shoots among them, and that this is what made them so tolerant of this unnatural sin. Whatever sophistries they used to justify the man's behavior, and their acceptance of it, the depravity of the Corinthian society in general would doubtless help deaden their consciences.

Now comes *the adjudication* (5:3–5). We note, first, *Paul's indignation:* "For I verily, as absent in body, but present in spirit, have judged already, as though I were present, concerning him that hath so done this deed" (5:3). Paul's source of information was so authoritative he knew the man to be guilty and therefore he did not hesitate to pronounce sentence. He was now acting both as an apostle and as a prophet.

When Naaman came to Elisha for cleansing, and obediently dipped himself in the Jordan, he came back to the prophet to give thanks, full of rejoicing, and wanted to show his gratitude by giving a handsome gift to Elisha. The prophet steadfastly refused to accept what might, later, be interpreted as payment for God's free gift of salvation, which is always offered "without money and without price" (Isa. 55:1). Gehazi, Elisha's servant, had no such scruples. As soon as the prophet's back was turned he hastened after Naaman. The Syrian general saw him and stopped his chariot. "All is well," Gehazi panted in answer to Naaman's question. "My master hath sent me," he continued, employing a convenient lie. "Behold, even now two young prophets have arrived from Mount Ephraim. He would like to give them a talent of silver and a couple of new suits." Delighted at being able to do something after all, Naaman gave Gehazi two talents of silver along with two suits of clothes. He even loaned Gehazi a couple of servants to carry the heavy bags of silver to the tower where Gehazi intended to hide them. Doubtless, like Judas, he went home rubbing his hands. His fortune was made!

He had forgotten Elisha. "Where have you been, Gehazi?" Elisha asked him when he came back into his presence. Gehazi told another lie. "I haven't been anywhere," he said. Then the ax fell: "Went not mine heart with thee, when the man turned again from his chariot to meet thee? . . . The leprosy therefore of Naaman shall cleave unto thee, and unto thy seed for ever." The stricken Gehazi "went out from his presence," we are told, "a leper as white as snow" (2 Kings 5:14–27).

The human spirit has strange powers, especially when under the active control of the Holy Spirit. In spirit Paul had already visited the church at Corinth. He had seen the evidence as clearly as though he had been there bodily. He had seen the saints arriving for morning worship. He had seen many a face he knew and others he did not know. He had seen them exchanging greetings in the foyer. He had seen one or two of the elders greeting the newcomers. He had seen a man and a woman come in. He had seen some of the elders exchange knowing looks and some of the people engage in winks and nods. He had seen the man and woman cordially received and welcomed by the elders and greeted warmly by others. He had seen the couple go in and take their places. He had seen them singing lustily and responding heartily to the various expressions of worship. He had seen the Lord's Supper being served and had seen the pair of them receive the emblems. He had seen them leave after the service, still enjoying the goodwill of the church. Maybe he had even seen the man's father standing bewildered, robbed, and forlorn somewhere on the edge of the crowd. He had been there in spirit. He had seen it as clearly as Elisha saw Gehazi and Naaman. All prophet, he had seen it. All apostle, he judged it. "I have already judged," he said, "as though I were present." The man would have been stopped at the door, had Paul been there in body. His indignation at the cordial and casual condoning of a crime overflowed.

We note also *Paul's injunction* (1 Cor. 5:4–5). First, he states the *source* of his authority to judge this matter: "In the name of our Lord Jesus Christ, when ye are gathered together, and my spirit, with the power of our Lord Jesus Christ" (5:4). They were to act. They were to act in solemn session. They were to act in the name and with the power of "our Lord Jesus Christ," giving Him His full title to add to the seriousness and solemnity of the occasion. They were to recognize that he, Paul, in his official capacity as their own apostle, would be there in spirit. Paul could see himself come into that church on this impending occasion as surely as though he could come in bodily. He could see himself, standing in their midst, as the man and the woman come in, perhaps like Ananias and Sapphira, ignorant of what was about to befall. He could see himself there in spirit, armed with the authority of Christ and with His power—an authority and power he now delegates to this local church. The Lord Jesus Christ did not die on the cross of Calvary in order to give His people license to sin (Rom. 6:1–2). God does not condemn sin in the sinner and then condone it in the saint. "Judgment must begin at the house of God" (1 Peter 4:17).

Paul next indicates the *force* of his authority (1 Cor. 5:5). He calls, first of all, for *excommunication:* "To deliver such an one unto Satan for the destruction of the flesh" (5:5a). No more terrible sentence could have been uttered. Job was delivered unto Satan, and Satan smote him with all kinds of disasters, including an outbreak of agonizing boils (Job 2:4–8). Even so, God drew the line and refused to allow Satan to go beyond a certain point. Normally, it would seem, Satan has no power over a believer. A deliberate and authoritative act is needed to withdraw the divine protection that the believer enjoys. This man was to suffer excommunication with an added horror, the horror of being put in Satan's hands, for God intended to make an example of this man that others might fear. Later on, similar punishment was inflicted on Hymenaeus and Alexander (1 Tim. 1:20). The authority to deliver a person to Satan seems to have been an apostolic authority.

"Such an one," says Paul, as though reluctant to even mention the man's name. The word for "destruction" is *olethros,* meaning "ruin." It indicates the physical consequences resulting from this particularly drastic form of excommunication. The word is used by Paul to describe the ruin to come upon mankind subsequent to the rapture of the church, which is God's Spirit-baptized vehicle for holding back the worst manifestations of evil in this age of grace (1 Thess. 5:3). Paul uses the word again, in a similar connection, to describe the "everlasting destruction" which will overtake unbelievers at the final return of Christ (2 Thess. 1:9). He uses the word one more time to describe the way money, and its power to snare people "in many foolish and hurtful lusts," can lead to a person's utter ruin (1 Tim. 6:9).

Along with the excommunication, however, there was to be *expectation* (1 Cor.

5:5b). Expelling the man from the fellowship of the church and clearing the way for Satan to get his hands on him was not an end in itself, but a means to an end: "that the spirit may be saved in the day of the Lord Jesus." The day of the Lord Jesus is the day of the Rapture and Resurrection, when the spirit, which returns to God at death, is reunited with the redeemed body. The "day" also embraces the period of "the coming of the Lord Jesus" (1 Thess. 3:13), when the saints of God will stand before the judgment seat of Christ (Rom. 14:12; 2 Cor. 5:10) to give account of the way they have lived their lives and used their spiritual gifts. This day is not to be confused with "the day of the Lord," when God enters into judgment with the ungodly.

So the man was to be handed over to Satan for his own highest good. God uses Satan at times for the discipline and correction of His own. He did so with Job, with Peter (Luke 22:31), and with Paul himself (2 Cor. 12:7). God, however, always draws the line beyond which Satan cannot go! He was to be permitted to wreak havoc in the body of this guilty man, but he was not allowed to touch the man's spirit. That was already quickened and indwelt by the Holy Spirit. So much for the charge.

Now comes *the challenge* (1 Cor. 5:6–13). Paul draws the attention of the Corinthians now to *the leaven* (5:6–8). First there is *a disclaimer:* "Your glorying is not good," he says (5:6a). The word for *glorying* is *kauchēma*—"boasting," or, rather, the ground of their boasting. The expression *not good* comes from the word *kalon,* of which one commentator says it is "almost untranslatable." It implies all moral beauty. The English *honorable* comes close to the meaning. The idea seems to be that the pride the Corinthians had in their church was woefully misplaced.

The disclaimer is followed by *a declaration:* "Know ye not that a little leaven leaveneth the whole lump?" (5:6b). The Corinthians thought themselves to be very sophisticated. Paul says they were ignorant. Throughout the Bible, leaven is used as a type of insidious evil. It does not take much leaven to permeate the whole loaf once it is introduced into the dough. However, its activity is arrested by the fire once the leavened loaf is put into the oven. Paul could clearly see that the immorality being tolerated in the Corinthian church would lead to a general breakdown of moral standards and the rapid spread of immorality in the church. Fire was the only remedy. Judgment!

So now comes *a demand* (5:7–8). Paul states *the reason* for discipline: "Purge out therefore the old leaven, that ye may be a new lump, as ye are unleavened. For even Christ our passover is sacrificed for us" (5:7). Mention of the leaven reminds Paul of the annual Old Testament Jewish practice of ridding the house of all the old leaven before the celebration of the Passover (Exod. 12:18–20; 13:6–7). This entailed a thorough-going spring cleaning, and was intended to depict the complete break with the old life in Egypt. It also anticipated the new life the Israelites were to live in fellowship with God once they had been redeemed. Every trace of leaven had to go. A diligent search through the whole house was pursued.

"Ye are unleavened," Paul exclaims. This referred to their standing in Christ rather than to their state. In the Old Testament offerings, leaven was permitted when the offering had to do with the *offerer*, because he was sinful, but it was forbidden when the offering represented *Christ* because He was sinless. In the case of the local church at Corinth, Paul called for the greatest diligence to be maintained to purge out all evil doctrinal and immoral influences. Ideally their local church was "unleavened" (Eph. 5:25–27). In actual fact, however, it contained the leaven of gross immorality. Discipline was in order so as to get rid of that which was corrupting the church.

Paul also states *the result* of discipline (1 Cor. 5:8): "Therefore let us keep the feast, neither with the old leaven of malice and wickedness: but with the unleavened bread of sincerity and truth." We do not celebrate the old Passover feast, which was strictly a Jewish feast. The true Paschal Lamb has been sacrificed for us. The Old Testament type has been replaced by the New Testament truth. We learn from John's gospel that the actual death of Christ coincided with the sacrifice of the paschal lambs throughout the land. The Jews slew their Passover lamb between noon and sunset on the fourteenth day of Nisan (John 19:14, 31; Exod. 12:6; Deut. 16:6). That was the very time Christ was on the cross. The Lamb has been killed, so now the leaven must be removed and the true feast enjoyed.

In Old Testament times the Passover feast was followed by "the feast of unleavened bread" (Exod. 23:15; Deut. 16:3), a feast which lasted a whole week. That was the old type. The new truth is that Christ has been sacrificed, once and for all, as the real Passover Lamb; therefore believers must rid themselves, once and for all, of everything leaven stands for. Away with malice and wickedness! On with sincerity and truth!

The word *malice* is *kakia*, meaning "depravity," a word which refers primarily to the vicious disposition and desires of the human heart. The word *wickedness* is *ponēria*, a word which suggests depravity, the active outworking of our wicked human nature. Together they express everything God hates. The man to be excommunicated was the embodiment of these things at Corinth. The word for *sincerity* is *elikrineia,* which suggests purity. It refers to something unalloyed, unadulterated. In Christ we are to put away evil and put on genuine Christian character.

Having spoken about the leaven, Paul now mentions *the letters* (1 Cor. 5:9–13). There was the *past letter.* It is generally believed that Paul refers here to an earlier letter he had written to the Corinthians, one which has not been preserved for posterity. Doubtless Paul kept up a voluminous correspondence with churches and converts in all parts of the empire. No doubt these letters would make interesting reading if they could be found. Doubtless, however, all that was of importance for the church, found in those letters, has found its way into his New Testament epistles.

He mentions here *the content* of that earlier Corinthian correspondence: "I wrote unto you in an epistle not to keep company with fornicators" (5:9). They were not to mix with immoral people! We get like the company we keep. Bad company often leads to bad behavior. Not even Solomon was able to escape the influence of bad company. He began by lowering his standards when he married an Egyptian princess to be his queen. No doubt he thought it a very fine thing at the time that Pharaoh of Egypt was willing to pay tribute to Israel, as an emerging regional power, to the extent of giving one of his daughters in marriage to Solomon. In actual fact, it was a sad compromise with the world. Before long Solomon cemented alliances with the various surrounding nations by marrying all kinds of pagan women. Perhaps he deluded himself into thinking he could convert them to the true faith. If so, he was seriously mistaken. He did not convert them, they corrupted him. Some of the religions they imported into Israel were foul in the extreme and, before he was through, Solomon was as involved in the lewd and licentious rituals of these religions as were the women themselves. It proved to be disastrous for himself and for his kingdom. God's standard is not one of compromise with immorality but complete separation from it.

When I was in the British Army in Palestine there were some sections of the city of Haifa which were posted "out of bounds" to the troops. They were mostly areas given over to prostitution. In His Word, God has written "out of bounds" over all aspects of immorality. Solomon tells us how he once watched a young man go down just such a forbidden street (Prov. 7:4–27). Indeed, he seems to have watched his encounter with a harlot with considerable interest. Solomon, it seems, knew the street and knew the harlot's house. Solomon's sensual indulgence had so deadened his conscience and corroded his character that, while he was quite able and willing to moralize on the young man's behavior, he did nothing to put the woman out of business or to send someone to warn the young man of his danger. We do well to keep away from those things in life posted out of bounds by God's Word.

Then, too, Paul mentions *the context* of that earlier letter: "Yet not altogether with the fornicators of this world, or with the covetous, or extortioners, or with idolaters; for then must ye needs go out of the world" (1 Cor. 5:10). It seems that Paul's previous injunction had been misunderstood, even ridiculed by some. Obviously we cannot abstain from all communication with unbelievers who practice fornication and other forms of wickedness. We cannot always choose our doctors, our taxi drivers, or even our workmates on the basis of their morals. Still less can we choose our next door neighbors on that basis. Paul ridicules the Corinthians in turn for imagining he had suggested any such thing. He not only sets them right, but he enlarges on the list of immoralities we cannot avoid in this world. He includes covetousness, extortion, and idolatry. The *world,* here, is human life and society, as organized at any given time and in any given place, with God left out. *Covetousness* is inordinate desire and it may apply to lust for sex, money, or power. *Extortion* comes from a word meaning "to ravish." It carries the idea of being rapacious. Zaccheus, before his conversion, was an extortioner, a man who became rich from the money he wrung out of taxpayers. *Idolatry* is a universal sin. It was rampant in Paul's day and is widely prevalent in our own. It is interesting that this is the first time *eidōloatrēs* occurs in the Bible (the word does not appear in the Septuagint), although, of course, the worship of graven images is roundly condemned throughout Scripture.

Paul now comes back to *the present letter* (5:11–13). He comes back, too, to the rule which had been professedly misunderstood by the Corinthians. We note the *expansion* of the rule (5:11). Certain types of behavior are incompatible with a Christian testimony and with church fellowship. He says: "But now I have written unto you not to keep company, if any man that is called a brother be a fornicator, or covetous, or an idolater, or a railer, or a drunkard, or an extortioner; with such an one, no, not to eat." Believers are not to maintain fellowship with, or to associate with, any professing believer who is known to be an immoral person, or a swindler, or an idolater, or possessed of a foul tongue, or one who is a drunkard or a thief. Nothing can do greater damage to a local testimony than to have such people acknowledged, as members in good standing, in the fellowship of the church. Such a person is to be cut off from all fellowship.

In Paul's day, the Lord's Supper was celebrated in close connection with the *agape* meal. The man under the church's interdict was to be cut off from both tables and, by extension, to be denied table fellowship in the homes of the other church members. This was an effective way for the church to disassociate itself from such professing believers. Indeed, the world itself would be impressed by such action. As for the person himself, if he were indeed a genuine believer, his isolation would be a sure way to bring him to his senses so that, by his repentance, he could eventually be restored to the fellowship. If the man were not genuinely saved, his excommunication would likely result in his returning completely back into the world.

We have also the *explanation* of the rule: "For what have I to do to judge them also that are without? do not ye judge them that are within? But them that are without God judgeth" (5:12–13a). The sphere in which church discipline operates is the church. Those within the church, that is, genuinely saved people, come under the jurisdiction of the church and are subject to its authority and to its discipline. The church has no right to try to pass sentence on unsaved people.

When I was a boy, there was an organization in Britain known as The Lord's Day Observance Society. Its chief function was to make sure that shops and businesses and places of amusement and, as far as possible, even transportation systems were kept closed, or limited to vital operations only, on Sunday. The Society, its rules, and its power were much resented by unsaved people. It was an attempt by the church to legislate for the world. Paul is not calling here for that kind of officiousness.

The apostles knew where to draw the line. The power of binding and loosing (Matt. 16:19) and of retaining or forgiving sins (John 20:23) was an apostolic function. Disciplining church members was a church function—one, indeed, that was anticipated by Christ Himself (Matt. 18:15–20). Peter judged Ananias and Sapphira (Acts 5:1–10) because they were believers but he did not judge Simon Magus, although he bluntly told him his true spiritual condition, because he was not a genuine believer (8:5–24)

Finally, we have *the execution* of the rule (1 Cor. 5:13b). Paul says, "Therefore put away from among yourselves that wicked person." The word for *wicked* here is *ponēros,* a word which expresses the active form of evil. It refers to something baneful. Paul's words are a direct echo of Deuteronomy 17:7, where God commanded the death of the person who embraced paganism, adding "so thou shalt put the evil away from among you." A similar death sentence was pronounced upon a consenting couple caught committing adultery. Again we have the formula "so shalt thou put evil away from Israel" (Deut. 22:22). False prophets were to be likewise put to death and for the same reason: "So shalt thou put the evil away from the midst of thee" (13:5). Sin in the local church was no more to be condoned than sin in the nation of Israel. Israel's failure to heed God's commands led in time to the corruption and judgment of the nation. The church's failure to heed God's commands has the same result.

B. Matters of a material nature (6:1–20)
1. Litigation (6:1–8)
    a. The court (6:1–4)
        (1) The secular court (6:1)
            (a) Paul describes it for us (6:1a)
            (b) Paul denies it to us (6:1b)
        (2) The sacred court (6:2–4)
            (a) Its higher spheres of operation (6:2–3a)
                i. To judge this world down here (6:2)
                ii. To judge that world up there (6:3a)
            (b) Its human sphere of operation (6:3b–4)
                i. Our competence indicated (6:3b)
                ii. Our competence illustrated (6:4)
    b. The critic (6:5–7)
        (1) Paul's chagrin (6:5a)
        (2) Paul's challenge (6:5b–6)
            (a) Their tacit confession (6:5b)
            (b) Their tactless conduct (6:6)
        (3) Paul's charge (6:7)
            (a) His repudiation of what they were doing (6:7a)
            (b) His recognition of what they weren't doing (6:7b)
    c. The crime (6:8)
        (1) The accusation reviewed (6:8a)
        (2) The aggravation revealed (6:8b)
2. Condemnation (6:9–11)
    a. A sobering declaration (6:9a)
    b. A searching denunciation (6:9b–10)
        (1) The warning expressed (6:9b)
        (2) The wicked exposed (6:9c–10)
            (a) Sins of a personal nature (6:9c–g)
                i. Lustfulness (6:9c–e)
                    a. Sexual sin—fornicators (6:9c)

    b. Spiritual sin—idolaters (6:9d)

    c. Social sin—adulterers (6:9e)

   ii. Lawlessness (6:9f–g)

    a. Sinning against normality—"effeminate" (6:9f)

    b. Sinning against nature—"abusers" (6:9g)

  (b) Sins of a public nature (6:10)

   Those with no control over

    i. Their wants (6:10a–b)

     a. The outward act—thieves (6:10a)

     b. The inward attitude—covetous (6:10b)

    ii. Their will—drunkards (6:10c)

    iii. Their words—revilers (6:10d)

    iv. Their ways—extortioners (6:10e)

 c. A sanctifying distinction (6:11)

  (1) What they had been (6:11a)

  (2) What they had become (6:11b–f)

   (a) The greatness of their transformation (6:11b–d)

    i. God has dealt with their state—they are washed (6:11b)

    ii. God has dealt with their standing

     a. They are set apart for God—they are sanctified (6:11c)

     b. They are set aright by God—they are justified (6:11d)

   (b) The ground of their transformation (6:11e–f)

    i. Through the Son of God, and His triumphant name (6:11e)

    ii. Through the Spirit of God, and His transforming nature (6:11f)

3. Fornication (6:12–20)

 a. A matter of perspective (6:12–13b)

  (1) The lawfulness of some things (6:12)

   (a) What Paul recognized (6:12a)

   (b) What Paul resolved (6:12b)

  (2) The limitations of some things (6:13a–b)

   (a) The body's legitimate needs discerned (6:13a)

   (b) The body's legitimate needs dismissed (6:13b)

b. A matter of principle (6:13c–18)
  (1) The principle validated (6:13c–15)
    (a) The negative principle (6:13c)
    (b) The new principle (6:13d–15)
        i. The main argument (6:13d–14)
            a. The body must be relinquished to the Lord (6:13d)
            b. The body will be raised by the Lord (6:14)
        ii. The mystical argument (6:15a)
        iii. The moral argument (6:15b)
  (2) The principle violated (6:16–18)
    (a) A contrast (6:16–17)
        i. A guilty union (6:16)
        ii. A glorious union (6:17)
    (b) A command (6:18a)
    (c) A consequence (6:18b–c)
        i. The distinctive nature of most sin (6:18b)
        ii. The deadly nature of moral sin (6:18c)
c. A matter of privilege (6:19–20)
  (1) The body is possessed by the Spirit of God (6:19)
  (2) The body was purchased by the Son of God (6:20)
    (a) A great truth (6:20a)
    (b) A great trust (6:20b)

Paul is still dealing with the question of *discipline in the church* (1 Cor. 5:1–6:20). He turns from matters of a *moral* nature (5:1–13) to matters of a *material* nature (6:1–20), although he soon reverts back to sins of carnality and corruption. He deals here with three subjects—*litigation* (6:1–8), *condemnation* (6:9–11), and *fornication* (6:12–20). So far as the issue of litigation was concerned there was, first of all, *the court* to be considered (6:1–4).

He turns his attention to *the secular court* (6:1) and first describes it for us and then denies it to us as Christians. He describes the law courts of the Gentiles as those of "the unjust." The word *unjust* is *adikos.* It is used in Acts 24:15 to distinguish between saved people and unsaved people. It was not that Paul thought it impossible to get justice in a secular law court. He himself had been exonerated by the Roman proconsul right there in Corinth itself (Acts 18:12–16). The point was that church matters should be settled within the church and not before the world.

"Dare any of you!" exclaims Paul. The word is *tolmaō*. It carries the idea of bringing oneself to do something. Paul thought it was shocking that they even consider washing their dirty laundry in public. Whatever would it do to the church's corporate testimony if its members engaged in public lawsuits? Every Jewish community in the world had its own internal arrangements for settling differences between Jew and Jew. Surely the church ought to have its own mechanism, too! He rules, right from the start, that secular courts are not appropriate places to settle internal squabbles. Such things should be kept within the family.

Paul turns now to *the sacred court* (1 Cor. 6:2–4). It has two spheres of jurisdiction. Paul begins by drawing our attention to *the higher spheres* of its operation (6:2–3a). First of all, the saints are going to judge *this world down here:* "Do ye not know that the saints shall judge the world? and if the world shall be judged by you, are ye unworthy to judge the smallest matters?" (6:2). Paul has already reminded the Corinthians of the judgment seat of Christ, where our position in the coming millennial kingdom will be determined by our performance in this life. Positions of vast power and great authority will be occupied by the saints of God who have won their spurs and earned their crowns. Daniel had a glimmering of it (Dan. 7:22). The Lord Jesus was more specific. The Lord had already told His immediate disciples, "Verily I say unto you, That ye which have followed me, in the regeneration when the Son of man shall sit on the throne of his glory, ye also shall sit upon twelve thrones, judging the twelve tribes of Israel" (Matt. 19:28). No small honor, indeed, as the tribes of Israel will be the human administrators, under Christ, of the nations of the earth during the Golden Age (Deut. 28:13; Zech. 8:22–23). The triumphant saints of the church age will wield similar authority, only from the heavenlies (Matt. 25:21, 23; Luke 19:17, 19).

If we are going to judge the world, Paul argues, how much more we should be able to judge the relatively minor matters which come up within the sphere of the church.

But there is more! We are going to judge *that world up there:* "Know ye not that we shall judge angels?" (1 Cor. 6:3a). The prophet Isaiah foresaw that time. He wrote, "And it shall come to pass in that day, that the LORD shall punish the host of the high ones that are on high, and the kings of the earth upon the earth" (Isa. 24:21). At the beginning of the millennial reign the Lord will overthrow the Antichrist at Megiddo and his armies and all the assembled armies of the world (Rev. 16:12–16). The returning saints will participate as spectators of this final dissolution of Gentile world power (Rev. 19:11–21). Thus will end the "times of the Gentiles" spoken of by the Lord (Luke 21:24). The surviving remnant of the Jewish people will go on into the millennial kingdom as Christ's ambassadors, viceroys, and administrators of the earthly kingdom.

We learn from the book of Daniel that Satan not only rules over the nations of the earth but he rules in the heavenlies. He sets his fallen angel princes over the various nations, kingdoms, and empires of this world. They wield enormous power and hold the kingdoms of the earth in thrall to Satan (Dan. 10:20–21; 12:1). These are the mighty beings against whom we wrestle when we pray (Eph. 6:10–13). These are "the high ones that are on high," of whom Isaiah speaks, who are to be overthrown at the second coming of Christ. The church age saints will reign with Christ in the very heavenlies where Satan and his angels now hold sway. Indeed we are already seated in those "heavenly places" with Christ (Eph. 1:19–23; 2:6). The seat of our operations in the heavenlies will be the celestial city (Rev. 21:9–22:5).

At the end of the millennial age, God will judge Satan (Rev. 20:4–10) and also the angels of Satan (Jude 6; 2 Peter 2:4). Paul here reveals to the Corinthian believers that we are going to have a share in this, the most dramatic and decisive judgment of all time. Such is the dignity, destiny, and duty of those who trust in Christ in this age

Paul moves at once from *the higher spheres* of operation (1 Cor. 6:2–3a) to *the human sphere* of operation (6:3b–4). "How much more," he says, "things that pertain to this life?" (6:3b). When it comes to judging angels, what mysteries will be revealed! What insights we shall be given into the secret war of the worlds. We shall know all about "extraterrestrials" then! Satan's machinations, his diabolic cunning, his whole vast hierarchical empire in the spirit world, his control over demons, disease, disasters, and death, and his powerful "wicked spirits in high places," who aid and abet him, will all be exposed. We will understand things then just as Job understood things when, at last, in the last chapter of his book, he received information, long hidden from him, but now revealed in the opening and closing chapters of his book (Job 1:1–2:10; 4:10–17). All of a sudden many of the seeming mysteries of life will be revealed. We shall see what part Satan and his angels played in the things which have happened on earth. And we shall judge those fallen angels! If we are to have the wisdom to do that, then, Paul says, we have that wisdom now for He who is "the Spirit of wisdom" (Eph. 1:17) lives within our hearts. We only have to ask Him for wisdom and it will be ours (James 1:5). It is well within our competence to judge the affairs that come up in the church.

Our competence is illustrated, by contrast: "If then ye have judgments of things pertaining to this life, set them to judge who are least esteemed in the church" (1 Cor. 6:4) "If you need tribunals," Paul says, intimating that there ought to be no such need. Still, civil disputes might arise, even among Christians, in which case, he says, "Why do you lay them before those who have no status in the church?" that is, before pagan judges. That is one interpretation of Paul's statement. Some would suggest, "Lay them [i.e., your civil disputes] before those church members who are least esteemed." If this is the right rendering, then Paul is being somewhat sarcastic. To resort to pagan magistrates would imply there was no one in the church gifted enough to arbitrate between two disputing parties—this to a church which prided itself on its gift and whose names included such an able man as Erastus, the city treasurer (Rom. 16:23).

We turn from *the court* (1 Cor. 6:1–4) to *the critic* (6:5–7). The critic is Paul himself, who can hardly believe the un-Christlike spirit abroad in the Corinthian church. We note *Paul's chagrin:* "I speak to your shame," he says (6:5a). The word for *shame* is *entropē,* which conveys the thought of turning in upon oneself and of producing a recoil from something vile or improper. It is linked with *aischunē* in the Septuagint version of the Psalms as, for instance, in Psalm 35, where David asks God to avenge him upon his enemies: "Let them be ashamed *[aischunē]* and brought to confusion *[entropē]* together that rejoice in my hurt" (35:26). The word *aischunē* carries the idea of ignominy. When David in his great messianic psalm (69:19) confessed to God his shame and revulsion at the thought of his sin, the word *entropē* is again used in the Greek translation. The word for *dishonor* in this same verse in David's psalm is *aischunē.* Coming back to the Corinthians, Paul says, they ought to be ashamed of themselves. We sense that he, himself, was ashamed of them or, at least, ashamed for them.

We note also *Paul's challenge* (1 Cor. 6:5b–6). He notes *their tacit confession:* "Is it so, that there is not a wise man among you? no, not one that shall be able to judge between his brethren?" (6:5b). Among *you,* you that set yourselves up to be so wise and so sophisticated! In his closing remarks in this letter, Paul says, "I beseech you, brethren (ye know the house of Stephanus, that it is the firstfruits of Achaia, and that they have addicted themselves to the ministry of the saints,) that ye submit yourselves unto such" (16:15–16). He goes on to mention Fortunatus and Achaicus, whose ministries were a benediction (16:17–18). And what about Lucius and Jason, Sosipater (Paul's own kinsman) or Tertius, who acted as Paul's personal secretary at times, or Gaius, famous for his generosity, or even Quartus "a brother" (Rom. 16:21–23)? Evidently Paul is being sarcastic when he challenges the Corinthians who were " unable to find" *(eni)* one man capable of arbitrating between the disputing parties. He could name a dozen.

He notes also *their tactless conduct:* "But brother goeth to law with brother, and that before the unbelievers" (1 Cor. 6:6). The shame of it! What would the unsaved think of the church and of its lofty claims to be the mystical body of Christ, heaven born and heaven bound, seated in Christ far above principalities and powers and every name which is named, not only in this world but also in the world to come? Had not the Lord Jesus, on the very night of His betrayal, prayed for the oneness of the body? "That they all may be one . . . that the world may believe that thou hast sent me" (John 17:21). What would this disgraceful squabbling, openly, in court, before pagan magistrates, do for the testimony? Would not the unsaved simply say, "These Christians, for all their lofty claims and high-sounding teachings, are no better than we are"?

Such was Paul's challenge. Now note *Paul's charge* (1 Cor. 6:7) in which he first *repudiates* what they were doing ("Now therefore there is utterly a fault among you, because ye go to law one with another") and *recognizes* what they weren't doing ("Why do ye not rather take wrong? Why do ye not rather suffer your-selves to be defrauded?"). There was a more excellent way. There was a higher and holier law, the law of love.

Years ago I fell into the hands of an unscrupulous businessman who persuaded me to invest money in what he knew to be a worthless enterprise. He gave me some equally worthless documents as security. When the first interest check was returned by the bank I knew I had been duped. I took the worthless check to him and demanded an explanation. It was a mistake, he said, he had meant to cover the check. I should redeposit it. It was the beginning of a long trail of lies and evasions. At last I took legal counsel. "A clear case of fraud," the attorney said. "Let me have the case and I'll see the man in prison." The man was a professing believer. He went to the same church as I did. I knew his wife and little children. After some agonizing heart searching, I decided to let the matter rest. The sum of money involved was considerable (at least for me it was) but it was not worth a lawsuit. I decided to "suffer myself to be defrauded."

"Ah!" the worldly wise would say, "then this brother was able to use 1 Corinthians 6 as a way to get away with fraud!" Well, yes and no! In actual fact the case was simply referred to a Higher Court. The man did not get away with his dishonesty, as I learned later. He paid in other ways. Nor was I the loser. A wealthy businessman friend of mine heard what had happened. He approached me one day and said, "I should have warned you about that man. I didn't know you were a potential victim. The Lord has put it on my heart to help you. Sell me those securities. Don't you worry about my taking a loss, I can absorb it easily enough. Anyway, I have more leverage than you have and I know more about him than you do. Leave him to me." The man was as good as his word. Within a few weeks he handed me a check for the full amount. Doubtless it does not always work out like that. But it will always work out—in the end.

A farmer who was an atheist wrote to a newspaper columnist, boasting of his unbelief and telling of an experiment he had just made. "This past spring," he said, "I plowed my fields on a Sunday. I cultivated them on a Sunday. I fertilized them on a Sunday. I planted them on a Sunday. I weeded them on a Sunday and I reaped them on a Sunday. This October I had as bumper a crop as I have ever had. So much for God and His Sunday! What do you think of that?" The newspaper columnist replied, "Sir, God does not always make full reckoning in October."

For here is the often-forgotten factor in this equation. "Suffer yourselves to be defrauded," Paul says. Even if the wrongdoer seems to get away with his wrongdoing—there remains the judgment seat of Christ; and Paul has already reminded his readers about that (1 Cor. 3:12–15).

Some time ago, my book *Exploring the Gospels: John* was reviewed in a Christian paper which has a considerable circulation among independent Baptists and others in this country. The editor was not content to pick malicious little holes in the commentary; he set out to destroy my good name and reputation among his readers. He warned them (falsely) that I was propagating "Campbellite" teaching and he urged them to beware of me as one unfit to preach in their pulpits. I have never met this man and have certainly done him no wrong. His charges were unfounded or, at best, based on a very narrow and bigoted view of Scripture. I felt I had been maligned and slandered. I considered writing a rebuttal, but was advised such action would only give him further occasion to attack me. The article he wrote doubtless did me some harm, both in terms of sales of my books and in invitations for meetings. My publisher suggested some kind of legal action, if only to make the fellow more careful in his attacks on other Christians, but in the end I decided to ignore the man. Why fight him? The Lord continues to bless the book, it continues to sell well, and, as for places to preach, I have as many as I can handle. And there remains that Higher Court. Let the Lord deal with him! I can even find it in my heart to pray for him.

Then Paul puts his finger on *the crime:* "Nay, ye do wrong, and defraud, and that your brethren" (6:8). In the original text the emphasis is on the words *ye* and *brethren.* All wrongdoing and fraud is criminal behavior, but for a brother to wrong and defraud another brother only aggravates the culpability of the guilty party. "And that your *brethren!*" exclaims the apostle. That was the last straw.

Having thus discussed the specific issue of *litigation* (6:1–8), Paul turns now to the broader scene in the Corinthian church, to behavior even more scandalous than going to law before the unsaved and defrauding fellow believers. He turns to *condemnation* (6:9–11), and begins with *a sobering declaration:* "Know ye not that the unrighteous shall not inherit the kingdom of God?" (6:9a). This categorical statement broadens out, in the following verses, to specific examples of what Paul means by "the unrighteous." It is a descriptive word for the unregenerate (John 3:3; Rom. 1:18).

Paul now questions whether some of the Corinthian church members were even saved at all. Their behavior certainly put the lie to their profession of faith in Christ. The kind of behavior he has just denounced, defrauding people and engaging in litigation in pagan courts, and the kinds of behavior he is about to denounce, is behavior characteristic of the unregenerate, not of the saved.

Now comes *a searching denunciation* (1 Cor. 6:9b–10). First, *the warning is expressed:* "Be not deceived" (6:9b). The expression occurs two other times in Paul's letters (1 Cor. 15:33; Gal. 6:7). The latter reference contains the well-known warning that "whatsoever a man soweth, that shall he also reap." James uses the word when warning that "when lust hath conceived, it bringeth forth sin: and sin, when it is finished, bringeth forth death." James adds, "Do not err [do not be deceived], my beloved brethren" (James 1:15–16). The word used is *planaō,* from which we derive our English word *planet.* The ancients were puzzled by the movements of the planets and considered them to be wanderers in space. Hence the word *planaō* means "to go astray or to wander." It often carries the idea of being self-deceived. The Lord used the word to describe the lost sheep (Matt. 18:12); so does Peter (1 Peter 2:25). People who think they can live immoral, scandalous lives and still go to heaven are self-deceived.

Now *the wicked are exposed* (1 Cor. 6:9c–10). First, Paul deals with sins of a *personal nature* (6:9c–g) and then with sins of a *public nature* (6:10). He begins with *lustfulness* (6:9c–e). There is *sexual* sin (fornicators), *spiritual* sin (idolaters), and *social* sin (adulterers). People who make a practice of such behavior should question whether or not they are saved at all. Perhaps their profession of faith is really spurious. The word for *fornicators* is *pornos,* which denotes the immoral person. Idolatry and immorality often go hand in hand. The word for *adulterers* is *moichos,* denoting one who has intercourse with the spouse of another. This is a social as well as a sexual sin, utterly demoralizing to family life and, eventually, destabilizing to a society.

Paul moves on from lustfulness to *lawlessness* (6:9f–g). There is the *sin against normality* (effeminate) and there is the *sin against nature* (abusers of themselves with mankind). Both these sins have always been present in society, but when a society is healthy, its practitioners hide their shame. It is a mark of an apostate society when such sins flaunt themselves and are given status as an alternate lifestyle. Such societies expose themselves to judgment (2 Peter 2:6; Jude 7). The word for *effeminate* is *malakos,* literally meaning "soft to the touch." The word is used to describe soft raiment (Matt. 11:8). Anyone who has toured the streets of San Francisco has seen men thus parading themselves as women, dressed in women's clothes and their faces painted like those of harlots. The word for *abusers* is *arsenokoitēs.* Paul describes these sins in Romans 1:26–28 as marks of total depravity and the kind of apostasy which results in being God-abandoned.

Paul continues the list, turning now to sins of a *public nature* (1 Cor. 6:10). There are those, for instance, with no control over *their wants.* There are *thieves* (the *outward act*) and the covetous (the *inward attitude*). The word for *thieves* is *kleptēs,* from which we get our word *kleptomaniac.* Judas was a thief, Barabbas was a thief, and before his conversion, Zaccheus was a thief. When he met Christ, however, all that was changed (Luke 19:1–9). The word for *covetous* is *pleonexia,* the desire to have more. The word is always used in a bad sense. The verb form of the word *(pleonekteō)* carries the idea of taking advantage of someone (1 Thess. 4:6).

There are also those with no control over their *will* (drunkards), no control over their *words* (revilers), and with no control over their *ways* (extortioners). The word for *drunkards* denotes habitual intoxication. The world uses the euphemism *alcoholic* and excuses their behavior by calling alcoholism a disease. The Bible calls it sin and holds those guilty of it responsible for their behavior. God does not send people to hell for a disease. The greatest force on earth for the reclamation of drunkards is the gospel. Some of the church's most honored members are people who were once hopeless drunkards and drug addicts. God does not damn a person for drunkenness—only for remaining a drunkard when Christ can save and change him.

The word for *revilers* is *loidoros,* meaning "to be abusive," "to rail." One lexicon uses the word *blackguard.* What a contrast with Christ, of whom it was said that men "wondered at the gracious words which proceeded out of his mouth" (Luke 4:22).

The word for *extortioners* is *harpax*, meaning "rapacious," and carries the idea of pillage, plundering, and robbery. The Lord Jesus depicted the Pharisees as extortioners (Matt. 23:25). False prophets are likened by the Lord to "ravening *[harpax]* wolves" (7:15). The wild character of Benjamin's descendants was foreseen by the dying Jacob, hence he said, "Benjamin shall ravin as a wolf"—*harpax* in the Septuagint translation (Gen. 49:27). Paul himself was a Benjamite and, in his unconverted days, he had helped fulfill dying Jacob's prophecy (Acts 7:58; 8:1, 3; 9:13, 14, 21; 22:4–8; 1 Tim. 1:13).

What a catalogue of sins! What a collection of church members! What an assembly of "saints"! The list reads more like a description of the inmates of a federal penitentiary than the description of a local church. Paul refused to have anything to do with such behavior. He repeats what he said before. Such people will not inherit the kingdom of God. People who profess to be saved but who live as though they weren't are self-deceived. It is not that a saved person cannot fall, and have a need to be restored to fellowship. It is a question, really, of the flow of a person's life. For instance, the river Nile flows north from the great lakes of Central Africa to the shores of the Mediterranean Sea. Between the fifth cataract and the fourth cataract the great river turns west and then south. Between the fourth cataract and the third cataract it turns again and heads northwest. At Derr, the river changes direction yet another time and flows south and east. Then it turns north again and heads straight for the delta. If someone at a point just beyond Derr were to be asked, "Which way does this river flow?" he would say "South," but he would be wrong. The river flows north. Its various twists and turns are not the normal and general direction of the flow but only temporary aberrations.

The same thing is true of the genuine believer. The great question is, in what direction does his life flow? Is it toward holiness? We see David commit adultery, we see Jonah run away from God's call, we hear Peter deny his Lord with oaths and curses, we see Elijah run away from Jezebel, and we hear Abraham deny Sarah in Egypt and again in Gerar. The stream seems to be bent. But look! There is David on his face weeping and writing his tear-drenched penitential psalms; there is Jonah heading for Nineveh after all; there is Peter preaching boldly to the multitudes; there goes Elijah confronting Ahab again; and there is Abraham heading for Mount Moriah. The real flow of life has simply reasserted itself. Things have straightened out. The life still flows toward holiness. The main direction of the life has again become clear. It is not that saved people cannot fall into the kinds of sins which characterized them in their unregenerate days. However, they do not continue in those sins. They bitterly repent of their fall and seek cleansing and a fresh filling of the Holy Spirit. They continue on their way toward heaven. The unregenerate have no such current toward holiness in their lives. They habitually sin and excuse themselves for it.

The sobering declaration and the searching denunciation are now followed by *a sanctifying distinction* (1 Cor. 6:11). First, Paul acknowledges *what they had been:* "And such were some of you," he says (6:11a). Fornicators, idolaters, adulterers, and so on. These were the very kind of people Paul evangelized when he came to Corinth. He had seen lives transformed. People had been picked up out of the gutter and turned toward heaven. As someone has said, punning Hebrews 7:25, the Lord Jesus can save "from the 'guttermost' to the uttermost!" And so He can.

Paul was not astonished that such people were to be found in the world, but he was outraged that such people should be found in the church. To belong to the church one must become a saved sinner, in other words, a saint. That is what the gospel is all about. It makes drunken people sober, crooked people straight, profligate people pure. It works! That is why Paul was not ashamed of it (Rom. 1:16). "Such *were* some of you," he says. He could give thanks "unto the Father, which hath made us meet to be partakers of the inheritance of the saints in light: who hath delivered us from the power of darkness, and hath translated us into the kingdom of his dear Son; in whom we have redemption through his blood, even the forgiveness of sins" (Col. 1:12–14).

Paul, then, acknowledges what they had been. He also acknowledges *what they had become* if, indeed, they were truly in the kingdom (1 Cor. 6:11b–f). He reminds them of *the greatness* of their transformation (6:11b–d). God has dealt with *their state,* they have been washed (6:11b), and God has dealt with *their standing,* they have been sanctified and justified, both *set apart for God* and *set aright by God* (6:11c–d). To be justified means to be declared righteous by God, to be acquitted of all charges. It is just as if we'd never sinned. To be sanctified means to be set apart by God for Himself, so that His righteousness might be reproduced in us by His Holy Spirit. Holiness becomes the prevailing characteristic of the life—the direction of its flow. A sinner accommodates himself to his sin; a saint abominates his sin.

I have read somewhere of a method used by trappers to catch ermine, a pretty little creature with a pure, white coat. The trapper waits until the ermine leaves the nest to hunt for food. Then he puts filth at the doorway of its home. The ermine sees the trapper, realizes its danger, and heads for its hole for safety. When it gets there, however, it sees the entrance covered with dirt and won't go in. It doesn't want to get its coat dirty. It would rather be dead than defiled. Such, too, should be the attitude, surely, of the Christian who has learned the truth of justification and sanctification. Such is the greatness of his transformation.

Paul reminds the Corinthians not only of the greatness of their transformation, but also of *the ground* of their transformation (6:11e–f). Our justification and sanctification are accomplished through *the Son of God* and His *triumphant name* ("in the name of the Lord Jesus") and through *the Spirit of God* and His *transforming nature* ("and by the Spirit of our God"). It is not by virtue of our own resolve and effort that we become new creatures in Christ. Salvation is *imputed* to us through the saving name of the Lord Jesus (Matt. 1:21; Acts 4:12). It is *implemented* in us by the indwelling Holy Spirit. The believer does not willingly or habitually disgrace the name of the Lord Jesus or distress the nature of the Holy Spirit.

Paul has discussed, then, the question of litigation (1 Cor. 6:1–8) and condemnation (6:9–11). He returns now to the matter of *fornication* (6:12–20). In the licentious climate of Corinth the problem of fornication was a most vexing question. Nobody thought anything of it. The Christian ethic was foreign to the world's thought. Many of the Corinthian believers had grown up as raw pagans who took immorality in their stride. It was a matter, after all, of doing what came naturally. Besides, everybody did it. So what was wrong with it? Similar views prevail in our modern world.

Paul begins with *a matter of perspective* (6:12–13a). There is, for instance, *the lawfulness of some things:* "All things are lawful unto me, but all things are not expedient; all things are lawful for me, but I will not be brought under the power of any" (6:12). There is also *the limit of some things:* "Meats for the belly, and the belly for meats: but God shall destroy both it and them" (6:13). As a Christian, one can do anything, within the bounds of God's law. That does not mean that everything is good for me. It certainly does not mean I should allow myself to be enslaved by anything I permit in my life. Food was meant for the stomach, but God has no permanent use for either. When we receive our resurrection bodies we shall be free altogether from the tyranny of physical appetite. Some would put the words "all things are lawful for me" in quotation marks, since they seem to have been the watchwords of a gnosticizing group in the church. Paul does not condemn their slogan out and out, because he himself was a strong proponent of a believer's personal freedom in Christ. He could understand this group's impatience with the ascetics in the church. To the extent, however, that their claim to freedom expressed impatience with traditional morality, Paul reined them in. Not all things really are part of true Christian living. A believer does not have liberty to do things which are wrong. Even some things which are within the bounds of permission are not necessarily helpful for Christian life and growth and should be avoided. It is said that C. H. Spurgeon, the great Victorian evangelist and Bible teacher, smoked—until he came across an advertisement promoting "the brand that C. H. Spurgeon smokes."

Not only is there the matter of perspective, there is also *the matter of principle* (6:13c–18). Some matters are cut and dried and leave no room for choice, especially when it comes to the body. One may, for instance, have some leeway, as a Christian, in matters of food and drink—food was a touchy issue in the early church, drink is a similar issue in the modern church. However, one has no leeway when it comes to the body and sex. First, Paul deals with *the principle as it is validated* (6:13c–15). He begins with *the negative principle:* "Now," he declares, "the body is not for fornication." And that is that. There is no room for discussion or negotiation. We are confronted with a flat and uncompromising negative. We are to say "No!" whenever the temptation to sexual sin is presented to us. Sex outside of marriage earns the unqualified disapproval of God.

The body is a marvelous piece of divine engineering and God expects us to keep it clean and under control. The more modern science discovers about its members and its mysteries, the more marvelous it becomes. Take, for instance, the chemistry of the blood. Consider, for a moment, just one of its molecules, the one we call hemoglobin. It is made up of 3,032 atoms of carbon, 4,812 atoms of hydrogen, 780 atoms of nitrogen, 4 atoms of iron, 880 atoms of oxygen, and 12 atoms of sulfur—a total of 9,520 atoms, each of which has to be hooked up to the other atoms in a precise and proper way. That is just one molecule of one part of the body. The greatest genius in the world cannot give us the chemical equation for one complete, functioning body. We know today, far better than David did (Ps. 139:14), how fearfully and wonderfully we are made. The chemistry of a single cell is awesome in its complexity, yet the brain alone contains 30 billion of them. The veins contain 20 trillion blood cells, the skin contains a million cells. In all, it is estimated that there are more than a million million cells in the human body, a number which staggers the imagination. During any given moment, in the life of any one cell, thousands of events are taking place. Indeed, each cell is a micro-universe of bewildering complexity. The nucleus of a cell, where all the complicated machinery is found, is actually less than four ten-thousandths of an inch in diameter. Moreover, the components of any given cell are enclosed in a membrane only half a millionth of an inch thick!

The evolutionary concept that all this "just happened," that the human body has resulted from "a fortuitous concourse of atoms," that blind chance produced such prodigious order out of chaos, is ludicrous. The body was *made,* and it was *made by God,* planned by His omniscient genius and produced by His omnipotence. That there should be no real purpose for such a complex organism is incredible. That God should leave us with no instructions as to the purpose for which He created our bodies is belied by the fact—one reason is given in the last two verses of this chapter (1 Cor. 6:19–20). That God would not warn us against the abuse or misuse of our bodies is belied by this verse (6:13). He bluntly states, "The body is not for fornication." We ignore God's warning at our peril. Dreadful diseases await the promiscuous. Mental anguish follows the violation of God's laws of purity. Guilt takes root and begins its deadly work both in the personality and in the body of the offender. We would do well to heed God's prohibition.

Having stated the negative principle, Paul now introduces *the new principle* (6:13d–15). He presents three arguments for chastity. First, there is *the main argument.* The body must be *relinquished* to the Lord because it will one day be *raised* by the Lord: "Now the body . . . is for the Lord, and the Lord for the body. And God hath both raised up the Lord and will also raise us by his own power" (6:13d–14). The body of the believer belongs to the Lord, something Paul expresses elsewhere with commanding force (Rom. 12:1–2). It is to be the instrument for accomplishing His purposes in the world. Moreover, it has a cosmic significance. Although death destroys it, nevertheless it will be raised, as Christ's own body was raised, because it will be an instrument for accomplishing His vast purposes in eternity. What those purposes are will be revealed in due time. How great they are is hinted at by Paul when he tells us that the whole creation is on "tiptoe" to see what will happen when the sons of God come into their own" (Rom. 8:19). God has great things in store for us in eternity and our bodies will be needed to be part of it.

The Lord Jesus, by becoming man, has forever glorified the human body (Heb. 10:5). That body of His was kept inviolate by Him so that through it He might accomplish God's eternal purpose (1 Peter 2:24; Heb. 10:10). God kept that body free from corruption and decay even in the grave (Ps. 16:10; Acts 13:35). Then He raised it from the dead (Acts 13:37) and in that body the Lord Jesus now administers the entire universe, seated at God's right hand in heaven (Heb. 1:3, 13; 2:6–9). God expects us to treat our bodies as Christ treated His. That is the main argument.

Then there is *the mystical argument:* "Know ye not that your bodies are the members of Christ?" (1 Cor. 6:15a). Paul takes it for granted that the believers at Corinth had some knowledge of the fact that the church is the mystical body of Christ—a truth he will develop later in his letter (chap. 12). While on earth, by virtue of the fact that we are thus mystically united with Christ, our bodies are part of that mystical body. When the Lord Jesus lived on earth it was through the instrumentality of His body that He spoke as never man spoke, with such insight and authority. It was by means of His body He made His way to the stricken home of Martha and Mary. It was with His hand He touched the leper and Jairus's little girl. It was by means of His hands He multiplied the loaves and fishes. It was His foot He planted on the stormy sea. It was His voice that stilled the storm, that dismissed demons, that summoned Lazarus from the dead. It was His eye which caught the eye of cursing Peter. It was His back that was bared to the smiter, His cheeks from which the beard was so terribly torn, His brow that was so insultingly crowned with thorns, His hands, His feet so cruelly nailed to the accursed tree.

Now He is in heaven and He "prolongs his days" (Isa. 53:10) through His mystical body. Our hands are to be His hands, our feet are to be His feet, our tongue is to be His tongue. If some sick person's pillow needs to be fluffed or someone's brow to be bathed, He has no hands but our hands. If some distant tribe is to be reached, He has no feet but our feet to go. If a book needs writing or a wrong needs righting, if a language needs translating or a truth needs proclaiming, our body must be His body. If He is to use my body as His body then it must be kept pure.

Moreover, there is *the moral argument:* "Shall I then take the members of Christ, and make them the members of an harlot? God forbid!" (1 Cor. 6:15c). The bare suggestion fills Paul's soul with horror. The very idea was outrageous. He could not think of a stronger argument against immoral behavior. All sin is a violation of the union of the believer and the Lord, but sexual sin is viewed as infamous, not to be thought of, a violation of the most sacred human relationships and high treason against our relationship with Christ.

So then, as a matter of principle, there can be no immorality permitted in the life of a Christian. The principle is *validated.* But now we see the principle *violated* (6:16–18). Again the argument is threefold. Paul begins with *a contrast* (6:16–17). First, there is *the guilty union* to be considered: "What? know ye not that he which is joined to an harlot is one body? for two, saith he, shall be one flesh" (6:16). Fornication, and union with a harlot, is a distortion of the holiness and happiness God intended for man and wife in the consummation of marriage. Normally the marital relationship leads to children and all the discipline, duties, and delights of family life. A Christian home, thus founded and fathered, is a suburb of heaven and the safeguard of society. Two become one and that unity produces fruit for the glory of God. Two become one and a bond is formed which impacts both personalities and which no power on earth can completely sunder. Deep emotions are stirred. God blesses the union. The foundation is laid for affinity and intimacy in all our being. Fornication is a sinful parody, a satanic substitute, a big cheat and lie. The two still become one but not in "holy matrimony" but in guilty lust. There is an interpenetration of personalities which is distorted, defiling, and demoralizing. For the gratification of a moment's carnal desire shame and guilt and sin are mutually exchanged. Damage is done to both partners in the illicit union. God's divine displeasure is actively evoked (Heb. 13:4) and sooner or later punishment follows, as night follows day. Those who become promiscuous multiply to themselves the distortion, damage, and defilement that stalk the steps of the immoral. They accrue the seeds of wrath in body and in mind, in heart and in soul, in conscience and in will. In the marriage bond a picture is painted of Christ and His church (Eph. 5:25–33). Just so, in the fornication bond, a picture is painted of the Devil and his dupe—for the father of sin is the Devil, the mother of sin is lust, and the offspring of sin is shame and death (James 1:15). What a high price to pay for immorality!

By contrast, Paul now points to *the glorious union:* "But he that is joined unto the Lord is one spirit" (1 Cor. 6:17). Evidently the bonding which takes place in the flesh in intercourse is a picture of the bonding which takes place in the spirit when a believer yields to the lordship of Christ. There is a mystical union between Christ and His church and between the Lord Jesus and the soul of the believer. The Lord Himself taught this truth (John 14:20; 15:4–5) and made it a matter of prayer (17:21–23). We become one spirit. That is to say, there is union between the human spirit of the believer and the Holy Spirit of God, which bears fruit in love and life, in happiness and holiness, and in goodness and godliness. Fornication grieves the Holy Spirit and abuses the grace of God.

The contrast is followed by *a command:* "Flee fornication" (1 Cor. 6:18). There are some sins that are too appealing, too subtle, too strong for us. The only thing to do is to run away. Joseph is the classical biblical example of a young man who did that very thing (Gen. 39:7–12). His brother Reuben and his brother Judah are both examples of men who did the opposite (Gen. 35:22; 49:3–4; 38:1–26) and who paid for it in shame and, in Reuben's case, with terrible loss in the kingdom. The supreme biblical example of a man who toyed with immorality is David (2 Sam. 11:1–27). How terribly he paid for his sin is detailed in subsequent chapters. The spiritual and mental anguish he suffered can be assessed by reading some of his tear-drenched, sob-choked, guilt-ridden penitential psalms. The best thing to do when faced with a situation which can only end in a lustful union is to run away. Better to be scorned and mocked than to incur the displeasure of God. Those who put themselves in the way of temptation, or who dally with it when it comes, are more than halfway to a fall.

Finally, Paul points to *a consequence* (1 Cor. 6:18b–c). First, he acknowledges *the distinctive nature of most sin:* "Every sin that a man doeth is without the body" (6:18b) and underlines *the deadly nature of moral sin:* "but he that committeth fornication sinneth against his own body" (6:18c). Sins such as lying, murder, theft, and so on are wrong and punishable, but still they are, by their nature, not sins against one's own body. Even such sins as gluttony, drunkenness, and suicide are, in a sense, "outside the body," since their cause and incentive come from without. Such sins may be done by means of the body and may injure the body but none of them militate against the sanctity of the whole well-being of the body as does fornication. Fornication involves not only a person's body but his or her whole being. The effects of other sins can usually be corrected by abstinence, but once a person has committed a sexual sin the damage can never be undone.

God visits His own judgment on the immoral person. The sinful union brings inevitable mental damage. It also leads to all kinds of rabid and foul diseases which lurk in the shadows, waiting to avenge God's broken law upon the bodies of the guilty parties. Moreover, by practicing immorality, the believer largely disqualifies himself from further usefulness in the Lord's service. After David sinned with Bathsheba he never won another victory. On the contrary, he had ever-increasing family problems and constant disruptions in his kingdom.

Paul has one more matter to discuss in relation to the Christian and fornication, *the matter of privilege* (6:19–20). In the first place, the believer's body is *possessed by the Spirit of God:* "What? know ye not that your body is the temple of the Holy Ghost which is in you, which ye have of God, and ye are not your own?" (6:19). How terrible a thing it is to commit fornication, using a body which not only now belongs to the Holy Spirit but which is actually indwelt by Him. The Spirit of God has various names and titles in the New Testament, but, supremely, He is known as the Holy Spirit. Throughout the entire immoral liaison the Holy Spirit is present, in the body being thus abused, grieved beyond words, witnessing the whole shameful thing, wounded in His heart, His holiness outraged, His immediate vengeance held back only by His grace. Surely this has to be Paul's crowning argument against fornication!

Not quite! He has one more. The believer's body was *purchased by the Son of God*: "For ye are bought with a price"—*what a great truth!* "Therefore glorify God in your body, and in your spirit, which are *God's*"—*what a great trust!* (6:20). The price is infinite—the precious blood of Christ (1 Peter 1:18). Before plunging into sexual sin we need to go back to Calvary. We need to see the body of our Savior nailed to the accursed cross. We need to remember that He bore our sins in His own body on the tree. We need to see Him hanging there, paying the price for our sin. Paul, with true spiritual genius, leaves this final and unanswerable argument to the last. As the hymn-writer has put it,

> Lest I forget Gethsemane,
> Lest I forget Thine agony,
> Lest I forget Thy love for me—
> Lead me to Calvary.[1]

Who can come away from Calvary and not say what Joseph said when that immoral woman offered him her body? He said, "How can I do this great wickedness, and sin against God?" (Gen. 39:9). To him, that was the sum and substance of the whole matter.

---

1. "Lead Me to Calvary." Copyright © 1921. Renewal 1949 by Hope Publishing Company, Carol Stream, IL 60188. All rights reserved. Used by permission.

PART 4

Difficulties in the Church

1 Corinthians 7:1–14:40

Paul now turns his attention to matters about which he had been asked specific questions. New converts always have a lot to learn, especially those coming to Christ out of a completely pagan background. He has dealt at length with *divisions* in the church at Corinth (1 Cor. 1:10–4:21) and has discussed *discipline* in the church (5:1–6:20). Now he turns his attention to *difficulties* in the church (7:1–14:40). These can be divided into two categories: those connected with *our personal walk* (7:1–11:1) and those connected with *our public worship* (11:2–14:40). The two major issues he discusses have to do with the matter of *marriage* (7:1–40) and the matter of *meat* (8:1–13). However, Paul surrounds these two subjects with all kinds of advice and illustration.

As we begin to review what Paul has to say about *our personal walk* (7:1–11:1), we start with *Paul's exhortation* (7:1–8:13), which, itself, takes in the two matters at issue. From there on we have *Paul's example* (9:1–27) and *Paul's explanation* (10:1–11:1). The matter of *marriage* has always been one of great interest, concern, and exercise among God's people. Whether or not to remain single, who to marry, when to marry are questions that relate to the very stuff of which life is made. After the decision to accept Christ, the decision we make with regard to marriage is the most important. A person's chosen partner in life can make or break that person's life. When King Saul wanted to get rid of David he employed his daughter Michal's infatuation with David as a most useful opportunity. "I will give him her," he said, "that she may be a snare unto him" (1 Sam. 18:20–21).

As the modern marriage vow affirms, marriage is intended by God to be for life—"for better or for worse." Nor can marriage be entered into on an experimental basis, as many seem to think in these days of easy, "no-fault" divorce. The Bible never, for one moment, countenances the "throw-away marriage" concept so common in our day. In God's ideal, marriage vows are to be kept.

We come then to *Paul's discussion* (1 Cor. 7:1–17). He begins with *the single person* (7:1–9). He comes straight to the point. We have his *candid statement:* "Now concerning the things whereof ye wrote unto me: It is good for a man not to touch a woman" (7:1). The word for *good* here is not *agathos,* which has to do with something good in its very nature and character and beneficial in its effects, but *kalon,* which can be rendered "fair," or "an excellent thing," something well adapted to its circumstances or its purpose. In verse 26 the same word is used but limited by the clause "good for the present necessity."

There seem to have been two things in the background, both of the question and the abrupt answer. There were two extremes at Corinth. Some had Essene ascetic tendencies and were inclined to regard marriage as a form of defilement; there were those who had antinomian tendencies and who were inclined toward lasciviousness. The spirit of Gnosticism, as reflected by these opposite tendencies, was abroad in the church long before it received its actual name. Both views were wrong. This extremism, in both directions, lay behind the question. Paul himself inclined toward the ascetic view, but he kept his balance and sense of proportion.

Another matter in the background of the question and in especially Paul's answer, was the character of the times. The near return of Christ was still a lively hope in the church. On the other hand, Paul sensed that severe trials were on the way. Nero had recently been proclaimed emperor (A.D. 54). Within ten years the terrible Neronic persecution against the church would break out (A.D. 64), and while, as yet, there were few outward signs of Nero's unbridled wickedness, a man as naturally astute and as spiritually alert as Paul might well have had a foreboding of trouble to come. When the terror leaped upon the church in all its ferocity, it would be well indeed to be wifeless and childless. Jesus had said much the same (Matt. 24:19).

Paul's words, therefore, were not dictated by asceticism but by reality. More! Paul's wisdom in this matter was tempered by caution. Celibacy might be the way for some, but it certainly was not the way for all. It should not be mandated, nor should some church hierarchy make it a rule for its priests. Paul had no such an idea in his mind. After all, the celibate state is no holier than the married state (1 Tim. 4:1–4; Heb. 13:4). Several of the Lord's apostles were married and Paul asserted his right to get married if he so desired (1 Cor. 9:15). And as for pressing his words about the desirability of remaining single in view of the perils of the hour, supposing Amram and Jochabed had refrained from having children (Exod. 1:8–2:2)? What then would Israel have done for its Moses? Or what if the parents of Elijah had decided that the days were too full of apostasy to get married and found a family? What would Israel have done then for its great prophet of fire?

Indeed, we are immediately faced in the text with Paul's *common sense* (1 Cor. 7:2–5). First, *he recognizes the fundamental of marriage:* "Nevertheless, to avoid fornication, let every man have his own wife, and let every woman have her own husband" (7:2). In other words, marriage is a desirable, necessary, and practical estate. It was ordained by God (Gen. 2:18–25), and it is necessary for the continuance of the human race, for the welfare of the state, and for the well-being of children. It is also God's wise and benevolent safety valve against unbridled lust. The twice-repeated *all* here shows that, under normal conditions, marriage was a duty.

We can see what happens when celibacy is forced upon men and women by reading the history of the Roman Catholic Church,[1] by studying Father Chiniquy's disclosures, for instance,[2] or, nowadays, by simply following the news.[3] Not, of course, that Rome has any monopoly on scandals. The evangelical church has provided its own unsavory crop of miscreants in recent times. All the more reason, indeed, for a man and a woman to be happily married.

Next, Paul *regulates the function of marriage* (1 Cor. 7:3–5). There is to be *mutual responsibility:* "Let the husband render the wife due benevolence: and likewise also the wife unto her own husband" (7:3). The word for *benevolence* is *eunoia,* meaning "good will." Some think the word should be *opheilē,* which has

---

1. Malachi Martin, *Decline and Fall of the Roman Church* (New York: Bantam Books, 1983).
2. Chas. Chiniquy, *Fifty Years in the Church of Rome* (New York: Christ's Mission Book Dept., 1885).
3. "Sins of the Fathers," *Time,* 19 August 1991, 51.

the more comprehensive meaning of "her due." The translators of the revised text seem to have employed a needless euphemism. The word for *render* is *apodidōmi,* meaning "to give back." In other words, there is to be a reciprocal recognition of each other's wishes and rights. The word signifies not the granting of a conjugal favor but the discharge of an obligation between husband and wife. Each is to be considerate of the other. After all, one of the purposes of marriage is to defuse the desires which, if not legitimately satisfied, might sadly find expression in immorality.

When I was in the British Army in Palestine, I met one godly old couple who lived truly saintly and Spartan lives. They believed, however, that sex within marriage should be restricted absolutely to the procreation of children—a notion obviously negated by this verse. This couple had no children. I never had the nerve to ask them what that signified—total abstinence or sterility. Moreover, they sought to impose their Spartan and ascetic views on the church and even invoked the extreme penalty of excommunication against one couple when they admitted to using birth control. The aged elder wrote to me to ask me my opinion. I replied that, according to 1 Corinthians 7:3–5, what a married couple did in the privacy of their own home was their own business and no concern of the church. I discovered that the godly old couple had adopted their harsh views based on God's command to Adam and Eve to "be fruitful and multiply"!

There is not only to be mutual responsibility within the framework of marriage, there is also to be *mutual respect:* "The wife hath not power ["rule over," *exousiazō,* denoting the exercise of authority] of her own body, but the husband: and likewise also the husband hath not power of his own body, but the wife" (7:4). The marriage vow involves the surrender of rights by each partner. Each shares body rights with the other. One partner can be unreasonably demanding, the other can be unfairly frigid. Either attitude can lead to resentment and friction within the marriage and can even lead to marital unfaithfulness. The answer is love and respect. Sometimes desire must be curbed because of the other's physical, emotional, or even spiritual condition. Sometimes, regardless of one partner's personal preference, the physical and emotional needs of the other must be the overriding factor. Neither is to exploit or dominate. As there is to be equality before God within the marriage state, so there is to be equality between each other. Paul points out the need for give and take in this whole area of life.

There is, furthermore, to be *mutual restraint.* We note the *exactness* of the rule: "Defraud ye not one the other;" the *exception* to the rule: "except it be with consent for a time;" and the *explanation* of the rule: "that ye may give yourselves to fasting and prayer: and come together again, that Satan tempt you not for your incontinency" (7:5).

The word for "defraud" is *opostereō*, which means "to rob, despoil or defraud." Paul has already used the word in this epistle—when urging the Corinthians, in matters of money, to allow themselves to be defrauded rather than suing each other in secular courts (6:7). The word was used by Jesus when He summarized the commandments for the rich young ruler. "Defraud not," He said (Mark 10:19). Evidently it is no light thing, in God's sight, for one partner to hold out on another partner in this area of life, or to use its possibilities as a weapon.

However, there may be times when, by mutual consent, the husband and wife agree to a period of abstinence. One reason for such an agreement, suggested by Paul, is to give opportunity for a season of prayer and fasting. Fasting is a legitimate spiritual function. If this is what Paul has in mind he may be echoing the Old Testament. Israel had come to Sinai. In three days the Lord planned to come down upon Mount Sinai in the sight of all the people. The Law in all its majesty would be given, under the most awesome circumstances. We read, "The LORD said unto Moses, Go unto the people and sanctify them today and tomorrow, and let them wash their clothes" (Exod. 19:10). In conveying God's demands Moses warned, "Be ready against the third day; come not at your wives" (19:15). When the Law was given it was made clear that, under its provisions, ceremonial uncleanness attached to the entire reproductive process, even within the bonds of marriage (Lev. 15:15–33; 12:1–8). We are free from the Law in this regard now. However, the Mosaic Law reflects the holiness of God and it might well be that occasional purposeful abstinence from sexual intercourse might serve, as does fasting, to add an edge to our prayers.

Paul, however, having made the suggestion, immediately warns against prolonged or permanent abstinence. Once the agreed period of abstinence has expired a married couple should resume normal relations. Otherwise they might expose themselves to the obvious temptation of the Devil. God knows our frame. So does the Devil.

In the Old Testament a Nazarite vow set an Israelite apart for God for a special purpose and for a specific period. Such a vow was not intended to be permanent. When it was terminated it had to be done in such a way that the devotee could not indulge fanciful dreams about his own superior spirituality. On the contrary, he was reminded in a most forceful way that he was, by nature, a very great sinner (Num. 6:1–21). There were only three lifelong Nazarites in the Bible: Samuel,

Samson, and John the Baptist. Samson's Nazarite vows proved of little help to him in resisting the lusts of the flesh. Perhaps that is why Paul is so cautious in this whole matter of vows and abstinences and why he advocates strict time limits on their practice.

For the remainder, vows of abstinence and chastity and poverty (so beloved by medieval ascetics) have little part in dynamic Christianity. At best they are to be undertaken for limited periods and, when the vow affects someone else who has a right to be considered and consulted, as is the case in marriage, only with that person's consent and cooperation. Even the best intended acts of consecration can be a snare if carried beyond the bounds of one's strength.

In the case of the Corinthians (as is so in our contemporary society) most of them came from promiscuous lifestyles which had been given the full approval of an all-permissive society. This made it all the more imperative that they not shoulder ascetic burdens God never intended them to bear. Repression of God-given appetites can be as harmful as unrestrained indulgence. Ascetic practices, when undertaken beyond what God demands, and without reference to one's own limitations and circumstances, do not dampen the fires of lust but feed them.

Paul's common sense is now followed up with *Paul's considered suggestion* (1 Cor. 7:6–9). We note *what he confesses:* "But I speak this by permission, and not of commandment" (7:6). He is referring to what he has just said. The word for *permission* here is *sungnōmē*. The word refers to "a joint opinion," or "a fellow feeling." The word *concession* has been suggested as a good rendering. He is not apostolically commanding this or that within the marriage bond. He protects the privacy of the individuals concerned, and their right to make up their own minds as to what is proper in their relationship. But he is making a divinely inspired concession. The concession is *not* that they can resume marital relations after a period of mutually agreed abstinence. The concession is that they can mutually refrain from marital relations for a period if they are so agreed and so desire. Paul is often quoted as though he discouraged marriage. In fact, the opposite is true. He was all for marriage as a general rule of life.

We note next *what he compares* (7:7–8). There was something he *desired:* "For I would that all men were even as I myself"; there was something he *discerned:* "But every man hath his proper gift of God, one after this manner, and the other after that"; and there was something he *declared:* "I say therefore to the unmarried and widows, It is good for them if they abide even as I." That Paul is not here mandating celibacy is evident from what he wrote to Timothy: "I will [I prefer— *boulomai*] that the younger women marry, bear children, guide the house, give none occasion to the adversary to speak reproachfully" (1 Tim. 5:14). Paul him-self had the gift of continence so that, although he was unmarried and celibate, he was content to be so and not imperiled by lust. The Lord said much the same in His own teaching on divorce and remarriage. He said that there were some people who were naturally celibate, "so born from their mother's womb"; that there were some people who "have made themselves eunuchs for the kingdom of heaven's sake," that is, they have deliberately opted for a life of celibacy; on the other hand some have celibacy forced on them by others, "there are some eu-nuchs which were made eunuchs of men"—a most unnatural, dangerous, and undesirable state savoring of unnatural and unusual punishment (Matt. 19:12). Paul, while able to handle celibacy for himself, and while desirous that others might have the same gift of remaining single and unharmed, certainly had no intention of imposing it on all, or even putting pressure on people to do as he did in this matter. He was constitutionally able to handle celibacy. Others would make shipwreck if they tried it. The Lord Jesus added, in His own command on this matter, "He that is able to receive it, let him receive it." Paul put it this way: "But every man has his proper gift of God." He himself was possibly a widower, a fact which would lend force to his advice to the unmarried "and widows." He thought it a desirable thing to remain unattached but he certainly was not going to mandate it. To remain unmarried did not bestow some kind of moral or spiri-tual superiority, only an advantage under certain circumstances.

Probably, for example, a man like David Livingstone would have been better off to remain unmarried when his life's calling was to the wildest regions of Africa. His wife was unable to keep the pace he set. His own heart burned with a passion to explore, to emancipate, and to evangelize. He wanted to strike a lasting blow against the slave trade, the horrors of which he saw at the source and which never ceased to haunt him. He was drawn deeper and deeper into the jungle in his obsession with finding the sources of the Nile. At last his wife went back home. Then the gossips started slandering him, so he called her back—to her death. In the Old Testament, God demanded that Jeremiah remain unmarried (Jer. 16:2), not only as a sign to the sinful nation but because it was not fitting that any woman be made to share the heartbreaks of this "man of sorrows."

We note not only what Paul confesses and compares, but also what he *concedes* (1 Cor. 7:9). He says, "But if they cannot contain, let them marry: for it is better to marry than to burn." The word for *burn* here is *puroomai,* which means "to glow with heat." It is translated "fiery" in reference to the fiery darts of the evil one (Eph. 6:16). Here, it may refer to burning with lust or to burning in Gehenna. The words *cannot contain* come from *engkrateuomai* and refer to lack of self-control. Paul is not being cynical but eminently practical. One authority points out that the tenses in the original add greater force and beauty to this statement. The word for *marry* is in the aorist, signifying "to marry once for all," whereas the word for *burn* is in the present tense, signifying "to be on fire." In other words, "marriage once for all is better than continuous lust." The former is sensible, the latter is sinful.

Years ago I worked in the same office as a woman who had taken a vow of celibacy. She was obviously a woman made for marriage and motherhood. It did not take long to discover that the woman was repressed and unhappy, although she put on a smiling face and adopted an outwardly cheerful demeanor. She once confided in me about her vow of celibacy and frankly confessed she wished she had never made it. I responded that she had seemingly made a foolish vow, just as Jephthah had done (Judg. 11:30–40), and that she would be well advised to reconsider it before she did something as foolish as Jephthah did. Her vow was a foolish one and one she was ill-equipped to keep. It was tormenting her rather than transforming her. I suggested she confess to the Lord that she had made a foolish promise and ask Him to release her from it. Then she should find herself a husband before she stumble and fall. My assessment was confirmed some time after that when a colleague told me of a rather disconcerting experience he had just had with this same woman.

Paul turns now from the single person (1 Cor. 7:1–9) to *the separated person* (7:10–17). First, we are invited to listen to *an authentic voice* (7:10–11). He gives us, initially, *a rule for married women* (7:10–11b) and begins with a *command:* "And unto the married I command, yet not I but the Lord, Let not the wife depart from her husband" (7:10). Paul counseled the unmarried and the widows to remain single; he commands married couples to remain married. The Lord is not in the business of breaking up homes in the interest of "consecration." Indeed, Paul had the Lord's own word for this command. The Lord summarized this ruling to His disciples with the brief statement, "Whosoever shall put away his wife, and marry another, committeth adultery against her. And if the woman shall put away her husband, and be married to another, she committeth adultery" (Mark 10:11–12). The exception to the rule, in this case, is given in Matthew 5:32; 19:9, and is assumed in Mark. Even where, for the direst of reasons, divorce was permitted by the Lord, He still points to the ideal and emphasizes the counsels of perfection (Matt. 19:3–8).

The marriage vow is invariably treated in the New Testament as binding and the marriage state as permanent. "Let not the wife depart," Paul says. In many marriages difficulties arise, especially in homes where the husband or the wife becomes a believer after the marriage. In that case the wife is not the same woman as the husband married, or the husband is not the same man the woman married. There are likely to be tensions, especially where the conversion radically changes the saved partner's thoughts and attitudes, likes and dislikes, choices and preferences. Things, maybe, they did together before, and enjoyed, the other now dislikes and barely tolerates.

A friend of mine, years ago, became a believer some considerable time after he was married. His wife remained an unbeliever. He at once gave up smoking, drinking, and dancing and became increasingly committed to the local church, to his Bible, to his new friends in Christ, and to the Lord's work. His wife's resentments grew. She intensely disliked the church and the believers because she felt they had robbed her of the man she had married. She devised ways to annoy him. Knowing of his love for music and his delight in the hymns he had learned, she pounded away at the piano when he was home, playing dance music and jazz. He had developed an antipathy for cigarette smoke, so she took up smoking, put ashtrays in every room of the house, and followed him around the house, from room to room, smoking. My friend was not the wisest person I have ever met and, doubtless, aggravated his wife with his zeal for a lifestyle foreign to the one he had lived before. Nowadays the solution would be separation or divorce, but Paul offers no such option. Had my friend shown his wife more consideration and tender, loving care, he might have won her. As it was he regarded her as his "cross," spent as much time as he could away from home, rarely spoke about her, and "put up" with her when he was home.

Having stated, as bluntly as possible, his command, Paul makes *a concession:* "But and if she depart, let her remain unmarried, or be reconciled to her husband" (1 Cor. 7:11a–b). The reference is to separation because of incompatibility or some other reason—one could think of a dozen ways in which some marriages become almost intolerable—not to divorce, which is a different matter, and which dissolves a marriage completely. The hope is that separation might lead to reconciliation. It is not so drastic a step as divorce and it leaves room for second thoughts. There can be no thought of another liaison in this case, that would only complicate things and negate the possibility of a healing of the breach.

The word for *reconciled* is *katallassō*. The word carries the idea of a change, especially from enmity to friendship. Usually the word is reserved in the New

Testament to describe our estranged relationship from God. The enmity is all on our side, but it is God, the offended One, who takes the initiative by offering His grace to us by virtue of Christ's propitiatory sacrifice. Because of this, sinners, despite all their natural alienation and hostility, are invited to be reconciled to Him. This involves a change of attitude. If God invites sinners to be reconciled to Him, how much more the estranged couple should seek reconciliation with each other.

There follows *a rule for married men:* "And let not the husband put away his wife" (7:11c). As we would say in our colloquial proverb, "What's good for the goose is good for the gander." The man gets no special treatment. Traditionally the woman gets shabby treatment in this whole area of life. The classic biblical example is the case of the woman taken in adultery and dragged by her captors before Christ for judgment. "Master," gloated the scribes and Pharisees, "this woman was taken in adultery, *in the very act*" (John 8:3). Then why was not the man taken as well as the woman? The case is typical. Paul, however, allowed no preferential treatment for the man in the case of separation. He, too, must remain single and seek reconciliation with his wife.

We are now invited to consider *an apostolic view* (1 Cor. 7:12–17). First, *mixed marriage* (a believer and an unbeliever) is considered (7:12–15). Paul begins with the case of *division in the home* (7:12–14). There is, for instance, *the rule* (7:12–13). There is the situation which exists when a husband has an unbelieving wife: "But to the rest speak I, not the Lord: If any brother hath a wife that believeth not, and she be pleased to dwell with him, let him not put her away" (7:12), and the comparable situation when a wife has "an husband that believeth not, and if he be pleased to dwell with her, let her not leave him" (7:13).

There are many adjustments to make in marriage, even when the couple come from the same cultural, social, educational, and religious background. Love, communication, patience, and understanding can ease the process. But when one of the partners becomes a Christian, a whole new array of adjustments becomes necessary.

The Lord Jesus recognized the impact the gospel would inevitably make upon family life when one member became a Christian. He said, "Think not that I am come to send peace on the earth: I came not to send peace, but a sword. For I am come to set a man at variance against his father, and the daughter against her mother, and the daughter-in-law against a mother-in-law. And a man's foes shall be those of his own household" (Matt. 10:34–40).

Suddenly there opens up in the home "a great gulf fixed," a chasm as deep as the pit and as wide as eternity. One partner has passed from death unto life, has been suddenly inhabited by God, has become a citizen of another country and a member of a new family. The things he used to love he begins to loathe and the things he used to loathe he begins to love. For that person old things have passed away and all things have become new. He has a new heart, a new hope, a new home, a new heritage, a new happiness, a new holiness. His life's partner, however, remains an entrenched unbeliever, wedded to the old life, to the old patterns, to the old perspectives, the old pleasures, the old plans and prospects. The bridge to reach across that great divide must be love.

Without love, the gulf will only widen. With love, all things are possible. Paul will bring us soon to a description of the love that never fails (1 Cor. 13). With love, the marriage might yet be saved. This is the earnest hope expressed by the apostle in the words "Let him not put her away," and the words "Let her not leave him." The fact that the unbelieving partner is willing to stay breathes hope. It would, on the human level, be so much easier to cut the ties and start afresh. To settle down instead to the long and often lonely process of trying, without compromise, to bridge that gulf is, indeed, the "more excellent way" of love.

Having stated the rule, Paul gives *the reason.* Involved is both the sanctity of their *partnership* and of their *parenthood:* "For the unbelieving husband is sanctified by the wife, and the unbelieving wife is sanctified by the husband: else were your children unclean; but now are they holy" (1 Cor. 7:14). The question might well arise as to whether the believing partner is defiled by continuing such close association with an unbeliever. In his next epistle Paul will warn the believer against deliberately marrying an unbeliever (2 Cor. 6:14–18), but that is quite a different matter altogether. Where the marriage tie has already been established, prior to the conversion of one of the partners, the tie is to be considered sacred. God always upholds the sanctity of marriage.

With the conversion of one of the members a new dimension of holiness and sanctity is brought into the home. A new, holy, and Christlike lifestyle is exhibited by the believer. God has invaded the home. The Holy Spirit has a firm foothold in the family. The unbeliever may remain an unbeliever, but now the Holy Spirit is at work on all levels of the family life. The invasion of the Lord Jesus has forever changed things in that home. The longer the unbelieving partner remains, and the more the believing partner becomes like Jesus, the more likely it becomes that the unbelieving partner will recognize the new atmosphere of goodness and godliness which has come into the home.

Indeed, to a certain degree, the unbelieving partner is actually "sanctified" by the believing partner. The word used is *hagiazō.* The thought behind the word is that of being set apart for God. In a sense the unbelieving partner has been corralled! Sometimes, out West, one sees a cowboy cut a chosen steer from the herd and pen it up for some special purpose. That is what happens when the husband or wife becomes a believer. The Holy Spirit corrals the unbelieving partner and sets that one apart for special exposure to the gospel.

Then, of course, there are the children—in themselves a powerful argument for not breaking up the home. The children of such a marriage are described by Paul as being "holy." The word is *hagios,* the adjectival form of the word for *sanctified.* The children, as well as the unbelieving partner, are brought into the corral. The believing partner can dedicate the children to God, and can begin to exert an influence on them for God and begin to pray for their conversion.

The apostle turns now from the case of division in the home (1 Cor. 7:12–14) to the more serious case of *defection from the home:* "But if the unbelieving depart, let him depart. A brother or a sister is not under bondage in such cases" (7:15). The believing husband or wife is to do all that can be done, under the new circumstances, to keep the home intact. However, if the unbelieving partner insists on leaving, then so be it. The word for *bondage* here is *dedoulōtai.* The thought seems to be that the one thus abandoned is in virtual widowhood and, presumably, free to marry again. When the Lord declared marital unfaithfulness to be the one ground for divorce He was not contemplating the issues now raised by the apostle. Paul speaks to these larger issues. The bonds, Paul says, are untied by virtue of the abandonment of the relationship by the unbeliever. "But God hath called us to peace," Paul adds. Peace is the atmosphere of the Christian life. If the unbelieving partner elects to remain, the goal should be to live together in peace. If the unbeliever decides to leave, there should be no squabbling. No pressure should be brought to bear to force the unbeliever to either stay or depart.

Finally, in this connection, Paul considers *what matters most* (7:16–17). There is, first, *a blessed prospect:* "For what knowest thou, O wife, whether thou shalt save thy husband? or how knowest thou, O man, whether thou shalt save thy wife?" (7:16). That, indeed, would be the happiest solution to the problem. As someone has said, "A mixed marriage has missionary potential."

Some years ago, I was preaching in a small church in a great Northern city. There was one family pointed out to me as a matter of interest. The wife had recently come to Christ as a result of a large, women's Bible class conducted in the city by one of the church members. In turn, the wife had won her children to

Christ. There remained the husband. He was a professor of mathematics in the university. He was a thoughtful individual and a thorough gentleman. He was confused by the extraordinary changes that had come into his family and invaded his home. The transformation of his wife and children into real Christians left him particularly bewildered because he had always considered himself a believer. When I was able to point out to him the difference between "believing" and "receiving" (John 1:11–13), he responded at once and accepted Christ as His own Savior. The whole family and, indeed, the entire church rejoiced. He went on to become an active member of the Christian community. This is the blessed prospect Paul holds out to all those involved in a mixed marriage. There is no guarantee that the unbeliever will eventually respond to the gospel, but there is the earnest hope.

Then, too, there is *a basic project:* "But as God hath distributed to every man, as the Lord hath called every one, so let him walk. And so ordain I in all churches" (1 Cor. 7:17). In other words, a person should seek to live his life with the gifts that God has given him and in the condition in which God has called him. "Accept yourself for what you are," Paul says. It is sound advice. There is a recognition here of the sovereignty of God in deciding many of the issues of life which affect us, many of which we should not try to change. Just because conversion has wrought all manner of changes within does not necessarily mean that God intends to change all the circumstances in which our lot is cast. This verse provides a bridge between what Paul has said so far and the new topic he introduces next.

> (2) The digression (7:18–24)
>   (a) A spiritual issue (7:18–19)
>   i. The divine comment (7:18–19a)
>   *a.* A religious rite neutralized (7:18)
>   *b.* A religious rite normalized (7:19a)
>   ii. The divine commitment (7:19b)
>   (b) A social issue (7:20–24)
>   i. The secular sphere (7:20–21)
>   *a.* The principle (7:20)
>   *b.* The precept (7:21)
>   *1.* Don't fret if you are not free (7:21a)
>   *2.* Don't fail if you are set free (7:21b)
>   ii. The sacred sphere (7:22–24)

       a. Our duty (7:22)

          1. Bound, but unbound (7:22a)

          2. Unbound, but bound (7:22b)

       b. Our debt (7:23)

          1. We are bought by Him (7:23a)

          2. We now belong to Him (7:23b)

       c. Our dwelling (7:24)

(3) The declaration (7:25–40)

  (a) Paul's considered advice (7:25–28)

     i. The context of his advice (7:25–26)

       a. His concern about the truth (7:25)

          1. As to its source (7:25a)

          2. As to its soundness (7:25b)

       b. His concern about the times (7:26)

     ii. The content of his advice (7:27–28)

       a. His statement (7:27)

          1. To those now still married (7:27a)

          2. To those not still married (7:27b)

       b. His satire (7:28)

          1. Marriage is no sin (7:28a)

          2. Marriage is no sinecure (7:28b)

  (b) Paul's confident admonition (7:29–35)

     i. A word about total commitment (7:29–31)

       a. Look at the clock! (7:29–31a)

          1. Reassess your marriage (7:29)

          2. Reassess your moods (7:30a–b)

             (i)   When gloomy (7:30a)

             (ii) When glad (7:30b)

          3. Reassess your materialism (7:30c–d)

             (i)   Getting things (7:30c)

             (ii) Grasping things (7:30d)

          4. Reassess your motives (7:31a)

       b. Look in the closet! (7:31b)

     ii. A word about temporal cares (7:32–35)

       a. Contrasts considered (7:32–34)

          1. Paul's sincere desire (7:32a)

          2. Paul's several distinctions (7:32b–34)

(i)   His comment (7:40a)

(ii) His claim (7:40b)

Paul's *discussion* (1 Cor. 7:1–17) is now followed by a *digression* (7:18–24) in which he reviews the whole area of one's calling in life, and then by a *declaration* (7:25–40) in which he returns to the matter of marriage. The digression begins with words about *a spiritual issue* (7:18–19). In verses 15–22 the word *called* occurs eight times. The first two occurrences (7:15, 17) have to do with remaining, if possible, in the marital state in which we were when we were called. God is fully aware of that state and all its difficulties, stresses and strains, and potentialities. The remaining half dozen occurrences support the idea that whatever our lot in life, when we respond to the call of God, we should not arbitrarily try to alter it.

There was, for instance, the troublesome matter of circumcision, a spiritual issue, and one that caused considerable controversy in the church in New Testament times. Paul says, "Is any man called being circumcised? let him not become uncircumcised. Is any called in uncircumcision? let him not be circumcised" (7:18). There was something far more important: "Circumcision is nothing, and uncircumcision is nothing, but the keeping of the commandments of God" (7:19).

Circumcision was the covenant sign between the Hebrew people and God (Gen. 17:10–14). There was a strong Judaistic faction in the New Testament church which believed Gentile believers ought to be circumcised and made to keep the Mosaic Law. In other words, they should become Jews in order to become Christians (Acts 15:1). Nobody crusaded more vigorously against the erroneous idea than the apostle Paul. He could clearly see that capitulation on this issue would reduce the church to just another Jewish sect. Moreover, to demand that Gentile believers be circumcised would greatly reduce the appeal of the gospel for Gentile men. Circumcision was not only a painful initiatory rite into Judaism, it was heartily despised by the majority of Gentiles. There was a "Cephas" party active at Corinth, made up of devotees of the apostle Peter. Doubtless one of the strong planks in their religious platform was circumcision. Doubtless, too, they zealously sought converts to their view among Gentile believers. Paul pours cold water on the whole idea. He does the same with the converse idea that, in order to demonstrate their complete emancipation from Judaism, Jewish converts should find some way to reverse the distinctive badge of their race and religion.

"Circumcision is nothing!" he exclaimed, "uncircumcision is nothing!" He had himself circumcised Timothy because Timothy was half-Jewish and such a step would increase his ministry to the Jews (Acts 16:3). He kept Titus uncircumcised and used this Gentile as a test case when he went to Jerusalem to fight for the complete emancipation of Gentile Christianity from all Judaistic demands (Gal. 2:3). Beyond that there was no merit one way or another. The whole pointless squabble was settled by the fact that God called Jews and Gentiles impartially regardless of whether or not they were circumcised. Indeed, the important thing was to bring one's life under the authority of the Word of God.

There was also *a social issue* to be considered (1 Cor. 7:20–24). Paul looks first at *the secular sphere* and states a principle and a precept: "Let every man abide in the same calling wherein he was called. Art thou called being a servant? care not for it: but if thou mayest be made free, use it rather" (7:20–21). He looks, thus, at the whole vexing issue of slavery in the Roman world, the great social issue of the day. If the believer was a slave, when he was converted he should not let that bother him. God knew all about that. The entire question should be left in God's hands. Well did Paul know the injustices that went with slavery, even the dire perils. A slave had no rights. He could be tortured and killed at his master's whim. Any revolt on his part could lead directly to a cross. Paul had not yet written his letter to Philemon, in which he struck the deathblow to slavery in the Christian community. Even then he did not directly attack the institution itself. He organized no marches, advocated no demonstrations, employed no lobbyists, encouraged no resistance. The converted slave should simply go on being a slave, but be the kind of slave he could envision the Lord Jesus being.

But suppose he had the opportunity to be set free? He should avail himself of the opportunity. (Some think the words *use it rather* mean that he should elect to remain a slave and use his position for the glory of God. In this case Paul, perhaps, was thinking primarily of Christian slaves who had Christian masters.) Either way, bond or free, he was to recognize that his condition in life was fully known to God when He called him.

Paul looks also at *the sacred sphere* (7:22–24). He points to a believer's *duty:* "For he that is called in the Lord, being a servant, is the Lord's freeman: likewise he that is called, being free, is Christ's servant" (7:22). The word for *freeman* is *apeleutheros,* meaning "absolutely free," a much stronger word than the one used in verse 21.

The word *apeleutheros* has an interesting etymology. The picture behind the word is that of manumission from slavery. Among the Greeks this was accomplished by employing a bit of legal play-acting. The manumitted slave was first purchased by a god. The slave, of course, had no money, so his master paid it for him into the temple treasury in the presence of the slave. A document was then executed which contained the words *for freedom.* Henceforth he was considered to be the god's property so no one could enslave him again.

In the case of the emancipated slave of verse 21, all he received was freedom from secular slavery. By contrast, the Lord's "freeman" had indeed been purchased by God and was "free indeed" (John 8:36), never to be enslaved again. He may, perhaps, continue to be the property of a human master, but now he really belonged to a heavenly Master.

As for the person who was free when called by God, he should henceforth consider himself to be the Lord's slave. Indeed, Paul saw himself as "the bondslave of Jesus Christ" (Rom. 1:1), and therefore everyone's slave (1 Cor. 9:19).

Paul points next to the believer's *debt:* "Ye are bought with a price; be ye not the servants of men" (1 Cor. 7:23). And what a price! Peter reminds us that we "were not redeemed with corruptible things, as silver and gold . . . but with the precious blood of Christ" (1 Peter 1:18–19). We have been set free! By the words *be ye not the servants of men,* Paul seems to be referring to the party leaders in the Corinthian church who were seeking to make proselytes to their various causes. We are not to allow ourselves to be brought under the domination of some ecclesiastical hierarchy, nor are we to surrender the keeping of our conscience and convictions to some man.

Then, too, Paul points to the believer's *dwelling:* "Brethren, let every man, wherein he is called, therein abide with God" (1 Cor. 7:24). That is what now dominates the believer's life—God! All else fades into insignificance. The believer now lives his life, whether bond or free, whether circumcised or uncircumcised, whether married, single, or separated, with God. God has moved in. Nothing else matters! God no longer dwells somewhere out there beyond the confines of time and space, in a light unapproachable and before which the shining seraphim veil their faces. He has come to live with us, not as He did with Israel in the Old Testament, when He took up His abode in the tabernacle but hid Himself behind an impenetrable veil and barred the way to His presence with threats and warnings. Oh, no. He has moved in! He makes Himself at home where we live, be it in a tumble-down slum or a palatial mansion. Our status makes no difference to Him. He ennobles all with whom He dwells. It is that to which we are called. We are called to "abide with God." If we do that, whether belonging to this persuasion or that, whether married or divorced, whether a slave or a prince, we have been lifted to life on a new plane.

Now comes Paul's *declaration* (7:25–40), as he returns to the question of marriage. The section begins with *Paul's considered advice* (7:25–28); it continues with *Paul's confident admonition* (7:29–35); and ends with *Paul's concluding acknowledgment* (7:36–40). We note first *the context* of Paul's advice (7:25–26). He was concerned about two things. He was concerned about *the truth:* "Now concerning virgins I have no commandment of the Lord: yet I give my judgment as one that hath obtained mercy of the Lord to be faithful" (7:25).

Evidently the Corinthians had asked Paul for a ruling, not only about married men and women, but also about single women. Some think the question also concerned unmarried single men. Certainly the question of celibacy concerned both of them. It seems, however, that the main focus of the Corinthians' question was whether or not a betrothed young woman should proceed with her plans for marriage or break off the engagement and remain single. Paul's ruling would affect not only the girl herself, but her fiancé and her father or whoever was responsible for the arrangements.

In responding to the question, Paul, in the interests of truth, prefaces his remarks by stating that while he had no direct command from the Lord about the matter (for, when all is said and done, it is not as though the matter were one vital to faith and doctrine); nevertheless his considered opinion was based on considerable experience of God's mercy and could therefore be trusted. He wanted to assure the readers of his letter that he was fully aware of the issues involved and sympathetic to the emotions involved. The word *mercy* implies that. The word is *eleeō,* which in itself means "to feel sympathy with the feelings of another and to act accordingly." Paul had been in need of sympathetic understanding himself, and a gentle touch from God (1 Tim. 1:13, 16), so he knew how to be tender, especially when handling truth which might hurt.

Even though he was giving his considered judgment here, it was still the inspired word of an apostle. Also it has been incorporated into the Holy Scriptures by the sovereign Holy Spirit of God, the ultimate Author of all Scripture (2 Tim. 3:16). Therefore it is of equal weight and authority as any other part of Scripture. Paul had "no commandment of the Lord" since the Lord had not spoken specifically to this subject. Now the Holy Spirit speaks to it in accordance with the Lord's promise (John 16:12–13). Paul's "judgment" was overruled by the Holy Spirit, in the same way all Scripture is overruled, to ensure that what was finally written was exactly, verbally, what the Holy Spirit wanted written.

Paul was concerned not only about the truth, he was concerned about *the times:* "I suppose therefore that this is good for the present distress, I say, that it is good for a man so to be" (1 Cor. 7:26). The word for *suppose* here is *nomizō*, meaning "to reckon." It is used of the mob who stoned Paul at Lystra who, "having stoned Paul, drew him out of the city, supposing he had been dead" (Acts 14:19). The word, which occurs fifteen times in the New Testament, always means to conclude from custom, law, or evidence, never simply to imagine. It was thus that the laborers who had toiled all day, when they saw the late arrivals receiving a full day's pay for part of a day's work, supposed that they should receive more. They thought they had justice on their side (Matt. 20:1–16). The most significant use of the word is in connection with Luke's genealogy of the Lord Jesus— "And Jesus himself began to be about thirty years of age, being (as was supposed) the son of Joseph" (Luke 3:23). Luke states that Joseph was "the son of Heli." In actual fact he was the son of Jacob (Matt. 1:15–16) and the son-in-law of Heli. He was regarded ("as reckoned by law"—*"nomizō"*) as the legal son of Heli, Mary's father.

Paul, then, arrived at a considered opinion, having weighed the evidence. His conclusion? Because of the difficulties and dangers of the times, unmarried people would do best to remain as they were. This was probably not the kind of advice the young people would welcome. Still, history proved Paul right. Within a decade Nero blamed the Christian community in Rome for the great fire and launched a holocaust against the church that has become proverbial for its savagery. As Paul weighed the pros and cons of getting married, when the times were so threatening, as he read them (and he had experienced the world's fierce hate), he concluded it would be better to suffer the pain of a broken engagement now than have to bear before long the anguish of seeing one's loved ones torn away to unspeakable tortures. By that time there would be little children to add to the pain.

We now turn to *the content* of Paul's advice (1 Cor. 7:27–28). We note, first, *his statement:* "Art thou bound unto a wife? seek not to be loosed. Art thou loosed from a wife? seek not a wife" (7:27). Remain as you are. Then we note *his satire:* "But and if thou marry, she hast not sinned" (7:28). It's no sin to get married! The word for *sin* here is *hamartanō,* meaning "to miss the mark" or "to wander from the right path." In the New Testament the word is always used in a moral sense. It can refer to either a sin of omission or of commission, whether in thought, word, or deed. Paul's inspired advice: "Don't get married" was only that, advice. It was not a divine command, the breaking of which would bring its appropriate penalty.

But if marriage was no sin, it was no sinecure either: "Nevertheless such shall have trouble in the flesh: but I spare you," Paul adds. The marital state, in those critical days, was bound to add an extra burden. Those who elected to get married anyway, regardless of Paul's advice, would be courting trouble. It is obvious that a single person facing persecution is in a stronger position than a married person who has to weigh the effect his stand will have on his dependents. Often one of the first moves of a terrorist is to seize the prisoner's family and hold them hostage for his cooperation with their demands. Paul knew all about this. He had been a terrorist himself once (Acts 22:4; 26:11).

Now comes Paul's *confident admonition* (1 Cor. 7:29–35). He now discusses two things, *our total commitment* (7:29–31) and *our temporal cares* (7:32–35). He begins his word about our total commitment by saying, in effect, *Look at the clock!* (7:29–31f.). He demands that we reassess four things. First, he calls upon us to *reassess our marriage:* "But this I say, brethren, the time is short: it remaineth, that both they that have wives be as they that have none" (7:29). The word for *short* is *systellō,* which means "shortened" or "contracted." The word is used in connection with the sudden death of Ananias under the judgment of God. Luke says: "The young men arose, wound him up *[systellō]* and carried him out and buried him" (Acts 5:6). The idea is that they wrapped up the corpse. The only other place *systellō* is used in the New Testament is here in 1 Corinthians 7:29. Time, it seemed, was about to be wrapped up. The second coming of Christ was as much "the blessed hope" of the church in New Testament times as it is today. It is always regarded as near or imminent. We are always to live in expectation of His return. We must not allow even the most sacred and binding of earthly relationships to blind us and bind us. At any moment things could be wrapped up. It was Paul's keen anticipation of the Rapture (1 Thess. 4:15–5:11) that kept him sold out at all times.

All too often married people allow domestic duties to get in the way of their commitment to Christ. Matters connected with husband, wife, or children are allowed to take precedence over the things of God. There seems to be almost a note of irony in the excuse one of the men gave for turning down the supper invitation. He said, in the Lord's own words, "I have married a wife, and therefore I cannot come" (Luke 14:20). The Lord refuses to accept that excuse.

We are also to *reassess our moods,* whether gloomy or glad: "And they that weep, as though they wept not; and they that rejoice, as though they rejoiced not" (1 Cor. 7:30a–b). This is no time for indulging our sorrows, Paul says. Sorrows come, but we are not to be overwhelmed by them, to continue wallowing in them, being increasingly taken up with ourselves and our own little world of woe.

Charles Dickens has caught the idea best in his *Great Expectations.* The story revolves around Pip, an orphan boy, being raised by his graceless sister and her husband, an illiterate but lovable village blacksmith. The great day in Pip's life was when he was chosen to visit Miss Havisham to keep occasional company with her ward.

"I had heard of Miss Havisham," he says, everybody for miles around had heard of Miss Havisham uptown as an immensely rich, grim old lady who lived in a large and dismal house barricaded against robbers, and who led a life of seclusion.

In due time the blacksmith's son arrived at the great house and was let in by a beautiful, proud, and scornful girl he learned was Estella, Miss Havisham's ward. She left him outside the door of Miss Havisham's room to make his own intro-duction. He found himself in a large room well lighted with candles. No peep of daylight ever entered there. He supposed it to be a dressing room. His eye finally fell on the strangest lady he had ever seen.

"She was dressed in rich materials, satins and lace and silks, all of white. Her shoes were white. She had a long white veil dependent from her hair and she had bridal flowers in her hair, but her hair was white." There were other dresses scat-tered around and half-packed trunks and jewelry. A second glance revealed some-thing else.

"I saw that everything within my view which ought to be white, had been white long ago, and had lost its luster, and was faded and yellow. I saw that the bride within the bridal dress had withered like the bridal dress and flowers." He noticed, too, that a clock in the room had stopped at twenty minutes to nine. He soon discovered that everything in the room had stopped a long time ago.

On a later visit he was sent into another room from which also all daylight was excluded. The room was cold and wintry. It was spacious and had once been handsome, but everything discernible in it was covered with dust and mold and was falling to pieces. The most prominent object was a long table with a table-cloth spread on it, as if a feast had been in preparation when the house and the clocks all stopped together. A centerpiece of some kind was in the middle of the table, but it was so heavily overhung with cobwebs that its form was quite indis-tinguishable. There were spiders running about on the table. Pip heard rattling behind the panels and black beetles could be seen groping about the hearth.

Miss Havisham appeared. "This," she said, pointing to the long table, "is where I will be laid when I am dead. They shall come and look at me here. What do you think that is?" she continued, pointing with her stick, "that, where those cobwebs are?" Pip confessed himself unable to guess. "It's a great cake. A bride cake. Mine!" she said.

"Call Estella," Miss Havisham ordered after a while. Estella was commanded by her old guardian to play cards with the blacksmith's son. "With this boy?" she said disdainfully. "Why, he is a common laboring boy!" Pip thought he heard Miss Havisham answer, "Well? You can break his heart."

"What do you play, boy?" Estella finally asked. "Nothing but beggar my neighbor, miss," poor Pip replied. "Beggar him," said Miss Havisham to Estella.

And so began the story of Pip's heartache. Many years before, Miss Havisham had been engaged to be married. She idolized the man, who pursued her with vows of devotion. He was able to play upon her love to get great sums of money out of her. The wedding day was set. The wedding gowns were bought. The honeymoon was planned. The wedding guests were invited. The day came, but not the bridegroom. Instead he sent a letter. What was in it nobody ever knew. The man had bled her for all he could get. It was suspected he was already married. Miss Havisham received the letter at twenty minutes to nine. She never recovered.

On the contrary, she planned revenge against her fate. She adopted Estella. She took the young girl in hand. She raised her to break men's hearts. Break Pip's heart she most certainly did.

Sorrow has its place. But sorrow indulged inordinately is destructive. Sorrow must be put away as soon as may be. It is foolish, even sinful, to build a shrine to our sorrow. The Comforter has come. There is a better way. The time is short. We cannot waste it brooding over the past and taking out our revenge on others.

The same is true of rejoicing. If we are not careful it, too, can turn sour, unless it is centered in Christ. We cannot go through life laughing. There are too many wretched people in the world, too much poverty, too much suffering, too much pain. When Solomon decided to go in for mirth he soon found out how barren was that path. "I said of laughter, It is mad!" he confessed" (Eccl. 2:1–2). There are few people more irritating than the person who is always hearty, always joking, always wanting to have fun. Even when we have legitimate cause for rejoicing we should remember that "the time is short." The call of Christ is to a cross, not a carnival.

Then, too, Paul calls upon us to *reassess our materialism:* "It remaineth that . . . they that buy, as though they possessed not" (1 Cor. 7:30c–d). There are more important things in life than accumulating things. The word for *possessed* here is *katechō,* meaning "to hold fast." *Getting* things is not what life is all about. *Grasping* them is even worse. The time is short. There is too much need in the world for us to be spending all our money on ourselves. In arguing with Job about his bankruptcy and his sufferings, Eliphaz the Temanite reminded Job that one of the sins of the Antediluvians was that they rejected God though "he filled their houses with good things" (Job 22:15–18). Materialism always deadens spiritual sensitivity. The things money can buy are transient at best and trivial in the light of eternity. We cannot take any of it with us. We would be far wiser to lay up treasure in heaven. A preacher friend of mine used to say, "If you want treasure in heaven you'd better give some money to someone who is going there."

Then, too, Paul advises us to *reassess our motives:* "And they that use this world, as not abusing it" (1 Cor. 7:31a). Every contact we make with this world must be a light one. It was not for nothing that Abraham, Isaac, and Jacob, although blessed with this world's goods and the heirs of great and precious promises and vast domains, retained their pilgrim character. The writer of Hebrews sums it up: "By faith Abraham, when he was called to go out into a place which he should after receive for an inheritance, obeyed . . . by faith he sojourned in the land of promise as in a strange country, dwelling in tabernacles with Isaac and Jacob, the heirs with him of the same promise . . . these all . . . confessed that they were strangers and pilgrims on the earth" (Heb. 11:8–9, 13). The only one of the patriarchs to build a house was Jacob—and he paid for it dearly (Gen. 33:17–34:31).

"Look at the clock!" says Paul. It's getting late. Time is short. We need to have eternity's values in view. He tells us also to *look in the closet:* "For the fashion of this world passeth away" (1 Cor. 7:31b). There is nothing permanent about this world, as its changing fashions eloquently reveal. A glance in the wardrobe will soon show how quickly this world's fashions change. Everything about this world is marked by change and decay. Today's latest model is tomorrow's antique. The world changes its mind almost as often as it changes its clothes. My brother, who is a research pathologist, tells me that, in medicine, they have what they call "a five-year half-life." He explained that every five years half the things researchers now know to be true are proven false and are replaced by new theory!

Since the world, and all that is in it, is so transient, we would do well to echo the words of the old hymn:

> Change and decay in all around I see;
> O Thou that changest not, abide with me.

Paul turns now from speaking about *total commitment* (7:29–31) to speak about *temporal cares* (7:32–35). First of all *contrasts are considered* (7:32–34) and then *consecration is commanded* (7:35). We note first *Paul's sincere desire:* "But I would have you without carefulness" (7:32a). The word is *amerimnos,* "free from anxiety." The word was used by the chief priests when bribing the soldiers who had been on guard at the tomb. They had brought news of the Resurrection. Instantly the Sanhedrin decided this must be hushed up. So serious did they consider this new development to be that they paid out large money to buy the soldiers. They gave them some propaganda to spread. They were to say that while they were asleep the disciples had come and stolen the body. The soldiers were naturally apprehensive for, although the story was a palpable lie, no Roman soldier would willingly confess to sleeping while on guard, still less to telling everyone they met. The penalty for that offense, aggravated by the theft of what was being guarded, was death (Acts 12:19; 16:27). The high priests sought to assuage their fears: "If this come to the governor's ears," they said, "we will . . . secure *[amerimnos]* you" (Matt. 28:14). They were to have nothing to worry about. The Sanhedrin would screen them from reprisal.

Paul could clearly see that a time of dreadful tribulation was coming upon the church. By remaining single, by preparing for the worst, by touching the things of this world with as light a touch as possible, by focusing on the Lord and His coming again, the Corinthians could be shielded from much anxiety and care. It is a good recipe at all times.

We note also Paul's *several distinctions* (1 Cor. 7:32b–34). First, he has a *message for the men* (7:32b–33). Men who are *single* seek to please *the Master:* "He that is unmarried careth for the things that belong to the Lord, how he may please the Lord" (7:32b); men who have *spouses* seek to please *their mate:* "But he that is married careth for the things that are of the world, how he may please his wife" (7:33). Paul has a corresponding *word for the women* (7:34). Women who are *single* seek to please *the Master:* "There is a difference also between a wife and a virgin. The unmarried woman careth for the things of the Lord, that she may be holy both in body and in spirit" (7:34a); women who have *spouses* seek to please *their man:* "but she that is married careth for the things of this world, how she may please her husband" (7:34b).

Paul is not depreciating marriage, only stating an obvious fact. Single men and women can devote more thought and time to the Lord's work than can married people. It is only right and proper that married people should be concerned with house and home. Being a Christian should make a person a better husband, a better wife, a better father, a better mother. Paul could send Timothy or Titus here, there, and everywhere to discharge important apostolic missions. He could not do that with Aquila. Aquila was a married man. True, he and his wife could consecrate their home to the Lord's work. It could become a base of operations for evangelism, a meeting place for the church, a quiet spot where those untaught in the faith could be shown more perfectly the truth of God (Acts 18:1–5; 24–26). Just the same, their commitment had certain built-in limits set by the fact that they were married and not single.

Contrasts have been considered, now *consecration is commanded:* "And this I speak for your own profit; not that I may cast a snare upon you, but for that which is comely, and that ye may attend upon the Lord without distraction" (1 Cor. 7:35). Paul was not trying to put hindrances in their way, he was setting before them the ideal, the way they could best serve the Lord without encumbrance and without worldly distractions.

The word for *snare* here is *brochos,* a word that refers to a noose or a halter. In a sense, marriage fastens a halter around the neck of a man or a woman. Both parties surrender some of their freedom of action once the marriage vows are spoken. Obligations and duties are shouldered which cannot be lightly set aside. A horse that wears a halter may enjoy the comfort of the barn but he can no longer go where he wants or do what he wants. It has surrendered a measure of its freedom, and the bit and bridle he bears is the proof of it. Paul's advice concerning marriage was pragmatic. He did not want believers, especially those contemplating, for instance, pioneer missionary work or those facing an imminent outbreak of persecution, to encumber themselves with marital restrictions. The halter, however padded, tailored, and comfortable, was still a halter.

We now come to *Paul's concluding acknowledgment* (7:36–40). He considers, first, *a father's duty to his unmarried daughter* (7:36–38). To begin with, there was *the parental decision* (7:36–37). The Bible does not envision our modern, Western ideas of dating and experimenting by singles before marriage. In Bible times the all-important decision as to who should marry whom was a parental decision. Doubtless, in many instances, the young people concerned were allowed some say in the matter. Often, however, the contract was arranged long before they came to the years of understanding and independence.

Paul addresses, then, the question of parental consent, the decision of a father *to release his unmarried daughter in marriage* (7:36). He makes allowance for the father's *conscience,* the father's *conclusion,* and the father's *consent:* "But if any man think that he behaveth himself uncomely [that he is not behaving honorably] toward his virgin [unmarried daughter], if she pass the flower of her age [if she is beginning to lose her first youth], and need so require [if the strain is beginning to show], let him do what he will, he sinneth not: let them marry." Even in a day when parental authority and control in these matters was considerably more rigid and effective than it is today, there was still the possibility of a grown woman deciding to take matters into her own hands and defy parental authority and public opinion alike. Paul was wise enough to see that, in such a case, a frustrated daughter might go sadly astray. Also, Paul was wise enough to know that, in the matter of marriage, he would do well not to command but to suggest. Indeed, he seems to have recognized the possibility that some of the things he has already said might be taken by some parents as a hard and fast law. There is always the legalist out there, all too eager to seize some word of Scripture and enforce it out of all context and original intent. Paul wisely refers the decision in this matter back to the parent and makes due allowance for the unmarried daughter's own needs and desires in the matter.

He also, however, modifies this by considering the opposite question, the decision of a father *to restrain his unmarried daughter from marriage* (7:37). He takes into consideration both the father's *resolve* and *rights:* "Nevertheless he that standeth stedfast in his heart, having no necessity, but hath power over his own will, and hath so decreed in his heart that he will keep his virgin, doeth well" (7:37). This refers to the parent who, having weighed all the issues, still decides it would be wiser if his unmarried daughter continue as she is, living at home. Paul concedes the partner's right to act according to his own decision. If the man were a slave he would have no such right, so Paul assumes there are no mitigating or restricting factors to prevent the father from asserting his will. Nowadays the daughter's will in the matter would certainly have to be given much more consideration than in Bible times. Doubtless a father could expect some scenes these days if he tried to force his will. He would certainly need to have his own emotions well in hand. It is surely assumed, too, that his decision is for the daughter's protection and long-term interest and not just the product of his own prejudice or dislike.

In our own culture the two verses we have just considered (7:37–38) could equally be applied to a man, and to the woman to whom he has become engaged, or to whom he has proposed, and been accepted. Should he or should he not go through with the engagement? Should he, in spite of a "frowning providence," go through with the engagement? Should he, out of consideration for the woman whose emotions he has stirred and whose expectations he has awakened, go ahead with the wedding? Is it fair to her to keep her "dangling on a string," as we would say? Time is passing. The woman is not getting any younger. The emotional strain of a prolonged engagement and a constantly postponed marriage is considerable. Indeed, his own heart inclines toward the marriage. Paul's advice is blunt: "Go ahead and get married. There's no sin in that!"

It may be, however, that, all things considered, it would be best, after all, to terminate the engagement. He must be prepared for some scenes perhaps, but let him terminate it. "There's nothing wrong with that either," Paul says. On the contrary, it is unfair to keep the woman on tenterhooks and wracked with uncertainty.

Having thus outlined the parental decision, Paul adds a word of his own. We have *the Pauline declaration:* "So then he that giveth her in marriage doeth well; but he that giveth her not in marriage doeth better" (7:38). It is not a question of one decision being morally better than the other but of it being more expedient—in view of the considerations Paul has already discussed—consecration on the one hand and persecution on the other hand.

So then, Paul has discussed a father's duties to his virgin; he now concludes this lengthy segment by discussing *a wife's duties to her vows* (7:39–40). There is, first, *the law of the wife* (7:39a). Paul says, "The wife is bound by the law as long as her husband liveth." The Old Testament law, of course, made provision for divorce (Deut. 24:1–4; Lev. 22:13; Num. 30:9). By the time of Christ, one rabbinical school had adopted very liberal views on the subject and permitted divorce on the most casual and trivial of grounds. Another school had much more restrictive views. It was to try to catch Christ, by setting Him for or against one or other of the views, that the Pharisees asked Him His views on divorce (Matt. 19:3–12). The Lord Himself acknowledged that marital unfaithfulness was grounds for divorce but, in answering their question, put marriage back on the lofty plain intended for it by God. Here Paul endorses the Lord's high standard and declares the marriage vow to be sacred and permanent. He knew, of course, the legal grounds for divorce as recognized both by the Law and by the Lord. Here he chooses to overlook them and to uphold the ideal—something, of course, which Jesus did Himself.[4]

Finally, there is *the law of the widow* (1 Cor. 7:39b–40). We note *what Paul admits:* "But if her husband be dead, she is at liberty to be married to whom she will, only in the Lord" (7:39b). There is a distinction made here by Paul between the unmarried daughter, still at her father's disposal, and the widow, who is a free woman able to dispose of herself. She is free to marry anyone she likes, subject, of

---

4. See John Phillips, *Exploring the Gospel of Matthew.* Forthcoming reprint from Kregel Publications.

course, to the obvious proviso that her intended husband be a believer. Later on in this epistle the apostle will militate more passionately against any kind of unequal yoke. Paul does not see it as within his province, apostle though he is, to tell a widow who she may or may not marry. However, she must marry "in the Lord." The clear implication in that statement is that she must marry within the bounds of the known will of God, who now plays for her the role of Father. He is the One who will protect her, if she will let Him, from a hasty, foolish, or inappropriate marriage.

Some commentators have pointed out the difference here between the Pauline phrases *in the Lord* and *in Christ.* The one has to do with our material relationships, the other with our mystical relationship; the one has to do with earthly things, the other with eternal things; the one has to do with our human circumstances, the other has to do with our heavenly circumference; the one has to do with matters where we can act sovereignly, the other has to do with matters where God has acted sovereignly; the one has to do with the secular sphere, the other has to do with the sacred sphere; the one has to do with our daily life, the other has to do with our divine location. All believers are " in Christ." All believers must make sure their decisions are "in the Lord."

Last of all, we note *what Paul advises:* "But she is happier if she so abide, after my judgment: and I think also that I have the Spirit of God" (7:40). If, as some think, Paul was himself a widower, then that would add some additional weight to his comment. That Paul was not actively opposed to remarriage is evident from his comments to Timothy on the subject of widows (1 Tim. 5:14). Still, given the need for unimpeded dedication and the nature of not improbable dangers soon to come upon the Christian community, Paul throws the weight of his advice on the side of not getting remarried. Still, he is not issuing a command, just stating his advice. The advice of an apostle, however, ought to be given its due weight. Paul expressly states in diffident terms, given the delicate nature of the subject and the opposing passions and pressures likely to be involved, that he is giving not only his own opinion but the will of the Holy Spirit as well. Even so, in this matter he was not prepared to give a mandatory ruling.

      b. The matter of meat (8:1–13)
          (1) A primary problem (8:1–3)
              (a) The substance of it (8:1–2)
                    i. What we know instinctively (8:1a)
                    ii. What we know inductively (8:1b–2)

        a. The clever man's danger (8:1b)

        b. The clever man's deception (8:2)

    (b) The solution to it (8:3)

(2) A potential problem (8:4–5)

    (a) A fact (8:4)

        i. A pagan devotion (8:4a)

        ii. A pagan delusion (8:4b)

    (b) A fallacy (8:5)

        i. The varied nature of pagan gods (8:5a)

        ii. The vast number of pagan gods (8:5b)

(3) A practical problem (8:6–11)

    (a) The wise believer (8:6)

        i. Truth about the solitary majesty of the Godhead (8:6a)

        ii. Two of the several members of the Godhead (8:6b–c)

            a. The Father: the Conceiver of all things (8:6b)

            b. The Son: the Creator of all things (8:6c)

    (b) The weak brother (8:7–11)

        i. His conscience (8:7–8)

            a. How it binds him (8:7)

                1. Mentally (8:7a)

                2. Morally (8:7b)

            b. How it blinds him (8:8)

                1. To the reality of God (8:8a)

                2. To the requirements of God (8:8b)

        ii. His confusion (8:9–10)

            a. The possibility of stumbling him (8:9)

            b. The process of stumbling him (8:10)

                1. What he discerns (8:10a)

                2. What he does (8:10b)

        iii. His condemnation (8:11)

(4) A profound problem (8:12–13)

    (a) Paul's pointed charge (8:12)

        i. Self-will is a serious matter (8:12a)

        ii. Self-will is a sinful matter (8:12b)

    (b) Paul's personal choice (8:13)

      i. Paul's holy extremism (8:13a)

     ii. Paul's humble explanation (8:13b)

Paul is still dealing with *difficulties in the church* (1 Cor. 7:1–14:40), especially with matters concerning *our personal walk* (7:1–11:1). We have noted *Paul's exhortation* (7:1–8:13) on *the matter of marriage* (7:1–40). We are now to consider his exhortation on *the matter of meat* (8:1–13). The discussion spills over to the next two chapters. At issue was whether or not meat offered to idols could be eaten with a clear conscience by a Christian. Much of the discussion hinges on principles. The "meats" issue, while still relevant in Christendom and throughout much of the world today, is not the burning issue. The issue would be more evident if today we were to think in terms of whether or not a Christian should drink alcoholic beverages. The whole discussion, indeed, can be enlarged, by application, to cover a variety of issues such as whether or not a Christian should smoke, watch certain movies, read certain books, indulge in questionable amusements of all sorts.

Paul begins this section by introducing *the primary problem* (8:1–3). He states first *the substance* of the problem (8:1–2), beginning with what we know *instinctively:* "Now as touching things offered unto idols, we *know* that we all have knowledge" (8:1a). The first word for *know* here is *oida,* which refers to things we know intuitively and without effort. The second reference is to things we know *inductively:* "We all have knowledge. Knowledge puffeth up, but charity edifieth" (8:1b). The word for *knowledge* here is *gnōsis,* which refers to knowledge acquired by learning, effort, or experience. The words *we all have knowledge* are thought to be an actual quote from the letter the Corinthians had written to Paul. The inquirers evidently thought they knew all about idol-worship and its implication. "It is easy to think that we know" over problems such as this, Paul responds.

But knowledge is by no means everything. The clever man's *danger* lies in that very thing—thinking that because he has certain knowledge, he has therefore "arrived." But knowledge only inflates the ego of some people. "Knowledge puffeth up," Paul says. Ever since Adam and Eve ate of the tree of knowledge in the Garden of Eden, mere knowledge has been a snare to the human race. There never was a time, for instance, when men had more knowledge than they have today. Our knowledge base is expanding so quickly we have to computerize it, and even then, with the enormous masses of information now available to us, we are as far from the truth as we ever were—which is what Paul later, just before his death, told Timothy (2 Tim. 3:7). What the world needs today is what the Corinthians needed when they wrote to Paul, saying, "We all have knowledge"— not more knowledge but wisdom. Jesus has a monopoly on that (Col. 2:3), however, so it is no wonder that, within a verse or two, Paul directs the thoughts of the Corinthians back to Him (1 Cor. 8:6).

The clever man's danger lies not only in the fact that his knowledge inflates his ego. It lies in the fact that his preoccupation with his cleverness causes him to overlook love. Learning and logic will never take the place of love in God's sight. Before long Paul will devote a whole chapter to the importance of love. "Knowledge puffeth up," he says here, "but charity [love] edifieth." The word *charity* here translates the highest word for love in the Greek vocabulary, *agapē*. The word conveys the idea of divine love, Calvary love, God's love, spontaneous love, love irrespective of one's "rights." It is not knowledge which edifies but love. The word for *edify* here is *oikodomeō*. It literally means "to build a house." It is used metaphorically of building up believers and of building up the local church (Acts 9:31). It refers to building Christian character and to spiritual growth. Airing of knowledge does not produce these kinds of results, but love does.

In the Lord's parable of the good Samaritan it was not the priest or the Levite who accomplished anything. The priest had a first-class technical knowledge of the sacrifices and ceremonies of Judaism. He knew how to inspect a sacrificial animal and how to prepare it for the altar. He knew the right thing to do when his turn came to minister in the sanctuary. He had plenty of knowledge, some of it highly specialized knowledge, but he was devoid of compassion.

It was the same with the Levite. He was an expert in biblical and rabbinical law. He could give you chapter and verse from the Pentateuch, or Hillel's interpretation of this, or Shamai's interpretation of that, but he had not an ounce of kindness in him for the bruised and broken figure lying half dead by the side of the road. Much good did the knowledge of the priest and the Levite do him! The Samaritan had none of the access to divine mysteries the priest had, and none of the knowledge of the fine points of the Law that the Levite had. But he had love. If we could have asked the unfortunate traveler, a few weeks later, which of the three had "edified" him, he would have said the Samaritan. Knowledge is not to be despised, but without love it amounts to very little.

Paul clinches the argument. A man may, indeed, know a great deal. Even so, he still has a lot to learn. That seems to be the force of verse 2. The complacent Corinthians thought they knew everything—that is the clever man's *deception*. The Corinthians even couched their inquiry regarding the question of meat in a way that suggests they thought they already knew. All they wanted was Paul's endorsement of their own opinions. Paul pricks their balloon. They still had a lot to learn.

For having stated the substance of the problem—and the question of eating meat offered to an idol was only an incidental problem, the true problem was with their intellectual conceit—Paul now states *the solution* to the problem: "But if any man love God, the same is known of him" (1 Cor. 8:3). There is a subtle twist in the argument here. Love and knowledge are still the predominant words but there is a slight change in the argument. Paul could have said: "If any man love God the same knows Him," but that might have helped foster the already inflated conceit the Corinthians had in their knowledge. So he used the passive form instead: "the same is known of him." What Paul is saying is simply this: "The Lord knoweth them that are his" (2 Tim. 2:19). When God thus "knows" a person, that person comes to know Him. However, any such knowledge of God is wholly dependent upon love. Knowledge based on love will solve all problems, even the most difficult and explosive ones.

Paul now turns from the primary problem to *the potential problem* (1 Cor. 8:4–5). Idolatry was, indeed, a potential problem then. It is a very real problem still, even in Christendom. When we think to what extent the worship of images, relics, saints, and icons has invaded the professing church, we can see how real this potential problem has become. Paul, while answering the immediate question as to whether or not a believer in that day and age could conscientiously eat meat offered to idols, enlarges the question and discusses the actual nature of the idols and images themselves.

First, we have *a fact* (8:4). There was the fact of *pagan devotion:* "As concerning therefore the eating of those things that are offered in sacrifice unto idols, we know that an idol is nothing in the world" (8:4a). There can be little doubt that this whole question was a vexing one in the early church, especially, as was the case in Corinth, where the church was made up of a mixture of converted Jews and Gentiles. The Gentile converts were inclined to be liberal in their views about the matter. If it were unlawful under any circumstances to eat meat offered to idols, then that would force the believers to adopt rules as stringent as those required under Levitical law. Nearly all the best meat offered for sale in the markets of a pagan city originally came from pagan temples. Only the finest animals were offered for sacrifice. It was customary for the priests to take their cuts and then to sell the remainder to the public in the meat market. The Gentiles had always bought their meat in the market regardless of where it originally came from. As Christians they would naturally do the same. Indeed, as a practical consideration they could never be sure about any meat they bought if they were to be tied by a restriction which said it was wrong to eat meat offered to an idol. The markets certainly did not separate such meat from that secured from other sources. More, if such a ruling were to be applied, how could a Gentile believer have table fellowship with unsaved family members or friends? He would find himself cut off from society in the same way the Jews were cut off from Gentile society. Indeed, Christianity, in that case, would be in danger of becoming just another Jewish sect. Consequently Gentile believers reacted strongly against any curtailment of their liberty.

Equally vociferous were the Jewish converts. They had been raised on Levitical law, which stated that only kosher food could be consumed. Every Jewish community had its own butcher. A Jewish kitchen had to be ritually antiseptic. A Jew could eat no meat that was not certified as free from ritual contamination. Besides, the Jerusalem Council had enjoined a prohibition against eating meat offered to idols as one of the four conditions for acceptance of Gentiles into the Christian fold by the Jewish church (Acts 15:29). It is evident, so far as this point went, that Paul was quite prepared to assert his own apostolic authority to annul that ruling so far as Gentile believers in general were concerned. He evidently saw the ruling as having only temporary and local significance. He was certainly not prepared to make it mandatory in such a city as Corinth. He was always viewed with great suspicion by the Jerusalem church for his stand.

It may well have been that the Jewish converts in the Corinthian church counted on Paul's earlier Pharisaic upbringing and rabbinical training as tilting Paul's ruling in their favor. Surely, on this issue, he would side with Cephas, who had already capitulated once to the Jerusalem legalists (Gal. 2:11–14).

On the other hand, it may well have been that the Gentile converts in the Corinthian church counted on Paul's wholehearted endorsement of their position. They all knew he had no such scruples.

Paul handled the vexing question with great tact and tenderness. He wanted to offend no man's conscience. He had a deep sympathy for the weak believer and his scruples. At the same time, he wholeheartedly endorsed the principle of freedom in Christ. He begins by looking at the broader issue—the actual nature of idolatry itself.

He begins with a fact, the fact of *pagan devotion*. He had been around Gentiles all his life. He knew what a hold idolatry had on the unregenerate human heart. He had come to Corinth from Athens where, so the Romans said, "It was easier to meet a god than a man," because images were so plentiful. "An idol is nothing in the world!" That was Paul's opening broadside in the debate. No idol has any real existence. It is a man-made thing, the product of human imagination and a craftsman's tools. It is nothing but a carved piece of wood, or a sculptured block of stone. It is no more a god than a chair. One might as well worship the kitchen table. That is not to say that idolatry does not get a fearful hold over the human heart. It does. Anyone who has read the story of Michelangelo will recall how that, after finishing his masterpiece, *The Pieta*, he came back later to admire it and ended up worshiping it—a piece of sculptured marble he had hewn with his own hands. Even the serpent of brass which God commanded Moses to make in the wilderness (Num. 21:4–9; John 3:14) had eventually to be destroyed by Hezekiah because the Jews had turned it into an idol (2 Kings 18:4). Idolatry is the most foolish of all human activities, since it involves offering homage and adoration to nothing but an inanimate, man-made object. Paul contemptuously writes the word "Nothing!" over all idolatry. It is the worship of something that does not exist.

Which brings us to *pagan delusion,* for the idolater imagines that there is some-thing there. "An idol is nothing," Paul says, "there is none other God but one" (1 Cor. 8:4b). Since there is only one God, any other entity which is supposed to be God is simply nothing! The idolater may be deluded into thinking that the graven image to which he bows is a god, but anyone who knows God knows better.

An illustration of this can be found in the story of Gideon. When God com-manded him to destroy the altar and the "asherah" (the pornographic sex-cult idol) on his father's property, Gideon obeyed. The next morning the villagers howled for Gideon's blood for committing sacrilege. Gideon's father, however, defended his son: "Will ye plead for Baal?" he demanded. "If he be a god, let him plead for himself" (Judg. 6:31). Similarly, Elijah mocked the false prophets of Baal when their wildest appeals to him received no answer. "O Baal, hear us!" they cried. Elijah scoffed at them. "Cry aloud," he said sarcastically, "for he is a god; either he is talking, or he is pursuing, or he is in a journey, or peradventure he is sleeping and must be awaked" (1 Kings 18:27). The whole scene had been staged by him to prove that Jehovah was a true and living God whereas Baal was nothing (18:22–29).

Next, Paul introduces *a fallacy.* He points out both the *varied nature* and the *vast number* of false pagan gods: "For though there be that are called gods, whether in heaven or in earth, (as there be gods many, and lords many)" (1 Cor. 8:5). There are scores of them mentioned in the Bible. The Egyptians, Assyrians,

Babylonians, Greeks, and Romans had whole pantheons of them. To this day the Hindus number their gods by the countless thousands. It is all a gigantic farce, at least so far as the actual worship of idols is concerned. That evil spirits lurk behind the graven images is something Paul discusses later (10:20). Here he wants only to show that no one should pay any attention to idols since they were only dead images corresponding to nothing at all (Isa. 44:6–20). So why should anyone pay any attention to whether or not meat, bought in all good faith in the market, had at one time been offered to an idol, which was a nonentity?

Paul turns next to *the practical problem* (1 Cor. 8:6–11). For the fact remained that some did make an issue of it, so the practical problems resulting from that still needed to be faced. He talks, first, to *the wise believer* (8:6). In contrast with the multitudinous idols of the pagans is the true and living God of the Jews and Christians: "But to us there is but one God, the Father, of whom are all things, and we in him; and one Lord Jesus Christ, by whom are all things, and we by him." Paul draws attention to the *truth about the solitary majesty of the Godhead.* There is only one God. Paul is here insisting on the truth of monotheism in contrast with the crowded and conflicting pantheons of the pagans. We have here an echo of the creedal statement of Israel: "Hear, O Israel, the LORD our God is one LORD" (Deut. 6:4). It is generally believed that idolatry was foisted on the human race by Nimrod, that its early home was Babel, and that, after the overthrow of the tower of Babel it spread throughout the world. The truth of monotheism was rediscovered by Abraham by divine revelation. He at once turned his back on his polytheistic home in Babylonia to become a pilgrim and stranger in a pagan world. The nation of Israel was called into being to bear witness to the world of the name and nature of the one true God. When Israel sank into worse paganism and idolatry than the heathen, God sent them to Babylon as captives. There the nation had idolatry forever burned out of its soul. As Christians we are heirs to the Judaistic belief in the one true God.

But there is more to it than that. God exists in three persons. Witness to this can be found in the very first verse of the Bible: "In the beginning God *[Elohim]* created the heaven and the earth" (Gen. 1:1). In this verse we have a plural noun, *Elohim* (indicating more than two persons), followed by a singular verb (indicating one God). Here Paul draws our attention to *two of the several members of the Godhead,* to the Father as the *Conceiver* of all things and to the Son as the *Creator* of all things. The whole universe was God's idea. It is "of God." We are His redeemed, are "in Him" or "for Him," as some render this. The whole universe was created by the Lord Jesus Christ. We are "by Him," or we "belong to Him," as some render it. He gives us life.

The point of all this seems to be that the idols of the heathen are nothing. By contrast, the God we worship not only conceived and created the universe but He is a Father to His people and has been revealed to us by the one and only Lord Jesus Christ. How trivial, in view of all this, is this question of "meats" and "idols" and all quibbling about whether or not meat offered to a nonentity can contaminate a Christian! Paul seems to be pleading with the Corinthians to get their minds off such unimportant things and get them fixed on the true realities. The wise believer does just that.

Now Paul turns to *the weak brother* (1 Cor. 8:7–11). This is the believer who still has a tender conscience about eating meat tainted, in his view, by having possibly come from a pagan temple.

There is, first, the matter of *his conscience* (8:7–8). His conscience *binds* him, both mentally and morally: "Howbeit there is not in every man that knowledge: for some with conscience of the idol unto this hour, eat it as a thing offered unto an idol; and their conscience being weak is defiled" (8:7). The *mental* problem lies in the fact that this person still believes idols are real. He still believes, in his heart of hearts, that the sacrifice offered to an idol is a real sacrifice to a real god. He still believes, therefore, that the surplus meat which finds its way from the temple to the market really is tainted by its association with the pagan temple and idol. He cannot shake himself free from this conviction, burned into his soul by years of paganism before he met Christ, or by the rigid upbringing he had as a Jew before his conversion to Christ.

The *moral* problem lies in the fact that, although this believer still has this belief, he eats the meat anyway. By so doing he injures his conscience. The defilement he incurs does not come from the meat, because the meat itself is not defiled. It comes from doing something his conscience has decided is wrong— even though, in actual fact, it may not really be wrong at all.

When I was in the British Army, I was stationed on Haifa docks and lived, with about twenty other men, in a small camp located at the far end of the dock. The small kitchen which serviced the men dished up the usual unpalatable British army food. Across the harbor from our camp was the breakwater which made Haifa port possible. Tied up to the breakwater were a number of old ships which the Zionists had used to try to land Jews on Palestinian soil in defiance of the British blockade.

One day some of the fellows borrowed a boat and rowed out to the breakwater to explore some of the abandoned ships. They came back with an unexpected contribution for our kitchen—some cans of American food: tomatoes, fruit, processed meat, and the like. It was a welcome addition to our drab army diet.

As we were eating one of these spiced-up meals, one of the fellows challenged me: "That food was stolen. You're supposed to be a Christian. How can you eat it?" he demanded. "With my knife and fork, just like you," I replied. Still, my mess-mate had raised an interesting question. If I had really believed that the canned goods had been stolen, it would have been wrong for me to eat it. The situation would have been analogous to that of the Corinthian believer who thought meat offered to idols was tainted. As it was, I took the position that the food had been abandoned and was in public domain.

The apostle continues. The weak brother's conscience not only binds him, it *blinds* him. It blinds him both to the *reality* of God and to the *requirements* of God: "But meat commendeth us not to God: for neither if we eat, are we the better, neither, if we eat not, are we the worse" (8:8). God is not small-minded. Our acceptance by Him is simply not affected by what we eat or drink. God is far more concerned as to whether or not one has a pure heart than whether or not the roast beef he had for supper came from an idol temple at some point in its journey from the farm to the table. We cannot help but admire Paul's sanctified common sense. The strong believer thinks he can eat anything. That does not make him any better. The weak believer thinks there are some things he cannot eat. He's no worse for that.

"Meat commendeth us not to God." The verse can be applied to the question of fasting. There may be times when fasting is beneficial to one's spiritual life. However, we must keep in mind the fact that God will not think any better of us if we do it. This verse ought to put an end to such a medieval notion as not eating meat during Lent.

Having dealt with the matter of the weak brother's conscience, Paul turns to the matter of *his confusion* (8:9–10). There is, for instance, *the possibility of stumbling him:* "But take heed lest by any means this liberty of yours become a stumblingblock to them that are weak" (8:9). Paul's great heart went out to the weak. He was not going to lend his name to any assault upon their consciences by the strong, much as all his instincts and insights sided with those who championed freedom. This is where love comes in. A man has a right to eat or drink anything he wants, but he has no right to stumble someone else in the process. We have no right to encourage someone, by our example, to do something that might be against his conscience. We might be responsible for tripping someone up. The word for *stumbling block* here is not *skandalon,* which suggests a trap or a snare, but *proskomma,* which suggests an obstacle against which a person might catch his foot. Paul does not have in mind here the deliberate tempting of a weak brother to do something that he believes to be wrong. He has in mind the careless setting of an example that might end up being harmful to someone else.

Paul goes further. He gives an illustration. He describes *the process of stumbling him:* "For if any man see thee which hast knowledge sit at meat in the idol's temple, shall not the conscience of him which is weak be emboldened to eat those things which are offered to idols?" (8:10). Evidently there were some Christians at Corinth who saw nothing wrong in that. A pagan might invite his friends to a meal in the temple. The host might possibly be a relative. The meal, held in such a place, would naturally be under the sponsorship or the patronage of the temple and would likely enough be opened by "saying grace," by a libation in honor of the god. A man of sophisticated habits might see nothing wrong in accepting such an invitation, even though doing so would be taking his liberty quite far.

That Paul does not approve of going to such lengths to demonstrate one's liberty is hinted at in the word he uses for *the idol's temple.* The word is *eidōlion,* which should have raised a warning flag in the minds of his readers. It was not a word used by the pagans but, rather, a word coined by the Jews and one which contained a taunt. Where the Greeks spoke of the Atheneum or the Apolloneum or the Posideum, linking the name of the temple to the name of the god, the Jews spoke of the *idoleum.* The very word *eidōlion* implied something shadowy and unreal. Doubtless those believers who accepted an invitation to a banquet held in an "idoleum" could find arguments to justify their behavior. Paul finds an argument to condemn it—the weak believer's conscience and the harm that might result to him if he followed such an example.

He might be "emboldened" to eat things offered to idols in defiance of his conscience. The word for *emboldened* is *oikodomeō* (as in 8:10). Here, however, Paul is using irony, for instead of building up the weak believer, such action will pull him down. The strong believer might be emboldened to accept an invitation to a banquet held in such a place because the idol enshrined there meant nothing to him. His example, however, might have disastrous consequences if emulated by a weaker brother. We can think of places in our modern world to which we would be well advised not to go and for the same reason.

Paul turns now from the weak brother's conscience and confusion to his *condemnation* (8:11). He puts it squarely at the door of the strong believer who allows his liberty to run ahead of his love: "And through thy knowledge shall the weak brother perish, for whom Christ died" (8:11). Surely, Paul says, you wouldn't want that, for a weak brother to experience spiritual disaster just because you, in your superior sophistication, wanted to indulge your rights as an emancipated believer.

The question of "meats" is not really an issue in our modern, Western society, although the influence of Eastern cults and modern dietary notions are tending to make it so. The corresponding issue, in evangelical circles today, would be whether or not a Christian ought to drink. Some Christians see no harm in it. I have been in countries such as Italy, France, and Argentina, where it is served as a matter of course.

Here, for instance, is a believer who has a tender conscience about drinking wine or alcohol of any kind. He is in the home of a peer who offers him a glass. The person is someone he admires, perhaps, and respects. Other Christians at this same table have accepted the wine without question. He concludes it must be all right, so he accepts the wine—and gets a taste for it. His conscience rises up in warning but now it is too late. He has developed a liking for wine. The viper has bitten him. He wants more. He finds himself at last a drunkard, a hopeless slave to drink. If he recovers at all, it will only be at fearful cost. In any case he has been destroyed. The word Paul uses here for *perish* is *apollymi,* meaning utter ruin and loss. Interestingly enough, the word is used by the Lord Jesus to describe the marring of the wineskins when subjected to the action of wine they were not meant to hold (Luke 5:37), the sheep that was lost (15:4, 6), and the condition of the lost prodigal (15:24). To be responsible for someone's ruin, someone, indeed, for whom Christ died, is a high price to pay for the indulgence of one's rights.

Paul concludes the whole discussion by pointing out *the profound problem* (1 Cor. 8:12–13). We note his *pointed charge.* Self-will, he says, is both a *serious* matter and a *sinful* matter: "But when ye sin so against the brethren, and wound their weak conscience, ye sin against Christ" (8:12). Christ died for the weak believer just as He died for the strong believer, something the strong believer sometimes forgets in his exasperation at the weak brother's scruples. No believer has any right to ride roughshod over the "shibboleths" of another believer.

"Ye sin against Christ." That is the climax of the whole discussion. The Lord Jesus had a special care for those who were weak. Orphans and widows, women and children, the downtrodden and fallen, the hungry, the lonely, the outcasts all found a place in His heart. The Lord Jesus always used His great strength to help the weak. We should do the same.

When the Lord stages His coming judgment of the nations in the Valley of Jehoshaphat, He will commend some and condemn others. The final explanation will be: "Ye did it unto me," or "Ye did it not unto me" (Matt. 25:40–41). What we do or do not do to one another we do or do not do to Him. "Ye sin against Christ." No really concerned believer will want to be guilty of that. We will not stand in the Valley of Jehoshaphat, but we shall certainly stand at the judgment seat of Christ. We shall be held accountable for our behavior there. We had better amend it here.

We note, in conclusion, Paul's *personal choice.* He sets before us *his holy extremism:* "Wherefore, if meat make my brother to offend, I will eat no flesh while the world standeth"; and *his humble explanation:* "lest I make my brother to offend" (1 Cor. 8:13). In both cases here the word for *offend* is *skandalizō.* He shuddered at the thought of casting a snare before anyone, especially a brother. He would rather starve. The word for *meat* is *brōma,* which really means not just meat but food of all sorts. The word for *flesh* is *kreas,* which refers to meat. There is almost a note of contempt here at the thought that any believer could be so insensitive in the exercise of his liberty as to actually stumble a weaker brother.

When it came to principle Paul would not yield an inch. When it came to self-denial he would go to any lengths. Of course the weak brother has responsibilities, too. He is not to use his scruples and prejudices in such a way as to hold the strong believer ransom. There are some religious bigots who use their inhibitions just to get their own way. They would rob others of all their liberty. Romans 15:2 takes care of that.

> 2. Paul's example (9:1–27)
>> a. His position (9:1–5)
>>> (1) He claims his apostolic position (9:1–2)
>>>> (a) The sum of his apostleship (9:1)
>>>>> i. The testimony of his liberty (9:1a)
>>>>> ii. The testimony of his Lord (9:1b)
>>>>> iii. The testimony of his life (9:1c)
>>>> (b) The seal of his apostleship (9:2)
>>>>> i. His critics dismissed—his claim really needs no more discussion (9:2a)
>>>>> ii. His claim declared—his calling really needs no more demonstration (9:2b)

(2) He clarifies his apostolic position (9:3–5)
    (a) His reasonableness (9:3)
    (b) His rights (9:4–5)
        i. To material provision (9:4)
        ii. To marital provision (9:5)
            a. This right indicated (9:5a)
            b. This right illustrated (9:5b)
b. His policy (9:6–15)
    (1) How Paul regarded his right to financial support (9:6–11)
        (a) The right of full-time workers declared (9:6)
        (b) The right of full-time workers discussed (9:7–11)
            i. The man who goes to fight (9:7a)
            ii. The man who grows the fruit (9:7b)
            iii. The man who guards the flock (9:7c)
        (c) The right of full-time workers defended (9:8–9)
            i. A question (9:8)
            ii. A quotation (9:9)
        (d) The right of full-time workers demonstrated (9:10–11)
            i. The Christian worker's hope (9:10)
            ii. The Christian worker's harvest (9:11)
    (2) How Paul resigned his right to financial support (9:12–15)
        (a) A personal exception (9:12)
            i. The rule restated (9:12a)
            ii. The right relinquished (9:12b–c)
                a. A deliberate policy (9:12b)
                b. A desirable policy (9:12c)
        (b) A practical exhortation (9:13–14)
            i. The Old Testament principle (9:13)
            ii. The New Testament parallel (9:14)
        (c) A pointed explanation (9:15)
            i. His method was quite personal (9:15a)
            ii. His motive was quite pure (9:15b)
c. His preaching (9:16–18)
    (1) Preaching by compulsion with choice (9:16–17a)
        (a) A humble nobility (9:16a)
        (b) A holy necessity (9:16b)
        (c) A happy notability (9:17a)

  (2) Preaching by compulsion without choice (9:17b–18)
   (a) A dispensational responsibility (9:17b)
   (b) A different reward (9:18)
 d. His passion (9:19–23)
  (1) His method in preaching (9:19–22a)
   (a) Indifference to one's social status (9:19)
    i. Whether of the upper class (free) (9:19a)
    ii. Whether of the under-privileged class (bond) (9:13b)
   (b) Indifference to one's spiritual status (9:20a)
    i. The Jew and God's commandments
    ii. The Jew and God's covenants
    iii. The Jew and God's commitments
   (c) Indifference to one's secular status (9:20b–22a)
    i. Whether positional (9:20b–21)
     a. The legalistic person (9:20b)
     b. The lawless person (9:21)
    ii. Whether personal (weak) (9:22a)
  (2) His motive in preaching (9:22b–23)
   (a) To win people to Jesus now (9:22b)
   (b) To win praise from Jesus then (9:23)
 e. His purpose (9:24–27)
  (1) An illustration (9:24–25)
   (a) A contest (9:24–25a)
    i. The explanation (9:24a)
    ii. The exhortation (9:24b–25a)
     a. The plea (9:24b)
     b. The price (9:24c)
      1. At all costs try to win (9:24c)
      2. At all costs train to win (9:25a)
   (b) A crown (9:25b)
   (c) A contrast (9:25c)
  (2) An application (9:26–27)
   (a) Paul's drive (9:26)
    i. He is in the race—to win (9:26a)
    ii. He is in the ring—to win (9:26b)
   (b) Paul's dread (9:27)

      i. A possibility systematically fought (9:27a)

     ii. A possibility squarely faced (9:27b)

Paul has not yet finished with his discussion of meats. However, he now enlarges his field of vision. The whole question of Christian liberty and of our "rights" as believers comes under review. We have considered *Paul's exhortation* (1 Cor. 7:1–8:13). Now we must consider *Paul's example* (9:1–27). It was typical of Paul that he did not say, "Do what I say." He said, "Do as I do!"

We begin with *his position* (9:1–5). First, he *claims his position* as an apostle (9:1–2). He puts down *the sum of his apostleship* (9:1), adding up the indisputable reasons why he has every right to the title. "Am I not an apostle?" he demands. He cites a threefold testimony to his apostleship. There was *the testimony of his liberty* (9:1a). "Am I not an apostle? am I not free?" In the early church God gave gifts to men (1 Cor. 12–14) and He gave gifted men to the church (Eph. 4:11–13). The gift of an apostle was the greatest of all.

In the Gospels the word *apostolos* (singular and plural) occurs only nine times. It occurs sixty-nine times in Acts and the Epistles and three times in Revelation. In the synoptic Gospels and Acts the term is almost exclusively reserved for the Twelve, the men chosen and commissioned by the Lord during His earthly ministry (Matt. 11:1; Luke 6:13). It was from this position of potential power and privilege that Judas fell. The remaining apostles thought it incumbent upon them to choose a successor and did so by ballot. The man they chose, Matthias, is never heard of again (Acts 1:26). There were others who are called "apostles" in the New Testament. Such were Paul and Barnabas (14:4, 14) and Andronicus and Junias (Rom. 16:7).

Paul calls himself an apostle nineteen times. He argues his claim here in 1 Corinthians 9 and in 2 Corinthians 12. On two occasions the word *apostolos* is translated "messenger," for that, essentially, is what the word means—"a sent one." He considered himself an apostle "born out of due time" (1 Cor. 15:9–10). He considered himself appointed of God to be the apostle to the Gentiles, just as Peter had been called to be the apostle to the Jews (Gal. 2:8). Special power and authority were vested in the apostles in general and in Paul in particular. Indeed, Paul seems to have had all the gifts. The apostles were used of God to write Scripture, perform miracles, execute judgment, and evangelize the world. Signs and wonders accompanied their ministry at times. In all these things Paul was outstanding and stood apart and ahead of all the others (1 Cor. 15:10; 2 Cor. 12:12).

He mentions, here, his freedom. He was under bondage to no man. He was free from the Law. He had a free hand to exercise his rights or to give up his rights. His critics, arguing from what they would have done themselves, given his standing and status in the church, thought that if he were really an apostle he would have asserted his rights (to financial support, for example), not abrogated them. With short, staccato questions Paul lets it be known that, despite the malignant slanders of his enemies, he was indeed an apostle and free to do what he wanted within the will of God.

Moreover, there was *the testimony of his Lord:* "Am I not an apostle . . . have I not seen Jesus Christ our Lord?" (1 Cor. 9:1b). In order to be an apostle it was an indispensable requirement that one be able to bear direct, personal witness to the resurrection of Christ (Acts 1:21–22). We have no means of knowing whether or not Paul had ever seen the Lord Jesus during the years of His public ministry. It is not at all improbable since he was "brought up at the feet of Gamaliel" (22:3), a rabbinical scholar we meet in Jerusalem (5:34). We do know that he met the risen Christ on the Damascus road (9:3, 17; 15:8). It was this special appearing of Christ to him which colored all of Paul's thinking about Jesus. He knew Him as "the Lord from heaven" (1 Cor. 15:47)

Then, too, there was *the testimony of his life:* "Am I not an apostle . . . are not ye my work in the Lord?" (1 Cor. 9:1c). Whoever else, on whatever grounds, might have wanted to argue Paul's claim to apostleship, surely the Corinthians should not have been in their number. He had evangelized their city with apostolic power and had led large numbers of them to Christ.

For there was also *the seal of his apostleship* (9:2). He summarily *dismissed his critics*—his claim really needed no more discussion: "If I be not an apostle unto others, yet doubtless I am to you" (9:2a). He summarily *declared his claim*—his calling really needed no more demonstration: "For the seal of mine apostleship are ye in the Lord" (9:2b). So far as the Corinthians were concerned the matter was closed. Paul had no more to say. Let the emissaries from Jerusalem come, let the Cephas party have their say, the Corinthians had Paul's stamp on them. All they needed to say was "Paul? Not an apostle? Nonsense! He has demonstrated his apostleship among us and he won us to Christ!"

Having claimed his position as an apostle, Paul now *clarifies his position* as an apostle (9:3–5). We note *his reasonableness:* "Mine answer to them that do examine me is this . . ." (9:3). He does not go off the deep end. He does not imperiously silence all debate as though he were some kind of pope. He does not say, "How dare you question me!" or "What right do you have to examine me?"

Where no matter of principle was involved, Paul was always the most open, pacific, and reasonable of men. He did not suffer from an inflated ego, or stand upon his dignity, or "pull rank" on his detractors. Sometimes men who hold high office get so that they cannot tolerate the slightest challenge to their authority or the mildest questioning of their demands. To do so is like knocking the inflamed toe of a man suffering from gout. Paul was not like that. So far as he was concerned, anyone could challenge him (Acts 17:10–11). He had nothing to hide or no carnal ego to defend.

The word for *examine* is *anakrinō.* It can be translated "investigate" or "judge." Luke uses the word when recording Pilate's early verdict concerning Christ: "I having examined *[anakrinō]* him before you, have found no fault in this man" (Luke 23:14). Luke uses it a number of times in the book of Acts (4:9; 12:19; 24:8; 28:18). One meaning of the word is examination by torture, a common enough practice in all ages. Evidently Paul's critics were not sparing him any pain in "putting him to the question." Evidently, too, Paul could take even that in his stride. If his Lord was willing to subject Himself to such hostile and injurious cross-examination, then why should he complain when he was similarly treated?

Still, he had an answer for his foes and critics. The word for *answer* is *apologia,* "defense." It was one thing to accept criticism amicably. It was something else again to take it lying down. When Paul thought that, for the cause of Christ, he ought to defend himself, he did not hesitate to do so. This, too, was reasonable.

We note, therefore, *his rights* as an apostle (1 Cor. 9:4–5). Doubtless Paul could have compiled a long list of his rights. He contents himself with spelling out his rights in just two areas—perhaps his critics had concentrated their attack upon him in these two areas. He had *material* rights: "Have we not power to eat and drink?" (9:4). The word he uses for *power* is *exousia,* meaning the authority or the right to do something or to enjoy something.

Here Paul insists on his right to be supported in the ministry by the church and to eat and drink what he pleases. But if he has the right to material support in the exercise of his apostolic ministry, he also has the right to support himself in the ministry if he wants to and if he considers that the wisest thing to do. There were times when Paul worked with his own hands to support himself and his colleagues in the Lord's work (4:12; Acts 18:1–2; 1 Thess. 2:9; 2 Thess. 3:8–9). There were times when he gladly accepted financial gifts from others (Phil. 4:14–18).

Paul often had good reasons for being a "bi-vocational" missionary. He is careful, however, not to impose this as a general rule because that might cause hardship to other full-time servants of the Lord. Nor did he wish to set a precedent others might find too restricting. Nor did he want to deprive other believers of the privilege of sharing financially in the Lord's work. He had his rights, but they were not to be regarded as rules.

A young preacher friend of mine was co-pastoring a large and thriving church. He confided in me that he barely received enough money to adequately support his family. Part of the problem was the senior pastor, who refused to take any salary at all from the church. "It's all well and good for him," the young man said. "He doesn't need any money. He's very well off. He sold a prosperous business before becoming pastor of this church. The trouble is that the deacons have developed a mind-set. They think that because they do not have to pay him, they do not have to pay me. At least, they don't think I need to be given very much!" The senior pastor had set an unfortunate precedent. Paul was careful to assert his right both to receive adequate compensation for his ministry and to decline compensation if he so desired.

Paul not only had monetary rights, he had *marital* rights: "Have we not power to lead about a sister, a wife, as well as other apostles, and as the brethren of the Lord and Cephas?" (1 Cor. 9:5). This verse is taken by some to prove that Paul was not, himself, a married man. Speculation ranges all the way, however, from Paul's being single, to his being married (and eligible on that count, at least, to qualify as a member of the Sanhedrin), to his being a widower, and to his being separated from his wife who, it has been conjectured, may have left him when he became a Christian. Paul's words in 7:7 add weight to the view that Paul was unmarried.

Still, that is not the primary point of this verse. The point is that the apostles had every right to be married, had every right to have their wives accompany them on their itineraries, and had every right to expect the churches to support both them and their wives—an affirmation that militates against the notion of enforced priestly celibacy. More, if that was true of the other apostles and full-time Christian workers, it was equally true of Paul! Why should his case be any different from theirs? He cites the cases of Cephas (Peter) and the Lord's brothers (the natural sons of Mary and Joseph, born after the birth of the Lord Jesus— Matt. 13:55–56; Acts 1:13–14). Maybe Peter had his wife (Mark 1:30) with him when he visited Corinth. Perhaps the reference to "Cephas" means that some of Paul's particular critics were of the Cephas party in Corinth.

People are the same all over. In Jesus' day they criticized John the Baptist for his asceticism and they criticized Jesus for His accessibility. Jesus likened them to children at play; when one group invited the others to come and play at weddings, they refused to do that; and when they invited them to play at funerals instead, they wouldn't do that either (Matt. 11:16–17).

It was the same with the apostle Paul. With some people nothing he did was right. If he accepted money for his ministry, that was wrong—he was just in it for the money. If he declined to be supported financially, that was wrong—he was being too independent. For him to remain single was suspicious, for him to get married would be wrong, too; it would hinder his freedom. If he were married but left his wife at home that would be wrong—people would say they didn't get along. If he were married and brought his wife along, what kind of life was that for a woman? And besides, why should they pay her travel expenses as well as his!

Having stated his position on these things, Paul next sets out *his policy* (1 Cor. 9:6–15). He tells *how he regarded his right to financial support* (9:6–11). First, he *declares* the right of all full-time Christian workers to be financially supported (9:6). It would be marvelous, of course, if God arranged for money to grow on trees for His servants. That would be very convenient. But that would rob His ministers, messengers, and missionaries of seeing Him work a thousand even more marvelous miracles in supplying their needs. Also it would rob the Lord's people of an opportunity to sacrifice and give and share in the ministry of the Lord's servants and of a subsequent reward in heaven.

Paul mentions the case of himself and Barnabas. "Or I only, and Barnabas, have we not power [the right] to forbear working?" he says. "Are Barnabas and I the only ones not allowed to leave our secular employment to give time to the ministry?" he demands. Although he himself sometimes voluntarily chose to be self-supporting, it was by no means mandatory that he or anyone else engaged in the Lord's work be obliged to do so. The reference to Barnabas is probably connected with their joint ministry at Antioch (Acts 11:22–26) and to their first missionary journey (13:1–14:28). It may well have been that the pair had agreed to earn their own living when funds were short in those early, pioneering days. This, however, was of necessity and out of propriety rather than the general rule.

There are advantages and disadvantages to both methods of support in the Lord's work. For a number of years I supported myself in the ministry as an accountant for a lumber company in Canada, while seeking to establish a church in what, in those days, was a remote frontier town. One advantage was that I was able to meet all kinds of people on their own level, as a fellow businessman. It provided many opportunities for making contacts and witnessing. Also, the church was in its infancy, was made up of poor people mostly, and could not afford to pay a pastor. The drawback was that a considerable amount of my time was committed to the company I worked for. Sermon preparation, visitation, supervision, and the scores of other things that needed attention had to be crowded into what time was left—sometimes my family had to suffer as a result.

For many years now I have been supported in the ministry. What a blessing that has been! I'm sure, for one thing, none of my books would ever have been written had not the Lord opened the way for me to devote many hours a day to the systematic study of His Word.

Both methods of support were appropriate in their proper time and place. And so Paul felt. Still, he declares the right of full-time workers to be financially supported by others in the exercise of their God-given call to the ministry.

Next he *discusses* the right of all full-time Christian workers to be adequately supported in the ministry. He gives three appropriate illustrations. There is, for instance, *the man who goes to fight:* "Who goeth a warfare any time at his own charges?" he demands (1 Cor. 9:7a). Nobody serves as a soldier at his own expense. Waging a war is a costly business. The soldier is called upon to make many sacrifices in his country's cause. He has to leave his family, leave his job, leave his sports and pleasures in order to suffer hardship, obey orders, and face battle, wounds, and death. He is not expected to equip himself, pay his own travel expenses, and provide his own meals and necessities as well. The full-time Christian worker who is expected to be just as *daring* as a soldier going into battle should be given no less.

There is, too, *the man who grows the fruit:* "Who planteth a vineyard, and eateth not the fruit thereof?" (9:7b). Bringing a vineyard into profitable production is a long and arduous business and one which calls for considerable expertise and skill. It calls for a capital investment of money and time. Nobody plants, prunes, and protects a vineyard out of sheer altruism and philanthropy. When the grapes ripen on the vine and the produce is merchandised, the husbandman expects to be reimbursed for his labor. The full-time Christian worker, who is expected to be just as *diligent* as a husbandman tending a vineyard, can expect no less.

There is, also, *the man who guards the flock:* "Or who feedeth a flock, and eateth not of the milk of the flock?" (9:7c). Shepherding is hard work. It calls for long hours. The sheep have to be guided to still waters and green pastures. They have to be rescued from danger and defended from their enemies. They have to be counted into the fold at night and their hurts and injuries tended with care. A good shepherd knows and loves his sheep. He endures the heat of summer and the cold of winter. He does battle with the lion and the bear, the wolf and the thief. He spends weeks away from his family. He watches over the birthing of the lambs. He goes after the ones that go astray. It would be strange, indeed, if he were to be denied the right to some of the milk. The full-time Christian worker, who is expected to be no less *devoted* than a shepherd, has an equal right to the more mundane and material things of life.

Thus Paul discusses the rights of full-time workers. Then, too, he *defends* the right of all full-time Christian workers to be adequately supported in the ministry (9:8–9). He raises a *question* and answers it with a *quotation:* "Say I these things as a man? or saith not the law the same also? For it is written in the law of Moses, Thou shalt not muzzle the mouth of the ox that treadeth out the corn. Doth God take care for oxen?" The quotation is from Deuteronomy 25:4. Yes, indeed! God does so care for the ox. He cares for all His creatures. He provides the raven with its food (Job 38:41) and attends the funeral of a sparrow (Matt. 10:29) and clothes the grass and spreads a banquet for the fowls of the air (6:26–30). It would be cruel to muzzle the ox that pulled the threshing implement through the corn. Why not let the poor beast have its fill of the corn it desired when there was plenty, enough and to spare? God does not begrudge the ox its due. Nor should we begrudge those who labor in God's harvest field the right to have their share of material blessings.

Yet it is amazing how grudging and mean-spirited some people are when it comes to the Lord's work. I remember many years ago driving up to our local church in a new car. I had only recently joined the staff of the Moody Bible Institute. The pay was very meager in those days and I and my family knew what it was like to have to pinch and scrape to make ends meet. The car I drove that Sunday morning was not a flashy car. Indeed, it was a very modest car—no power brakes, no power steering, no automatic transmission, no air-conditioning—but it was new. The car had been provided for me by a relative, but nobody knew that. As I was getting out of the car a young man came over. He looked at the new car. He looked at me. He said, "It must pay to be in the Lord's work." The jibe stung me. "Yes," I said, "it does. However, please remember, there's not one penny of your money in that car." The young man had never contributed a penny toward my support, and never did. Yet he felt he had the right to make the critical remark he did. Others have made similar comments over the years, and I have learned it's best to ignore them. Equally provoking are those who live high, wide, and handsome themselves but who expect the Lord's servants to be kept poor and to be satisfied with secondhand, worn-out cars and cast-off clothing. They would muzzle the ox that treads out the corn. The Holy Spirit wants no part of such discrimination and mean-spiritedness.

In concluding this part of his statement of policy, Paul *demonstrates* the full-time worker's right to adequate support (1 Cor. 9:10–11). He points to *the Christian worker's hope:* "Or saith he it altogether for our sakes? For our sakes, no doubt, this is written: that he that ploweth should plow in hope; and he that thresheth in hope should be partaker of his hope" (9:10). The law concerning muzzling the ox was obviously intended to have a much broader interpretation than mere consideration for the ox. Paul sees the spiritual principle behind the coded law.

He expands the thought. Both the plowman who goes to work at the beginning of the farming process, and the reaper who garners in the sheaves at harvest time, have the same stake in the outcome. Both are entitled to their just remuneration from the profits of the harvest. Their "hope" is the same. All too often the evangelist who comes along and reaps a harvest of souls in a church is lauded and glamorized and frequently given a very generous financial gift when he leaves. Everyone sees the results of his preaching. The man who comes along and plants the gospel seed in the soul of a listener or whose ministry of Bible teaching moves the unsaved listener along a little further in his understanding of the gospel is often looked upon as somewhat of a failure because nobody sees the "results" of his work. Accordingly, his honorarium is often much more modest than that of the evangelist. Paul puts both men on an equal footing. The one man plows "in hope"; the other threshes "in hope." The same expression is used, suggesting both should be equally valued and remunerated. After all, the evangelist's success largely depends on the faithful, often forgotten, plowing, planting, watering, and weeding work of others. Paul's illustration is drawn from the farming practice common to his day when all the laborers looked forward to the harvest, when each would receive his remuneration in grain, payment being in kind.

Which brings Paul to *the Christian worker's harvest:* "If we have sown unto you spiritual things, is it a great thing if we shall reap your carnal things?" The Christian worker has rich blessings to bestow. When he faithfully passes on to others blessings of a spiritual nature, it is a small thing, after all, that they should reciprocate with material benefits bestowed on him.

When Paul wrote his magnificent memo to Philemon, urging him to receive back as a brother his runaway slave Onesimus, he has many arguments. One seems to be conclusive. He acknowledges the fact that Onesimus not only ran away but, seemingly, robbed his master in the process. Paul urges Philemon to charge that to his account. "I will repay it," he says. It was only money, after all. Here was Paul's clincher: "I'm not stressing the fact," he says, "that you owe me your own soul." Looked at in that light, no understanding Christian can surely begrudge a minister or a missionary adequate financial support for his labor.

But Paul is not through. He has more to say about his policy in regard to financial support. He has shown us how he *regarded* his right to it. Now he tells us *how he resigned his right to financial support* (9:12–15).

He begins with *a personal exception* (9:12). He *restates the rule:* "If others be partakers of this power *[exousia]* over you, are not we rather?" (9:12a). He was an apostle and had been ordained an apostle by the Lord Himself. He was a missionary and his success as a missionary was evident everywhere he went. He had thrown himself into the work. He was a prophet, an evangelist, a pastor, a teacher. Both his status and his success in the ministry spoke for him. If anyone had a right to be financially supported by the Lord's people, he did. The Corinthians, especially, since they were part of his success and proof of his gifts and fruit of his unwearying labors, ought to acknowledge his claim. If anyone had a right to financial support, he did. If anyone had a right to financial fellowship from *them,* he did. He restates the rule.

But then he immediately *relinquishes the right.* He does this as a matter of *deliberate* policy: "Nevertheless we have not used this power [this right, *exousia*]"; and as a matter of *desirable* policy: "but suffer all things, lest we should hinder the gospel of Christ" (9:12b–c). He was willing to put up with all kinds of things to expedite the gospel. Nothing does more harm to the gospel than for people to get the idea that people are in it for the money. Some of our modern televangelists have given the unsaved great cause to blaspheme by their greed and by their flamboyant lifestyles and by their unblushing financial corruption. Paul would rather bend over backward to make sure nobody could ever accuse him of merchandising the gospel.

Now comes *a practical exhortation* (9:13–14). First, he states *the Old Testament principle:* "Do ye not know that they which minister about holy things live of the things of the temple? and they which wait at the altar are partakers with the altar?" (9:13); and then he states *the New Testament parallel:* "Even so hath the Lord ordained that they which preach the gospel should live of the gospel" (9:14).

Paul is referring here to the Jerusalem temple and the Levitical service. The priests were entitled to some share of the various sacrifices that were offered on the altar. Moreover, in the division of the Promised Land among the tribes, the tribe of Levi was given no territory. Instead the Levites were given cities here and there within the other tribes and the tithes and offerings of the general population were to be their portion. They ministered in holy things and administered the ritual side of the Law and were, consequently, supported by the other tribes. Numerous references to this system of support are to be noted in the Old Testament (Lev. 6:16, 26; Num. 18:8–9; Deut. 18:1–4). When the Lord sent out His disciples to announce the approaching kingdom to Israel, He told them they could look for Him to open doors for them so that their material needs would be met (Matt. 10:9–13). Similarly, when He sent out the seventy, He confirmed the same means of support (Luke 10:7). He Himself was content to live the same way, being dependent for His needs upon the generosity and gifts of others (8:1–3). The Jerusalem church, in its early days, practiced a widespread system of charitable donations for the support of the Lord's work (Acts 4:32).

Paul concludes this policy statement with *a pointed explanation* (1 Cor. 9:15). As to his *method,* it was quite *personal:* "But I have used none of these things" (9:15a). As to his *motive,* it was quite *pure:* "Neither have I written these things, that it should be so done unto me" (9:15b). He was not begging for their financial support. Far from it! "It were better for me to die," he says, "than that any man should make my glorying void." He would rather die than have his boast (of financial independence) be made an idle one!

Abraham took a similar stand. The kings of the East had come and the first battle in the Bible had been fought. Sodom and Gomorrah had fallen. Lot and his family had been taken prisoners. Abraham mobilized his men and went into action. He defeated the Eastern coalition and delivered Lot and his family. Subsequently he sat at the table of Melchizedek, the priest-king, gave his tithes and received a fresh revelation of the Lord as "The Most High God, possessor of heaven and earth" (Gen. 14:1–20). Then the king of Sodom came with his crafty proposition—"You keep the spoils; let me have the souls." Abraham answered him nobly and in the power of his fresh vision of God. "I have lift up mine hand unto the LORD, the most high God, the possessor of heaven and earth," he said, "that I will not take from a thread even to a shoelatchet, and that I will not take any thing that is thine, lest thou shouldest say, I have made Abram rich" (Gen. 14:21–23). It was a matter of principle. It was a matter of pride. It was a matter of prudence. Abraham and Paul were cut from the same piece of cloth.

Paul has had something to say about his *position* (1 Cor. 9:1–5), and about his *policy* (9:6–15). He is still dealing with his example (9:1–27) and now has something to say about his *preaching* (9:16–18). He has something to say about preaching by compulsion—*with choice* (9:16–17a): "For though I preach the gospel, I have nothing to glory of: for necessity is laid upon me, yea, woe is unto me if I preach not the gospel! For if I do this thing willingly, I have a reward." He has something to say, too, about preaching by *compulsion—without choice:* "But if against my will a dispensation of the gospel is committed unto me, what is my reward then? Verily that, when I preach the gospel, I may make the gospel of Christ without charge, that I abuse not my power in the gospel" (9:17b–18). While Paul found ground for boasting in his refusal to assert his right to financial support, he found no such ground for boasting in his determination to preach the gospel. There was no merit in his preaching the gospel. In a sense he was like Balaam. He was under a compulsion to preach the gospel.

Balaam did not want to preach a message of blessing on the children of Israel. He was under contract with the king of Moab, indeed, to do the very opposite. He was being paid to curse the people of God. Four times he tried to curse the Hebrew people and four times God forced him to bless them instead—much to the fury of Balak, king of Moab (Num. 23–24). Paul, of course, was no false and unwilling prophet like Balaam. However, he had the same overwhelming compulsion as Balaam to preach the gospel and to bless the people of God. Paul could see no particular merit or ground for boasting in that.

Paul gives voice to the compulsion that drives all true evangelists, reformers, and pioneer missionaries. "Woe is me if I preach not the gospel!" Paul was a conscript. He had been arrested on the Damascus road. He had been given a vision of the Man in the Glory. He had been sent forth as the bond slave of the ascended Lord to evangelize the great Gentile world. He had a driving force in his soul, a vision of the Lord from heaven, a realization that he dare not trifle with his call.

"Woe is me if I preach not the gospel!" The same compulsion gripped the soul of Jonah. Once he had thought he could flee his call. Now he knew better. We see him making all speed along the great north road for Nineveh, bearing in his body the stigmata, the slave brand of God. His sojourn in the whale's belly, in what he himself called "the belly of hell," had left its indelible mark upon him. We see him putting up at a wayside inn and seeking some dark corner where his fearful countenance, marred by the gastric juices of the whale, might not be seen! We see a wayfarer try to strike up a conversation.

"Hello, stranger. What's your destination?"

"Nineveh."

"Nineveh, eh? A great city! You a merchant?"

"No, I'm a preacher."

"You're surely not going to try to preach in Nineveh! Why, man, they'll flay you alive or impale you on a spike! Let me give you some advice, stranger. You'll get in trouble if you go and preach in Nineveh."

"Trouble? For preaching in Nineveh? Here, bring that candle. Look at my face! I've had trouble enough for *not* preaching in Nineveh!"

"Woe is me if I preach not the gospel!" The same compulsion gripped the soul of Ezekiel. He was told from the start what to expect. He would not be believed. He would have had a better response had God sent him to a pagan people. But, successful or not, he was to discharge his commission. Here were the terms: "Son of man, I have made thee a watchman unto the house of Israel: therefore hear the word at my mouth, and give them warning from me. When I say unto the wicked, Thou shalt surely die; and thou givest him not warning, nor speakest to warn the wicked from his wicked way, to save his life; the same wicked man shall die in his iniquity; but his blood will I require at thine hand. Yet if thou warn the wicked, and he turn not from his wickedness, nor from his wicked way, he shall die in his iniquity; but thou hast delivered thy soul" (Ezek. 3:17–21). A similar warning was given to the prophet later on (33:1–9).

Paul was heir and successor to the compulsion which motivated the prophets. We are heirs and successors of Paul. The great awakenings in church history have been heralded by men driven by the desperate need of the lost, by the greatness of the message, by the dreadful conditions of the times, by the compulsion of the Holy Spirit—"Woe is me if I preach not the gospel!" Let the world call them zealots or fanatics. Let the world threaten them with banishment or martyrdom. They must preach the gospel.

Paul took another look at his compulsion and his call. It came down to this. He *had* to preach the gospel. He could discharge it willingly, in which case he would receive a reward. He could discharge it unwillingly, but discharge it he must. He could not choose whether or not he would preach the gospel, he was under compulsion to do that, so there was no room for boasting there. His ground for boasting lay elsewhere altogether, in an area where he was not under compulsion. One such area was in the matter of financial support. Here he had a measure of freedom. He could exercise his rights. He could demand that he be supported by those to whom he ministered. That was a perfectly legitimate exercise of his will. Or, he could choose to preach the gospel free of charge. This was what he chose to do.

To Paul, it was important that, when he preached the gospel, he do so in such a way that his audience would never get the idea that, somehow or other, they must pay for it. In this he was following in the footsteps of Elisha. When Naaman was healed of his leprosy, he came back to Elisha, eager to give him a reward. He had brought with him ten talents of silver, six thousand pieces of gold, and ten changes of raiment (2 Kings 5:5), a king's ransom indeed. Elisha would take none of it. The Gentile captain must not, by any means, imagine that God's great salvation, so full, so free, could be bought. Gehazi, the prophet's servant, had other ideas. As soon as Elisha's back was turned, Gehazi ran after Naaman, told him a pack of lies, and conned him out of two talents of silver and two changes of raiment. Much good it did him. Elisha knew perfectly well what he was up to. He smote him with the leprosy of Naaman. Paul was as jealous as Elisha to make it perfectly clear to one and all that salvation is free. It cannot be bought. It is not for sale.

He turns now to *his passion* (1 Cor. 9:19–23), his passion for preaching, that is. First, he discusses *his method in preaching* (9:19–22a). We learn that when it came to preaching, Paul was indifferent to three things. He was indifferent, for instance, to a person's *social status* (9:19). A man might be of the upper class or of the underprivileged class, he might be numbered among "the free" or among slaves, it made no difference to Paul. He himself was adaptable to any stratum of society. He says, "For though I be free from all men yet have I made myself servant unto all, that I might gain the more." He has just finished telling us of his determined financial independence. Now he says that although he was no man's slave, yet, owing allegiance to no man, dependent on no man, at the same time, for the cause of Christ, he was everyone's slave.

Paul's personal social standing is one of considerable interest. He was born a Jew, of the tribe of Benjamin, and strictly raised as a Pharisee. He seems to have come from a well-to-do family. He was well educated, moved in high society in Jerusalem, and was known in ruling Jewish circles. It has been suggested that he might even have been a member of the Sanhedrin. He possessed Roman citizenship by birth, something very rare indeed. This, in itself, would place him high on the social ladder. He was at home, too, in the Greek world and could converse at ease and as an equal with the Athenian intellectuals on Mar's Hill.

At the same time, Paul was a tentmaker by trade, since every Jewish boy was required to learn a trade, and he was not ashamed, at times, to work at his trade.

Thus he could rank himself among artisans of the working class as well as among the lions of the social world. He was as much at home plying his needle in a workshop in the marketplace as he was talking to kings and governors. Moreover, he spent time in prison, for the cause of Christ, and so was at home with men from the criminal class. Indeed, on occasion, he proved his ability to exert enormous influence over such men (Acts 16:22–28). Soldiers and sailors, governors and jailers, slaves and slave owners, the rich and the famous, and the poor and the down-and-out, were all the same to Paul—people for whom Christ died. There was no social barrier he recognized. He moved with ease in all strata of society, nobody's slave, yet everybody's slave.

Moreover, a person's *spiritual status* made no difference to Paul, when it came to preaching Christ. He says, "Unto the Jew I became as a Jew" (1 Cor. 9:20a). We know that, on his missionary journeys for instance, he always went to the Jew first. If there was a synagogue in town it was where he always began. His first major arrest resulted from his earnest effort to secure Jewish goodwill for his beloved Gentile converts (Acts 21:18–33). Nor was this mere play-acting on Paul's part. He describes himself as having been, indeed, "a Hebrew of the Hebrews" (Phil. 3:5). He had been a trained rabbi, a disciple of the renowned Gamaliel, a zealous Pharisee, a Jewish fanatic. Nobody knew better than Paul the religious advantage and spiritual blindness of the Jewish people.

He could think, for instance, of the Jew and *God's commandments*. He knew by heart all 613 commandments of the Mosaic Law and in his unconverted days had made a noble, but vain, effort to keep them (Rom. 7:7–17). He knew from bitter experience that the Law could not save, it could only condemn and that, at best, it was a schoolmaster designed to bring people to Christ (Gal. 3:24).

He could think of the Jew and *God's covenants*. There were various ones, beginning with the Abrahamic covenant and proceeding on through the Mosaic and Palestinian covenants to the Davidic covenant and the promised new covenant.[5] The nation of Israel occupied a unique position among the nations, being the only nation with which God had entered into a treaty relationship. The unique and far-reaching commitments made by God to the Hebrew people gave this people a status given to no other people. They were the "Chosen People." Some of the covenants contained conditional clauses, but some of them were absolutely unconditional. The seal of the Abrahamic covenant, the foundational covenant and the greatest of them all, was circumcision. The Jews had turned this covenant seal into a religious totem, an icon, a kind of charm, and given it

---

5. See John Phillips, *Bible Explorer's Guide* (Grand Rapids: Kregel, 2002).

merit in itself. To be circumcised became the symbol of national and religious pride, and the test of whether or not a person could be in the family of God. Among the Jews the rite itself became the important thing, not that of which it was a mere symbol. Similarly in many churches baptism, infant and otherwise, has become the "open sesame" that unlocks the doors of heaven (Col. 2:11–13). The death of Christ activated the new covenant, foretold by Jeremiah, but most Jews remained stubbornly wedded to the old covenant (Jer. 31:31–34; Heb. 8:7–13). Paul saw through the fallacy of rabbinic Judaism and all that it stood for.

Paul could think, also, of the Jew and *God's commitments.* The prophets were not only the conscience of their day and age, they gave voice to many precious promises, most of them focusing on the nation of Israel. Many of these promises had to do with the great purpose of God to send His Son into the world to redeem and to reign. Well, that Son was born and the Jews rejected Him. They handed Him over to the Romans to be crucified, and then remained indifferent to His resurrection. The Sanhedrin, indeed, concocted a silly story to account for the disappearance of His body from its sealed and guarded tomb. Moreover, as the book of Acts demonstrates, the majority of the Jewish people, in the homeland and throughout the Diaspora, continued to reject Christ whenever He was preached to them.

There were many advantages to being born a Jew, but the Jews remained blind to them (Rom. 3:1–4). Indeed, Paul devotes an important section of his great Roman epistle to a discussion of the past, present, and promised situation of the Christ-rejecting Jewish people (chaps. 9–12). But with Paul, the case of the Jewish people was proof enough that a person's religious status cut no ice so far as the gospel was concerned. Religious people need to be saved as desperately as anyone else.

Then, too, a person's *secular status* made no difference to Paul when it came to preaching the gospel (1 Cor. 9:20b–22a). Take, for instance, a person's *positional* status. A person might be a *legalistic* person. Paul says of such, "To them that are under the law, [I became] as under the law, that I might gain them that are under the law" (9:20b). Or a person might be a *lawless* person. Paul says of them, "To them that are without law, as without law, (being not without law to God, but under the law to Christ,) that I might gain them that are without law" (9:21). In other words, Paul always began with a person where he found him and in the condition of soul in which that person was. He sought common ground. He did not try to force the Mosaic Law on a Gentile. He did not try to persuade a Jew to ignore God's law, only to see its glorious fulfillment in

Christ. As already stated, Paul was quite willing to circumcise Timothy (because he was already half Jew by birth and circumcising him would give him greater acceptance in the Jewish community), but he did not see any point in circumcising Titus. On the contrary, he made use of the fact that Titus was uncircumcised to put the Jerusalem church to the test (Acts 16:1–3; Gal. 2:1–3). Paul, in stating here his willingness to meet a man on his own ground, is careful to emphasize that he was never lawless himself. He had decided views as to the Mosaic Law as a system; he had equally emphatic views as to the law as a standard. He gladly set aside the system but, bound by the law of Christ, a higher and holier law indeed, it was impossible for him to consider doing anything morally or ethically wrong.

Paul related himself not only to a person's positional status, but also to his *personal* status: "To the weak became I as weak, that I might gain the weak" (1 Cor. 9:22a). The "weak" here are those with religious scruples and an overactive conscience. He has already discussed his attitude toward such (8:1–13).

Such, then, was his method in preaching the gospel. No wonder he was such a great soulwinner! He now explains *his motive in preaching* (9:22b–23). He had a twofold motive. First, he wanted *to win people to the Lord:* "I am made all things to all men, that I might by all means save some" (9:22b). Doubtless, this magnificent open-mindedness of Paul opened him up to criticism from smaller and meaner men, but Paul was not nearly so much concerned with that as he was in being like Christ and with winning the lost (Gal. 1:10). The Lord's enemies called Him "a man gluttonous, and a winebibber, a friend of publicans and sinners" (Matt. 11:19) because of His unconventional approach to sinners. Paul was content, in this too, to be like Jesus.

I was in London some years ago. A young missionary friend of mine had made arrangements with the owner of a restaurant to borrow a large upper room over the restaurant for a special meeting. It was special, all right! All the missionary's friends and colleagues were sent out on the adjacent streets to round up a congregation with the promise of free coffee and donuts as bait. By the time my friend was ready to preach, the room was full, and the service began.

My missionary friend is a man who lives by faith. He seldom has money in his pocket. He would as soon give away his watch or his wallet as keep them. His preaching is dynamic and challenging. He walks with God. After this impromptu meeting was over, the missionary mingled with the crowd. It was the height of the hippie craze when many considered it important to damn the Establishment, defy all moral and conventional codes, wear long hair and straggly beards, dress in scruffy, dirty, and outlandish clothes, indulge in every form of immorality, smoke pot, avoid washing, and herd in noisy and noisome communities. One such individual was the missionary's special target that night.

He sat down beside this fellow and engaged him in conversation. The young man scoffed at Christianity. He pointed out abusively some of the more glaring and obvious failures of the church and professing Christians. The missionary was unperturbed. He agreed that there were plenty of phonies around. He offered to prove to this young man that there was reality in Christ. He said, "I'm leaving next week for India to further the cause of Christ there. I'd like you to come along as my guest. You can come just as you are. I'll pay all your expenses. You can live with me, travel with me, eat with me. You can argue with me, listen to me, disagree with me, watch me. I'm going for three months. How about it? You say Christianity is phony. I'll prove to you it is real." The fellow decided it was time for him to leave!

"I am made all things to all men, that I might by all means save some," said Paul. That was Paul's motive—to win people to the Lord. But he had another motive: *to win praise from the Lord:* "And this I do for the gospel's sake, that I might be partaker thereof with you" (1 Cor. 9:23). The following verses make it clear that he has the judgment seat of Christ in view. He had one great goal in life, to share in the triumphs of the gospel. He knew it to be "the power of God unto salvation" (Rom. 1:16).

Paul concludes this section by stating *his purpose* (1 Cor. 9:24–27). First, he has *an illustration* (9:24–25). He sees *a contest* (9:24–25a), a crown, and a contrast. He begins with the contest: "Know ye not that they which run in a race run all, but one receiveth the prize? So run, that ye may obtain. And every man that striveth for the mastery is temperate in all things."

Just outside the city of Corinth, on the Isthmian Plain, triennial Greek games were held. These games were famous. At the time of Paul's writing they even overshadowed the Olympian games. The Corinthians were proud of these games, the chief glory of their city. Paul draws on this important athletic event for an illustration as to how we should live in view of the judgment seat of Christ.

Paul pictures a race. The word he uses is *stadion,* denoting a stadium or a racetrack. The stadium with which the Corinthians were familiar measured about 600 feet (Greek) or about an eighth of a Roman mile. Traces of the great Corinthian stadium where the games were held are still discernible on the isthmus.

"Run!" says Paul. He urges the believer to get into the race, to *try* to win, to *train* to win. Christianity is not a spectator sport—or, if it is, we are not the spectators; other eyes than ours are watching (Heb. 12:1); we are the contestants. "Run!" he says. We are all in the race, like it or not. The great thing, once in, is to win. Not all will win the prize. "Try to win!" he says. We are to give it all we have. "Train to win!" he says. "Strive for the mastery. Be temperate in all things." The expression *striveth for the mastery* is *agōnizomai,* the usual term for contending in the games. The word gives us our English word *agonize.* The expression *is temperate* is *enkrateuomai.* It refers to the exercise of self-control and self-denial. When a person enters an athletic contest he goes at once into vigorous training. He has to get his body trim, his weight under control. He has to build up his muscles, his lungs, his reflexes, his endurance. He restricts his diet. He denies himself. He starts a program of strenuous physical exercise. Can we do any less? How can we hope to win if we do not put ourselves into a disciplined program of daily preparation for usefulness to the Lord?

Paul sees not only a contest, he sees *a crown:* "Now they do it," he says, "to obtain a corruptible crown" (1 Cor. 9:25b). In the context he uses two words. The word *prize* is *brabeion,* which refers to the prize bestowed in connection with the games. The word is akin to *brabeus* (an umpire) and to *brabeuō* (*to decide, to arbitrate*). The *crown* is the *stephanos,* a chaplet made of perishable material such as wild olive, parsley, wild celery, or sometimes pine. Greek athletes would go to great lengths to win such a crown. We see the same thing even to this day, only now the Olympic Games are televised and watched by millions, and the prizes for outstanding and extraordinary feats of skill and endurance are medals.

Paul sees, too, *a contrast:* "But we [do it to obtain] an incorruptible [crown]" (9:25c). His eye is on that coming day when the Lord will reward those who have been overcomers in the race down here. A forgotten poet has captured the idea. He says,

> Proud were the mighty conquerors
> Crowned in Olympic games;
> They thought that deathless honors
> Were entwined about their names.
> But dead was soon the parsley leaf,
> The olive and the bay;
> But Christian's crown of amaranth
> Shall never fade away.

Having given us his illustration, Paul closes with *an application* (9:26–27). He returns to himself and his own goals and ambitions.

We are to note *Paul's drive.* He is in *the race!* He is in *the ring!* He is in to win. He says, "I therefore so run, not as uncertainly; so fight I, not as one that beateth the air" (9:26). The word for *uncertainly* is *adēlōs.* It occurs only here. It means that Paul was in the arena with a clear understanding of the conditions and the object in view. He knows what he is up against. He is determined to be a winner. He makes no apology for his desire to win the prize. Many Christians do not seem to have this understanding. They take a casual, indifferent, lackadaisical attitude toward the Christian life. They are easily distracted. A shower of rain is all it takes to keep them home. A cottage at the beach can occupy their whole summer. A concert, Jimmy's ballgame, the chance for a free game of golf is all it takes to divert them from the things that really count. They are not in the race to win. All they are doing is playing games.

Paul was in the race to win. He was also in the ring to win. "So fight I," he says. The word he uses is *pykteuō.* It, too, occurs only here. It means to fight with the fist, that is, to box. It was a serious matter, in Paul's day, to get into the ring. Instead of being covered with a padded boxing glove, the hand was covered with the *cestus.* This consisted of leather bands studded with pieces of metal. It could inflict terrible punishment.

Paul was in the ring. He had no intention of "beating the air." This was called *skiamachia,* "shadow boxing." No, indeed! Paul was up against a diabolical and determined enemy, one who would do all in his power to deliver a knockout blow. Paul was determined to get his punches in first and deliver them with skill and power.

Finally, we have *Paul's dread* (9:27). There was a possibility he *systematically fought:* "But I keep under my body, and bring it into subjection" (9:27a). For much of our temptation comes by way of the body. Paul uses two expressions here. The expression *keep my body under* comes from *hypōpiazō,* which means "to strike beneath the eye, or to give himself a black eye." The expression *bring it into subjection* comes from the word *doulagōgeō,* which means "to reduce it to slavery." Paul is not advocating the medieval practice of self-flagellation. He is using figurative language and illustrating the need for constant moral and physical discipline. The possibility he systematically fought was the possibility of his body getting the upper hand.

Then, too, there was a possibility he *squarely faced:* "Lest that by any means, when I have preached to others, I myself should be a castaway" (9:27b). The word for *castaway* is *adokimos,* meaning "to be disapproved or rejected for the prize." Paul was horrified at the thought that, having told others the laws of the contest, he should himself violate them and be ignominiously rejected by the Judge.

    3. Paul's explanation (10:1–11:1)
      a. The type (10:1–14)
        (1) The approach (10:1–5)
          (a) Shared experiences ("all") (10:1–4)
            i. Salvation: under the cloud (10:1a)
            ii. Separation: through the sea (10:1b–2)
              a. A permanent break with Egypt (10:1b)
              b. A pictorial baptism unto Moses (10:2)
            iii. Satisfaction: around the table (10:3–4)
              a. Sustained with bread from the highest heaven (10:3)
              b. Satisfied with water from the riven rock (10:4)
                1. The mention of the spiritual rock (10:4a)
                2. The meaning of the spiritual rock (10:4b)
          (b) Shattered expectations (10:5)
            i. The outrage of many (10:5a)
            ii. The overthrow of many (10:5b)
        (2) The application (10:6–10)
          (a) A warning against wicked wants (10:6)
            i. In the past (10:6a)
            ii. In the present (10:6b)
          (b) A warning against wicked worship (10:7)
            i. The false objects of their worship (10:7a)
            ii. The foolish outcome of their worship (10:7b)
          (c) A warning against wicked works (10:8)
            i. Their immoral passions (10:8a)
            ii. Their immediate punishment (10:8b)
          (d) A warning against wicked ways (10:9)
            i. Their provocation of God (10:9a)
            ii. Their punishment by God (10:9b)
          (e) A warning against wicked words (10:10)
            i. Their discontent (10:10a)

Paul is still dealing with *difficulties in the church* (1 Cor. 7:11–14:40) and especially with matters concerning *our personal walk* (7:1–11:1) He has set before the Corinthians *his exhortation* (7:1–8:13) regarding matters relating to *marriage* (7:1–40) and *meat* (8:1–13), and he has set before them *his example* (9:1–27). The letter now moves on to *Paul's explanation* (10:1–11:1), and the discussion revolves around three basic areas. He deals with *the type* (10:1–14), with *the table* (10:15–22), and with *the tests* (10:23–11:1). Here we are concerned with the type.

We begin with *the approach* (10:1–5). Paul is about to revert to his discussion regarding meats and conscience, but first he prepares the ground some more. He goes back to the Old Testament and seizes on one of its great illustrative passages to press home his point.

The typology of the Old Testament is rich and varied. "Types" are simply divinely planned and recorded illustrations. They can be connected with persons (such as Melchizedek, Joseph, and David), with objects (such as the tabernacle and the temple), with rituals (such as the offerings and the feasts), with things (such as the ark of Noah, the burning bush, the serpent on the pole, and Aaron's garments), and with events (such as the redemption of Ruth, the healing of Naaman, and the history of David). Indeed, much of the historical section of the Old Testament can be viewed typologically. Some say that the only legitimate types are those which are used as such in the New Testament. This view is obviously too narrow. Joseph is an outstanding type of Christ but is never so depicted in the New Testament. The ones which are discussed in the New Testament are samples. They are samples, however, of a whole species. Properly understood, Old Testament types are as accurate as mathematics. They are, indeed, a form of prophecy. Apart from typology some parts of the Old Testament would be virtually unintelligible, if not wholly irrelevant, to us today. This is true of Old Testament passages that deal with the tabernacle, the offerings, the ritual of the Levitical priesthood, and both Solomon's and Ezekiel's temples. Once the typological significance of these and similar subjects is grasped, then the passages leap to life and point us directly to Christ.

Paul begins with some *shared experiences* (10:1–4). This passage comes into focus when we look at these verses in their entirety and note the constant repetition of the little word *all*—"*all* our fathers," "*all* baptized," "did *all* eat," "did *all* drink." These were experiences common to the whole Hebrew community as well as to "the mixed multitude" which shared in those things that accompanied the salvation of the Old Testament people of God. We have the same inclusive and comprehensive *all* used later by Paul in this letter to describe something very similar: "For by one Spirit are we *all* baptized into one body, whether we be Jews or Gentiles, whether we be bond or free; and have been all made to drink into one Spirit" (12:13). The connection is too obvious and exact to have been accidental. So much, then, for those who would reserve the baptism of the Spirit to a special, privileged class in the church. All believers share in some of the things which are common to the saving experience. This *all* stands in contrast with the *many* and the four-times-repeated *some* of verses 5–10.

Paul, in developing the Old Testament type, details some of these shared experiences. First, there were those events which speak of *salvation:* "Moreover, brethren, I would not that ye should be ignorant, how that all our fathers were under the cloud" (10:1a). The incidents to which Paul refers in verses 1–14 are detailed in Exodus 13–17 and Numbers 10–15. The apostle picks up the story at the point at which the "mixed multitude" which accompanied the Hebrews out of Egypt became part of this great salvation movement.

The mixed multitude evidently had some measure of faith (and it does not take much faith to be saved) and were tired of the oppression of Pharaoh. They saw an opportunity to escape from bondage and they took advantage of that "so great salvation," which was being offered to the Hebrew people. They, like the Hebrews, set out for the Promised Land and were baptized unto Moses. However, they were not the ones to whom the message was first preached. They must have been aware of all the things which had preceded the actual baptism. That some of the common people in Egypt responded at a relatively early stage to the salvation process is expressly stated in connection with the seventh plague (Exod. 9:20–21). After the eighth plague, even some highly placed Egyptians saw the hand of God in what was happening (10:7). It is not unlikely that some, when they saw the Hebrews sheltering behind the blood, did the same. In any case, multitudes threw in their lot with the Hebrews, once the truth of salvation through the shed blood of the lamb became common knowledge on the morning after the Passover. When the Gentiles saw what God had done for Israel, many decided to make a decision for Moses and for the Hebrews' God.

This mixed multitude, at the beginning at least, was imperfectly taught but God graciously allowed them to join His blood-bought people in this great salvation movement. He put them "under the cloud" as well as the Hebrews themselves. In a way they were like Lot, who had a secondhand faith and whose behavior was terribly suspect (Gen. 12:5; 13:5–13; 14:10–16; 19:1–38) but who was declared righteous by the Holy Spirit (2 Peter 2:6–9).

The heart of God is most wonderfully kind and He reaches out to all classes and conditions of men. He evidently is much more willing to accept those who can exhibit the merest token of faith than some people are prepared to give Him credit for. The "mixed multitude" were doubtless a source of disturbance in the camp from time to time (Exod. 12:38; Num. 11:4), but God did not forbid them to come nor did He deny them the experience of being baptized unto Moses in the cloud. We have a similar "mixed multitude" in the church. They profess to be saved. They doubtless have a share in some of the great universals of salvation. They keep company with others of bolder and more enlightened faith. Yet they are carnal and worldly and often a source of trouble in the local church. They never seem to grow in grace or increase in the knowledge of God. It is hard to say if they are saved or not. Before we are too hard on them, we would do well to remember our own shortcomings and to recall that in the type now being developed for us by Paul, true-blooded Hebrews with much more truth in their backgrounds lusted, murmured, rebelled, and died short of Canaan just as did the mixed multitude.

There were three movements in the salvation experience recorded in the book of Exodus. First, God put His people under the blood. They had to learn that the mighty miracles of Moses could not save them. They only made Pharaoh (a type of Satan) more determined than ever to keep God's chosen people enslaved in Egypt (universally, when used as a type in Scripture, a type of the world). It was not until the blood of the Passover lamb was shed that salvation was possible.

Then the blood could be applied and protection made available from the judgment of God.

Then the people were brought through the water. The people took a step of faith, and salvation was followed by separation. Paul sees this experience of crossing the Red Sea as a kind of baptism. The baptism did not save—it was the blood that saved. Our understanding of that may vary as much as did the understanding of the Hebrews themselves. They evidently had a more robust understanding of the blood and its power to save than did the mixed multitude, whose comprehension at best was limited. Even at that, the understanding of the Hebrews was dim. Few, if any, could see Calvary in it, for instance, as we can now. But, be their understanding great or small, it was the blood that saved. As the people, one and all, moved forward, they were all put under the cloud. Paul mentions the "fathers" since they, presumably, would have a more mature understanding of the significance of the great events in which all were now sharing.

Then God gathered His people around the table in the wilderness so that they might feast, as it were, on Christ and grow up to be mature believers, able to take on the giants of Canaan.

This, then, is the background. Paul begins with the "fathers" all being placed "under the cloud." The cloud is evidently the *shekinah* glory cloud. The word *Shekinah* was coined by the rabbis. It means "that which dwells." It is described by Moses as "a pillar of cloud, to lead them the way; and by night a pillar of fire, to give them light; to go by day and night. He took not away the pillar of the cloud by day, nor the pillar of fire by night, from before the people" (Exod. 13:21–22). The living God was present in the *shekinah* glory cloud. Its normal place, when Israel was on the march, was in front to lead and direct. It is often pictured as a pillar ascending toward the sky and spreading out, like a vast umbrella, in protection over all of God's people. The psalmist seems to have had this in mind when he said: "The Lord is thy keeper: the Lord is thy shade upon thy right hand. The sun shall not smite thee by day, nor the moon by night" (Ps. 121:5–6). When the camp was halted the *shekinah* came to rest upon the mercy seat, between the cherubim, upon the ark in the Holy of Holies in the tabernacle, and later in the temple (Exod. 40:34–38). When Pharaoh changed his mind about letting his captives go, and mobilized his cavalry to bring them back, the *shekinah* simply moved its position from the front to the rear of the camp to hold the Egyptian army at bay (14:19). Thus God took the newly saved people, made them His own, flung the mantle of His protection over them, and led them on to the Red Sea. Such is salvation! It is all of grace and all of God. He will accept even the feeblest and most faltering faith.

Salvation was followed by *separation.* There was to be *a permanent break with Egypt:* "And all passed through the sea" (1 Cor. 10:1b). Once the saved people were over on the other side of the Red Sea, the Egyptian threat was at an end, for the Egyptian army was destroyed by the returning waters. Then it was that the redeemed people raised their voices in song—in the first song in Scripture, indeed (Exod. 15), for only a saved people can really sing. There were no songs in Egypt, only slavery, sadness, and sorrow. The water of the Red Sea now flowed between Israel and Egypt. There was to be no going back to the old way of life. The people had come through the Old Testament equivalent of water baptism, a typological experience of death, burial, and resurrection. A new life stretched before them, to be lived on different principles. Faith, hope, and love were to be their portion as they journeyed on toward the Promised Land.

There was also to be *a pictorial baptism unto Moses:* "And were all baptized unto Moses in the cloud and in the sea" (1 Cor. 10:2). Paul lifts the type from mere water baptism to much higher ground—to our baptism into Christ, of whom Moses was a type. The children of Israel doubtless had little apprehension of these deeper and more mystical aspects of their experience. Paul, guided by the Holy Spirit, clothes it in magnificence. There was a sense in which the newly redeemed people were now united with Moses in a new and living way. He was their head, they were his people. They were to be one with him. Paul does not develop the concept of Spirit baptism into Christ here. But he will develop it later (12:13), as we have already noted. The believer today is mystically united with Christ by the baptizing work of the Holy Spirit. He is the believer's head; the believer is a member of His body. The union is both perfect and permanent. There can be no going back to the world and to the old way of life. Our water baptism speaks of our union with Christ, in death, burial, and resurrection, which makes such a return impossible. We have died with Christ to all that we were by natural birth. We have been buried with Him and we have been raised with Him to walk in newness of life. Our water baptism is thus an outward expression of our inward experience. These things happened typically to those who were baptized unto Moses and truly to us who are baptized into Christ.

Salvation and separation were to be followed by *satisfaction* (10:3–5). The believer was to be *sustained by bread from the highest heaven:* "And did all eat the same spiritual meat" (10:13). The various wilderness experiences of Israel were all divinely planned. What happened to Israel in the *wilderness* illustrates what happens to us in the *world.* The wilderness was a hostile environment for Israel;

this world is a hostile environment for us. Israel was to be taught how to make their way through that hostile environment as they walked by faith and not by sight. They experienced God's tender loving care each step of the way. The things which happened to them physically happen to us spiritually.

The Exodus began on the fifteenth day of the first month. Manna was provided a month later. On the fifteenth day of the second month, the people complained bitterly because they were hungry. Already they were glamorizing their old way of life in Egypt. Forgotten already were the blows, the slavery, the constant fear of death. They said to Moses, "Would to God we had died by the hand of the LORD in the land of Egypt, when we sat by the flesh pots, and when we did eat bread to the full; for ye have brought us forth into this wilderness, to kill this whole assembly with hunger" (Exod. 16:3).

God's answer was one of grace: "Behold, I will rain bread from heaven for you; and the people shall go out and gather a certain rate every day, that I may prove them, whether they will walk in my law, or no" (16:4). Thus came the manna. The psalmist says that God gave them "the corn of heaven. Man did eat angels' food" (Ps. 78:24–25). This was not "the drops of the tarfu or tamarisk tree," as the liberals claim. This was food supernaturally rained down from heaven. Paul calls it "spiritual meat." The Lord Jesus told the Jews that He was the true bread from heaven (John 6:47–52). The wilderness was unable to furnish a table for God's Old Testament people. Their needs had to be supernaturally and daily supplied from heaven. All they had to do was gather enough for each day's need. Similarly this world can provide nothing which will nourish the reborn soul of the child of God. We must feast upon the Word of God, the inspired Word (the Bible) and the incarnate Word (Christ), and on the spiritual food supernaturally supplied to us from heaven. Our responsibility is to gather our daily portion that we may grow in grace and increase in the knowledge of God. We cannot nourish the inner "spiritual man" with man-made books and magazines. We must feast upon Christ in His Word.

Then, too, the believer was to be *satisfied with water from the riven rock* (1 Cor. 10:4–5). Paul says, "And did all drink of the same spiritual drink: for they drank of that spiritual Rock that followed them: and that Rock was Christ." Some have made heavy going of that, trying to imagine the Rock following the Hebrew people from place to place on their wilderness journey! The meaning is very simple. The incident of the riven rock followed the other incidents experienced by Israel and here mentioned by Paul.

In time the people came to Rephidim, and there was no water for the people to drink. Again they turned bitterly on Moses, even threatening to stone him. God told Moses to go on ahead with some of the elders of Israel until he came to "the rock in Horeb." He was to smite the rock "and there shall come water out of it, that the people may drink." He did as he was told, and water came gushing out of the smitten rock (Exod. 17:1–7). Again, all this pointed forward to Christ, and illustrates Calvary.

The rock was evidently a type of Christ. Not only does Paul say so but it is frequently and variously referred to thus in the Old Testament (Deut. 32:4, 15, 18, 31, 37; 1 Sam. 2:2; Ps. 62:2, 6). We read of the rock of life (Deut. 32:18), of salvation (2 Sam. 22:47), of refuge (Pss. 27:5; 62:6–7), of rest and of refreshment (Isa. 32:2). The Lord Jesus Himself claimed to be the Rock (Matt. 16:18), and Peter understood this to be so (1 Peter 1:7–8).

The type was fulfilled when Christ, the "Rock of Ages," was smitten at Calvary. On the day of Pentecost the river flowed from that Rock when the Holy Spirit came in all His abundant fullness to satisfy our thirsty souls.

Now all these were *shared experiences* by the children of Israel and those who accompanied them, in the days of Moses. Paul turns abruptly to the *shattered expectations:* "But with many of them God was not well pleased: for they were overthrown in the wilderness" (1 Cor. 10:5). Not all those who left Egypt entered Canaan. Canaan does not typify heaven, the eternal home of the blessed. It typifies what Paul calls "the heavenlies." He develops the theme in his letter to the Ephesians. It is the place where all our blessings are (Eph. 1:3), and where most of our battles are (6:12). We are seated there in Christ in victory and power (1:20–23). The tragedy is that many who trust the Lord to get them out of Egypt never trust Him to get them into Canaan. They never cross Jordan and live in victory in the heavenlies. The theme is developed at some considerable length in the second warning passage in Hebrews (4:7–5:13). The warning is that it is possible to have a saved soul and a lost life. It is possible to live a defeated Christian life in the world and to miss all the good things God has for us in Christ.

Now comes *the application* (1 Cor. 10:6–10). It contains ten warnings, based on what happened to the Hebrews in the wilderness, addressed to believers in general in this age of grace, and to the Corinthians in particular. There is a warning against *wicked wants:* "Now these things were our examples, to the intent we should not lust after evil things, as they also lusted" (10:6). The word for *examples* is *typos* and is the same word as *examples* (10:11). The word is transliterated into our word "types." The first time the word is used in the New Testament is in connection with the unbelief of Thomas. He said, "Except I shall see in his hand the print *[typos]* of the nails . . . I will not believe" (John 20:25). A type is not something we imagine. It is something substantial and real.

The word for *lust after* is *epithymētēs*. The root word is often connected with evil desire. The lusting to which Paul refers is recorded by Moses. It was part of a pattern of bad behavior on the part of the people and one which God judged: "The mixed multitude that was among them fell a lusting: and the children of Israel also wept again and said, Who shall give us flesh to eat? We remember the fish, which we did eat in Egypt freely; the cucumbers, and the melons, and the leeks, and the onions, and the garlick; but now our soul is dried away: there is nothing at all, beside this manna, before our eyes" (Num. 11:4–6). It was utter carnality to speak disparagingly of the manna and yearn after the food given to them by their oppressors in Egypt. It revealed a serious backslidden condition. They actually longed after the old way of life, and that which sustained it. They spoke disparagingly of the "angels' food," the bread from heaven, so graciously given by God. They craved the "good things," so to speak, of the old way of life. Moses followed up his account of this lusting by an interesting description of the manna itself (11:7–9). He adds that "the anger of the LORD was kindled greatly" (11:10). "Say thou unto the people," he said, "Sanctify yourselves against to morrow, and ye shall eat flesh: for ye have wept in the ears of the LORD, saying, Who shall give us flesh to eat? for it was well with us in Egypt: therefore the LORD will give you flesh, and ye shall eat. Ye shall not eat one day, nor two days, nor five days, neither ten days, nor twenty days; but even a whole month, until it come out of your nostrils, and it be loathsome unto you" (11:18–20).

That in itself should have taught them a lesson. Our bodies are not made to live for long on a straight meat diet. They soon begin to crave farinaceous food. Without greens, scurvy develops. But that was not all. The Lord sent the quails in enormous flocks. The people ran about gathering this unexpected windfall in great quantities. Their terrible criticism of the manna, their harking back to the old life before their redemption, soon brought even more drastic results: "And while the flesh was yet between their teeth," Moses says, "ere it was chewed, the wrath of the LORD was kindled against the people, and the LORD smote the people with a very great plague. And he called the name of that place Kibroth-hattaavah: because there they buried the people that lusted" (Num. 11:33–35). The name means "graves of lust." The psalmist's comment on this is instructive, too. He said that God "gave them their request: but sent leanness into their soul" (Ps. 106:15).

Paul is building here onto the foundation he laid earlier in this Corinthian letter—regarding making the eating of meat such an issue in their lives and in their assembly.

Now comes the second warning. It has to do with *wicked worship:* "Neither be ye idolaters, as were some of them; as it is written, The people sat down to eat and drink, and rose up to play" (1 Cor. 10:7). The word for "play" is *paizō*. It occurs only here in the New Testament. It means "to play as a child." It also refers to dancing and making merry. The word is kin to *empaizō*, used almost entirely in the New Testament for mocking Christ. It is only a short step, indeed, from idolatry to mocking Christ and using His blessed name as a curse word.

The incident to which Paul refers here took place when Moses was on Mount Sinai receiving the tables of the Law (Exod. 32:6). The people arrived at Sinai in the third month from their departure from Egypt. Their stay at Sinai was prolonged. Indeed, in the course of the making of the Mosaic covenant and the attendant giving of the Law, Moses ascended and descended Mount Sinai no less than seven times. The incident to which Paul refers took place during Moses' fifth ascent (24:9–32). The Ten Commandments had already been given. The death sentence had already been pronounced on a number of sins, including sacrificing "unto any god, save unto the LORD only" (22:20). The details concerning the making of the tabernacle were now being given to Moses. He was gone this time for a prolonged period.

Down in the valley, the people grew impatient. They mobbed Aaron, Moses' brother and Israel's high priest. "Up, make us gods, which shall go before us," they said, "for as for this Moses, the man that brought us up out of the land of Egypt, we wot not what is become of him" (Exod. 32:1). Aaron, cowed by the people, told them to collect the golden earrings from the people and bring them to him. From these, he made a golden calf.

While in Egypt, the people could not help but observe the gross idolatry of the country. The Egyptians worshiped cats and crocodiles, bats and beetles, frogs and falcons. All sorts of creatures were objects of adoration, not least of which was the sacred bull, which was supposed to be the incarnation of the god Apis, just as Pharaoh was supposed to be the incarnation of Ra, the sun god. When the bull, which was imagined to be the embodiment of Apis, died, it was embalmed, placed in a worthy sarcophagus, and entombed in the city of Serapium. Evidently it was this false Egyptian god Aaron had in mind when he made the golden calf. Adding insult to injury, the people spoke of the calf in the plural of majesty, saying, "These be thy gods, O Israel, which brought thee up out of the land of Egypt" (Exod. 32:4). Carried away now by the prevailing fervor, Aaron built an altar and proclaimed, "Tomorrow is a feast to the LORD," thus identifying Jehovah, the living God, with the wretched idol he had just made with his own hands. The next day the people sacrificed burnt offerings and peace offerings to the idol and, as quoted by Paul, "the people sat down to eat and to drink, and rose up to play" (32:6). It is evident (32:19) that this "play" included dancing, doubtless the lascivious kind of dancing common to much idolatry.

Still on the mount, Moses knew nothing of all this, but God did. Had it not been for the intercession of Moses, the guilty people would have been wiped out then and there (32:7–14). Moses, accompanied by Joshua, who had evidently been waiting for him on the mountain, hastened down the mountain. Then they heard a sound coming up from below. "When Joshua heard the noise of the people, as they shouted, he said unto Moses, There is a noise of war in the camp. And he said, It is not the voice of them that shout for mastery, neither is it the voice of them that cry for being overcome: but the noise of them that sing do I hear" (32:17–18). What a comment on the music of the world! Noise! The noise of war! This is the second mention of singing in the Bible, and it is set in glaring contrast with the first mention of singing, the singing of a newly redeemed people (chap. 15). Joshua first identified the "noise" with war. The translators of the King James Bible seem to have been almost inspired in rendering the Hebrew word for " sing" here as "shout," "cry," and "sing." It is certainly an apt description of much that passes for music and singing in today's world. This kind of din is identified here with rebellion against the Establishment, as represented by Moses, and as part of a revolt against God by His own, redeemed people.

The sequel came quickly: "And it came to pass, as soon as he came nigh unto the camp, that he [Moses] saw the calf, and the dancing: and Moses' anger waxed hot, and he cast the tables out of his hands, and brake them beneath the mount. And he took the calf which they had made, and burnt it in the fire, and ground it to powder, and strawed it upon the water, and made the children of Israel drink of it" (32:19–20). Almost as a footnote, it is added that "Moses saw that the people were naked." Such is idolatry.

Judgment was not long delayed. Moses took his stand in the gate of the camp and said, "Who is on the LORD's side?" (32:26). It was at this point that the tribe of Levi responded and redeemed the blot upon the tribal history (Gen. 35:22; 49:3–4), and, furthermore, earned the right to become the consecrated tribe. Armed, and under divine warrant, the Levites executed about three thousand guilty men that day (Exod. 32:28).

The Corinthians, many of whom came from pagan backgrounds, are thus warned by Paul of the sinfulness and seriousness of any lapse into idolatry. It would be a good policy for them to stay away altogether from pagan temples, feasts or no feasts.

The third warning was against *wicked works:* "Neither let us commit fornication, as some of them committed, and fell in one day three and twenty thousand" (1 Cor. 10:8). This incident occurred over thirty years after the incident of the golden calf. A new generation had grown up, and many of those who had originally gone out of Egypt were already dead. The march toward the Promised Land had been resumed, but the new generation had to learn for itself the painful lessons taught to their parents years before.

The Hebrews, who had already tasted victory, now arrived at the borders of Moab. The king of Moab resorted to guile. He hired Balaam, a Mesopotamian psychic, to come and curse the people of God, promising him a handsome reward. Balaam made four attempts to earn his wages, but each time God turned the curse into a blessing. The enraged king of Moab was beside himself. It was then that Balaam made that wicked suggestion of his, so frequently denounced in the Bible. It became known as "the doctrine of Balaam." "My lord, King," he said, "since you cannot curse them, why not corrupt them? You cannot overcome them with the men of Moab, so why not try the women?" Balaam had learned enough about God to know that, if Israel were to become corrupted, God would judge them.

Balak, king of Moab, followed Balaam's wicked advice, and we read, "the people began to commit whoredom with the daughters of Moab. And they called the people unto the sacrifices of their gods: and the people did eat, and bow down to their gods. And Israel joined himself unto Baal-peor" (Num. 25:1–3). The name *Baal* meant "Lord." Peor was the name of the mountain on which he was worshiped. The worship of Baal was accompanied by acts of immorality. Probably the women who seduced the Israelites were the consecrated prostitutes who were kept in the service of this foul religion.

Judgment fell swiftly. The judges of Israel were commissioned by Moses to slay all those involved in this affair. The "heads of the people," that is, the leaders, were taken and publicly hanged (25:4). There was also a plague which broke out that caused an even greater number of deaths. "Those that died in the plague were twenty and four thousand," Moses says (25:9). Some discrepancy is imagined between this figure and the figure of "three and twenty thousand" mentioned by Paul. The full figure is given by Moses. This figure included the ringleaders who were hanged before the plague broke out. He does not give their number, but evidently it totaled a thousand men. The twenty-three thousand were those who "fell in one day" in the subsequent plague.

The fourth warning was against *wicked ways:* "Neither let us tempt Christ, as some of them also tempted, and were destroyed of serpents" (1 Cor. 10:9). This incident took place shortly before the matter of the Moabites. The people had recently won a resounding victory over Arad the Canaanite in the Negeb. Instead of being elated because the wilderness wanderings were over and the tribes were now proceeding slowly but surely toward the Promised Land, we read that "the soul of the people was much discouraged because of the way. And the people spoke against God and against Moses, Wherefore have ye brought us up out of Egypt to die in the wilderness? for there is no bread, neither is there any water; and our soul loatheth this light bread" (Num. 21:4–5). This sounds like the surviving remnant of the old generation which had come out of Egypt. The same old complaints and caustic remarks are aired again, the same wicked criticism of the manna, the same harsh words about lack of water. On the previous occasion, God had acted in grace, but this time there was swift and unannounced judgment: "And the Lord sent fiery serpents among the people, and they bit the people; and much people of Israel died" (21:6).

Paul's comment is that they "tempted Christ." The word he used was *ekpeirazō*, an intensive form of the word for "tempt." It means to put someone thoroughly to the test. It was what Satan tempted Christ to do when he urged Him to cast Himself down from the pinnacle of the temple so that He could test the truth of God's promise in Psalm 91:11–12. The Lord, in answer, quoted Deuteronomy 6:16, which says, "Ye shall not tempt the Lord your God, as ye tempted him in Massah." The reference is to Exodus 17:2–7 and to the first bitter complaint of the people that there was no water to drink.

It is a sin to try God's patience, to put His grace to the test, to see how far we can go, to see if He means what He says. It is folly to trade on His kindness and forbearance. At least this time, when bitten by the fiery serpents, the people, on their own initiative, "came to Moses, and said, We have sinned, for we have spoken against the Lord, and against thee; pray unto the Lord, that he take away the serpents from us" (Num. 21:7). The cure was unusual but appropriate. Moses was told to make a serpent of brass and fasten it to a pole where it could be plainly visible. "Every one that is bitten," the Lord said, "when he looketh upon it, shall live" (21:8). The Lord Jesus Himself recognized the type and used it as an illustration of His own crucifixion when preaching the gospel to Nicodemus (John 3:14–16).

The Corinthians, in their carnality and pride, in their abuse of gift and grace, in their divisions and tolerance of immorality, in their quarrels and attacks upon the leadership of Paul, who was a veritable Moses to them, in their lawsuits and in their abuse of the Lord's Table and in their intellectualism and compromise with idolatry, were on the same path as the Israelites of old.

The final warning is against *wicked words:* "Neither murmur ye, as some of them also murmured, and were destroyed of the destroyer" (1 Cor. 10:10). The word for *murmur* is "to mutter, to say things in a low tone." The word *gonguzō* gives us our English word "song." The word for *destroyed* is *olothreutēs,* which occurs here only, although the verb is used of the destroying angel who slew all Egypt's firstborn sons (Heb. 11:28). All murmuring has its root in unbelief and expresses itself as a denial of the goodness and mercy of God.

The grumbling of the children of Israel began at once, even before they had shaken the dust of Egypt off their feet. When they saw the Egyptian cavalry bearing down upon them and the waters of the Red Sea before them, they turned on Moses: "Because there were no graves in Egypt, hast thou taken us away to die in the wilderness? Wherefore hast thou dealt thus with us, to carry us forth out of Egypt?" (Exod. 14:11). They murmured when they reached Marah and found bitter water there (15:24); when they were in the wilderness of Sin because they were hungry (16:2); when they came to Rephidim and found no water at all (17:3). They murmured against the manna and cried for flesh to eat (Num. 11:4). They murmured when the ten spies told that the Promised Land was inhabited by giants (14:2). They decided to go back to Egypt. This was the most serious and crucial of all their murmurings, for God, at this point, locked the door to the Promised Land against them for a whole generation. Korah, Dathan, and Abiram and a large number of princes of the tribe of Reuben criticized the leadership of Moses and the priesthood of Aaron (16:1–3). All the congregation murmured against Moses and Aaron when Korah, Dathan, and Abiram were spectacularly swallowed up in an earthquake (16:41). They murmured again when they found no water at Kadesh (20:2–5). They murmured because they were hungry and tired of the manna on their way around Edom (21:4–5). It seems they did little else but grumble and complain all the way from Egypt to Canaan.

And the destroyer marched on their heels. With the sole exception of Joshua and Caleb, every single man and woman over twenty years of age was condemned to death in the wilderness, in answer to their own prayer when they criticized the Promised Land of Canaan (Num. 14:2–32). Thereafter, the wilderness way became the wilderness wanderings as, for forty years, they went from place to place, leaving their bones scattered along the whole sad trail.

And that was what Paul was up against with the Corinthians, grumbling, complaining, and criticizing.

But now the application of divine truth is succeeded by *the appeal* (1 Cor. 10:11–14). First, *truth is discussed:* "Now all these things happened unto them for ensamples: and they are written for our admonition, upon whom the ends of the world are come. Wherefore let him that thinketh he standeth take heed lest he fall" (10:11–12). In writing up the history of the Old Testament people of God the Holy Spirit left much unsaid. What He did include had the double purpose of recording key incidents and of teaching timeless principles.

God's dealings with people in Old Testament times passed through various phases, often referred to as dispensations. He used different methods with the human race at different times and entered into various covenant relationships with men and nations. The Old Testament ages passed through the age of innocence in the Garden of Eden before the Fall, the age of conscience from Adam to the Flood, the age of human government from Noah to Abraham, the age of promise from Abraham to Moses, and the age of law from Moses to the time of Christ. All these ages have climaxed in the present age of Grace. It is upon us that "the end of the ages are come." When our age is over, events will move rapidly to a final fulfillment of all that was anticipated in the Old Testament. In the meantime, the experiences of the Hebrew people afford valuable lessons for us.

Paul chose his examples with care. A distinct moral order can be discerned in the five stages of misbehavior he cites from the wilderness experiences of Israel. They were all downward. They mark stages in the life of the backslider. The first observable trait of backsliding is a distaste for the Bible (the heavenly manna) and a craving for the spicier fare of the world. Next, Christ is replaced by some kind of worldly religion, one which has about it the elements of idolatry. Immorality in some form or other usually follows, not just spiritual adultery, but some kind of moral sin. These downward steps lead to skepticism and to some form of tempting God. The final stage is reached when the resolve is made to go back to the world completely. Such behavior brings the certain displeasure and judgment of God.

The process is very subtle and the downward slope very slippery. Hence Paul warns the Corinthians, "Wherefore let him that thinketh he standeth take heed lest he fall." The word for *take heed* is *blepō*—"Look to it!" or "Beware!" The word suggests more than ordinary caution. It is when we are most sure of ourselves that we are most likely to fall. Thus Peter boasted, in his self assurance, "Though all men shall be offended because of thee, yet will I never be offended."

The Lord told him that before the cock crowed, he would deny Him three times. Peter boasted again, "Though I should die with thee, yet will not I deny thee" (Matt. 26:33–35). Little did Peter know that Satan desired to have him and that the Lord had had to pray especially for him that his faith fail not (Luke 22:31–32). Within hours Peter had denied the Lord with oaths and curses. The best of us, when all is said and done, are like poor Mephibosheth, who was "lame on both his feet" (2 Sam. 9:13).

Next, *temptation is discussed* (1 Cor. 10:13–14). First, Paul talks about *sporadic temptation* (10:13), the kind of temptation we encounter all the time. He tells us *how to evaluate temptation* (10:13a–b). In the first place it is *common to man:* "There hath no temptation taken you but such as is common to man" (10:13a), a fact he has amply illustrated in the various incidents he has just cited from the wilderness experiences of the Hebrew people. All temptation comes to us from one of three sources: from the lust of the flesh, from the lure of the world, or from the lies of the Devil. It is half the battle to know the enemy. Satan has had some six thousand years to study human nature. He knows us better than we know ourselves. He knows how to use his three great lures of "the lust of the flesh, and the lust of the eyes, and the pride of life" (1 John 2:16). He found them effective with Adam and Eve and he finds them effective with us. No one is immune from temptation. There is no advance in holiness which renders us safe from temptation. The Lord Jesus Himself was tempted by Satan, who tried these same three primeval and prevalent temptations on Him that he found so successful with Eve. Fortunately, Satan's tricks have been unmasked for us in the Word of God. We know about "the wiles of the devil" (Eph. 6:11). We are "not ignorant of his devices," as Paul will later remind the Corinthians (2 Cor. 2:11). Satan orchestrates temptation using the world, the flesh, and evil spirits to assail us. However, he has no new tricks in his bag. His temptations are such as are "common to man."

Then, too, temptation is *controlled by God:* "But God is faithful, who will not suffer you to be tempted above that ye are able" (1 Cor. 10:13b). He knows us better than Satan knows us. He drew the line in the sand again and again in Satan's temptation of Job, and beyond that line the Evil One, for all his might and malice, was not allowed to go. God knew His man (Job 1:8) and knew just exactly how much he could take. It may seem that the enemy is having it all his own way but that is not so. The tapestry of our lives is being woven with consummate skill. We only see the back side of it down here, and the strands often seem to be tangled and meaningless and the things which come upon us to be utterly senseless. However, God is weaving a wondrous picture. When we see it, we shall praise Him for all eternity. As someone has put it,

> Not 'til the looms are silent
> And the shuttles cease to fly,
> Will God unroll the fabric
> And explain the reasons why;
> The dark threads are as needful
> In the Weaver's skillful hand
> As the threads of gold and silver
> In the pattern He has planned.

Paul tells us how to evaluate temptation. It is common to man, it is controlled by God. Our case is by no means unique. He tells us, furthermore, *how to escape temptation:* "But will with the temptation also make a way to escape, that ye may be able to bear it" (1 Cor. 10:13c). When Eve faced fallen Lucifer it would have seemed that all the advantages were on his side. She was a fair young woman, wholly innocent, unconscious of the malice of her visitor, unversed in sin, blissfully ignorant of the subtlety and wickedness of the Evil One. He, on the other hand, was the greatest of all created intelligences. He possessed great gifts and a wisdom unsurpassed, although now warped and twisted by sin into diabolical cunning. What was Eve's "way to escape"? All she had to say, to each of Lucifer's suggestions, was "thus saith the Lord." She had the Word of God and, so long as she held fast to that, she was invulnerable, and well Satan knew it. He bent all his skill to disarming her of the one weapon she had, the one weapon he feared, the one weapon he fears still. That is one way for us to escape from temptation—hold fast, in faith and obedience, to the Word of God.

But then, too the triune God is on our side. We find from Scripture that our three enemies, the world, the flesh, and the Devil, are opposed by the Father, the Holy Spirit, and the Son. The flesh is opposed by the Holy Spirit. God said, in the days of Noah, "My *Spirit* shall not always strive with man, for that he also is *flesh*" (Gen. 6:3). The Lord said to Nicodemus, "That which is born of the flesh is flesh; and that which is born of the Spirit is spirit" (John 3:6). Paul wrote, "Walk in the Spirit, and ye shall not fulfil the lust of the flesh. For the flesh lusteth against the Spirit, and the Spirit against the flesh: and these are contrary the one to the other" (Gal. 5:16–17).

Similarly, we find the world is opposed by the Father. These, for instance, are constantly set, the One against the other, in the Lord's High Priestly Prayer (John 17). John wrote also, "If any man love the world, the love of the Father is not in him" (1 John 2:15–16). Jesus, describing His incarnation and ascension, said, "I came forth from the Father, and am come into the world; again, I leave the world and go to the Father" (John 16:28)

In like manner the Son is opposed to the Devil. This is seen most plainly in the Temptation (Matt. 4:1–11) and in the parable of the wheat and the tares (13:37–39). It is seen in the Lord's constant activity in casting out evil spirits and in delivering all those who were oppressed of the Devil. He came to "destroy him that had the power of death, that is, the devil" (Heb. 2:14) and also to "destroy the works of the devil" (1 John 3:8).

So then, our enemies, great as they are, fearful as they may seem to us, are really impotent because they are opposed by Omnipotence. Here we have another way to escape.

Then, too, with every temptation there comes a moment, however brief, when the initiative is ours to decide which way the result will go. We have two options. We can give in to the temptation, or we can give in to the Holy Spirit. That is one way to escape. Paul says, "Sin shall not have dominion over you. . . . Know ye not, that to whom ye yield yourselves servants to obey, his servants ye are to whom ye obey: whether of sin unto death, or of obedience unto righteousness" (Rom. 6:14, 16). James wrote, "Submit yourselves therefore to God. Resist the devil, and he will flee from you" (James 4:7). Paul told Timothy to "flee these things," that is, the love of money, which he described as "the root of all evil" (1 Tim. 6:10–11) and to "flee also youthful lusts" (2 Tim. 2:22). So, no matter how fierce the temptation, God sees to it that the way to escape is available to us. We cannot help being tempted, but we can help yielding to temptation. Often the best thing to do is simply run away, as Joseph did (Gen. 39:7–12).

Paul has not quite finished. He has talked about sporadic temptations, the everyday temptations so prevalent in a world of sin. Before leaving the subject he talks about *special temptation:* "Wherefore, my dearly beloved, flee from idolatry" (1 Cor. 10:14). Down through the ages, idolatry has been associated with every form of sin. It was an ever-present snare to the Hebrew people throughout all their Old Testament history. Idolatry insults God (Rom. 1:20–24). It degrades man. It is hand-in-glove with deception, immorality, superstition, cruelty, and crime. It is false, through and through, and is a sure and certain road to hell. It is by far the most persistent and pervasive form of error on this planet. It began early in the history of the race, and has been entrenched deeply in man's religious thinking ever since. It has its tentacles in all lands and can be found everywhere in the modern world. Paul tells us to flee from it. It is deadly.

    b. The Table (10:15–22)
      (1) The provision of the Lord's Table (10:15–17)
        (a) Who Paul summons (10:15)
        (b) What Paul says (10:16–17)
          i. About the Lord's memorial body (10:16)
           a. The communion of the cup—His blood to be remembered (10:16a)
           b. The breaking of the bread—His body to be remembered (10:16b)
          ii. About the Lord's mystical body (10:17)
      (2) The protection of the Lord's Table (10:18–22)
        (a) A foundational fact (10:18)
          i. A sacrificial meal (10:18a)
          ii. A sanctifying mystery (10:18b)
        (b) A further fact (10:19–20a)
          i. A searching question asked (10:19)
          ii. A searching question answered (10:20a)
        (c) A frightening fact (10:20b–22)
          i. No compromise with demons (10:20b)
          ii. No communion with demons (10:21–22)
           a. A terrible participation in demon worship is possible (10:21)
           b. A terrible provocation of divine wrath is possible (10:22)

Paul has adequately dealt with the type (1 Cor. 10:1–14). He now turns his attention to *the Table* (10:15–22). He speaks first about *the provision* of the Lord's Table (10:15–17). We note *who Paul summons* to consider his words: "I speak as to wise men; judge ye what I say" (10:15). Paul takes it for granted that the Corinthians are intelligent people, able to make the transfer from the type in the Old Testament to the situation in the Corinthian church and able also to follow the ensuing argument about the Lord's Table and the idol feasts which some of them had been attending—and then boasting of their liberty in Christ.

We note, also, *what Paul says* (10:16–17). He has something to say about *the Lord's memorial body* (10:16). There is *the communion of the cup:* "The cup of blessing which we bless, is it not the communion of the blood of Christ?" There is also *the breaking of the bread:* "The bread which we break, is it not the communion of the body of Christ?" The order here is reversed from the actual order in which the elements are served at the Lord's table (Matt. 26:26–29; 1 Cor. 11:23–25). The cup is put first here because it is the blood of Christ, which secures all spiritual blessings, and also because Paul intends to dwell further on the significance of the bread. Paul points out that, when we drink the cup, there is a spiritual sharing in the blood of Christ and that, when we break the bread, there is a spiritual sharing in the body of Christ.

The use of the pronoun *we* in connection with the breaking of bread seems to indicate that each believer can break the bread for himself. There is no priestly mediator envisioned. The loaf is passed from one to another and each believer tears off a piece for himself—a vivid picture, indeed, of what we did to Christ and of what He has done for us. The blood of Christ and the body of Christ are the two focal points in the communion. They are graphically represented by the wine and the bread, the two elements on the table.

Paul has something to say also about *the Lord's mystical body:* "For we being many are one bread, and one body: for we are all partakers of that one bread" (10:17). The bread on the table not only reminds the believer of the material body of Christ, which was broken at Calvary, it also reminds him of the mystical body of Christ, which was brought into being as a result of the Lord's death, burial, and resurrection. Paul will have more to say later to the Corinthians about the mystical body of Christ (12:12–27).

Paul now moves on to *the protection of the Lord's Table* (10:18–22). He marshals three facts. First of all there is *a fundamental fact:* "Behold Israel after the flesh: are not they which eat of the sacrifices partakers of the altar?" (10:18). Paul here draws another analogy from the history of the Jewish people. In some of the Old Testament offerings, after certain parts had been burnt upon the altar, and other parts given to the priests, the offerers sat down to eat the remainder in a sacrificial meal in the tabernacle court. Earthly Israel was still keeping up this Levitical ritual when Paul wrote this letter. To participate in the sacrificial feasts (when they were still valid; before Calvary, that is) was to have fellowship with God, whose altar it was. Just so, those who participate at the Lord's Table have fellowship with Him whose table it is. That is a fundamental fact.

Next there is *a further fact*: "What say I, then? that the idol is any thing, or that which is offered in sacrifice to idols is any thing? But I say, that the things which the Gentiles sacrifice, they sacrifice to devils [demons], and not to God" (10:19–20a). By this time the "wise men" who were to judge what Paul had to say must have been alerted to where Paul's argument was taking them. If those who ate the flesh of animals offered in the Jewish sacrifices were having fellowship with the God whose altar it was, and if those who participate in the Lord's Supper are having fellowship with the One whose table it is, the conclusion is inescapable. Those who eat meat which has been offered to idols are having fellowship with those idols and become partakers of the pagan altar. Paul takes it for granted that the wise men will make the connection. Accordingly he anticipates their expected objection.

"You have already conceded that idols have no real existence and that there is only one God" (8:4), he can hear them say. "I am not saying," he replies, "that false gods really exist or that sacrifices made to them have some value. No indeed! However, behind these foolish graven images, imagined by the pagans to be gods and goddesses, there are sinister realities—demons." The pagans, and all those who worship graven images, are actually worshiping evil spirits, the emissaries of Satan, who instigate and perpetuate idolatry. For demons do exist, and they exist in great numbers. They appear to be disembodied spirits, for they have a craving to seize the bodies of men and beasts. Idols provide them with excellent cover for gaining hold over those who worship the imagined "gods," represented by the graven images in their temples and shrines. In many cases those who worship idols become possessed by evil spirits.

All of which leads Paul to *a frightening fact* (10:20b–22). Since it is possible for a believer, knowingly or unknowingly, to actually become a communicant of demons, there is to be *no compromise with demons:* "And I would not that ye should have fellowship with devils" (10:20b). Paul does not want any believer to run the risk of having any fellowship with demonic powers. There can be no compromise in this matter. To have fellowship with a demon, consciously or unconsciously, is a dangerous thing to do. A person may feel himself a strong enough believer to go where he wants and do as he pleases in these matters. He is still in peril. To go to a spiritist seance or to play with a Ouija board opens a believer to similar perils. The safe thing to do is to stay away from all such things. Paul has already told us to "flee from idolatry" (10:14). Now we know why.

There is to be *no communion with demons* (10:21–22) for two reasons. *A terrible participation in demon worship is possible:* "Ye cannot drink the cup of the

Lord, and the cup of devils: ye cannot be partakers of the Lord's table, and the table of devils" (10:21). Because it is possible it is prohibited. Moreover *a terrible provocation of divine wrath is possible:* "Do we provoke the Lord to jealousy? are we stronger than he?" (10:22). No Christian can have anything to do with idolatry. The prohibition goes back a long way. The second commandment says, "Thou shalt not make unto thee any graven image, or any likeness of any thing that is in heaven above, or that is in the earth beneath, or that is in the water under the earth: thou shalt not bow down thyself to them, nor serve them: for I the LORD thy God am a jealous God, visiting the iniquity of the fathers upon the children unto the third and fourth generation of them that hate me; and showing mercy unto thousands of them that love me and keep my commandments" (Exod. 20:4–6). To that commandment Paul added another one, for those who love the Lord and participate at His table: "Thou shalt not compromise with idolatry."

    c. The tests (10:23–11:1)
       (1) Some basic regulations (10:23–30)
          (a) Our freedom indicated (10:23–24)
             i. The extent of that freedom (10:23)
             ii. The exception to that freedom (10:24)
          (b) Our freedom illustrated (10:25–30)
             i. The conscience and its liberty (10:25–27)
                a. When at the butcher's stall (10:25–26)
                b. When in the banqueting hall (10:27)
             ii. The conscience and its liabilities (10:28–30)
                a. When to refuse meat offered to idols (10:28a)
                b. Why to refuse meat offered to idols (10:28b–30)
                    1. A scriptural reason (10:28b)
                    2. A secondary reason (10:29–30)
                        (i) The weak brother's conscience is to be respected (10:29)
                        (ii) The wise brother's conduct is to be protected (10:30)
       (2) Some basic responsibilities (10:31–11:1)
          (a) Our great exercise (10:31–32)
              i. To bring glory to God (10:31)
              ii. To bring grace to men (10:32)
                  a. To the Hebrew people (10:32a)

        b. To the heathen people (10:32b)

        c. To the heavenly people (10:32c)

    (b) Our great example (10:33–11:1)

       i. Paul's motives (10:33)

         a. To woo people for Christ (10:33a–b)

           1. By living a sacrificial life (10:33a)

           2. By living a selfless life (10:33b)

         b. To win people to Christ (10:33c)

      ii. Paul's Master (11:1)

         a. Just follow me (11:1a)

         b. Thus follow Him (11:1b)

Paul now approaches his concluding remarks about *our personal walk* (1 Cor. 7:1–11:1). His *exhortation* (7:1–8:13) and his *example* (9:1–27) have been followed by his *explanation* (10:1–11:1). In this explanation he has discussed *the type* (10:1–14) and *the table* (10:15–22). In the background of much of this discussion has been the vexing question of meats (commencing at 8:1), and to what extent a believer may or may not eat meat offered to an idol. From 9:1 to 10:22 he has digressed, but never very far, from the subject.

For instance 10:1–22 has been, really, a discussion of two tables—a table provided by the Moabites for God's Old Testament people in the wilderness and a table provided by the Master for God's New Testament people in the world. The one was a table of rebellion, the other a table of remembrance. The one was designed to lead astray; the other designed to lead aright. The one was a lewd table; the other was the Lord's Table. The one was designed to be a snare, a provision for their lusts; the other was designed to be a spur, a provision by the Lord. At the one table there was a repudiation of all the Lord had done for them; at the other there is a recognition of all the Lord has done for us. In the one case the kinsman-redeemer was absent, he was on Mount Sinai accepting a great revelation; in the other case the Kinsman-Redeemer is absent, He is on Mount Zion anticipating a glorious return. The one table was a monument to their infidelity, idolatry, and immorality; the other was a memorial to His Person, passion, and position. They sat down at the one table to eat and drink and rose up to play. We sit down at the other table to eat and drink and rise up to pray. The one table brought the people face to face with judgment; the other table brings us face to face with Jesus.

It is not hard to see that, in each case, the question of eating, drinking, and idolatry are not far away. God's Old Testament people were also given another table, spread for them in the holy place of the tabernacle. There could be no fellowship between that table and the idols they had been snared to worship by the Moabite king. God has now given us yet another table. There can be no fellowship, either, between that table and the idols set up in even some professedly "Christian" churches. Indeed, Paul has just made the point: "Ye cannot drink the cup of the Lord, and the cup of devils: ye cannot be partakers of the Lord's table, and the table of devils" (10:21). Such behavior on our part is as provocative as was Israel's of old (10:22).

Paul is now ready to resume the discussion of "meats" and bring his argument to a final conclusion. He sets forth *the tests* (10:23–11:1). First, *some basic regulations* (10:23–30). *Our freedom is indicated* (10:23–24). As to the *extent* of that freedom, Paul says, "All things are lawful for me, but all things are not expedient: all things are lawful for me, but all things edify not" (10:23). As to the *exception* to that freedom he says, "Let no man seek his own, but every man another's wealth" (10:24). He gives us a wide enough latitude when it comes to such things as "meats," things over which there is honest difference of opinion. But then he reins it in by emphasizing our basic Christian duty of being mindful of the advancement and well-being of other people. Christian liberty sets vast horizons before us, but we must not push other people down in our desire and determination to take advantage of them.

In the days of the Old West, in Oklahoma, for instance, new territories would be opened up from time to time. These distant horizons beckoned one and all. The day would be set when the pioneers could go in and stake their claims. They would line up by the hundreds at the starting point, eyes straining westward where the virgin lands called, where vast ranches could be staked out and fortunes made. Out there was land and liberty. Men with horses, men with wagons, men with families, men with all-too-ready guns lined up for the signal and there would be a mad rush for the horizon! The weak would be trampled by the strong. The law-abiding would be exploited by the ruthless.

There can be no such stampede where love rules. Our freedoms, our possessions in Christ, may be vast as those distant prairies. But, in Christ, love rules, and consideration for the weak, not a selfish determination to enjoy all our liberties regardless of others. On the contrary, the believer who thinks first of others gets further and gets more in the end than the one who looks out only for himself. Liberty? Yes, indeed! License? Never!

Then, too, *our freedom is illustrated* (10:25–30). Paul now speaks of *the con-*

science and its liberty (10:25–27). First, he takes us to *the butcher's stall:* "Whatsoever is sold in the shambles, that eat, asking no question for conscience sake: for the earth is the Lord's, and the fulness thereof" (10:25–26). This is just plain common sense. The word for *shambles* is *makellon,* and simply denotes a market, here a meat market. Paul could see no point in asking whether or not meat sold on the open market had once been dedicated to an idol. What difference did it make to the meat? Meat was meat! Nobody would suspect one of having leanings toward idolatry simply because some of the meat in the butcher's shop had arrived there by way of a heathen temple. One went to the butcher to buy beef, not pay respect to a graven image. Why raise needless questions and arouse a needless nagging conscience over so trivial a matter?

Paul appeals to one of the great messianic psalms (Psalm 24) to support his contention that the whole world belongs to the Lord and its "fullness" is for our benefit. So what if pagan priests have laid claim to the meat that eventually showed up in the butcher's shop? Did that nullify the superior fact of God's ownership? No, indeed! Never mind the pagan priests, the meat came originally from a bountiful Lord and that should satisfy the weakest conscience.

Then Paul takes us to *the banqueting hall:* "If any of them that believe not bid you to a feast, and ye be disposed to go; whatsoever is set before you, eat, asking no question for conscience sake" (10:27). Any scruples should have been settled before accepting the invitation. It would be not only bad manners but downright insulting to question the host about whether or not the roast beef on the table had originally carried the stamp of the local idol temple. Paul evidently could see nothing wrong in accepting a dinner invitation extended by an unbeliever. He could see something wrong in embarrassing a well-meaning host by making a fuss over what shop the meat had come from, once seated at his table. That would not only be rude, it would be counterproductive and would likely prejudice the host against the gospel. It is a word in season. Many well-meaning but legalistic believers unnecessarily prejudice people against the gospel by their thoughtless appeal to their own religious scruples. Nowadays they declaim against mixed bathing, head coverings, long hair on men, and the like. Not that it is necessarily wrong to hold strong views on such things. It is wrong, however, to insist on one's own scruples at the wrong place and time, to someone's acute embarrassment and chagrin. There is a time and place for everything, as Solomon once said (Eccl. 3:1).

Paul now turns to *the conscience and its liabilities* (10:28–30). First, he mentions *when one should refuse to eat* meat offered to idols: "But if any man say unto you, This is offered in sacrifice unto idols, eat not for his sake that shewed it, and for conscience sake" (10:28a). This raises quite a different issue. Now it is no longer a question solely of one's own conscience. Now somebody else's spiritual well-being is at stake. Now, for the sake of that other person and for the spiritual well-being, perhaps, of others at the table, a stand must be taken. Indeed, one's own testimony might also be involved. A challenge has been issued. Now it is no longer a matter of politeness. It is a matter of principle.

Father Chiniquy, in his fascinating book *Fifty Years in the Church of Rome*, tells of an incident which happened when he was still a zealous Roman priest in Quebec. He and another priest had been to visit a recently bereaved parishioner. The woman asked her priest to say a mass for the soul of her recently departed husband. The priest insisted on being paid for his services; the woman pleaded her extreme poverty. She had nothing. She was too poor to pay. The priest spotted a small piglet and demanded if it was hers. She confessed that it was, but pleaded it was all she had in the world. She counted on feeding it slops so that, when it was grown, she could sell it to help support her bereaved children. The priest was angry and told her that either she give him the piglet or her husband could do without his mass.

Chiniquy was upset by the dialogue but held his tongue. In the end the priest stalked off, the mass unsaid. The woman had her piglet and an anguished heart. Chiniquy had a conscience that accused him of cowardice.

Shortly afterward, he was seated at the table in his colleague's manse. A number of other priests were guests. Supper that night was a roast of particularly tender pork. Someone congratulated the host on the savory meat, and the priest, laughing, said he had received it for saying mass for the soul of one of his recently departed parishioners. Father Chiniquy looked up. He inquired if it was the piglet about which his colleague had argued with the widow. Laughingly, his host admitted that it was.

Chiniquy put down his knife and fork. He pushed back from the table and rose to his feet. He denounced his colleague for his callousness and heartlessness and declared that his conscience would not permit him to eat meat, however tender, procured by such despicable means. Then he walked out of the room, his conscience appeased and, doubtless, the consciences of all the others who remained sorely stung.

Yes, indeed! There is a time when larger issues are at stake, when one's conscience comes before all else.

Paul not only tells us when to refuse to eat such meat, he tells *why one should refuse* to eat such meat (1 Cor. 10:28b–30). He gives a *scriptural* reason, quoting again, from Psalm 24: "For the earth is the Lord's, and the fulness thereof" (1 Cor. 10:28b). The emphasis here would surely be on the lordship of Christ. For now the issue is quite different. The believer has actually been challenged. "This meat has been offered in sacrifice to an idol." Now the issue is no longer one of liberty. It has to do with lordship. And, when it comes to that, it is the lordship of Christ the believer owns. If it becomes an issue between eating meat offered to an idol or owning the absolute sovereignty of the Lord, well, the Lord it is! No matter even if the host is upset.

Nowadays, few occasions would arise where an issue could be made over meat, at least in our Western society. But an issue could be made over drink. Some people are total abstainers on principle. Such a person might be a guest of one who was not a teetotaler. The guest would do well not to ask for the recipe of a particularly palatable fruitcake, for instance. However, if the hostess, while handing him a serving, were to say, "There's brandy in that!" the guest might well take it that his convictions were being challenged. In that case he would do well to decline his portion—for conscience sake.

Which brings us to Paul's *secondary* reason (10:29–30). First, *the weak brother's conscience is to be respected:* "Conscience, I say, not thine own, but of the other: for why is my liberty judged of another man's conscience?" (10:29). The strong believer, by accepting the invitation to the unbeliever's feast, may be very well aware that, by so doing, he is not sanctioning idolatry, even if he is bluntly told that the meat was bought from an idol temple. But, if the weak believer *supposes* that he has sanctioned idolatry by such behavior, then, to that extent, the strong believer has wounded the weak brother's conscience.

But that only raises another question: "Why should my freedom to eat be held ransom by someone else's conscience?" Just because someone *thinks* I am doing wrong does not mean that I actually *am* doing wrong. We answer directly to the Lord. It certainly does not seem fair that the strong believer must sacrifice himself to the scruples of the weak one. Paul has already shown, however, the high ground he took on the whole issue: "If meat make my brother to offend, I will eat no flesh while the world standeth, lest I make my brother to offend" (8:13). Now *there's* a strong believer.

If the weak brother's conscience is to be respected, then, by the same token, *the wise brother's conduct is to be protected:* "For if I by grace be a partaker, why am I evil spoken of for that for which I give thanks?" (10:30). Why should anyone speak evil of me when I eat something for which I am thankful and for which I have given God thanks? Paul is being fair. A strong believer should put limits on his liberty out of regard for another man's scruples. Paul refuses to endorse a philosophy of liberty at all costs. At the same time, the strong believer does not have to allow others to sit in judgment on his exercise of his liberty, nor does he have to make the conscience of a bigoted, superstitious man the standard by which he has to regulate his life. Neither weakness, on the one hand, or strength, on the other hand, can be allowed to become tyrannical. Paul adds a word of caution here, for the strong believer—just because we give thanks for something does not, necessarily, mean that what we are doing is right.

Paul turns now to *some basic responsibilities* (10:31–11:1). He speaks, first, of *our great exercise* (10:31–32). It is twofold. We are to be exercised to *bring glory to God:* "Whether therefore ye eat, or drink, or whatsoever ye do, do all to the glory of God" (10:31). That should settle most issues. "What would Jesus do?" is a question we might well ask when confronted with the issue of questionable amusements or the freedom of conscience to do this or that. It is a basic axiom of hermeneutics that God does all things for His own glory. Paul affirms here that it should be a basic axiom of behavior for the believer, too, to do all things for the glory of God. There is no glory brought to God when a believer exercises his liberty to the detriment of a weaker brother. There is no glory brought to God when a believer uses his own scruples as a weapon with which to bludgeon a stronger brother. So, even such mundane things as eating or drinking can, should, and indeed must be governed by the unifying factor of the glory of God.

We are to be exercised also to *bring grace to men:* "Give none offence, neither to the Jews, nor to the Gentiles, nor to the church of God" (10:32). This is an important verse since it defines the three classes into which God divides all mankind. Following Bible chronology, for the first 2,000 years of human history God dealt solely with "Gentiles," with mankind in general. For the next 2,000 years, beginning with Abraham, God dealt primarily with "the Jews," the Hebrew people. Since Pentecost, for the past 2,000 years, God has been dealing supremely with the church. All divine revelation has to do with one or other of these three divisions of mankind. All Bible prophecy concerns the Jews, the Gentiles, or the church of God. God's plans and purposes embrace Jews, Gentiles, and the church. The believer has relationship to all three. He must not cause offense to the Jews. Although "blindness in part is happened to Israel" (Rom. 11:25), the believer is to love the Jewish people. They gave us the Bible. They gave us Jesus. The hateful things done to the Jews by so-called Christians have given many Jews a distorted view of Christianity and given them ample cause to view the church with great suspicion. We are to make sure we do not add to this, but do all we can to remove it.

The believer must not cause offense to the Gentiles, to the vast multitudes which make up the various nations of the world. Racial prejudice has no place in a believer's heart. He is not to cause offense to those who do not know and love the Lord. He is not to ridicule their religion, their customs, their speech. He is to see them as people for whom Christ died.

The believer must not cause offense to the church of God. The church is divided into many denominations and sects. Some of the views held by sincere, believing people may seen (or even be) odd, extreme, erroneous. Still, we are not to cause them offense.

Paul concludes his discussion of causing offense by pointing to *our great example* (1 Cor. 10:33–11:1). Paul speaks of *his motives* (10:33). All he wanted to do was *woo people to Christ:* "Even as I please all men in all things, not seeking mine own profit, but the profit of many" (10:33a–b), and to *win people to Christ:* "that they may be saved" (10:33c). Not content with the negative aspect of things, simply not giving offense to anyone, Paul embraced the positive—trying to please everyone, with one end in view, their salvation. He would allow no liberty of his, no right to do this, that, or the other, to hinder his master passion of winning people to Christ. Who would want his right to drink a glass of wine, for instance, to stand in his way of winning a bartender to Christ? Paul was motivated by a consuming passion for souls.

Finally, Paul speaks of his *Master:* "Be ye followers of me, even as I also am of Christ," he said (11:1). Paul modeled himself on Christ, who "pleased not himself" (Rom. 15:1–3). Indeed, he modeled himself so perfectly on Christ that he could challenge people to model themselves on him. How many of us could challenge people to copy us as we copy Christ?

> B. Our public worship (11:2–14:40)
>> 1. The gift of the Lord's Supper (11:2–34)
>>> a. Order in the fellowship (11:2–16)
>>>> (1) A word of commendation (11:2)
>>>>> (a) For remembering Paul personally (11:2a)
>>>>> (b) For remembering Paul practically (11:2b)
>>>> (2) A word of comprehension (11:2–16)
>>>>> (a) The matter of man and his headship (11:3–12)
>>>>>> i. The fact of his headship categorically declared (11:3)
>>>>>>> *a.* The human order of things (11:3a–b)

   1. The man has a head to acknowledge (11:3a)
   2. The man has a headship to administer (11:3b)
   b. The highest order of things (11:3c)
ii. The fact of his headship correspondingly displayed (11:4–7)
   a. The principle (11:4–5)
      1. The man must display his supremacy in the church (11:4)
         (i) When (11:4a)
         (ii) Why (11:4b)
      2. The woman must display her subordination in the church (11:5)
         (i)   When (11:5a)
         (ii) Why (11:5b)
         (iii) What (11:5c)
   b. The practice (11:6–7)
      1. The woman must display her covering (11:6)
         (i) Her "covering" (her hair) is to be shaved as a symbol of her disobedience (11:6a)
         (ii) Her covering (her veil) is to be shown as a symbol of her obedience (11:6b)
      2. The man must display his calling (11:7)
         (i) The man's head shorn (11:7a)
         (ii) The man's headship shown (11:7b)
iii. The fact of headship comprehensively discussed (11:8–12)
   a. There is an order in creation (11:8–9)
   b. There is an order in Christ (11:10–12)
      1. The observing angels (11:10)
      2. The obvious angle (11:11–12)
         (i) The mutual dependence of the creature on the creature (11:11–12a)
         (ii) The mutual dependence of the creature on the Creator (11:12b)
(b) The matter of man and his hair (11:13–16)
   i. A final contrast (11:13–15)

    a. The first question (11:13)

    b. The further question (11:14–15)

        1. Nature and a man's hair—its length (11:14)

        2. Nature and a woman's hair—its loveliness (11:15)

    ii. A final caution (11:16)

Paul is still dealing with *difficulties in the church* (1 Cor. 7:1–14:40). He has dealt with matters relating to *our personal walk* (7:1–11:1), specifically the matter of *marriage* (7:1–40) and the matter of *meat* (8:1–11:1). Now he turns to matters relating to our *public worship* (11:2–14:40). He now discusses the *gift of the Lord's Supper* (11:2) and especially emphasizes *order in the fellowship* (11:2–16) and *order at the feast* (11:17–34). He will finally come to the vexing question of *the gifts of the Lord's servants* (12:1–14:40). The matters under discussion, despite all Paul has to say about them, remain the most controversial and complex in church life. Opinions differ as widely over the interpretation of these half dozen chapters, as they did over the original issues centuries ago in the Corinthian church.

Before beginning with the question of disorderly conduct at the Lord's Table, Paul makes his plea for *order in the fellowship* (11:2–16). At issue here is the controversial matter of the woman's role in the church. The rise of the feminist movement in our culture has made this portion of Scripture a veritable battleground. Paul is accused of narrow-mindedness (although how anyone could be broader-minded than Paul is difficult to say) and of a bias against women (which is totally unfair, since no one was more courteous to women and considerate of women than Paul). What Paul does insist on is order in the church, order based on experience, common sense, observation, nature, and, above all, Scripture and divine revelation. Anyone who has a quarrel with the order, especially where men and women meet together on the grounds of a common salvation, upon which the apostle insists, have a quarrel not with him but with the Holy Spirit. Paul is not airing prejudice or male chauvinism in this passage. He is writing under the direct inspiration and illumination of the Holy Spirit, who certainly knows what is best for the church He created, and who makes no mistakes.

Paul begins with *a word of commendation:* "Now I praise you, brethren, that ye remember me in all things, and keep the ordinances, as I delivered them to you" (11:2). The word for *ordinances* is *paradosis,* usually used in a negative sense in the New Testament. It is used of "traditions," especially the traditions of the Jewish rabbis. The word is used here and in 2 Thessalonians 2:15; 3:6, positively. It seems, when used in this way, to refer to church order and to the two specific ordinances the Lord did give to the church—baptism and the communion feast. Always eager to find something to praise, Paul commends the Corinthians for their exercise about these things. However, he evidently has weightier matters on his mind. His *but* rings out with haste, before the ink is dry on his commendation.

There follows *a word of comprehension* (1 Cor. 11:3–16), in which Paul develops the whole subject of the woman's role in the local church. Two subjects are discussed—headship (11:3–12) and hair (11:13–16). The headship of the man is made immediately and abundantly clear. *The fact of man's headship is categorically declared* (11:3). As to *the human order* of things, Paul says, "But I would have you know that the head of every man is Christ; and the head of the woman is the man" (11:3a); and as to *the higher order* of things, "The head of Christ is God" (11:3b).

This brings us back to basics. God is a God of order (1 Cor. 14:40), an order that reaches back into His own nature. He insists on order in the universe. Science is predicated on the fact that this universe is based on order. This order extends into human affairs, to government, to the home, to the church. In terms of human life the woman has a head, the man; the man has a head, Christ, who by virtue of the fact that He is God, absolutely and eternally, takes priority and preeminence over the headship vested in the man. The man is answerable for his actions, ultimately and inescapably, to Christ.

By the same token the woman is answerable to the man. This does not imply male superiority, nor does it imply female inferiority. It simply states it to be a fact that, in their respective roles in society, in the home, and in the church, this is God's ordained order and state of affairs. No amount of argument is going to change it. All attempts to defy it can only lead to breakdown and chaos.

When a person purchases an appliance or a piece of equipment it normally comes with the manufacturer's instructions and warranty. Usually the warranty is valid only so long as the instructions are heeded. The manufacturer knows the nature and complexity of the equipment better than anyone. After all, he designed and made it. If the instructions come with the warning, "Press button 'A' *before* you press button 'B'" it is because of some basic requirement connected with the structure and nature of the machine. If a person reverses the order and insists on pressing button B before button A, and things go wrong, what can he expect? The instructions were clear and plain. Human life and society are far more complex than any man-made appliance. We would do well to heed the Maker's instructions. He categorically states that the head of the man is Christ and that the head of the woman is the man. That is the way things are. The feminist lobby, for all its noise, anger, organization, and resentment, is not going to change the way things are. This is true of society in general, the home in particular, and the church above all. In this chapter, of course, Paul is more concerned with order in the church.

He carries the principle of order even higher by affirming that even Christ has a head—God. He places this statement after the one which says that the head of the woman is the man, as though to soften any possible blow to the woman's pride.

God has His own order within the Godhead itself. This is not an order based on being. Father, Son, and Holy Spirit are each eternally, equally, and essentially God. What is revealed here is a voluntary subordination of Christ in terms of office. By virtue of the Incarnation He became man, although in no sense did He cease to be God. He "took upon him the form of a servant, and was made in the likeness of men" (Phil. 2:7), even though "being in the form of God, [he] thought it not robbery to be equal with God" (2:6). He became man in order to fulfill the law, to be man as God intended Man to be, and to carry out God's purpose in redemption. The Lord Jesus saw no reason for resenting the subordinate role He voluntarily assumed in becoming man. He could cheerfully say, "I do always those things that please [the Father]" (John 8:29).

So then, in the human order of things and in the highest order of things Paul establishes categorically the fact of headship. But he has only just begun. We note next that *the fact of man's headship is correspondingly displayed* (1 Cor. 11:4–7). First comes *the principle* (11:4–5). In the first place, *the man must display his supremacy in the church:* "Every man praying or prophesying, having his head covered, dishonoureth his head" (11:4). Since this statement follows right on from the previous one, it is evident that "his head," which he thus dishonors, is Christ. When a man takes a leading role in a church activity, such as praying or preaching, he is to leave his physical head uncovered in order to display his headship in spiritual things and in order to acknowledge the headship of Christ.

This is a very remarkable statement. In the synagogue exactly the opposite was enjoined. To this day a Jew, reading the Torah in the synagogue, puts on a cap known as a *yarmulke.* Some of the stricter Jews always cover their heads in public. The Jewish custom of the man covering his head when the Scriptures are read goes back before Paul's day. The Holy Spirit, by requiring the very opposite practice in the church, is evidently striking a blow at the Judaizers, who were forever trying to corrupt Christianity into a mere extension of what Paul calls elsewhere "the Jews' religion."

The "covering" to which Paul refers in verse 4 is technically a veil which covers the man's whole head and conceals all his hair. Possibly there were men in the Corinthian church who were going to this extreme of self-abnegation in worship, thinking they were pleasing God by such a display. Paul repudiates any such practice. The contrary was what was called for: the man must pray and preach with his head completely uncovered to display his headship and the Lord's.

By contrast, *the woman must display her subordination in the church:* "But every woman that prayeth or prophesieth with her head uncovered dishonoureth her head: for that is even all one as if she were shaven" (11:5). The woman's head, here, is the man. If and when a woman takes a public part in church worship she must cover her physical head in order to honor the man who is her spiritual head. By so covering her head she displays her subjection to the man and witnesses that she is functioning, in a public capacity, under the authority of the man.

That women did take part in public worship in the early church is evident. Philip the evangelist, for instance, had four daughters who prophesied (Acts 21:8–9). However, public ministry by women in the congregation was reined in by the Holy Spirit. They are told to be silent in the church and are forbidden to speak (1 Cor. 14:34). The context there, however, has to do with the abuse of the gift of tongues. There seems little doubt that if the same stricture were to be enforced on women in the modern "tongues" movement, it would likely die a natural death. Women are forbidden to teach or, in any way, to assume the man's role (1 Tim. 2:11–15). They are to "learn in silence," Paul says. He bases the rule on God's order in creation. The subsequent reference to them being "saved in child-bearing" may possibly refer to their emancipation from this ruling in their role as teachers to their children. It is evident that both Priscilla and Aquila were active in teaching the gifted preacher Apollos "the way of God more perfectly," although doubtless this was done privately and not publicly. Also Paul told his young colleague Titus, who was engaged in putting in order the affairs of the church in Crete, that the older women should teach the younger women (Titus 2:3, 5) and, indeed, be "teachers of good things."

From all this it seems fairly evident that women did have a teaching role in the church, but that it had certain somewhat rigid restraints placed upon it. These restrictions are related not only to God's order in creation, by which order he made man first and invested him with headship, but also to the woman's leading role in the Fall. The idea of women taking the man's role in teaching is frowned upon. Where, however, she does teach it must be subject to the authority of the man and, according to 1 Corinthians 11:5, when she does so teach, or pray, it must be with her head covered to display her subjection to the man's authority. None of which, however, finds much favor with today's emancipated women, many of whom see all this as some kind of sex discrimination. It would be better to adopt the attitude that God knows best what is good for church, home, and society, that it is impossible for God to be unfair or biased, that He loves women as much as He loves men, and that these restrictions are imposed, not by a misogynic male but by the Holy Spirit Himself.

Here Paul, writing under the direct inspiration of the Holy Spirit, states that for a woman to pray or prophesy with her head uncovered means that she dishonors her head (the man) and that is the same, in God's sight, as though she were "shaven." If she disregards the covering, which is the symbol of her position, she may as well discard the natural covering God has given her (her hair) as well. This does not appear to have anything to do with the woman's presence at a church service, where she adopts the role of a silent worshiper, but to those occasions when, under the man's supervision, she adopts a more public role.

The word here for *uncovered* is *akatakalyptos.* It stems from *kalyptō,* which means "to veil," to which is added the preposition *kata (down).* The reference is not to some token, such as a doily, but to a veil, a proper covering. The word for *shaven* is *xuraō,* which implies being shaved with a razor. If it would be a disgraceful thing for a woman to be thus shaven, it is equally a disgraceful thing for her to pray or prophesy in such a way as to disgrace God's order in the church. For her to do so would, indeed, be tantamount to a denial of the man's role as her head in the church.

During the German occupation of France and other European countries during World War II, some women collaborated with the Germans and consorted with German soldiers and officials. After the war their fellow citizens showed their anger at such compromise by seizing the women and shaving off all their hair. They then became objects of public shame and disgrace. Paul uses a similar picture here to illustrate how strongly the Holy Spirit feels about the respective roles of men and women in the church.

Having set forth the principle, Paul now turns to *the practice* of that principle (1 Cor. 11:6–7). First, *the woman must display her covering* (11:6). Either *her covering (her hair) must be shorn as a symbol of her disobedience* ("for if a woman be not covered *[katakaluptomai],* let her also be shorn") or else *her covering (her veil) must be shown as a symbol of her obedience* ("but if it be a shame for a woman to be shorn or shaven, let her be covered *[katakalyptomai]* "). It is to be either one or the other.

Paul here uses two words to describe the disgrace the Holy Spirit associates with a woman assuming a public role without acknowledging, by wearing a veil, her submission to the authority of the man. He uses again the word *xurao* and adds the word *keiro,* which means "to crop." The word is used of shearing sheep (Acts 8:32). In the middle voice, as here in 1 Corinthians 11:6, it means to have one's hair cut off. Evidently for a woman to have her hair cropped or cut very short is as disgraceful, in God's eyes, as for her to actually be shaven. This should give us some idea how strongly He feels about this whole issue. It is no light thing for a woman to occupy a man's role without due authority from the men in the church and without modestly covering her head as outward evidence of an inward compliance to God's rules of order in this matter.

If the woman must display her covering (her veil), *the man must display his calling* (1 Cor. 11:7). Again, there are two factors in the equation. First, *the man's head must be shown*—"For a man indeed ought not to cover his head"; for *the man's headship must be shown*—"forasmuch as he is the image and glory of God: but the woman is the glory of the man." Again, the word for *cover* is *katakaluptomai,* as in the preceding verse. It means "to cover up," to be veiled. The *kata* in this word is intensive.[6] The man must not do this. He must pray and prophesy with his head uncovered to display both his own headship and that, also, of Christ, whose representative he is. Paul says that the man is "the image and glory of God." This takes us back to the beginning. The word for *image* is *eikon,* a word that conveys the two ideas of representation and manifestation. It is used "of man as he was created as being a visible representation of God, I Cor. II:7, a being corresponding to the Original."[7] Even the drastic damage done to that image by the Fall has not entirely destroyed it. The word is used of Christ as "the image of God" (2 Cor. 4:4) for, in Him, the image and likeness was perfectly restored—so much so that He could say to Philip, "He that hath seen me hath seen the Father" (John 14:9). Man was intended to display the wisdom, goodness, love, and power of God and was created to that end. He was also created to display God's glory and to manifest His greatness and His majesty. He was indeed a noble being when he came fresh from the hands of his Creator. Much of the original image and glory has been tarnished as a result of sin but enough remains to set man apart from the rest of creation. In the church an arena has been designed where man can again approach the

---

6. Vine, *Expository Dictionary of New Testament Words,* 1:252.
7. Ibid., 2:246

divine ideal by being conformed to the image of God's Son (Rom. 8:29). Man, in the church, leaves his head uncovered, because he is to draw attention to Christ, his Head, in whom the divine ideal, in creating man, has been fully realized. What God intended in the creation of Adam has been realized in the coming of Christ.

Paul adds the footnote that "the woman is the glory of the man." He does not say that she is his "image and glory." The image of Adam was borne by Seth, not Eve (Gen. 5:3). Paul does not deny that the woman also bears the image of God. On the contrary, he clearly implies that she does, by deliberately avoiding completing the parallel, by *not* saying that she is man's image and glory. The woman, he implies, was just as much created in God's image as Adam was. He thus endorses again the fundamental equality of the sexes.

However, the woman is said to be "the glory of the man," just as the man was said to be "the glory of God." Paul is careful to put the woman in her place as subordinate to man in the order of creation and in the very nature of things. Adam was made first. Eve, it might almost be said, owes her origin to him. So, as the moon reflects the glory of the sun, so the man reflects the glory of God and the woman reflects the glory of the man.

The fact of man's headship has now been both categorically declared (1 Cor. 11:3) and correspondingly displayed (11:4–7). *The fact of man's headship is now comprehensively discussed* (11:8–12). First, Paul says, *there is an order in creation:* "For the man is not of the woman; but the woman of the man; neither was the man created for the woman, but the woman for the man" (11:8–9). This statement backs up the previous one that the woman is the glory of the man. Adam was created directly by the hand of God. Eve was also created directly by God but she was actually taken out of Adam (Gen. 1:26–30; 2:18–25). Moreover, she was created for Adam and to be a help meet for him. There is a difference in both origin and purpose. The man was created directly for God, the woman was created directly for man.

There is an order in Christ (1 Cor. 11:10–12). Here Paul pauses. He introduces an intriguing and unexpected side of things. He mentions *the observing angels:* "For this cause ought the woman to have power on her head because of the angels" (11:10). The word for *power* here is *exousia,* which means "authority." When a woman prays or prophesies in the church she must display her authority for doing so. With that covering on her head she reveals that she has been given authority to take such a role. Without the veil she is out of order. Wearing the veil, she shows that she has been given the authority.

This really has little or nothing to do with either ancient Jewish or pagan culture, and it certainly has nothing to do with our own modern culture. Its roots and reason are greater than that. It is bound up with the will of God, the order of creation, the fall of the human race and its restoration in Christ, and the watching angels. As has often been pointed out, a woman played little or no part in the synagogue service. Devout Jewish men actually thanked God that they had not been created women. A woman could not even make up the necessary quorum of ten to organize a synagogue. There had to be ten men, no matter how many women, or there could be no synagogue. In Christ women are emancipated. In the meetings of the early church she was permitted to pray and prophesy. However, the veil had to be worn when a woman did so. "Because of the angels," Paul adds, as an additional reason for this rule.

There has been much speculation over this statement. It is very germane to the subject. Again we are taken back to the beginning. Sin was introduced into this planet by an angelic being of the highest rank. He gained his victory over the human race by means of a woman (Gen. 3).

When God made man He made him to be ruled from his head. When He made woman He made her to be ruled from her heart. The distinction is as real as the physical difference between men and women. The fact that man is made to be ruled from his head and woman to be ruled from her heart does not mean that women cannot think. We all know some women who can out-think some men. Nor does it mean that men cannot feel. We all know some men who can feel far more deeply than some women. Just the same, the basic fact remains. Men tend to be ruled from the head, women from the heart.

What Satan did in the temptation was to reverse God's order. He first of all directed temptation to Eve's head and engaged her in an intellectual discussion as to whether or not it was right to do something God said was wrong. Her attempts to fend him off were all too clumsy. Three times she misquoted the two verses which, for her, constituted the entire Word of God and which was her sole defense. He raised in her mind a doubt about God's Word, followed it up with a denial, and ended with a delusion. He offered to set her free from the hampering restrictions imposed upon her by God's Word and bestow upon her godlike status and power. This overwhelming appeal to her intellect and vanity was more than she could withstand. She was deceived and overthrown.

Then, reversing his tactics, Satan directed temptation to Adam's heart. Indeed, he made no attempt, himself, to storm the citadel of Adam's soul. He let Eve do that. When Adam saw Eve in her fallen condition he was overwhelmed.

He loved her. He listened to her. He looked at her. He was not deceived. He knew what he was doing. It was "through one man's disobedience" that sin entered (Rom. 5:12, 19). God does not attribute the Fall to Eve but to Adam, who was given the headship and the responsibility. Thus Adam was disobedient and Eve was deceived, all because the Evil One was able to twist God's order.

The angels, it seems, were witnesses of all this. Lucifer, their one-time lord in the guise of a serpent, engineered the whole thing. Hence the reference here to the angels. They are watching with keenest interest those things which have to do with the church (1 Peter 1:12). They look to see God's order reestablished and reaffirmed in the church—and God's order calls for the woman to cover her head when she prays or prophesies.

There are not only the observing angels, there is *the obvious angle* (1 Cor. 11:11–12). There is, first of all, *the mutual dependence of the creature on the creature* (11:11–12a). Paul writes, "Nevertheless, neither is the man without the woman, neither the woman without the man, in the Lord. For as the woman is of the man, even so is the man also by the woman." We see here another example of Paul's sensitivity. He keeps on reiterating the fact that though the woman is subordinate to the man in terms of position, office, and responsibility, and must always bear witness to that when assuming a man's role, she is in no way inferior to the man. This is especially so "in the Lord," in the new sphere where those who love the Lord operate, "live and move, and have their being."

Paul illustrates this graphically enough. Although, in the first instance, at the time of creation, the woman was taken from the man, ever since then in the ordinary process of natural birth, the man is taken from the woman—an obvious enough fact indeed!

There is also *the mutual dependence of the creature on the Creator* (11:12b). Paul adds, "But all things of God." Eve did not create herself. No person is responsible for his or her own being. Nothing exists apart from God's creative power. God's wisdom, love, and power lie behind the entire universe of created things, whether Adam and Eve, who were made, and all their descendants, male and female alike, who were born and appointed their place in the scheme of things.

Thus Paul brings to a conclusion the matter of man and his headship. He winds up the discussion of order in the fellowship by taking up *the matter of man and his hair* (11:13–16). Since a woman's hair has been in the background of much of the preceding discussion, these concluding remarks are appropriate as they tie together the loose ends of the argument.

There is, first, *a final contrast* (11:13–15). Paul asks two questions. Here's *the first question:* "Judge in yourselves: is it comely that a woman pray unto God uncovered?" (11:13). The word for *uncovered* here is the same as in verse 5. Having established again the equality of the man and the woman before God, the apostle guards against that equality being used as any argument to undermine the previous teaching—that when a woman takes the man's role she is to wear a covering on her head. "Can't you see that for yourselves?" he says. "Do you need an apostle and a divine revelation to teach you what is seemly and what is not?" It ought to be obvious! The word for *comely* is *prepō* and refers to that which is pleasing to the eyes. We would use the word *becoming* today. Paul challenges his readers. Surely they could instinctively see the difference between when a woman usurped a man's role and displayed her hair and when she covered her head when taking a man's role. Simply in terms of modesty alone such a procedure was fitting and ought to be instinctively recognized as such. In Paul's day pagan prophetesses prophesied with their heads uncovered and their hair disarrayed. Perhaps Paul had this picture in mind. What devout, godly woman, standing up to speak in the church, would want to be like one of them? Surely, again, there should be an instinctive shrinking from such manifest disorder.

Then comes *the further question,* this time a question in two parts. The first part has to do with *nature and a man's hair,* especially with *its length:* "Doth not even nature teach you, that, if a man have long hair, it is a shame unto him?" (11:14). The word for *shame* here is not the same as in verse 5. The word here is *atimia.* Literally it means to be without honor. It is a dishonorable thing for a man to let his hair grow long. During the hippie craze in our Western society, those who dropped out of the Establishment deliberately adopted an interesting and significant way of displaying their revolt against the established norms of society. The men let their hair grow long. That long hair of theirs was worn as a badge and symbol of their contempt for the norm—what Paul calls here "nature." Along with this long hair went a militant drug culture, a flagrant defiance of all established moral standards, a preoccupation with poverty, dirt, and squalor, a fascination with the occult, a craze for rock music and filthy lyrics, and orchestrated mass demonstrations against everything that displeased them. The total breakdown in our society of the Judeo-Christian ethic stems from those days and the failure of the Establishment to deal firmly and decisively with the problem. The symbol of the revolt was everywhere evident—men with long, unkempt hair.

The convention of men wearing their hair short and women wearing their hair long goes back a very long way. It was so established a custom in Paul's day, for instance, that he could speak of it as a natural state of affairs. The custom can be traced back at least as far as Moses, for under the Mosaic Law it was only in the rare case of the Nazarite that long hair was allowed to be worn by men. In that case it was not a mark of rebellion but of consecration. As soon as the period of the vow was over the Nazarite had to cut off his long hair and burn it. It was second nature, then, even in Paul's day, for a man to wear short hair. For a man to have long hair, he said, was a shame. It proclaimed the man to be without honor. It might even have been regarded as having more serious complications—a tendency toward effeminacy and serious moral problems.

The second part of Paul's question takes up the obvious counterpart to all this. It has to do with *nature and a woman's hair,* especially with its *loveliness:* "But if a woman have long hair, it is a glory to her: for her hair is given her for a covering" (11:15). Some have taken this verse as an excuse for annulling all the previous teaching on the need for a woman to wear a covering on her head when she prays or prophesies. That cannot be. Paul does not devote a dozen verses to building his case only to knock it down casually and carelessly in the last verse. The woman's long hair is indeed her covering—but it is not the covering under discussion in the previous verses.

Paul uses a different word altogether here from the ones he has used elsewhere in the chapter. He uses the word *peribolaion.* It denotes something thrown around someone. It is a composite word made up of *peri (around)* and *hallō (to throw).* The thought behind the word is that a woman's long hair is a mantle, a wrapper, provided by nature for a woman's covering. Her hair, indeed, is her glory. Many women, indeed, know how to make the most of it and use it to advantage to catch the eye and excite the admiration (or envy) of others. As long hair on a man is a shame to him, so long hair on a woman is a glory to her.

This only adds weight to Paul's previous ruling. The woman, when she prays or prophesies, must put another covering over this natural covering. When she stands up to participate in worship she must not draw attention to herself. She must not put her hair on display. That would draw attention away from her words to her person. Her glorious, natural covering must be veiled. Only in this way can she honorably participate in audible public worship. The man, then, is to have short hair, the woman is to have long hair. The man is to participate in public worship with his head uncovered, the woman is to participate in public worship with her head covered. The man, with his head uncovered, acknowledges the headship of Christ. The woman, with her head covered, acknowledges the headship of the man.

Paul is through. However, he adds *a final caution:* "But if any man seem to be contentious, we have no such custom, neither the churches of God" (11:16). Paul, it seemed, realized that this teaching would be unpopular. He concludes with a sharp warning. The word for *contentious* here is *philoneikos.* It is a composite word made up of *phileo* (*to love*) and *neikos* (*strife*). It means to love strife or to enjoy squabbling. A companion word, *philoeikia,* is used to describe an incident in the Upper Room just after the Lord had instituted the communion feast, and just after He had bluntly stated that one of them would betray Him. We read "there was also a strife *[philoneikia]* among them, which of them should be accounted the greatest" (Luke 22:24). How sad! A love of strife leading to such an argument at such a time! Paul sensed this same un-Christlike spirit would motivate some to pick on his teaching and argue about it.

"We have no such custom!" Paul bluntly declares. That is, we have no such custom, here or anywhere else in the churches, to quarrel, especially over divinely revealed truth. The subject matter he had been discussing was of the highest order. It was not open for debate by those who simply liked to argue for argument's sake.

    b. Order at the feast (11:17–34)
        (1) The preliminary feast (11:17–22)
           (a) Paul's introduction (11:17)
           (b) Paul's information (11:18–22)
               i. There were divisions in the church (11:18–19)
                  a. What Paul heard (11:18a)
                  b. What Paul held (11:18b–19)
                     1. As to the reality of schisms (11:18b–19a)
                     2. As to the reason for schisms (11:19b)
               ii. There was disorder in the church (11:20–22)
                  a. What Paul denied (11:20)
                  b. What Paul deplored (11:21–22)
                     1. His scalding exposure of their behavior (11:21)
                         (i) Some were feasting wantonly (11:21a)
                       (ii) Some were fasting woefully (11:21b)
                     2. His scathing exclamation at their behavior (11:22)
                       (i) A justifiable exclamation (11:22a–c)

   (a) At their secular misconduct
    (11:22a)

   (b) At their spiritual misconduct
    (11:22b)

   (c) At their social misconduct
    (11:22c)

  (ii) A judgmental exclamation (11:22d)

(2) The primary feast (11:23–34)

 (a) Paul's concern (11:23–32)

  i. Significance of the Lord's Supper (11:23–26)

   a. When it was instituted (11:23a)

   b. Why it was instituted (11:23b–26)

    1. To remember the Lord's person (11:23b–25)

     (i) The emblem of His body (11:23b–24)

      (a) What the Lord did (11:23b–24b)

       (1) He blessed the bread
        (11:23b–24a)

       (2) He broke the bread
        (11:24b)

      (b) What the Lord desires (11:24c)

     (ii) The emblem of His blood (11:25)

      (a) What the Lord did (11:25a–b)

       (1) The taking of the cup
        (11:25a)

       (2) The making of the cov-
        enant (11:25b)

      (b) What the Lord desires (11:25c)

    2. To remember the Lord's passion (11:26a)

    3. To remember the Lord's promise (11:26b)

  ii. Seriousness of the Lord's Supper (11:27–30)

   a. The warning recorded (11:27–28)

    1. A very real danger (11:27)

    2. A very reasonable decision (11:28)

     (i) Preparation for the Supper (11:28a)

     (ii) Participation in the Supper (11:28b)

   b. The warning repeated (11:29–30)

    1. The judgment deserved (11:29)

(i)   Slighting the Lord's memorial body (11:29a)

(ii)   Slighting the Lord's mystical body (11:29b)

2. The judgment described (11:30)

(i)   Physical disability (11:30a)

(ii)   Physical death (11:30b)

(b) Paul's conclusion (11:31–34)

   i. A call to behave (11:31–32)

   a. How to foil judgment (11:31)

   b. How to face judgment (11:32)

      1. Its chastening work (11:32a)

      2. Its changing work (11:32b)

   ii. A call to begin (11:33–34a)

   a. Exercising mutual concern (11:33a)

   b. Exercising minimum care (11:33b–34a)

      1. To avoid causing jealousy (11:33b)

      2. To avoid courting judgment (11:34a)

   iii. A call to beware (11:34b)

The apostle now turns to the question of *order at the feast* (1 Cor. 11:17–34). Two feasts are in view, the love feast and the communion feast. Paul begins with *the preliminary feast* (11:17–22). First we have *Paul's introduction:* "Now in this that I declare unto you I praise you not, that ye come together not for the better, but for the worse" (11:17). Paul tells us, to start with, that he is now going to discuss the meetings of the church. The word for *come together* is *synerchomai.* The word refers to a voluntary assembly of people, rather than an authoritative gathering. The problem was that, at Corinth, their meetings were doing more harm than good. "I praise you not!" Paul indignantly exclaims.

We come now to *Paul's information* (11:18–22). First, there were *divisions in the church.* He says, "For first of all, when ye come together in the church, I hear that there be divisions among you, and I partly believe it. For there must be also heresies among you, that they which are approved may be manifest among you" (11:18–19). Paul was not surprised at what he had heard. There will always be problems in the church down here.

The word for *divisions* is *schisma,* from which we derive our English word "schism." The word pictures a cleft or a rent. It was used by the Lord to depict the rending of a garment (Matt. 9:16). A cognate word is used to describe the rending of the temple veil and also the rending of creation's rocks at the time of the crucifixion (27:51).

Paul also describes these dissentions as "heresies." The Greek word *hairesis* refers to that self-willed opinion which opposes truth and which leads to division and to the formation of sects. The word does not denote heresies as we commonly understand the word today, meaning radical departure from the truth.

We know that there was a regretable party spirit at Corinth because Paul has already dealt with it at some length (1 Cor. 1:10–16). The reference here is to a somewhat different problem. There, people were vying for position and rallying around sectarian names. Here, the reference is not so much to party spirit as to social snobbery. There was discrimination against the poor members of the fellowship.

Paul recognized the inevitability of such carnality and worldliness in the church. Much as he might deplore it, he could see a reason for it. God allowed it so that "they which are approved may be made manifest among you." The word *approved* comes from *dokimos,* a word often used of testing metals, as in Zechariah 11:12–13, to see if they are genuine. In such a heterogeneous fellowship as existed at Corinth, it was necessary that attitudes and behavior surface so that the genuine might be distinguished from the false.

But there were not only divisions in the church, there was also *disorder in the church* (1 Cor. 11:20–22). Note *what Paul denied:* "When ye come together therefore into one place, this is not to eat the Lord's supper" (11:20). The reference here is to the communal meal that preceded the communion service itself. The disorders in the Corinthian church were such that it was impossible for the Lord's Supper (the emphasis is on the word *Lord*) to be eaten. True, they came together for supper, and they might even have persuaded themselves that it was the Lord's Supper of which they were partaking, but the facts proved otherwise. At the Lord's Supper, rich and poor alike partake together of His bounty. What they were doing was such a mockery of the Lord's Supper as to negate the idea behind that supper altogether. When the Lord fed the five thousand He did not show partiality to the rich or to the socially elite members of the crowd. He didn't seat them together in a special group, make sure they were served first, that the chief apostles waited on them, and that their table was kept supplied even though others seated farther away had not yet had anything to eat. The idea is ludicrous. No wonder Paul regarded the behavior at the "Lord's Supper" at Corinth as a mere travesty of the feast it was supposed to be.

Note also *what Paul deplored* (11:21–22). We note, first, his *scalding exposure of their behavior* (11:21). Some were *feasting wantonly:* "For in eating every one taketh before other his own supper" (11:21a) and others were *fasting woefully:* "and one is hungry, and another is drunken" (11:21b). It was a shameful exhibit of pride and greed and discrimination on the part of the well-to-do members of the fellowship. Evidently each member brought to the meal his own supply of food and drink. While some indulged themselves to the point of satiety and drunkenness, others went hungry. There was no sharing, no spirit of compassion, nothing Christlike about the thing at all. The Lord's Supper, indeed!

We note also Paul's *scathing exclamation at their behavior* (11:22). He gives *a justifiable exclamation* (11:22a–c). They were guilty of *secular misconduct:* "What? have ye not houses to eat and drink in?" If they were going to behave like gluttons they would be better off to stay at home and indulge themselves there, not come to the Lord's Supper in order to show off their rich pantries, their greed, and their bad manners. They were guilty of *spiritual misconduct:* "Or despise ye the church of God?" Their behavior was an insult to the church of God, which was the very arena in which God was demonstrating Christ to a lost and dying world. Such conduct negated everything the church was in essence and everything it was supposed to represent in a pagan, godless world. They were guilty of *social misconduct:* "and shame them that have not?" Poverty is a big enough burden without having it shown up and exhibited by the ostentation, abundance, and ill-manners of the rich. Surely the church was one place where rich and poor could meet together on common ground. The rich, indeed, ought to furnish a lavish table for the poor on all such occasions, with "bread enough and to spare," with many basketfuls, indeed, for the poor to take home to their needy families. That would indeed be the Lord's idea of such a table.

Paul's justifiable exclamation is followed by *a judgmental exclamation:* "What shall I say to you? shall I praise you in this? I praise you not" (11:22d). He began this chapter by praising them for what he could (11:2), but the praise soon turns to blame. On the contrary he begins and ends these verses on their debasement of the Lord's table with rebuke (11:17, 22). Paul could see no redeeming feature whatsoever in this unbecoming and almost unbelievable conduct on the part of people who professed to love the Lord Jesus. It is no wonder this preliminary feast dropped into abeyance if this was the way it was conducted. What a disgraceful preliminary to participation in the communion service!

Paul turns abruptly to that service, to *the primary feast* (11:23–34), the feast we now commonly call the Lord's Supper. We note, first, *his concern* (11:23–32).

The Lord left only two ordinances with His church—baptism and breaking bread. In the one we commemorate our death with Him; in the other we demonstrate His death for us. Satan has attacked both these ordinances, since he hates and fears the twin truths they teach. He has distorted the Lord's Supper into the Mass, a near blasphemous ritual in which a man-ordained priest claims, by the utterance of five Latin words *(hoc est enim corpus muem),* to be able to turn a piece of bread into the body, blood, soul, and divinity of the Lord Jesus Christ. The Roman Church calls this "an unbloody sacrifice" and uses it to perpetuate its mind control over millions of deceived people. Its theological implications are horrendous. Anyone who wants to see how this dogma works out in practice should read Father Chiniquy's *Fifty Years in The Church of Rome.* That is one extreme! The other is to jettison the feast altogether or commemorate it as seldom as possible and as an appendix to an already crowded program, or keep the feast often in a perfunctory sort of way so that it becomes ritualistic, lacking in character and often more like a funeral service than a feast.[8]

Paul's particular concern, in this passage, was that people understand two things. First that they understand *the significance of the Lord's Supper* (11:23–26) and then that they understand *the seriousness of the Lord's Supper* (11:27–30). He begins with the question of *when it was instituted:* "For I have received of the Lord that which also I delivered unto you, that the Lord Jesus the same night in which he was betrayed took bread" (11:23). This feast of remembrance was instituted on the most solemn night of the Lord's life. The storm clouds were already gathering. The Passover feast commemorated by Jesus in the Upper Room was over—forever! Its significance was ended. The true Passover Lamb was about to be killed and His blood shed. Redemption from a greater bondage than that of

---

8. Satan has attacked baptism with equal vigor. Some groups discard the rite altogether, either because they cannot see its importance or because of ultra-dispensational views. Others baptize infants in order to bring them into the church or assure their salvation. No doctrine has been more instrumental in persuading lost people that they are really saved than the doctrine of baptismal regeneration. Here, Rome has taken the lead, but many Protestant churches have followed that lead using "covenant theology" as their justification for doing so. Other groups repudiate baptismal regeneration but embrace the view that baptism, nevertheless, is essential for salvation—bad news for the dying thief (Luke 23:40–43). Still others hold sound views on baptism, but push people into it without any understanding of the solemn significance of what they are doing. Others go to the other extreme and make candidates for baptism wait for months on end until they have demonstrated their fitness for it.

Israel in Egypt was about to be purchased for all mankind. Judas had already left to carry out his nefarious mission, and the Sanhedrin was awaiting his arrival. Pilate had been alerted that an urgent capital case might be referred to him soon. The Lord's last night on earth had come. Ahead loomed Gethsemane, Gabbatha, Golgotha, and the grave. By three o'clock on the day soon to dawn He would be dead. The shadow of the cross lay over that room. Before going out to face the terrible ordeal ahead, the Lord paused to institute this new feast. That was when it was instituted. The occasion could not have been more sobering.

Paul makes an affirmation in introducing this subject. "I have received . . . I also delivered," he says. The first *I* is emphatic. He had received the truth concerning the Lord's Supper directly from the Lord Himself, not from some intermediary source. He says the same thing of his gospel (Gal. 1:11–12). The other apostles had been in the Upper Room when the Lord actually instituted this feast. However, Paul had not derived his information about this great ordinance from any of them but by direct revelation from the Lord. Paul reminds the Corinthians further that he had communicated the truth about this ordinance to them verbally when he was among them. Doubtless he had led their first faltering steps in the path of obedience to the Lord's dying command and taught them how to spread the table and keep the feast. He is now confirming that oral instruction with written instruction which would safeguard it from the accretions of error and superstition. Those concerned could now always come back to the written Word when concerned that this precious provision was being either neglected or abused.

Paul now turns to the question of *why it was instituted* (1 Cor. 11:23b–26). The commemoration of the Lord's Supper (and, incidentally, of all true worship) revolves around three focal points. We come to remember, first of all, *the Lord's Person* (11:23b–25). Two specific emblems were brought forward by the Lord Jesus to emphasize this. First, there was *the emblem of His* body (11:22b–24). We read that the Lord Jesus "took bread: and when he had given thanks, he brake it, and said, Take, eat: this is my body, which is broken for you: this do in remembrance of me." There is enough in that simple but sublime act to fill a book.

How many times He had taken bread before! It was such an ordinary, everyday, commonplace act! Once before He had taken bread and blessed it and fed people by the thousands! But now He invests that simple commodity with a significance all its own. "This is my body!" He said.

First, however, He gave thanks—not just for the bread; this was not just an ordinary grace said before an ordinary meal! He gave thanks, then deliberately broke it, then solemnly said: "This is my body." In other words, He stood there with that bread in His hands, which symbolized His body, and gave thanks for the impending breaking of His literal human body on the cross of Calvary. What an extraordinary act of faith. Soon that body of His would be battered, bruised, and broken beyond our imagination. He would be punched and slapped, crowned with thorns, and scourged to the bone. His very beard would be torn from His cheeks. He would be hammered to a cross of wood and every bone in His body would be wrenched out of joint—yet He gave thanks for all that! Such was His trust in His Father! Such, too, was His understanding of the work of the Cross. Beyond the agony and pain wrought upon His mortal body was the joy of anticipation of the creation of His mystical body.

"This is my body!" The Roman church has seized upon this simple statement and used it to justify their dogma of transubstantiation. Martin Luther likewise insisted on taking it literally to perpetuate his own form of the Romish error. But obviously what we have here is a metaphor. The bread used at the communion feast is not magically changed into the material body of Christ by the incantation of certain words. The Lord meant that the bread was henceforth to be regarded as His memorial body. It was a picture of His material body soon to be broken at Calvary.

"Take, eat," He said, as He passed the broken bread around the table. As the bread was passed from hand to hand, each one tore off a piece, adding to its mutilation, and thereby testifying to the part his sin played in the breaking of the Lord's material body on the cross. It is a very personal thing. It is to be remembered, too, that the bread was broken, not cut up into little pieces. In Bible times bread was customarily broken, not sliced with a knife.

Next came *the emblem of His blood* (11:25). There were two symbolic acts here. First, there was *the taking of the cup:* "After the same manner also he took the cup, when he had supped"; and there was *the making of the covenant:* "saying, This cup is the new testament in my blood: this do ye, as oft as ye drink it, in remembrance of me."

This new feast was instituted after the Passover and was distinct from it. Nevertheless, the bread and wine, already on the table, and used in connection with the Passover, were now used for an entirely new purpose. There is much debate as to whether or not the Lord used wine in instituting this feast of remembrance. Matthew says it was "the fruit of the vine" (Matt. 26:27–29). The other synopticists do not say anything at all about the actual contents of the cup. However, it seems almost certain it was wine. The drinking of wine at the Passover has always been the custom. Since the wine used in that connection was red wine, it would serve well the purpose the Lord had in mind when using it as an emblem of His blood about to be shed for sinful men.

It is worth noting, however, that neither Paul nor the gospel writers actually say what was in the cup. The cup itself is always mentioned by means of *metonymy*, a figure of speech for what is in the cup. Doubtless this was done by the Holy Spirit for practical reasons. There have surely been many occasions when God's people have desired to have the Lord's Supper in places or under circumstances that have made it impossible to obtain wine. The best available substitute could, surely, be used. Then, too, there are many who have a conscientious objection to the use of wine, even at the Lord's Supper. There can be no objection to them using grape juice. The cup is mentioned, the wine is implied.

In any case, the contents of the cup were clearly intended to symbolize the blood shed on the cross of Calvary for the sin of the world. Throughout the Old Testament period rivers of blood flowed in countless animal sacrifices, but all that blood could not give a guilty conscience peace or wash away a single stain. Now "richer blood has flowed from nobler veins." The Lord would have us to never forget the breaking of His body and the shedding of His blood.

The shedding of His blood, however, was to serve another purpose. It was to ratify the new covenant *(diathēkē)*. The coming of this new covenant was foretold by the prophet Jeremiah (31:31–34). This new covenant had two distinctly different sets of clauses. There were eschatological clauses, which belong exclusively to the nation of Israel and which still await fulfillment. There were also soteriological clauses, which belong inclusively both to Israel (to be enjoyed at the time of Israel's national repentance at the Lord's second coming) and to the church. The Lord here activates the clauses in the new covenant, which has to do with salvation. His shed blood, symbolized in the cup, made the new covenant possible. Christians are brought into the new covenant to become partakers of all its salvation blessings.

So, then, the Lord would have us remember His *person*. "This do," He says, "in remembrance of me!" At the Lord's Table we should be occupied with "no man save Jesus only." We should focus our thoughts, our hymns, our Scripture reading, our ministry on His Person, on who He is in all the fullness of His nature and His personality. We should think about Him as the eternal, uncreated, self-existing second Person of the Godhead, coequal, coexistent, coeternal with the Father, possessed of all the attributes and prerogatives of deity. We should remember how He stepped out of eternity into time, how He lived among us as a man among men, man as God intended man to be, man inhabited by God. We should trace His pathway here below, the life that He lived, the truth that He taught, the way that He was. A thousand texts, a hundred hymns will come to mind. His Person! The subject is inexhaustible.

At the Lord's Table, however, we come to remember something else—*the Lord's passion:* "For as often as ye eat this bread, and drink this cup, ye do show the Lord's death" (1 Cor. 11:26a). The emblems in the Lord's Supper take us directly to Calvary. The feast was instituted on the eve of the Cross, with its dark shadow lying heavy on the Lord's heart. They speak of His body broken and of His blood poured out. They speak with eloquent voice of His passion. Therefore, at the Lord's Table we concentrate on the theme of the Lord's death. Again, our Scripture readings, our hymns, our ministry should focus on Calvary. Again, we have an abundant supply of Bible passages which take us to the cross. Old Testament typology, Old Testament prophecy, many psalms, the Gospel records, the Epistles, even the book of Revelation all take us to Calvary. Our hymnbook never tires of reminding us of the cross.

But there is something else. We come to remember *the Lord's position:* "Ye do shew the Lord's death till he come" (11:26b). For the Lord is no longer on the cross, He is on the throne—and He is coming again! Our meditation at the Lord's Supper should include thoughts of His sure and certain return. He is now our Great High Priest, our Advocate with the Father, seated at the right hand of the Majesty on high. There He sits, "henceforth expecting until all his enemies be made his footstool." Throughout Scripture, when the Bible speaks of the sufferings of Christ, it speaks also of the glory to follow. He arose from the dead. He ascended on high. He transcends all time and space. He is coming for His church, and then with His church He is going to reign. These are fitting themes for the Lord's Supper. Once more our Bibles and our hymnbooks supply us with many variations on this glorious theme.

Paul reminds us, too, of the words *as oft* and *as often* as he reviews the whole subject of the Lord's Table. The way this ordinance is often neglected one would think the Lord had said "as seldom," not "as often." God does not legislate how often, but He most certainly intimates how often. The first day of the week was the customary day when the early church met to remember the Lord (Acts 20:6–7). Paul arrived at Troas on Monday. He was in a hurry to get to Jerusalem having a desire, as a Jew, to be in the holy city in time for the Passover feast. He curbed his impatience and remained in Troas for a whole week. There was something more important to Paul than being in Jerusalem in time for the Passover—being at Troas to participate in the Lord's Supper, which, it seems, was celebrated on Sunday.

Having discussed the significance of the Lord's Supper, Paul turns to *the seriousness of the Lord's Supper* (1 Cor. 11:27–30). First *a warning is recorded* (11:27–28). He mentions *a very real danger:* "Wherefore whosoever shall eat this bread, and drink this cup of the Lord, unworthily, shall be guilty of the body and blood of the Lord" (11:27). The word translated "unworthily" is *anaxiōs,* occurring only here and in verse 29. It means to participate in the Lord's Supper without proper preparation. The warning may have reference to the unsaved, although it is difficult to see how a person can remember One he does not even know. The warning certainly has reference to believers. We are not to participate at the Lord's Table lightly or flippantly. Since the celebration of the Lord's Supper followed the fellowship meal, it is evident that some, at Corinth, were actually participating while intoxicated (11:21).

Paul underlines how serious a matter it is to partake of the emblems at the Lord's Supper in an unworthy way. Such a person becomes guilty of the body and blood of the Lord. It would be difficult to imagine a more terrible charge. The word for *guilty* is *enochos.* It means to be liable to a charge to face a legal action. The word was used by the Sanhedrin when it condemned the Lord Jesus to death (Matt. 26:65–66).

Paul mentions also *a very reasonable decision* (1 Cor. 11:28). There should be *preparation* for the supper: "But let a man examine himself" (11:28a), followed by *participation* in the supper: "so let him eat of that bread, and drink of that cup" (11:28b). We should not be apprehensive about partaking of the emblems at the Lord's Table but we do need to prepare our hearts first. There should be a measure of heart-searching. Is there unconfessed sin in my life? Does anyone have anything against me? Am I walking in fellowship with the Lord in the light of His Word? John reminds us that none of us is free from sin (1 John 1:8–9) and that the means to deal with it is readily available (2:1–2).

Then *the warning is repeated* (1 Cor. 11:29–30). First, *judgment is deserved* (11:29). Two sins are mentioned. The first has to do with slighting the Lord's *memorial* body: "For he that eateth and drinketh unworthily, eateth and drinketh damnation to himself" (11:29). The word *damnation* can be rendered "judgment." The related sin has to do with slighting the Lord's *mystical* body: "not discerning the Lord's body." The truth of the mystical body is in the near context (12:12–27).

Some churches are dedicated to guarding the Lord's Table from intruders.

Those wishing to participate must be members in good standing of their local fellowship or one of which they approve. Even when they approve of the sister fellowship, if the person wishing to join them at the table is coming from afar, he will often be required to produce "a letter of commendation" accrediting him to be a believer who holds all the right views. When a stranger without the proper credentials shows up at the Lord's Supper, the elders interrogate him. Sometimes he is refused admission altogether, and shown to a seat outside the circle of those allowed to actually participate. He is to sit there in silence, ostracized by "those in fellowship," permitted only to look on and listen. The person may be a true believer, far more spiritual than those in the inner circle around the table. No matter! He could not pronounce their "shibboleth" or meet their criteria. All that really offends them in this brother might be his denominational affiliation or the fact that he does not know some of the prominent people in their circles, or the distressing circumstance that he does not have a letter of commendation signed by someone they recognize, or the unpardonable sin of wearing the wrong kind of clothes or that his hair is too long or that he has a beard or that he admits an admiration for Billy Graham or someone else of whom they disapprove, or, if it is a woman, that she has her hair too short or she is not prepared to put a covering on her head even though they produce a dubious doily for her to wear.

One admires the zeal to protect the Lord's Table. But surely Paul says, "Let a man examine *himself,* and *so* let him eat." The sin to which the apostle refers here, of "not discerning the Lord's body," is surely the sin of cutting off true members of that body from the Lord's Table. To discriminate on the kinds of grounds mentioned above is to be guilty of not discerning the Lord's body, which is much bigger and far more diversified than any one local fellowship. The criterion should be life, not light. The Lord's body includes all those who know and love Him, and all such, unless living sinful lives or holding heretical views, ought to be welcomed at the Lord's Table. It is His Table, after all, not ours. To receive a visitor to the Lord's Table is one thing. To receive someone permanently into the fellowship of the local church is something else and does, indeed, merit a more thorough examination. Even so, we are to discern the Lord's body as including millions of members whose light on certain doctrines may be uncertain.

In the Old Testament, stringent rules were enforced as to who could or could not participate at the Lord's Table in the tabernacle. The basic requirement was one of birth. Generally speaking, only the priests could eat the showbread, and to be a priest it was necessary to be born into the priestly family. A blind priest, or a lame priest, or a priest who was improperly developed, while he was barred from service, was welcomed to the table (Lev. 21:17–23). The criterion for sitting at the Lord's Table is not how well we can see certain truths, or how noble and straight our walk or our present state of development. The Lord could overlook such things. Poor Mephibosheth was allowed to come to David's banqueting hall and hide his lame feet under the table (2 Sam. 9). A priest's bondslaves could come to the table and so could his widowed or divorced daughter (Lev. 21:11–12). However, if a priest was a leper he was not allowed to eat (21:4)—leprosy in the Bible is a picture of sin. People living in sin are barred from the Lord's Table as a matter of course. No absolute strangers were allowed to eat (21:10), and just because a man was visiting a priest or worked for the priest, that did not give him access to the Table. It is not a matter of who we know but a matter of being in the family. Judgment is not only deserved, if we fail to discern the Lord's body, but *judgment is described.* It might take the form of *physical disability:* "For this cause many are weak and sickly among you" (1 Cor. 11:30a), or it may take the form of *physical death:* "and many sleep" (11:30b). It is hard to escape the literal force of this warning. We do not need to guard the Table. It is the Lord's Table and He is well able to protect it Himself. Many at Corinth were not discerning the Lord's body. That was evident from the way they were treating the poorer believers at the love feast. The Lord has a whole arsenal of weapons at His disposal when it comes to judging His people. Weakness and sickness may not always be the result of a careless attitude toward His Table but evidently, at times they are.

Persistence in sin, even when the Lord's hand has been laid on one in displeasure, can result in premature death. The word for *sleep* here is *koimaomai.* It is never used of spiritual insensitivity. It is used of natural sleep, but that is evidently not what is referred to here. It is used of the death of the body, but only of the death of believers and especially of the death of believers since the Lord's ascension (Acts 7:60; 1 Cor. 7:39; 11:30; 15:6, 18, 51; 1 Thess. 4:13–15; 2 Peter 3:4). We derive our English word *cemetery* from the noun *koimētērion.* That word was used by the Greeks of a rest house for strangers, but, according to W. E. Vine, it was adopted by the Christians for a place where the bodies of loved ones were laid to rest. The word *cemetery* literally means "the sleeping place."[9]

We come now to *Paul's conclusion* (1 Cor. 11:31–34). There is *a call to behave* (11:31–32). First, Paul tells us *how to foil judgment:* "For if we would judge ourselves, we should not be judged" (11:31). Years ago, Allan Redpath was staying in a home where there were two boys. One night the family went off to the service, leaving the

---

9. Vine, *Expository Dictionary of New Testament Words,* 1:81.

boys home alone on their promise to be good. When they arrived back a strange silence reigned over the house. They called the boys but there was no answer. They went into the living room and there on the table was a pile of broken pieces and a note. The note read, "Dear Mom and Dad, we broke your vase. We are very sorry. We have put ourselves to bed without any supper. (signed) Jimmy and Joe." Said Allen Redpath, "What do you think that father did? Do you think he rushed upstairs and hauled the boys out of bed and gave them a thrashing for breaking the vase? No, indeed! They had judged themselves, and judgment was disarmed."

In like manner Paul calls on us to judge ourselves. Self-judgment is not morbid introspection. It is not a matter of dredging up sin long since forgiven. It is not a sad wallowing in shame and guilt over sin already exposed and confessed and forgiven and put right so far as is humanly possible. The context here is the Lord's Table and eating and drinking so unworthily as to be actually eating and drinking judgment to oneself. Indeed, the first word for *judge* here is the same word translated "discern" in verse 29. We are to discern ourselves, see in ourselves the sad state of soul that would hinder us from seeing the Lord's body. That way we can foil judgment

If we neglect to take care of our sin ourselves, God will take care of it for us. So Paul tells us *how to face judgment* (1 Cor. 11:32). In God's judgment of the believer there is a *chastening* process: "But when we are judged, we are chastened of the Lord." There is also a *changing* process: "that we should not be condemned with the world." The Lord chastens His own (Rev. 3:19). He makes a distinction between the saint and the sinner, between His own children and the world. Our responsibility, as believers, is to keep close to the Lord so that we might be sensitive to all that displeases Him. We should keep our lives open to His inspection. As the little chorus puts it, we should pray,

> Search me, O God, and know my heart today;
> Try me, O Savior, know my thoughts, I pray.
> See if there be some wicked way in me;
> Cleanse me from every sin and set me free.

If we allow wrongdoing to continue unjudged it gets worse and eventually becomes the norm. We no longer see sin as sin. God then has to do what we won't. He judges us and chastens us. He does this so that we can escape God's discipline, so often meted out to the godless people of this world.

Now comes *a call to begin:* "Wherefore, my brethren, when ye come together to eat, tarry one for another. And if any man hunger, let him eat at home" (1 Cor. 11:33–34a). This takes us back to the love feast. When the food is set out, it should be shared.

There should be no inconsiderate haste. If a man is so hungry he cannot wait for his turn, he should eat at home. It seems incredible that it should be necessary for an apostle to have to write such instructions into the very Word of God! The disorderly conduct at Corinth must have been very serious indeed. Such was Paul's godly concern that all things be done decently and in order in God's house that he does not hesitate to speak to even such mundane things as this, things which should have been settled by ordinary good manners.

Finally comes *a call to beware:* "That ye come not together unto condemnation [judgment]. And the rest will I set in order when I come" (11:34b). What a tragedy it would be if our gatherings were a source of condemnation and judgment instead of a source of grace and blessing. Evidently there were other issues in connection with the fellowship meal and the Lord's Supper that needed to be addressed. These, however, could wait until Paul's next visit. Hopefully by then the Corinthians would have put their own house in order.

> 2. The gifts of the Lord's servants (12:1–14:40)
>> a. Confusion (12:1–31)
>>> (1) Information (12:1–11)
>>>> (a) The subject of the gifts (12:1–3)
>>>>> i. A truth to be apprehended (12:1–2)
>>>>>> *a.* The danger of present ignorance (12:1)
>>>>>> *b.* The danger from previous influence (12:2)
>>>>>>> *1.* Their Gentile background (12:2a)
>>>>>>> *2.* Their genuine bondage (12:2b)
>>>>> ii. A test to be applied (12:3)
>>>>>> *a.* A terrible renunciation of the truth (12:3a)
>>>>>> *b.* A true recitation of the truth (12:3b)
>>>> (b) The source of the gifts (12:4–6)
>>>>> i. There are different endowments, but the same Spirit (12:4)
>>>>> ii. There are different enterprises, but the same Lord (12:5)
>>>>> iii. There are different enablements, but the same God (12:6)

(c) The scope of the gifts (12:7–11)
    i. Why gifts were given (12:7)
    ii. What gifts were given (12:8–10)
       a. Gifts of comprehension (12:8)
          1. The gift of inspiration—the word *(logos)* of wisdom (12:8a)
          2. The gift of insight—the word *(logos)* of knowledge (12:8b)
       b. Gifts of confirmation (12:9–10a)
          1. The ability to triumph over our mundane ways—faith (12:9a)
          2. The ability to triumph over our mortal woes—healing (12:9b)
          3. The ability to triumph over our material world—miracles (12:10a)
       c. Gifts of communication (12:10b–e)
          1. Primary gifts (12:10b–c)
             (i) The ability to express truth—prophecy (12:10b)
             (ii) The ability to expose error—discernment (12:10c)
          2. Passing gifts (12:10d–e)
             (i) The ability to excite the mind of some—tongues (12:10d)
             (ii) The ability to explain the message to others—interpretation (12:10e)
    iii. Ways gifts were given (12:11)

Paul turns now from *the gift of the Lord's Supper* (1 Cor. 11:2–34) to *the gifts of the Lord's servants* (12:1–14:40). This is a long and a highly controversial segment of this epistle. Paul's discussion of the subject revolves around three centers—*confusion* (12:1–31), *correction* (13:1–13), and *comparison* (14:1–40).

Gift is by no means the same as grace. Unsaved people can have natural gifts, great gifts, even gifts of genius. We think of people like Shakespeare, Einstein, and Beethoven. We do not equate gift with morality. Some men and women of tremendous ability are wholly without ethics or morality. Some have been scoundrels without conscience.

It is the same in the sphere of salvation. A believer can have spiritual gifts, even some of the greatest gifts, without any regard to spirituality or Christlikeness. It is a common mistake to imagine that just because a believer is gifted he is also godly. A successful evangelist, a brilliant Bible teacher, a compassionate pastor may or may not be spiritual. It is one of the mysteries of the faith, often demonstrated, readily observable, that gift does not necessarily go hand-in-hand with either grace or godliness in the Christian life. The Corinthians had all the gifts. They were also the most carnal and worldly of believers. Some great Bible teachers have been known to be veritable tyrants at home. More than one admired pastor has been known to run off with the church organist. Some evangelists who can get tearful responses from audiences have been eaten out with worldliness, pride, and greed.

Paul had to tackle this kind of problem at Corinth. At Corinth there was nothing but *confusion* (12:1–31) so far as the gifts were concerned. Paul deals with this along the line of *information* (12:1–11), *illustration* (12:12–27), and *indication* (12:28–31). By way of *information* he deals with the *subject* of the gifts (12:1–3), the *source* of the gifts (12:4–6), and the *scope* of the gifts (12:7–11).

So far as the *subject* of the gifts was concerned there was, first of all, *a truth to be apprehended* (12:1–2). Two dangers filled Paul's mind. There was, for instance, the danger of *their present ignorance:* "Now concerning spiritual gifts [spiritual things], brethren, I would not have you ignorant" (12:1). Ignorance is the mother of all kinds of mischief. A great deal of ignorance still surrounds the subject of spiritual gifts. People make the most outrageous claims and statements. People who have never done a structural analysis of 1 Corinthians 12–14 and who have never carefully exegeted what the Holy Spirit has to say in these chapters set themselves up as authorities. They parrot other people's opinions, or base their beliefs on some ecstatic experience and allow that "experience" to override sound doctrine, or take texts from these three chapters wholly out of context and parade these "proof" texts as sufficient authentication of their views. Some of them command vast audiences on radio and television. Some of them lead large congregations. Some of them can produce strange phenomena which, supposedly, support their claims to be right. The fact remains they are wholly out of touch with the thrust, teaching, and certainties developed by Paul in these three chapters. The fact that some of these people are "nice" people, or good people, or that they have a reputation for being taught in the Word proves nothing. The test is how they handle these chapters. The question of whether we are right or wrong about the teaching of these chapters is not merely academic. It is critical. We are up against a host of hostile intelligences in the spirit world eager to exploit our ignorance in this area of the Christian life.

For there is another danger. Paul reminds the Corinthians of the danger from *their past influence:* "Ye know that ye were Gentiles, carried away unto these dumb idols, even as ye were led" (12:2). Many of the Corinthian Christians had been won to Christ from a background of raw paganism. Behind the "dumb idols" lurked malignant evil spirits. These Gentile converts were familiar with ecstatic utterance, tongues, and frenzied prophecy. Apollo was believed to inspire Cassandra of Troy, the Delphic oracle, and the Sibyl of Cumae. The demon-possessed girl who followed Paul and Silas around Philippi was controlled by a pythonic spirit. So there was a counterfeit spirit world out there, real, menacing, waiting to deceive even God's elect. How vitally important it was to be right as to gifts which could and can be counterfeited by Satan and his demon hosts. The Corinthians were better equipped in this area than people are today. At least the Corinthians knew about demon oracles. Most modern Christians have never had direct contact with the demon world, that they know of, at least. The double danger at Corinth was that incautious believers might be susceptible to demonic attack and that, by rejecting sound doctrine, they might accept the counterfeit for the genuine. Some of the Corinthians had been deceived by "dumb idols" and had known the bondage of demon possession and demon obsession in their unconverted days.

There was a truth to be apprehended. There was also *a test to be applied:* "Wherefore I give you to understand that no man speaking by the Spirit of God calleth Jesus accursed; and that no man can say that Jesus is Lord, but by the Holy Ghost" (12:3). Now it is quite evident that unsaved people can say both these things. The blessed name of Jesus Christ is commonly taken as a curse word by the unregenerate, who thus expose themselves to the penalty of the third commandment (Exod. 20:7), and reveal of what spirit they are. Anyone can say the actual words "Jesus is Lord," so there must be more to this statement than appears on the surface.

The subject of the chapter is spiritual gifts and their use, especially the speaking gifts of tongues, interpretation, and prophecy. These were supernatural gifts, made operational by the Holy Spirit, who controlled the speaker at the time the specific utterance was being made. However, they were capable of being imitated by evil spirits. Hence the warning. The test was in the *content* of what was said while the speaker was evidently under the control of a supernatural power. It was not, and never has been, safe simply to assume that the inspired speaker is speaking from

God under the control of the Holy Spirit. The Holy Spirit Himself recognizes the danger of deception and builds in tests and safeguards that need to be employed whenever someone supposedly speaks in tongues or prophecies or gives a word of knowledge.

Should the speaker in any way detract from the Person, the work, the name, or the glory of the Lord Jesus, that speaker is *not* speaking by the Holy Spirit, no matter how true, brilliant, encouraging, or inspiring the rest of his "message" might be. Should the speaker fail to declare the fact that Jesus is Lord, his message should be regarded as highly suspect. Indeed, the communicating spirit, speaking through the believer who is in a trance-like state, should be challenged to make the confession that Jesus is Lord.

Moreover the listeners should pay strict attention to the reply. Since we are up against deceiving spirits, we need to beware. There are three ways a deceiving spirit can respond to the question. It can ignore the question altogether. It can respond with some true, even admirable statement about the Lord Jesus, which does not include the confession that "Jesus is Lord." It can release the believer from its control and let the believer himself answer the question. Each of these fraudulent responses reveals the presence of a deceiving spirit. Of course, the deceiving spirit may betray itself less subtly by cursing Christ. Cases are on record where Christians, speaking in tongues, have cursed and blasphemed in the most horrible way and where someone present, who knew the language in which they were speaking, has been able to expose the fearful deception.

Nor is the test given here by Paul the only one which must be applied whenever a person supposedly speaks in tongues or prophesies in the power of the Holy Spirit. Toward the end of the first century, when Gnostic sects were beginning to flourish, and when the most flagrant lies about the person of Christ were being circulated, the apostle John added a further test: "Beloved, believe not every spirit, but try the spirits whether they are of God: because many false prophets are gone out into the world. Hereby know ye the Spirit of God: Every spirit that confesses that Jesus Christ is come in the flesh is of God: and every spirit that confesseth not that Jesus Christ is come in the flesh is not of God: and this is that spirit of antichrist, whereof ye have heard that it should come; and even now already is it in the world" (1 John 4:1–3).

Both tests must be complied with. The confession that Jesus is Lord is a confession of the Resurrection and Ascension and of the Lord's true deity; the confession that Jesus Christ is come in the flesh is a confession of the Incarnation; of the Lord's true humanity.

No evil spirit can give voice to either truth. During His earthly ministry the Lord invariably cast out evil spirits and either ignored their testimony to Himself or silenced them—as He did, for example, when one of them spoke of Him in the synagogue where the Lord's people were gathered (Luke 4:33–35). Paul likewise got rid of the demon which possessed the slave girl and which tried to bear witness to the truth of Paul's ministry (Acts 16:16–18). The Lord has now imposed a ban of total silence on all unclean, deceiving spirits so that it is impossible for them to make either of the two confessions which now comprise the test. Only the Holy Spirit and good spirits in the service of God can make these confessions. Since the Holy Spirit requires these tests, it is evident that He will make the appropriate confession when asked. It is the height of gullibility, surely, to accept "tongues" or "prophecies" or "words of knowledge" as being from God if the Holy Spirit's own precautions are ignored or evaded.

Paul turns now to *the source of the gifts* (1 Cor. 12:4–6). There are *different endowments,* but the same Spirit: "Now there are diversities of gifts, but the same Spirit" (12:4); there are *different enterprises,* but the same Lord: "And there are differences of administrations, but the same Lord" (11:5); and there are *different enablements,* but the same God: "And there are diversities of operations *[energēma],* but it is the same God which worketh all in all" (11:6). Father, Son, and Holy Spirit unite in bestowing these varied gifts upon various believers. The gifts may differ in character and purpose, but behind the bestowal of each one is a member of the triune Godhead. The gifts are thus backed by all the fullness of the Godhead. Whatever discords and divisions and disagreements Satan may introduce into the church over the matter of the gifts, there is nothing but unity in the Godhead over their bestowal.

Various gifts, one God! God is a God of boundless diversity. No two fingerprints are alike, no two snowflakes, no two blades of grass, no two leaves, no two sunsets, no two personalities. God delights in variety. God is also a God of order. There are three Persons in the Godhead but there is only one God, and they are one in power and purpose. Paul is about to describe a number of gifts. He begins by emphasizing the oneness of their divine source. Believers have different gifts and different ways of serving God, but it is the same Spirit who bestows the gifts and the same Lord who is served by them. God works through different people in different ways, but it is the same God who achieves His purposes through them.

Paul turns now to *the scope of the gifts* (12:7–11). First, he tells *why gifts were given:* "But the manifestation of the Spirit is given to every man to profit withal" (11:7). Each and every gift is given by the Holy Spirit for the common good of all. The "manifestation" is not the outshining of human talent and ability but of the implanted power of God.

Now we are told *what gifts are given* (12:8–10). They can be divided into three general kinds. There are gifts of *comprehension* (12:8), gifts of *confirmation* (12:9–10a), and gifts of communication(12:10b–e).

First, there are gifts of *comprehension* (12:8). The first of these is *the gift of inspiration:* "For to one is given by the Spirit the word *[logos]* of wisdom" (12:8a). The early church had no New Testament, or at least only a partial, fragmentary, and incomplete New Testament. When Paul wrote this letter, for instance, he had written previously only to the Thessalonians and, probably, the Galatians. None of the other apostles except for James, the Lord's brother, seem to have written anything. The gospels of Matthew and Mark may have been *in* circulation. Beyond that, there remained "much land to be possessed" so far as writing the New Testament was concerned. One of the most necessary gifts, at this stage of the church's development, was the gift of "the utterance of wisdom." This gift gave the early church access to New Testament truth even though some of it had not yet been formally given by means of the written Word. The word for *wisdom* is *sophia.* It is joined with *revelation* as partaking of the same character (Eph. 1:17) or put instead of it as its equivalent (1 Cor. 14:6). This was the highest of the gifts and was possessed in special measure by the apostles and prophets.

Accompanying "the utterance of wisdom" was "the utterance of knowledge," *the gift of insight:* "to another the word *[logos]* of knowledge by the same Spirit" (12:8b). The ability to speak the word of knowledge was similar to the ability to speak the word of wisdom. It was inspired and inerrant teaching, but had reference to communications already made by God in His written Word. This gift was particularly needful in the early days of the church. Truth written to the Thessalonians, for instance, might be needed in a church in Galatia. Those with the gift of wisdom would be inspired to express that truth and those with the gift of knowledge would be able to expound that truth. This gift, like the word of wisdom, appears to be associated with the prophet and the apostle.

The first two gifts, then, were gifts of comprehension, essential at a time when the New Testament had not been completed, let alone been in general circulation. The Holy Spirit, who knew exactly, verbally, plenarily, just what would eventually comprise the New Testament, gave the word of wisdom and the word of knowledge here and there in the local churches as occasion required.

The next three gifts were *gifts of confirmation.* The church was supernaturally injected into history on the day of Pentecost just as it will be ejected back out of history supernaturally at the Rapture. The church represents a radical departure from all God's previous and promised dealings with mankind. It is unique! It is not an extension of Israel and it is radically different from Judaism. For two thousand years Israel had been *the chosen people* and God's instrument for speaking to the human race. Calvary put an end to Judaism. The rent veil in the temple bore eloquent testimony to that (Matt. 27:51). Pentecost marked the setting aside of Israel, as God's channel of revelation and blessing, until such time as "the fulness of the Gentiles be come in" (Rom. 11:25), that is, until God's purposes in and through the church on earth are completed.

It is evident that such a radical departure from the past would be bound to raise the wrath and envy of the Jews. They had rejected Christ. It was to be expected that they would reject Christianity, that they would cleave to their dead and divinely discarded Judaism and reject the church.[10] Just as the Lord was accredited by many marvelous miracles, so that the Jews were wholly without excuse for rejecting Him, so the church was accredited by many marvelous miracles, too, so that the Jews would be equally without excuse for rejecting Christianity. The Gospels record how the Jews rejected the Son of God, and the book of Acts records how the Jews, first in the homeland and then in the Diaspora, rejected the Spirit of God.

The Lord promised that the church would have ample accreditation (Mark 16:14–20).[11] The author of Hebrews bears witness to the fact that just such miracles as Mark mentions did accompany the proclamation of the gospel to the Jews. "How shall we escape, if we neglect so great salvation," he says, "which at the first began to be spoken by the Lord, and was confirmed unto us by them that heard him: God also bearing them witness, both with signs and wonders, and with divers miracles, and gifts of the Holy Ghost, according to his own will?" (Heb. 2:3–4).[12]

10. Paul deals with the whole issue at length in a great parenthesis in his Roman Epistle. He reviews God's *past* dealings with Israel (chap. 9) in terms of the *sovereignty* of God; with God's *present* dealings with Israel (chap. 10) in terms of the *salvation* of God; and with God's *promised* dealings with Israel (chap. 11) in terms of the *sincerity* of God. See Phillips, *Exploring Romans.*

11. Some have seen fit to challenge the authenticity of the last twelve verses of Mark's Gospel, probably because of their emphasis on the supernatural. These verses are found in all the ancient MSS. They are found in the Syriac versions and in the Latin versions. Jerome, who had access to Greek MSS older than any now extant, includes these verses. The Egyptian Armenian and Ethiopic versions all contain them.

12. Signs and wonders for the Jews; diverse miracles for the Gentiles; gifts of the Holy Ghost for the church. The Holy Spirit sovereignly gave or withheld these supernatural manifestations according to His own will. He never allows such power to get out of His own control.

Paul now discusses these gifts of confirmation, which were primarily intended to accredit the church as being divine departure from the norm of two millennia.

The first of these three gifts gave ability to triumph over *our mundane ways:* "to another faith, by the same Spirit" (1 Cor. 12:9a). This, of course, is not saving faith but miraculous faith. Saving faith is well within reach of any lost sinner. Saving faith does not differ in character from the ordinary, everyday faith we exercise thousands of times a day—as, for instance, when we put money in a bank, mail a parcel, board a bus, enter a building, sit on a chair, believe a politician, swallow some medicine, and so on. Instead of trusting a doctor or an architect or a philosopher or a guru we trust Christ. That is what makes ordinary faith saving faith.

Miraculous faith is of quite a different nature. It is one of the gifts of the Spirit. It enables certain people to move mountains, to see continual and extraordinary answers to prayer. The Lord Jesus spoke of this kind of faith when He said, "If ye have faith as a grain of mustard seed, ye shall say unto this mountain, Remove hence to yonder place; and it shall remove; and nothing shall be impossible unto you" (Matt. 17:20). This kind of faith gives the ability to command certain things to be done and instantly they are done. In other words, our commands become not only legislative but executive, as were the commands of the Lord Jesus to evil spirits, stormy seas, and dead people. Paul demonstrated this kind of commanding faith when he smote Elymas the sorcerer with instant blindness (Acts 13:11).

George Mueller of Bristol, who saw God provide, in extraordinary ways, for the hundreds of orphans entrusted to his care, did not claim to have the gift of faith. He said he had the grace of faith and attributed the miracles of divine supply to prevailing prayer, not to a supernatural gift. Along with this went a deep consciousness of God's will and a simple, childlike trust in God. Those today who command God to do this, that, or the other, sound to many as arrogant, presumptuous, and self-deceived, to say the least. Some seem to be downright tricksters.

Then, too, there was the ability to triumph over *our mortal woes:* "to another the gifts of healing, by the same Spirit" (1 Cor. 12:9b). The Lord Jesus gave this gift to the Twelve and to the Seventy when He sent them throughout the Promised Land to preach to the Jews that the kingdom was at hand (Matt. 10:1–6). This gift, so far as the Twelve were concerned, extended beyond the immediate mission, to the early days of the church (Acts 3:1–10; 9:36–43; 14:8–12; 28:8) and will be bestowed again upon the Lord's ambassadors during the tribulation age (21:42).

The gift of healing was supernatural. Medical science can work wonders today using medicine and surgery, but the gift of healing enabled those who possessed it to perform instant and permanent cures. Much that passes for "healing" today is psychosomatic, hypnotic, and often fraudulent. Nobody denies that God can and sometimes does heal people in answer to prayer, but it is highly doubtful that anyone has the *gift* of healing today. In the New Testament, those who had the gift of healing cleansed lepers instantly, gave sight to the blind, and restored strength to crippled limbs so that the lame could leap; their miraculous healing could be verified beyond all doubt.

A modern "healing" meeting is far removed from the New Testament model. The modern healer has to have a crowd. He or his agents, sometimes with hidden microphones, comb and screen the crowds so that only certain ones get anywhere near the healer. There is a great deal of hype and hoopla and the audience is worked up to the proper degree of hysteria. Those who come forward are "slain in the Spirit" by some process entirely foreign to the New Testament. And, of course, offerings are taken and a great deal of money changes hands. Everyone would be much more impressed if the so-called healer were to go to the local hospital, pick out the hardest case, as Jesus did (John 5:5–9) and as Peter did (Acts 3:1–10) and as Paul did (14:8–11), and instantly heal that person. Strange to say, modern healers stay as far away as possible from hospitals and sanitariums.

The gift of healing was present in the early church. In time, however, it passed away. As time went on Paul, who had the gift of healing, could speak of Trophimus being left at Miletum because he was sick (2 Tim. 4:20). He could write to the Philippians about Epaphroditus, who had been "sick nigh unto death: but God had mercy on him" (Phil. 2:25–30). He could advise Timothy to take some wine for his stomach's sake and because of his frequent infirmities (1 Tim. 5:23). The nation of Israel had fallen into a pattern of persistent unbelief. The "sign" gifts were mainly for them, anyway (1 Cor. 1:22), so it is no wonder that the gift of healing should gradually be withdrawn.

Another gift of confirmation was the ability to triumph over *our material world:* "To another the working of miracles" (12:10a). The word *miracles* comes from the Greek word *dynamis,* which suggests untrammeled, unhindered, unequaled power. The word occurs thirty-eight times in the Synoptic Gospels but, for some reason, John's gospel never employs it. John prefers the word *sēmeion,* which indicates a sign. Indeed, he selects eight signs which all manifest Israel's need and its condition of helplessness and death and the Lord's ability to meet that need. In the first, the Lord displayed His glory (John 2:11) and in the last He manifested Himself (21:14). When John wrote, Israel had ceased to be a nation, the signs had ceased, the church itself was facing apostasy, the old power, *dunamis,* was gone, the church was no longer performing miracles, it was in need of the refiner's fire.

Miracles, or power, were evident in the early church. Paul could smite a man with blindness (Acts 13:8–12), and both he and Peter could raise the dead (20:8–12; 9:36–42). Peter was miraculously released from prison (12:1–10) and the shackles fell from Paul's hands (16:23–26). Paul could be bitten by a snake and suffer no harm (28:3–6).

Actually, miracles are a rare phenomenon in Scripture. There are only five periods when they had any prominence and all five were during periods of crisis and transition.[13]

---

13. There was a blaze of miracles associated with the ministries of Moses and Joshua. These were designed to get Israel out of Egypt and into Canaan. The miracles then ceased and were replaced by the Word of God—the Pentateuch, the poetic books, and the early historical books.

There was another outbreak of miracles in the days of Elijah and Elisha. These stopped as suddenly as they started. They occurred at a critical time in the history of the monarchies. Apostasy was rampant in Israel and had affected Judah. The deportations loomed on the distant horizon. The miracles were designed to recall the nation to God. They ceased and were replaced by the Word of God—the writings of the pre-exilic prophets and an addition or two to the historical books and a few more psalms.

There was a brief flurry of miracles in the days of Daniel. The nation of Israel had long been in exile. Judah was undergoing a similar judgment. Babylon was becoming far too attractive for the majority of exiles. There was a need, in view of the foretold return to the Promised Land, for people to be reminded that God was still alive and on the throne. Again, the miracles ceased and were replaced by the Word of God. A few more historical books were written, some more prophetic books were added, and the Old Testament canon was closed. God had no more to say and no more sign miracles to perform for 400 years.

The only other time in Scripture where we have an outbreak of miracles is during the period covered by the Gospels and the book of Acts. This was the mightiest of all such periods. The Lord's miracles were countless (John 21:25), although only about three dozen are recorded. The apostles performed marvelous miracles and saw multitudes experience the greatest miracle of all—salvation (Rom. 1:16). As on all other occasions, the period of sign miracles was replaced by God's written Word. God would have us place the emphasis on His Word, not on miracles.

There will be another outbreak of miracles after the Rapture of the church, when the two witnesses will hammer away at the conscience of the world, as Moses did, only to be countered by Satan's miracles (performed by the Beast and the False Prophet) as Moses was. These miracles will cease and the Living Word will be revealed.

Miracles can be counterfeited. Satan can perform miracles. Miracles can act like a drug. The appetite grows with indulgence. A person who has seen one miracle soon craves to see another one. God does not satisfy that kind of craving.

Jesus refused even to answer Herod Antipas when he, all too evidently, was not interested in seeing justice done to his prisoner, only in seeing a miracle (Luke 23:8). Peter, after describing the supernatural he had experienced on the Mount of Transfiguration, immediately added, "We have a more sure word of prophecy . . . scripture" (2 Peter 1:17–20). It was probably to defuse the excitement of Peter and the others that, on their way down from the Mount of Transfiguration, the Lord told them to keep this experience a secret for the time being (Matt. 17:9).

When the rich man in a lost eternity implored Abraham to send Lazarus back to earth with a message for his five lost brothers, Abraham refused. The following dialogue sums up why God will not put a premium on miracles. The rich man was reminded, "They have Moses and the prophets." That is to say, "They have the written Word of God." The rich man insisted on a miracle: "Nay, father Abraham: but if one went unto them from the dead, they will repent." Abraham was unimpressed. He replied, "If they hear not Moses and the prophets, neither will they be persuaded though one rose from the dead" (Luke 16:30–31). How true! The next man Jesus raised from the dead was a man called Lazarus and, far from being convinced, the Jewish authorities tried to kill him (John 11:1–12:11). Indeed, John goes on to say of Jesus that "though he had done so many miracles before them, yet they believed not on him" (12:37).

Even when Jesus arose from the dead they refused to believe. On the contrary, the Sanhedrin bribed the sepulcher guard to circulate a false story to explain away the unexplainable (Matt. 28:11–15)—a story still popular among the Jews.

No wonder miracles are depreciated rather than dramatized in the Bible. The gift of performing miracles died out in the early church along with the other sign gifts. What people get for their money today, when they go to see those who supposedly perform miracles, is anyone's guess. No one denies that God can, and does, perform miracles. These happen in answer to prayer and in accordance with God's own will. They cannot be commanded. The power to perform miracles will not be restored until after the Rapture, when God's two witnesses will shake the world with their miracle-working power (Rev. 11:1–6). That Satan does empower people to perform miracles cannot be denied. However, he uses miracles to deceive.

Paul turns next to *gifts of communication* (1 Cor. 12:10b–e). These are divided into two, into *primary* gifts (12:10b–c) and *passing* gifts (12:10d–e). There are two primary gifts. First, there is *the ability to express truth:* "To another prophecy" (12:10b). The gift of prophecy is generally taken to be synonymous with preaching. Throughout Scripture, however, it refers uniformly to the declaration of things hidden to the natural mind. Frequently the word has to do with foretelling the future, and it is frequently used in this way in the New Testament (Matt. 11:13; 13:14; 15:7; Acts 19:6; 2 Tim. 4:14; Rev. 10:11). In its highest sense, prophecy has to do with declaring hidden secrets or with foretelling future events. The Lord revealed this when teaching his disciples about the coming of the Holy Spirit: "Whatsoever he shall hear, that shall he [the Holy Spirit] speak: and he shall shew you things to come" (John 16:13). This was one of the apostolic gifts, promised to the disciples and intended to enable the apostles to declare and write the truths that now compromise the New Testament.

Paul will have much more to say about this gift in chapter 14, where he contrasts it with the gift of tongues. All we need to say here is that the gift of prophecy enabled a believer to convey to a local assembly of Christians, and that by direct Holy Spirit illumination, truth already apostolically revealed but not yet in general circulation.

Along with this gift went another one, the *ability to expose error:* "to another discerning of spirits" (1 Cor. 12:10c). This gift was necessary because of the prevalence of evil spirits and false prophets (1 John 4:1–3). The same gift enabled a discerning believer to read the thoughts and intents of a wicked human heart. Thus Peter was able to read the thoughts and secret plans of Ananias and Sapphira, as well as the sin of the impostor, Simon Magus (Acts 5:1–11; 8:9–24). Similarly in the Old Testament, Elisha was able to read the secret thoughts of Hazael and of Gehazi (2 Kings 8:12–13; 5:25–26).

There were also two passing gifts, gifts of a *temporary* and transient nature among the gifts of communication. One of these gifts was the ability to *excite the minds of some:* "to another divers kinds of tongues" (1 Cor. 12:10d). This was an extraordinary gift demonstrated on the Day of Pentecost when Peter was able to preach to thousands, drawn from diverse backgrounds, and speaking numerous languages and dialects, and have his message understood by one and all as though he were actually speaking not only their mother tongue but their local idiom (Acts 2:1–12). Tongues such as this would be a marvelous asset on the mission field.

This, however, is not what was happening at Corinth. The tongues spoken were foreign languages. They were languages intelligible to some who were present but not known by the speaker himself and equally unintelligible to many in the congregation. This gift, for some reason, was highly prized by the Corinthians and its practice was accompanied by all kinds of abuse.

A parallel gift was the ability to *explain the message to others:* "to another the interpretation of tongues" (1 Cor. 12:10e). No translation was necessary on the Day of Pentecost. This was not the case at Corinth. Because many could not understand the tongue being spoken, the gift of interpretation was necessary. One reason for this appears in the attitude of the Jews. Their receptiveness on the Day of Pentecost had turned to open hostility. The gift of tongues was designed especially for the Jew (14:21–22) and, by the time Paul came to write this letter, it was very definitely a judgment sign. More will be said about this when we come to chapter 14. Paul makes it clear in chapter 13 that the gift of tongues was transitory and would come to a natural end when it had accomplished its purpose.

Like the other gifts, tongues was liable to satanic imitation. It still is. The Corinthians themselves were familiar, long before they came to Christ, with this phenomenon. Pagan oracles spoke in tongues. Modern missionaries tell of witch doctors who speak in tongues. Among modern "charismatics" we find practicing Roman Catholics who speak in tongues in one breath and pray to the Virgin Mary in the next. It is incredible that anyone could attribute this kind of confusion to the Holy Spirit.

Paul concludes this section on the scope of the gifts. Having explained why gifts were given and what gifts were given, he describes *ways gifts were given:* "But all these worketh that one and the self-same Spirit, dividing to every man severally as he will" (12:12). The gifts were various, the source only one. Behind the distribution of the gifts is the Holy Spirit, who brings all the divine genius of His omniscience to bear on the bestowal of this or that gift on this or that believer. Every believer has at least one gift. The Holy Spirit, who makes no mistakes, gives that gift.

It has been suggested that Paul reiterated this because of the opinion of some that the apostles themselves had the power to give spiritual gifts at their own pleasure. Simon Magus evidently thought Simon Peter had the power to give the Holy Spirit at will and that he would be open to a bribe to have the same power bestowed on him (Acts 8:14–23). It is true the apostles laid hands on people and that gifts were bestowed. Paul acknowledges this, for example, in the case of Timothy (2 Tim. 1:6). He here denies that he or anyone else had control over the gift that was imparted. The apostles may have served as channels, but that was all. In any case, the Holy Spirit did not need an apostle, a prophet, an elder, or anyone else to mediate the distribution of His gifts. He was in sovereign control of the entire process. No man could know what gift was best suited to an individual. Still less could a mere man know what was good for the whole church.

    (2) Illustration (12:12–27)

        (a) The mystical body of Christ (12:12–13)

            i. The members of the body (12:12)

           ii. The miracle of the body (12:13)

              a. The baptism of the Spirit (12:13a)

              b. The bestowal of the Spirit (12:13b)

        (b) The material bodies of Christians (12:14–27)

            i. The function of the body's members (12:14–20)

              a. The unity of the body (12:14)

              b. The uniqueness of the body (12:15–20)

                1. The noted diversity of its members (12:15–16)

                  (i)   The humbler members (12:15)

                  (ii)   The higher members (12:16)

                2. The needed diversity of its members (12:17–18)

                  (i)   Their separate duties (12:17)

                  (ii)   Their sovereign design (12:18)

                3. The normal diversity of its members (12:19–20)

                  (i)   An obvious fact of body life (12:19)

                  (ii)   An obvious facet of body life (12:20)

            ii. The fellowship of the body's members (12:21–27)

              a. Things absent from the body (12:21–24)

                1. There is no contention in the body (12:21)

                2. There is no contempt in the body (12:22–24)

                  (i)   No going by appearances (12:22)

                  (ii)   No going by applause (12:23–24)

              b. Things apparent in the body (12:25–26)

              1. Mutual accord (12:25–26a)

                (i)   How compact it is (12:25)

> (ii) How caring it is (12:26a)
> 2. Mutual acclaim (12:26b)
> *c.* Things affirmed by the body (12:27)
>   *1.* How personal is our place in it (12:27a)
>   *2.* How positive is our place in it (12:27b)

Paul turns now to *illustration* (1 Cor. 12:12–27), still seeking to clear up the confusion about the gifts in the minds of the Corinthians. He sets before them truth concerning *the mystical body of Christ* (12:12–13) and truth concerning *the material bodies of Christians* (12:14–27). First, there is truth about the mystical body of Christ. Paul speaks of *the members* of the mystical body: "For as the body is one, and hath many members, and all the members of that one body, being many, are one body: so also is Christ" (12:12). Paul will later come back to this apposite comparison in later letters (Rom. 12:4–8; Eph. 1:22–23; 3:5–6; 4:4). The complexity of the human body is awesome. Each day the medical community discovers new wonders. David could say, "I am fearfully and wonderfully made" (Ps. 139:14). He could add, "In thy book all my members were written, when as yet there was none of them" (139:16). The same could be said of the mystical body of Christ

Think for a moment of the human body. The basic unit in the human body is the cell. Each cell comes complete with a copy of the master plan that controls its particular function in the body. The blueprint, often called "the code of life," is carried in large chemical molecules known as DNA—deoxyribonucleic acid. It is the DNA that tells the cellular components how to behave. It is this code that makes us different from everyone else. Along with the DNA there are companion molecules of RNA—ribonucleic acid—that decipher the code in the DNA so that the various parts that make up the body can be built.

Such, too, is the mystical body of Christ, except that He is the One who controls the code of life so that while each one of us is different from everyone else, we all have our place and purpose, and who ensures that although we all come and go the body itself continues on, generation after generation, as the perfect vehicle through which Christ can express His own life on earth. The Holy Spirit is the One who interprets the code so that the various members can be incorporated into the mystical body and properly equipped to play their various divinely appointed roles.

Paul speaks, too, of *the miracle* of the body. First, there is *the baptism of the Spirit:* "For by one Spirit are we all baptized into one body" (1 Cor. 12:13a). A basic failure to understand the meaning of the baptism of the Spirit is at the root of much error. There is some discussion among scholars as to whether the verse should read "by one Spirit" (in which case the Holy Spirit does the baptizing) or "in one Spirit" (in which case Christ does the baptizing). That it is the Holy Spirit who does the baptizing, and that He thus incorporates us into the mystical body of Christ, seems to be more consistent with the context. On the other hand, the half dozen references to this supernatural baptism in the New Testament (Matt. 3:11; Mark 1:8; Luke 3:16; John 1:32–33; Acts 1:5; 11:15) suggest that it is the Lord Himself who does the baptizing and that we are baptized with the Holy Spirit. In any case, the baptism is what puts us into the mystical body of Christ.

The baptism of the Holy Spirit has nothing whatsoever to do with speaking in tongues, which was a temporary sign gift intended primarily to convince unbelieving Jews that God had injected the church into history and created a new vehicle of expression, one which was to have a large Gentile constituency.

The claim of some that this baptism is a kind of second blessing, reserved for a spiritual elite, and that those who have been baptized with the Holy Spirit will demonstrate it by speaking in tongues, is clearly false. Paul says that we are *all* baptized. He elaborates—"whether we be Jews or Gentiles, whether we be bond or free." Neither race nor rank makes any difference. Every true believer is baptized by (or with) the Holy Spirit and is thus incorporated into the body of Christ. The word *all* gives the lie to "charismatic" claims. As for this baptism being reserved for a spiritual elite, the fact of the matter was that the Corinthian church to which Paul was writing was the most worldly and carnal of all his churches. Yet there was not a genuine believer, regardless of spiritual status, who had not been included in this baptism. Paul continues with *the bestowal of the Spirit:* "and have been all made to drink into one Spirit" (1 Cor. 12:13b). The baptism puts the believer into the body of Christ; the drinking puts the Spirit into the body of the Christian. They are simultaneous, sovereign acts of God that comprise two of the many marvelous things which happen to a poor, lost sinner of Adam's ruined race when he accepts Christ as Savior. That is not to say that the believer knows, still less understands or appreciates, what is involved at the time. We learn of the mighty things accomplished at the time of our conversion only as we grow in grace and increase in the knowledge of God. Some believers never learn them. They remain true just the same. Happy is the believer who not only apprehends these things but appreciates them and appropriates them as well.

Paul now turns to the subject of *the material bodies of Christians* (12:14–27), which provide him with a forceful illustration of the mystical body of Christ. He speaks of *the function of the body's members* (12:14–20) and of *the fellowship of the body's members* (12:21–27).

He begins with *the unity of the body:* "For the body is not one member, but many" (12:14). How many? Nobody really knows, but certainly very many. A physician has to study for years just to get his medical degree. Then, if he so desires, he can go back to school for a few more years and specialize in one of the many branches of medicine. He can then devote the remainder of his life to studying just one member of the body and its functions and disorders. In other words, he can become a specialist—one who knows more and more about less and less! With the advent of biochemistry, molecular biology, and genetic engineering, and with the new tools available for research, the wonder and complexity of the human body and its many members is seen to be more amazing than ever. And so does the unity of the body and the harmony that prevails throughout the whole.

Now Paul turns to *the uniqueness of the body* (12:15–20). There is *the noted diversity of its members* (12:15–16). Paul looks first at some of *the humbler members* of the body: "If the foot shall say, Because I am not the hand, I am not of the body; is it therefore not of the body?" (12:15). Imagine, for instance, being the big toe on the left foot. Imagine it saying, "I'm only a big toe and I'm so ugly I spend my days wrapped up in a sweaty sock and stuck in a shoe. It's hot down here!" Suppose the foot were to envy the hand! After all, the hand is such a useful, agile member of the body. Think what a pianist or a typist or an artist can do with a hand!

A hand! It has eight wrist bones, five bones in the palm, fourteen in the digits. The two hands together command a quarter of all the bones in the body. Each hand has thousands of nerve endings per square inch, with the heaviest concentration in the fingertips. Two of the largest spaces in the motor cortex of the brain are concerned with the hands. The hands are rarely still. The finger joints alone are extended and flexed some 25 million times during a lifetime. Yet the hands rarely get tired. A hand is far more complicated and sophisticated than any machine. The hands can compensate for the loss of eyesight by reading Braille and for the loss of the ability to hear and speak by means of sign language. The hands can tell the texture of the soil or the weave of a fabric. A hand can even distinguish between the various coins in one's pockets. And each of its fingerprints is unique.

The foot may well be envious of the hand, but it isn't. It's got more sense! For the foot to so envy the hand as to deny that because it is not a hand it doesn't belong to the body is nonsense. Of course it belongs, and a useful member it is. It is a marvel of engineering with its 26 bones, 107 ligaments, and 19 muscles. It can balance upright a 6 foot, 200-pound man. When walking, even at a moderate pace, each foot takes a pounding—with a 200-pound man each foot receives a 200-pound jolt each minute. It's far worse when the man runs or jumps or jogs. The average man walks something like 65,000 miles in a lifetime.

The body is very thankful for its feet, humble members though they may be. A body without feet would be a hopelessly crippled body, greatly handicapped in the accomplishment of its goals.

Then there are some of the *higher members* of the body: "And if the ear shall say, Because I am not the eye, I am not of the body; is it therefore not of the body?" (12:16) The ear might say, "I am so ugly! I am just stuck on around the side of the head. I stick out as though to advertise my ugliness. But the eye. What a beautiful member that is! How it sparkles and glows How expressive it is! All the personality is centered in the eye. It is the very index of the soul! I would just as soon not belong to the body at all as be an ear, not an eye."

An eye! It has a dime-size cornea to bend light rays into orderly patterns and a pupil to control the amount of light coming into the eye. It has a small lens surrounded by tiny but extremely strong muscles. It has a retina which, although covering less than a square inch, contains 137 million light-sensitive receptor cells. Of these, 130 million are rod-shaped and control black-and-white vision and the rest are cone-shaped and control color vision. Messages are passed from the eye through the optic nerve to the brain and back again at a speed of about 300 miles per hour. Each transaction takes about 0.002 second.

Still, for all that, an ear has no need to be jealous of the eye. For the ear itself is a wonder of creation. The outer ear, which is attached to the side of the head, is simply a sound-gathering trumpet. An inch-long canal leads to the inner ear. The canal contains numerous hairs and four thousand wax glands that trap dust and other foreign matter. Hearing starts with the eardrum, which picks up sound from the airwaves. It can pick up a whisper, which will move the drum slightly— some think only the billionth of centimeter. On the other side of the eardrum are three little bones that work in harmony to amplify the movements of the drum twenty-two times. The amplified sounds are passed on to the inner ear. There the sound is transmitted to the cochlea, which contains thousands of nerve cells that look like hair. Each one is tuned to one vibration that it identifies, waving in a watery fluid. This waving, in turn, generates a minute electrical charge that is fed through the auditory nerve to the brain. This nerve contains over thirty thousand circuits. The ear not only enables us to hear. It also contains semicircular canals that control the balance of the body.

It is no small thing to be an ear. How foolish it would be for an ear, which is an important member of the body in its own right, to be jealous of the eye simply because the eye is aesthetically more attractive than itself. How silly to disassociate itself from the body because it cannot be an eye. Yet we see this kind of thing all the time in the church. Because this member can't play the piano she won't do anything. Because this brother cannot teach the new members' class he refuses to teach another class. Or, in terms of the gifts, especially at Corinth, because this one doesn't have the gift of tongues he refuses to exercise the gift he does have, the gift of showing mercy. Paul thought the whole thing childish and ludicrous.

Paul now moves on to *the needed diversity of its members* (12:17–18). He speaks of *their separate duties:* "If the whole body were an eye, where were the hearing? If the whole were hearing, where were the smelling?" (12:17) He speaks also of *their sovereign design:* "But now hath God set the members every one of them in the body, as it hath pleased him" (12:18). A body simply would not be a body without diversity. A properly functioning body pays tribute to its Designer, to His wisdom, love, and power. If the body had only one member, be it this one or that one, it would not be and could not be a body.

"The whole body an eye!" Here we come across an unexpected vein of humor in Paul. The idea of the whole body being an eye is ludicrous.

Some years ago I developed severe internal discomfort and the doctor sent me to a local hospital for tests. I was checked in, disrobed, and then arrayed in one of those dreadful hospital gowns, the kind you never know which way to put on and which, when finally donned, leave you feeling naked and vulnerable.

There were about a dozen of us lined up in a dreary corridor, awaiting the arrival of the radiologist, who was to do the X-rays. Presently he arrived. As he approached the nursing station he called out, "Who do we have today?" The nurse called back, "Seven stomachs and five gall bladders!" That was the first time I had ever been so described! It struck me as funny.

It struck Paul as funny, too! But that was the Corinthian mentality. They all wanted to be a tongue.

Incidentally, as W. E. Vine points out, the tenses of the two words "God hath *set*" and "as it *hath pleased* Him" are aorist, or point tenses, and should be translated *set* and *pleased*. He adds, "This marks the formation of the human body in all its parts as a creative act at a single point of time."[14] This strikes another blow at the theory of evolution, which imagines the gradual development of the body over immense periods of time.

The body bears all the marks of sovereign design. It is the work of omniscient genius and of omnipotent power. Each member is not only complex beyond all thought but perfectly suited for the part it has to play in relation to every other part. The same is true of the members of the mystical body of Christ, of which our bodies are but a picture. When we get to heaven and see the entire mystical body of Christ, in all its beauty and perfection, we shall marvel at the skill that designed and created it.

Paul speaks, also, of *the normal diversity of its members:* "And if they were all one member, where were the body? But now are they many members, yet but one body" (12:19–20). This is a summary statement that reemphasizes the folly of imagining that there can be a body at all unless there is both unity and diversity. Clamoring for the same few gifts was just as foolish.

This thorough discussion of the function of the body members (12:14–20) leads to a discussion of *the fellowship of the body's members* (12:21–27). Paul speaks first of *things absent from the body* (12:21–24). There is *no contention* in the body: "And the eye cannot say to the hand, I have no need of you: nor again the head to the feet, I have no need of you" (12:21). If I get some dust in my eye, it is the hand which comes to the eye's aid. If I were to step off the sidewalk onto the road only to see that I am in the path of an oncoming car, it would be folly for the head to say to the foot "I have no need of you!" No, indeed! The head would say, rather, to the foot, "Come on! Do your thing! Get a move on!" The whole body would have occasion to thank the foot! There is no contention in the body

Furthermore, *there is no contempt in the body* (12:22–24). In a body there is *no judging by appearances:* "Nay, much more those members of the body, which seem to be more feeble are necessary" (12:22). Take, for instance, the tongue. James calls it "a little member" (3:5). But what strength it controls! And what an intricate member it is! It is really a mucus membrane, surrounded by a complex battery of muscles and nerves, complete with taste buds designed to perform complex chemical actions. It assists in mastication, swallowing, and speech. It is able to adopt a great variety of shapes so that an astonishing battery of sounds can be articulated. Small! But mighty. A tongue can soothe a child to sleep or mobilize men by the million to march. It can whisper sweet nothings in a dear one's ear or pour out

---

14. W. E. Vine, *1 Corinthians* (Grand Rapids: Zondervan, 1961), 173.

vitriolic gossip, hate, and spite. It's not much to look at. Indeed, it is considered an insult in most places to poke it out at someone. When it comes to the tongue it would never do to judge by appearances. The same is true of many a member of the mystical body. D. L. Moody was not much to look at. He was illiterate, pushy, and unpolished. But what a mighty member of the body he was! Men of great learning, influence, wealth, and power came to hear him preach and, as was true of his royal Master, "the common people heard him gladly."

In a body there is *no judging by applause:* "And those members of the body, which we think to be less honourable, upon these we bestow more abundant honour; and our uncomely parts have more abundant comeliness. For our comely parts have no need: but God hath tempered the body together, having given more abundant honour to that part which lacked" (1 Cor. 12:23–24). There are some parts of the body that we do not hesitate to display. There are other parts we conceal. The expressions "more abundant honor" and "more abundant comeliness" have to do with clothing. The "less honorable" members are usually clothed; the "uncomely parts" are always clothed; the "comely parts" are not clothed. We openly display face and hands. We clothe other parts of the body.

However, things are evened out. The parts we clothe are honored, for the clothing itself can add grace and form to the body as a whole. Moreover, the parts of the body which we either clothe or which are unseen because they are internal have a special honor all their own. We usually call them "vital organs." A body can get along without a hand or an arm or a leg or an eye. It cannot get along without a heart or without a stomach, liver, or kidneys.

God has sovereignly "tempered the body together" and has deliberately given more abundant honor to the part that lacked. The word *tempered* is *sunkerannumi,* which means "to blend together." Blending things together calls for sophistication. We blend various kinds of coffee beans or different varieties of tea to achieve certain desired results. It is a process that calls for discrimination. In cooking we blend and mix ingredients to produce a special dish. The result could be disastrous if some vital ingredient were to be left out or the wrong ingredient put in. My wife once put baking soda in an omelet she was baking instead of baking powder! The result was indescribable! The only other place in the New Testament where *sunkerannumi* occurs is in Hebrews 4:2, where the apostle explains why, in some cases, the gospel fails to achieve the desired results. It is not "mixed with faith" in those who hear it. A vital ingredient is left out. God has carefully "tempered the body together." Nothing is left out. Nothing is left to chance. Each member is designed to function where it is and the way it does. The same is true of the body of Christ.

Paul turns now from those things which are absent from the body, rivalry, jealousy, contention, and so on, to those *things which are apparent in the body* (1 Cor. 12:25–26). There is *mutual accord* (12:25–26a) Paul shows *how compact* a body is: "That there should be no schism in the body; but that the members should have the same care one for another" (12:25), and *how caring* a body is: "And whether one member suffer, all the members suffer with it" (12:26a). If I cut my finger, my whole body is instantly informed of the fact. If I fall off a ladder and break my leg, the whole body enters into the pain. No member suffers in isolation. What happens to even the smallest or weakest member is of crying concern to one and all. So it should be in the body of Christ. It is to be a caring body. We should care for every member, whether a feeble one or an outstanding one, whether one we see every day or one in a remote Amazon tribe!

There is not only mutual accord in the body, there is *mutual acclaim:* "Or one member be honoured, all the members rejoice with it" (12:26b). When a person sits down to eat a tender, perfectly cooked T-bone steak, the whole body rejoices. When he goes to a concert and hears beautiful music, it is not just the ear that benefits, the whole body rejoices. When he stands, looking in awe, at the snow-clad Rocky Mountains, rising tall and rugged across the western horizon, the whole body enjoys it, not just the eye. The voice wants to shout, "Well done, God!" and the hands want to applaud. The feet want to hurry the person closer. The very heart wants to beat a little faster.

It should be thus in the body of Christ. David Livingstone is heaped with honors and given a state burial in Westminster Abbey and the whole church should rejoice. Billy Graham is given an audience with the queen or invited to lead the nation in prayer at a presidential inauguration, or asked to come to Moscow to conduct a great evangelistic crusade and the whole church should rejoice. He is being honored and we are being honored; the whole church is being honored. There is no schism in the natural body; there should be no schism in the mystical body.

Paul concludes this section of illustration by restating *things affirmed by the body* (12:27). How *personal* is our place in the body of Christ: "Now ye are the body of Christ" (12:27a); and how *positive* is our place in it: "and members in particular" (12:27b). The word *ye* in this statement is emphatic.

> (3) Indication (12:28–31)
>> (a) Positional limitations (12:28)

     i. The leading gifts of the body (12:28a–c)
       a. The limited gifts (12:28a–b)
         1. Those who had seen and who were sent by the Son of God—apostles (12:28a)
         2. Those who had sought and who were taught by the Spirit of God—prophets (12:28b)
       b. The lasting gift of the body—teachers (12:28c)
    ii. The lesser gifts of the body (12:28d–g)
       a. The sign gifts (12:28d–e)
         1. Power over situations—miracles (12:28d)
         2. Power over sickness—healings (12:28e)
       b. The simpler gifts (12:28f–g)
         1. Ability to do things—helps (12:28f)
         2. Ability to direct things—governments (12:28g)
   iii. The least gift—tongues (12:28h)
(b) Personal limitations (12:29–30)
     i. Do all have the supreme gifts? (12:29a–c)
       a. Gifts for the founding of the church (12:29a–b)
         1. Apostles to pioneer the work (12:29a)
         2. Prophets to proclaim the word (12:29b)
       b. Gift for the furthering of the church—teachers (12:29c)
    ii. Do all have the sign gifts? (12:29d–30b)
       a. The special gifts (12:29d–e)
         1. To move mountains—miracles (12:29d)
         2. To heal hurts—healers (12:30a)
       b. The speaking gifts (12:30b–c)
         1. To transmit truth to those who speak only foreign languages (12:30b)
         2. To translate truth to those who speak only familiar languages (12:30c)
(c) Proposed limitations (12:31)
     i. A word about superior gifts (12:31a)
    ii. A word about superior grace (12:31b)

Information (1 Cor. 12:1–11) and illustration (12:12–27) now give way to *indication* (12:28–31). Paul now intends to deal, once and for all, with the foolish clamor in the Corinthian church for the tongues gift. To do that he adds three additional gifts to the list, then puts the gifts in a descending order of importance. He deliberately puts tongues and interpretation at the bottom of the list because that is where they belonged. They were soon to be set aside altogether as no longer useful or relevant. They would become like vestigal organs in a body which once had a useful function but which are now no longer needed. Paul knew that, although the Corinthians didn't in his day, and the so-called charismatics don't in our day. We have only to compare Ephesians 4:8–16 with this Corinthians listing of gifts to see the difference. The Ephesian list contains no mention of miracles, healing, or tongues. The church had grown up. There was no more need of them.

In these verses now before us, Paul lists three sets of limitations as he descends from the apostolate, which heads the list, to tongues, which is put at the end. First, there are *positional limitations* (1 Cor. 12:28). Paul begins with *the leading gifts* of the mystical body (12:28a–c). There are, first and foremost, *those who had seen and who were sent by the Son of God:* "And God hath set some in the church, first apostles" (12:28a). An apostle had to be one who had seen the Lord. The apostolic gift was a miraculous gift. Paul will later remind the Corinthians that "the signs of an apostle were wrought among you in all patience, in signs, and wonders, and mighty deeds" (2 Cor. 12:12). An apostle was not an apostle unless he could prove it by the miracles that went along with apostleship. Moreover, God revealed His secrets to the apostles (and secondarily to the prophets) and used the apostles (supported by the prophets) to lay the foundation of the church (Eph. 2:20; 3:4–6). The gift of the apostle died out with the death of John, the last of the apostles to die. Nobody who has seen and has been sent by the Son of God, armed with apostolic power, has been in the church since the apostolic age.

Then there are *those who had sought and were taught by the Spirit of God:* "secondarily prophets" (1 Cor. 12:28b). The early church was handicapped. It had at its disposal the Old Testament Scriptures, supremely the Septuagint, the Greek translation of the Hebrew Bible. It had the substance of the four gospels in oral form, as it was passed along by the disciples. It had scraps of truth culled from "the apostles' doctrine" (Acts 2:42), but it did not have a complete New Testament. Instead it had apostles and prophets. Prophets were inspired by the Holy Spirit to make known "the apostles' doctrine."

In time the Holy Spirit fulfilled the Lord's pledge to his disciples and used them to write the New Testament: the Gospels (John 14:25–26), the book of

Acts (15:26–27), the Epistles, and Revelation (16:13–14). In time it was all reduced to writing and the New Testament canon was completed.

However, there was a transition period. New Testament truth, revealed to the apostles, was available but still not in circulation. Hence, the need for local churches to have prophets in their midst. Their ministry was to pass along to the local churches truth made available to the church at large by the apostles.

As more and more truth was committed to writing and put into circulation, the need for prophets declined. Once the New Testament canon was complete, the unique prophetic gift was withdrawn (1 Cor. 13:8).

Doubtless many who had the gift of prophecy were anointed preachers as well. The prophets, when inspired, were under the control of the Holy Spirit. This control was never rigid or mechanical or by violent compulsion (14:32), such as is often seen when "tongues" are displayed by those who claim to have the gift. In thus conveying truth, God always respected and enhanced the personality of the speaker. Just the same "prophecy [utterances of a prophet] came not in old time by the will of man [it was conceived in no human mind]: but holy men of God spake as they were moved by the Holy Ghost" (2 Peter 1:20–21). Paul knew the difference and made a conscious distinction—"spoke as they were moved [*pherō,* borne along] by the Holy Ghost"—between his words when inspired and when uninspired, when speaking by "permission" and when speaking authoritatively by the Holy Spirit (1 Cor. 7:6, 12, 25).

In due time the New Testament Scriptures were born, "cradled in miracle" as D. M. Panton once put it. In time "the religion of the church became the religion of the Book." That Book now stands supreme, exalted above the church as its sole and sufficient authority. Any so-called prophet who would add to or subtract from that Book in any way comes under the closing curse of the Bible (Rev. 22:18–19). All extrabiblical revelation is to be refused, whether it comes at a "charismatic" meeting or at a spiritist seance.

Paul follows this up with reference to *the lasting gift* of the mystical body: "thirdly, teachers" (1 Cor. 12:28c). This gift is high on the list and is to be greatly prized. How grateful we should be for those, like Aquila and Priscilla, who are gifted to show us the things of God "more perfectly" (Acts 18:24–26). How much we owe to those who show us how to rightly divide the word of truth (2 Tim. 2:15) and who teach us sound hermeneutic principles and how to exegete properly a passage of Scripture. Where would most of us be without good books written by sound men? Daniel "understood by books" (9:2) and so do we. Thank God for gifted teachers!

Paul turns next to *the lesser gifts* of the mystical body (1 Cor. 12:28d–g). There were, for example, *the sign gifts* (12:28d–e). There was the gift that gave *power over situations:* "after that miracles" (12:28d); and the gift that gave *power over sickness:* "then gifts of healings" (12:28e). The ability to teach the Word of God was to be preferred before the ability to work miracles or heal people. After all, these two gifts, much as they might have been prized and appreciated, dealt only with the temporal and the material side of life. Those who teach the Word deal with the eternal and spiritual side of life.

Then there are *the simpler gifts* (12:28f–g). Paul adds these, as he adds teachers, to the earlier list. There is *the ability to do things:* "helps" (12:28f). Not many people clamor for this gift, but what a precious and necessary gift it is! It is, in fact, a Godlike gift. It is inherent, indeed, in the name the Lord Jesus gave to the Holy Spirit. He is "the Comforter," the *paraklētos,* the One "called alongside to help" (John 14:16). Paul tells the Romans that the Holy Spirit "*helpeth* our infirmities." The word used is *synantilambanomai*—the same word used of Martha's request that Mary come and help her in the kitchen (Rom. 8:26; Luke 10:40). The word used here of *helps* is *antilēpsis.* It occurs only here in the New Testament. It occurs in the Septuagint in Psalm 83:8, where Assur is said to have helped the children of Lot (Ammon and Moab) against Israel. One authority suggests that, as used here in 1 Corinthians, the word embraces anything that could be done for poor or weak or outcast believers. The Holy Spirit ranks such a gift above the gift of tongues.

Then, *too,* there is *the ability to direct things:* "governments" (1 Cor. 12:28g). The word comes from the Greek word *kybernēsis,* which literally means "to guide" or "to steer" or "to pilot." This is an administrative gift, the ability to make sound decisions and oversee the administration of a local church. There are always decisions that have to be made. A modern church has buildings and staff and programs. All need to be steered. Happy is the church that has men at the helm who can think through the pros and cons of a decision before ever it is made, and decide what is the right and proper thing to do. So many churches make foolish decisions. They involve the believers in unnecessary debt or saddle them with incompetent or unspiritual personnel or lead them into unproductive or unprofitable programs. Often churches find themselves in a muddle or meddling in things that would have best been left alone. One or two men gifted with "governments" are worth more to a church than a whole balcony full of people babbling in tongues.

Paul comes at last to *the least gift:* "diversities of tongues" (12:28h). There it is, at the bottom of the list. So much for those who put it at the top! So much for those who claim it is the mark of those who, blessed above all others in the church, have received a "baptism of the Holy Spirit," a "second blessing" indeed. So much for those who crave this gift and who will go to any lengths to get it (or what passes for it) because of the imagined spiritual status it is supposed to give. I have met people who have been terribly inhibited because of their failure to speak in tongues. I have met people who have been given all kinds of foolish, even dangerous, advice. They have been told to start to babble, like a baby, babble anything, until they take off in tongues. They have been told to relax and put their minds in neutral and let themselves go so that the "spirit" can take over their beings. Some of this advice is foolish and results in some kind of self-hypnosis that, in turn, produces what passes for "tongues." Some of this advice is downright dangerous and results in demonic activity.

Having stated positional limitations in connection with the relative importance of the various gifts, Paul continues with some *personal limitations* (12:29–30). He asks two series of questions. First, *do all have the supreme gifts* (12:29a–c)? What about the *gifts for founding the church* (12:29a–b)? "Are all apostles?" That is, are all called to do the unique *pioneering* gift we associate with Peter and Paul? Obviously not! There was only a handful of apostles. Are all called to have the unique *proclamation* gift of inspired utterance? "Are all prophets?" (12:29b). Again the answer is "No!" In any case, both gifts were ultimately withdrawn so that those today who claim to be apostles or prophets are deceived and deceivers. Such deception was known in the church at the end of the apostolic age (Rev. 2:2). The classic modern example of a cult that claims to have "latter-day" apostles and prophets is the Mormon cult. The deep deceptions practiced by the Mormons are all too well known.

What about *gifts for furthering the church?* "Are all teachers?" (1 Cor. 12:29c). Again, obviously not. Although the teaching gift, like that of the evangelist and pastor (Eph. 4:11), is for the entire church age, certainly not everyone possesses the gift.

Paul continues with his second series of questions. He asks, *Do all have the sign gifts?* (1 Cor. 12:29d–30b). What about the *special gifts* (12:29d–e)? "Are all workers of miracles?" (12:29d). *Can all move mountains?* Of course not. Even when the gift of working miracles was operational not everybody had it. "Have all the gifts of healing?" (12:30a). *Can all heal hurts?* Once more, the obvious answer is "No!"

He asks, *Do all have the speaking gifts?* (12:30b–c). "Do all speak with tongues?" (12:30b). Do all have the ability to *translate truth to those who speak only foreign languages?* "Do all interpret?" (12:30c). Do all have the ability to *translate truth to those who speak only familiar languages?* Again, the answer to both questions is a uniform and resounding "No!" Thus Paul drives the last nail in the coffin of the tongues enthusiasts. The gift, even when valid, was not for everyone.

Positional limitations (12:28), personal limitations (12:29–30), and now, finally, *proposed limitations* (12:31). Paul has a word about the desirability of *superior gifts:* "But covet earnestly the best gifts," he says (12:31a). How anyone can read these chapters (chaps. 12–14) and still imagine tongues to be a superior gift is a mystery. The word for *covet* is *zēloō.* It means "to be zealous for" or "to strongly desire." The "best gifts" are those that head the list—except that of the apostle, which was not open to those not already members of the apostolate. If a believer is going to covet any gift at all it could be almost any gift except the gift of tongues. Paul will later show that the prophetic gift far surpassed the tongues gift.

He has one more word to add, a word about *superior grace:* "And yet shew I unto you a more excellent way" (12:31b). A whole chapter is devoted to that way—the way of love.

> b. Correction (13:1–13)
> > (1) The need for love (13:1–3)
> > > (a) Possessing great gifts—without love (13:1–2)
> > > > i. Gifts of communication (13:1–2a)
> > > > > *a.* The ability to speak different tongues
> > > > > *b.* The ability to see divine truth
> > > > ii. Gifts of comprehension (13:2b–c)
> > > > > *a.* A great grasp of hidden secrets
> > > > > *b.* A great grasp of Holy Scripture
> > > > iii. Gifts of confidence (13:2d)
> > > (b) Possessing great goodness—without love (13:3)
> > > > i. Great human compassion (13:3a)
> > > > ii. Great heartfelt compassion (13:3b)
> > (2) The nature of love (13:4–8a)
> > > (a) Love's chief concerns (13:4)
> > > > i. To be Christlike in suffering (13:4a)
> > > > ii. To be Christlike in sympathy (13:4b)
> > > (b) Love's charming contentment (13:4c–6a)
> > > > i. Love is never envious (13:4c)
> > > > ii. Love is never egotistical (13:4d–c)

        a. It is not pushy (13:4d)

        b. It is not puffed-up (13:4e)

    iii. Love is never eccentric (13:5a)

    iv. Love is never exacting (13:5b)

    v. Love is never enraged (13:5c)

    vi. Love is never evil-minded (13:5d–6a)

        a. It does not nurse grudges at wrongs done to itself (13:5d)

        b. It does not nurture glee at wrongs done to others (13:6a)

  (c) Love's changeless convictions (13:6b–8a)

    i. Love's focus (13:6b)

    ii. Love's forbearance (13:7a)

    iii. Love's faith (13:7b)

    iv. Love's future (13:7c)

    v. Love's fortitude (13:7d)

    vi. Love's fidelity (13:8a)

(3) The nobility of love (13:8b–13)

  (a) That which is passing (13:8b–12)

    i. Paul's definite expectation (13:8b–d)

        a. An end to prophecies (13:8b)

        b. An end to tongues (13:8c)

        c. An end to knowledge (13:8d)

    ii. Paul's definitive explanation (13:9–12)

        a. A word of illumination (13:9–10)

            1. The problem of partial knowledge (13:9)

            2. The promise of perfect knowledge (13:10)

                (i) A total revelation of the truth (13:10a)

                (ii) A total replacement of the temporary (13:10b)

        b. A word of illustration (13:11–12)

            1. The childish stage of things (13:11)

            2. The changed state of things (13:12)

  (b) That which is permanent (13:13)

    i. That which is enduring (13:13a)

    ii. That which is endless (13:13b)

"A more excellent way!" Less emphasis on gift and more emphasis on grace! It is unfortunate that chapter divisions split up the continuous discussion which takes up this long section on the gifts. As the chapters stand, this love chapter stands alone. Paul never intended that. The Corinthians excelled in gifts (1 Cor. 1:7). That was excellent! There was something more excellent—love. Let them add that ingredient and they would come behind in no grace as they now came behind in no gift. The problem at Corinth, as so often elsewhere, was that the Corinthians had fallen in love with their gifts. That kind of thing often happens. It is possible to love one's denomination more than the body of Christ, or to love one's doctrine more than we love the Lord. Paul is now going to argue for the absolute supremacy of love.

He deliberately uses the highest word for love in the Greek vocabulary and immediately takes it far beyond any definition of such love known to the Greeks, or anyone else. The word *phileō* refers to tender affection. It refers to love that is reciprocal, to brotherly love. It is subject to abuse. It occurs about 415 times in the New Testament, and about half the time it is used negatively. It does not last under pressure. Imagine the shock sustained by a marriage, based on the kind of emotional attachment implied by the word *phileō,* when the bridegroom takes off his wig before going to bed, revealing a bald head instead of the luxurious waves, or when the bride takes out her false teeth and appears with her hair all screwed up in rollers and her face an inch thick with complexion cream! The word *phileō* is never used in any command to man to love God. The Lord Jesus knew that *phileō* love was not a sufficient basis for Peter's continuing loyalty (John 21:15–17).

Paul uses the word *agapē* here. This is the great New Testament word for love. It has a meaning all its own. It is used of the love of the Father for the Son (John 17:26), of His love for the human race (3:16), and of His love for His own (14:21). This kind of love is perfectly enshrined in the Lord Jesus (2 Cor. 5:14; Eph. 2:4). It does not arise from our feelings. It is commanded (John 13:34; 1 John 2:7–8). It does not always coincide with our natural inclinations, nor is it concerned only with those for whom we have some natural affinity. It seeks the welfare of everyone (Rom. 15:2). It is Godlike and divine and is a fruit of the Holy Spirit in the life of the believer (Gal. 5:22; Eph. 5:9). The word occurs some 320 times in the New Testament. It is rarely used negatively. Since it is commanded it cannot be based on an emotion. On the contrary, it is based on the will. It is used as a command about nineteen times so, evidently, what is being called for is a decision. It is costly, as we learn from

John 3:16. It demands the care and welfare of the loved one regardless of whether that welfare involves hurting or healing; *agapē* love always involves helping. Most of us know little or nothing about it, although it is the very essence of the Christian life.

Paul begins here with *the need for love* (1 Cor. 13:1–3). He raises two problems. First, there is the possibility one might possess *great gifts—without love* (13:1–2). For instance, one might possess *great gifts of communication* (13:1a). He might possess *the ability to speak different tongues:* "Though I speak with the tongues of men and of angels, and have not charity, I am become as sounding brass, or a tinkling cymbal" (v. 1). The case is only *supposed.* The word *though (if)* is followed by the subjunctive mood, and it expresses a hypothetical but possible condition. The future will prove whether or not such was the case. The languages are known languages (Acts 2:7–8), human languages. We have no way of knowing whether or not angels speak a heavenly language, of their own. There is no reason why they should not do so. Paul is simply saying that although he were able to speak such a lofty language that in itself would prove nothing. The acid test of genuine Christianity is not language but love. It is no accident, of course, that he puts "tongues" first here. It was the last and least of the gifts, yet the one the Corinthians put first. Paul puts it first to show its utter worthlessness if not exercised in love. All "tongues" does, if not accompanied by love, is produce a din. He likens such tongues-speaking to a booming gong or a clanging cymbal, both of which instruments simply make a noise. The Corinthians, of course, were all too familiar with pagan rituals and ceremonials which employed these instruments to produce much noise, but apart from any sense. "Tongues," without love, become a mere discordant, obtrusive, and annoying noise, almost entirely without significance.

He might also possess *the ability to see divine truth:* "And though I have the gift of prophecy . . ." (1 Cor. 13:2a). This is the other communication gift which was so prominent in the transitional stage of the early church, at which time Judaism was being discarded by God and replaced with Christianity. Both Balaam and Caiaphas were enabled to prophesy. Both were devoid of love. It profited neither of them. Love is an indication of new birth; prophecy isn't. In the Sermon on the Mount, where the law of love is codified, the Lord warns of those who, on the day of Judgment, will plead, "Lord, Lord, have we not prophesied in thy name? and in thy name have cast out devils? and in thy name done many wonderful works?" only to hear the Lord reply, "I never knew you: depart from me, ye that work iniquity" (Matt. 7:22–23).

One might possess not only great gifts of communication without love, but also *great gifts of comprehension* (1 Cor. 13:2b–c). One might have, for instance, *a great grasp of hidden secrets:* "Though I understand all mysteries" (13:2b); and also *a great grasp of Holy Scripture:* "and all knowledge" (13:2c). It is evident that God has made His mind and purposes known "at sundry times and in divers manners" (Heb. 1:1–2). He kept many things secret, for instance, in Old Testament times, things which were not revealed at the time but which have now been "revealed unto his holy apostles and prophets by the Spirit" (Eph. 3:5). The word *mustērion* is connected with various concealed or secret things in the New Testament.

It is used, for instance, in connection with the secrets of the kingdom of heaven (Matt. 13:10–11), secrets the Lord both revealed (to the disciples) and concealed (from the multitudes) by speaking in a series of mystery parables. The word is used of the duration of Israel's blindness during this church age—although the blindness itself had long since been foretold (Isa. 6:9–10). It is used of the Rapture (1 Thess. 4:13) and of the subsequent reign of iniquity on this earth (2 Thess. 2:7). The great secret, however, is the secret of the church itself, kept secret since the world began (Rom. 16:25) and all through the Old Testament era (Eph. 3:5), a secret hid in God (3:9), hidden from all other ages but now made known (Col. 1:26). That Gentiles would one day come into blessing was no secret and is the subject of many Old Testament Scriptures (Gen. 12:3; Deut. 32:8; Ps. 18:49; Isa. 11:10; 49:6). That Gentiles would be baptized into the mystical body of Christ and become equal members with the Jews in that body was not a subject of Old Testament prophecy. When Paul wrote to the Corinthians, some of the mysteries had not yet been revealed—the mystery of the harlot church, for instance (Rev. 17:1–6).

If one, however, should have a grasp of all these mysteries and also be in possession of "all knowledge" and be able to reveal the deeper meaning of all the Scriptures and yet be devoid of love, it would all add up to nothing.

And not only great gifts of communication and comprehension but *great gifts of confidence* as well: "and though I have all faith, so that I could remove mountains, and have not charity [love], I am nothing" (1 Cor. 13:2d). This does not refer to saving faith, which always manifests itself in works (James 2:14–26). It refers to miracle-working faith, that absolute confidence in God and of being in the will of God, as can see God remove obstacles from the path. This kind of faith, in itself, does not prove one to be a genuine believer, let alone a super-believer. Judas could work miracles (Matt. 10:1–8). The greatest miracle is love.

In one of her books Corrie Ten Boom tells of meeting a man who had been one of the guards in the Nazi concentration camp where she and her sister were imprisoned, brutally treated, starved, and terrorized, and where her sister had died a slow and cruel death. Years later, although memory of the terrible wounds had healed, the scars still remained. When Corrie Ten Boom met the man, unexpectedly, face-to-face, all the horrors of the camp rose like ghostly specters, and when the man asked her to forgive him, all her old nature revolted. But forgive him she did, for Christ's sake. It was a miracle of love. Love comes far ahead of faith in Paul's listing of the fruit of the Spirit (Gal. 5:22–23). Moreover, it has as its near neighbors goodness on the one hand and meekness on the other.

The possibility is that a person might possess great gifts—without love. The possibility exists, too, that a person might possess *great goodness—without love* (1 Cor. 13:3). He might, for instance, display *great human compassion:* "And though I bestow all my goods to feed the poor . . ." (13:3a). Here we have charity without love. Its epitome is the welfare state, where aid is doled out according to socialistic philosophy rather than Christian love. The words *bestow . . . to feed the poor* translate the one Greek word *psōmizō* and, even so, fail to give its full force. It is derived from the word *psomiōn* (a mouthful), and it means literally "to give away mouthful by mouthful." We get the idea best from our word *dole.* The word primarily means "to feed by putting little bits into the mouth" (of an infant or animal, for instance). The person doling out the allowance might derive some sort of satisfaction from this. It is doubtful that the person on the receiving end of the dole does. Paul envisions a person doling out thus his entire estate and doing so out of a sense of duty, perhaps, but certainly not out of a deep, abiding love. Such charity, he says, is worthless. When the Lord Jesus fed the hungry multitudes it was no dole! He spread the table with such a lavish and prodigal hand that not only was every man, woman, boy, and girl filled to capacity, there were a dozen basketfuls left over for the disciples! Paul elaborates on the idea when he says, "God loveth a cheerful [*hilaros,* 'hilarious'] giver" (2 Cor. 9:7).

Finally, a person might display *great, heartfelt compulsion:* "And though I give my body to be burned, and have not charity [love], it profiteth me nothing" (1 Cor. 13:3b). This, surely, has to be the ultimate sacrifice, to become a martyr for a cause, to be committed even unto death, even to be burned at the stake. Millions of people have become such martyrs, committed to a wrong cause, even to such hate-filled ideologies as communism or fundamentalist Islam. In the early days of the church, Christians often seemed to covet and court such deaths.

Paul shows here that there is nothing intrinsically meritorious about death by martyrdom, and that such a death, divorced from love, profits a person nothing.

Nothing! Love is the one factor in the equation essential if the answer is not to be, in the end, a distressing zero. But what does Paul mean by love? He goes on to describe *the nature of love* (13:4–8a) in one of the most magnificent passages ever penned.

He begins with *love's chief concerns* (13:4). Nobody can contemplate the verses that follow without constant reference to Henry Drummond's great pamphlet, *The Greatest Thing in the World*. He reminds us that "Love was not Paul's strong point . . . the hand that wrote 'The greatest of these is love,' when we meet it first, is stained with blood."[15] Paul had come a long way, growing in grace, increasing in the knowledge of God, developing the fruit of the Spirit, by the time he wrote this passage.

"You can take nothing greater to the heathen world," says Drummond, "than the impress and reflection of the love of God upon your own character. That is the universal language. It will take you years to speak in Chinese, or in the dialects of India. From the day you land, that language of love, understood by all, will be pouring forth its unconscious eloquence. It is the man who is the missionary, it is not his words. His character is his message."[16]

It takes Paul only three or four brief verses to tell us all about love. There are eight negatives and four positives, eight ways in which love "suffers long" and four ways in which love "is kind." There are eight things love expels from the character and four things it exhibits.

The first of love's chief concerns is to be *Christlike in suffering*. "[Love] suffereth long," Paul says (13:4a). The quality exhibited here is patience. "Love understands," says Drummond, "and therefore waits."[17] Long-suffering, however, is more than patience; it is self-restraint when faced with provocation. Love does not retaliate. Love is never in a hurry to punish. David displayed this kind of patience in his relationship with King Saul. David knew he was now the Lord's anointed, God's chosen successor to Saul. Yet he waited. On no less than twenty-four separate occasions, one way or another, in this way or in that, Saul tried to murder David. David never retaliated, never hit back. He waited for God's time. His forbearance and patient love and persistent loyalty almost won Saul over (1 Sam. 26:17–25).

---

15. Henry Drummond, *The Greatest Thing in the World* (London: Collins, 1978), 48.
16. Ibid., 50
17. Ibid., 51

The second of love's chief concerns is to be *Christlike in sympathy:* "[Love] . . . is kind" (1 Cor. 13:4b). Where patience and long-suffering passively wait, kindness is eager to be in action. Drummond reminds us how much of Christ's life was spent in doing kind things. David, as soon as the throne was firmly under his control, set out to show the kindness of God to poor, lost Mephibosheth (2 Sam. 9). "In the heart of Africa," says Drummond, "among the great lakes, I have come across black men and women who remembered the only white man they ever saw before—David Livingstone: and as you cross his footsteps in that dark continent men's faces light up as they speak of the kind doctor who passed there years ago. They could not understand him but they felt the love that beat in his heart."[18] Love is kind. We all have it in our power to be kind to those around us.

Paul moves on to describe *love's charming contentment* (1 Cor. 13:4c–6a). In the first place, *love is never envious:* "[Love] . . . envieth not" (13:4c). The word translated "envieth" here is *zēloō*, which embraces both envy and jealousy. When used of man, the distinction is that, whereas envy desires to deprive someone of something he has, jealousy desires to have the same sort of thing for itself.[19] These are ugly sins. By contrast, love is generous in the face of competition. Envy and jealousy appear most often when we find ourselves up against people in the same line of ministry, service, or activity we are, only doing it better than we do. It is that mean-spirited feeling of ill-will and detraction that so insidiously takes root in our hearts. Love, on the other hand, is magnanimous, open-handed, and generous with sincere praise for the other man. This envious jealous spirit was at work in Corinth over the question of the gifts. There was a tendency to want what someone else had, especially the gift of tongues because that was such a spectacular gift. Since love is an act of the will, the best way to deal with envy or jealousy is to crucify it and to begin to actively pray for and support the one whose gift and success you covet.

Moreover, *love is never egotistical* (13:4d–e). In particular, *love is not pushy:* "[Love] vaunteth not itself" (13:4d). A person who vaunts himself parades his own imagined superiority. The word comes from the Greek word *perpereuomai.* It means "a braggart." It refers to a boastful person, to the person who likes to show off and draw attention to himself. Love is not like that. Love is not anxious to impress other people. When Abraham negotiated the purchase of a burial site, he described himself to the people of the land as a stranger and a sojourner among them. Mindful of Abraham's resounding victory over the kings of the east (Gen. 14) some time

---

18. Ibid., 50–51.
19. Vine, *Expository Dictionary of New Testament Words,* 2:37.

before, they replied, "Thou art a mighty prince among us" (23:4, 6). That is by far the best recognition to have.

Moreover, *love is not puffed up* (1 Cor. 13:4e). The Greek word is *phusioo*, "to be inflated." This is the person who has an exaggerated idea of his own importance. At Corinth the boastful, ostentatious people were the "tongues" people. Love is humble. Love comes out of the shade to do its kind deed, then retires back into the shade again. Love does not think that what it has done is at all out of the ordinary. It does not exhibit pride or self-esteem.

Moreover, *love is never eccentric:* "[Love] . . . doth not behave itself unseemly" (1 Cor. 13:5a). In other words, love has good manners. The word used is *aschēmoneō*. The only other place it occurs is in 7:36, where it has to do with a man behaving properly toward his fiancée. Love does not exhibit inappropriate behavior. It knows how to behave itself at a wedding, a graduation, or a funeral. It has something to contribute. This is love in action in little things such as complimenting the bride or congratulating the groom or comforting the bereaved. Love knows how to behave as a gentleman or as a lady, not artificially but genuinely. It does not speak or act in an inappropriate way. Drummond defines this characteristic as "Love in society, love in relation to etiquette."[20]

Then, too, *love is never exacting:* "[Love] . . . seeketh not her own" (13:5b). Love is not selfish. Love does not pursue its own interests. It does not insist on having its own way. When Abraham's and Lot's cattle began to multiply so that there was acrimonious squabbling among their herdsmen for the available pasturage, Abraham was quick to put a stop to it. He recognized the fact that the unsaved were looking on and taking note. He magnanimously suggested that he and Lot divide the land between them and go their separate ways. More! He generously told Lot he could have first choice. The land was all his. God had deeded it to him, not to Lot. But "[love] seeketh not her own." Abraham was not long in learning that God rewards such unselfishness. He at once reaffirmed that all the land was Abraham's, including the eastern vales that Lot had so eagerly chosen for himself (Gen. 13:14–18). Love does not insist on having its own way. It does not seek its own advancement. As Drummond says, "There is no happiness in having, or in getting, but only in giving. Half the world is on the wrong scent in the pursuit of happiness. They think it consists in having and getting and in being served by others."[21]

---

20. Drummond, *The Greatest Thing in the World,* 52–53.
21. Ibid., 54.

Furthermore, *love is never enraged:* "[Love] is not [easily] provoked" (1 Cor. 13:5c). In the original text there is no word for *easily*. The statement is absolute. The story is that King James had a hot and quick temper and that the translators supplied the word *easily* to soften the absolute for their royal patron. The Greek word is *paroxunomai,* from which we derive our English word *paroxysm*. The cognate word *paroxusmos* is used to describe the "sharp contention" between Paul and Barnabas over the issue of John Mark (Acts 15:39). Love refuses to be provoked into a wrong action. Love is not roused to a spirit of anger and bitterness. It refuses to be exasperated, even though it may be justly aroused to righteous indignation. Love does not carry a chip on its shoulder. It is not insulted. It doesn't play psychological games. It doesn't say to itself, "I wonder why Mrs. Sniffbetter didn't speak to me today" or "I wonder why Mr. Blacktooth snubbed me at the board meeting yesterday." Love doesn't know what it is to be irritable over things like that.

Moreover, *love is never evil-minded* (1 Cor. 13:5d–6a). It *does not nurse grudges at wrongs done to itself:* "[Love] . . . thinketh no evil" (13:5d). The word used is *logizomai*. It is an accounting term. The word *kakon* refers to all kinds of evil and wrong. In other words, love does not keep account of wrongs it suffers. Nor does it look for opportunities to get its own back. Nor does love go around looking for pity. When Paul and Silas were arrested, given a mock trial, beaten with rods, thrust into the inner prison at Philippi, and locked into the cramping stocks, they did not sulk. They sang (Acts 16:22–25). Love bears no resentment. Love nurses no grudges.

In addition, *love does not nurture glee at wrongs done to others:* "[Love] . . . rejoiceth not in iniquity" (1 Cor. 13:6a). Love does not gloat when bad things happen to other people. It does not secretly rub its hands and enjoy the misfortunes even of those who have done it wrong. The thought goes even deeper. Love does not find satisfaction in the wrongdoing of other people. The word *schadenfreude* aptly expresses the thought. It means "malignant joy." Our hearts indeed are "deceitful above all things and desperately wicked." La Rochefoucald said, "There is something not altogether disagreeable to us in the misfortune of our best friends." Love shudders at such a thought.

There is an interesting footnote to the story of Jacob's night-long struggle with the Jehovah-angel. In the morning, blessed but broken, and limping on his thigh, Jacob made his way across the Jabbok and into his camp. He would limp for the rest of his life. Then comes the puzzling footnote: "He halted upon his thigh." Moses said, "Therefore the children of Israel eat not of the sinew which shrank, which is upon the hollow of the thigh, unto this day: because he touched the hollow of Jacob's thigh in the sinew which shrank" (Gen. 32:31–32). What does that mean? Simply this: we must not feast on the failures and shortcomings of others! Love does not do that.

Still describing the nature of love, Paul turns to *love's changeless convictions* (1 Cor. 13:6b–8a). First, we have *love's focus:* "But [love] rejoiceth in the truth" (13:6b). Like love, truth is here personified. Love expresses itself in truth. It is glad when truth prevails. Love does not tell lies, it does not cheat or deceive. It is characterized by integrity. By the same token love rejoices at the establishment of theological truth. It enthusiastically endorses all the great truths of Scripture.

Then we have *love's forbearance:* "[Love] . . . beareth all things" (13:7a). The word translated "bears" is *stego,* which can be rendered "covers" or "protects." It means "to put a roof over." That is what love is like. It finds ways to cover and protect, ways to forgive and forget. The Lord Jesus sought to put a cover over those who nailed Him to the tree. He called upon His Father to forgive them, the poor, ignorant mortals who were actually nailing their Maker to the cross, and who were in danger of the avenging twelve legions of angels who, with drawn swords, were straining over the battlements of heaven prepared to visit instant wrath upon them. When Ham came to tell his brothers he had discovered his father's nakedness, Shem and Japheth responded at once, but not in the way Ham had done. They took a garment and walked in backward and covered his shame (Gen. 9:20–29). Such is the way of love. Subsequently Noah blessed these two boys, passed Ham over in ominous silence, and pronounced a curse on the Canaanite branch of Ham's family. He did so as a prophet.

Next comes *love's faith:* "[Love] . . . believeth all things" (1 Cor. 13:7b). That does not mean that love is gullible, that love blindly accepts everything it is told. Love is not to be taken in like that. However, love is always ready to believe the best and put as good a construction as it can on an action. It gives the benefit of the doubt. Love prefers to be generous rather than censorious. Often that is all some poor delinquent needs—to have someone trust him and put some confidence in him.

We all remember Mr. Grimwig and Mr. Brownlow. Mr. Brownlow had taken poor Oliver Twist into his home. He was willing to believe Oliver's story as to how he had fallen among thieves. Mr. Grimwig was skeptical and scornful. A test was proposed. Oliver was summoned by Mr. Brownlow and sent off on an errand with some books to return to a local bookstore and with a sizable sum in his pocket. Mr. Grimwig offered to eat his own head if Mr. Brownlow ever set eyes on Oliver again. What happened, of course, takes up the rest of Charles Dickens' classic. The difference between the two men was that Mr. Brownlow loved little Oliver and Mr. Grimwig didn't. Therefore Mr. Brownlow was willing to put his belief in Oliver to the test. Mr. Grimwig remained cynical. In the story, Mr. Brownlow had to wait a very long time before he was proved right. But then, that is another characteristic of love. Love knows how to wait.

Then comes *love's future:* "[Love] . . . hopeth all things" (13:7c). Love is optimistic. Love refuses to acknowledge defeat. *Hope* is a word which we associate with the future. It hopes against hope. It forgives not just seven times but seventy times seven times (Matt. 18:22). Love entertains great expectations.

We are not overly fond of the word *hope*. We treat it as though it were a second-class word. If we ask someone if he is saved and he says, "I hope so," we feel that is a most unsatisfactory answer. We feel he needs more than just hope. But, in its own sphere, *hope* is a very strong word indeed. The second coming of the Lord Jesus is spoken of as a "blessed hope" (Titus 2:13). That is what keeps us going, which enables us to rise above our circumstances, to face the future, to laugh at death itself. We have something the world does not have, something the world cannot give, something it cannot take away. We have hope. The person who abandons hope soon succumbs. Hope is something more than simply having been blessed with a sanguine temperament. Hope is love's sister. Hope is born and bred in the believer by the Holy Spirit. Love is the driving force behind hope. Love is of God and love hopes in God. That was the great challenge of the psalmist, facing fears within and foes without. He said, "Why art thou cast down, O my soul? And why art thou disquieted in me? Hope thou in God: for I shall yet praise him for the help of his countenance" (Ps. 42:5). As each successive wave of depression threatened to overwhelm him he kept on saying it (42:11; 43:5). Poor William Cowper learned, in spite of his disability, to let love activate hope in his soul. Yes, and to teach others to sing when strong tides and stormy wakes threatened their lives:

> Ye saints of God, fresh courage take,
> Those clouds ye so much dread
> Are big with mercy, and shall break
> In blessings on your head.

For the future belongs to God, and God is love, so hope, which deals in the future, looks at God and sings.

Then, too, there is *love's fortitude:* "[Love] . . . endureth all things" (1 Cor. 13:7d). The word for *endure* is *hupomenō.* It means "to remain under the load." Love is strong. Love remains under the load no matter how long it takes and no matter what else is piled on top. Love bears up courageously no matter what the suffering. Love is the stuff of which true martyrs are made. This is the love that "will not let us off and that will not let us go and that will not let us down," as Preston Moore, a preacher friend of mine, likes to put it. This is the love that is stronger than death, the love that many waters cannot quench (Song 8:6–7). This was the kind of love Paul had for the Corinthians. They depreciated him and listened to cult leaders. They said unkind and untrue things about him. They resisted his authority although he was an apostle and had led many of them to Christ. Paul went on loving them just the same, went on writing to them, and went on sending his aides to talk to them. His was a love that endured.

Finally, there is *love's fidelity:* "[Love] never faileth" (1 Cor. 13:8a). Gifts fail. At Corinth they were already being abused. They had been given by God to build the church, they were being used instead to tear it down. Most of the gifts Paul writes about to the Corinthians were soon to fail altogether. They were about to come to an end. Love, however, was not like that. Love was lasting. Love could not fail or fall or be rendered obsolete. Love could never cease to be active. The Corinthians had become so obsessed with the gifts they had stopped loving one another. Paul puts love back on the throne. Love is the one thing in the universe on which we can count. It is made out of the very stuff of eternity. It belongs to the ages. Time will fail. The created universe will fail. The sun and stars will fail. Love will never fail.

As we read once more this magnificent description of love, one thought keeps returning to our minds—this is a description of Jesus! And so it is! He is God and God is love. Jesus is love incarnate. So, at the risk of producing a somewhat informal paraphrase, let's take one more look at this description of love, only this time let us substitute the glorious word *Christ!* for that awkward King James word *charity.* And this is what we get:

"Though I speak with the tongues of men and of angels, and have not [Christ], I am become as sounding brass, or a tinkling cymbal. And though I have the gift of prophecy, and understand all mysteries and all knowledge; and though I have all faith so that I could remove mountains, and have not [Christ], I am nothing. And though I bestow all my goods to feed the poor, and though I give my body to be burned, and have not [Christ], it profiteth me nothing.

"[Christ] suffered long, and was kind.[22] [Christ] envied not; [Christ] vaunted not Himself, was not puffed up, did not behave Himself unseemly, sought not His own, was not provoked, thought no evil, rejoiced not in iniquity, but rejoiced in the truth; bore all things, believed all things, hoped all things, endured all things. [Christ] never failed. . . .

"And now abideth faith, hope, [Christ], these three; but the greatest of these is [Christ]!"

Hallelujah! What a Savior! And that is what Paul is after in this hymn of love. He wants us to be like Jesus.

Paul turns, finally, to *the nobility of love* (13:8b–13). Love outlasts everything. Love takes precedence over all. Love is of God. Love is greater than any gift, certainly greater than any transitory gift. He speaks, first, of *that which is passing* (13:8b–12). We notice *Paul's definite expectation* (13:8b–d). Three gifts, he states, specifically and significantly, will come to an end. There will be an end to prophecies, to tongues, and to knowledge: "But whether there be prophecies, they shall fail; whether there be tongues, they shall cease; whether there be knowledge, it shall vanish away." It would be hard to find three more definite statements than that. Other gifts would cease, too, the gift of the apostle, for example. Paul deals here specifically with the ones that were causing all the trouble at Corinth.

First, he says that "prophecies" will fail. When Paul said of love that it "never faileth," he used the word *piptō*. It is used of the Word of God, for instance, which, in its smallest detail, will never lose its authority or cease to have force (Luke 16:17). One authority says that technically the word means "is never hissed off stage" (like a bad actor). It can also mean that it never "falls away like the petals of a withered flower," as in James 1:11. That is because love is eternal. It will play its part on the eternal stage. It is deathless as God is deathless.

Paul now drops that word and picks up another one to describe the "failure" of prophecies. He does this to draw attention to the difference between love and the gift of prophecies. He now uses the word *katargeō*, which literally means "to reduce to inactivity." There would come a time, he said, when prophecies would be put out of business. They would cease to function. They would be abolished. In the Greek language there are three basic voices which govern verbs—active, passive, and middle. The active voice is used when the subject is doing the acting. The passive voice is used when the subject is being acted upon by another party.

---

22. Note: By putting some of the verbs in the past tense (just for the sake of this experiment), we get an even more graphic picture of love incarnate in Christ.

The middle voice is used when the subject is doing the action upon itself. For instance, if we say "The mother washes the child," that would be the active voice of the verb *to wash*. If we say, "The child is washed by his mother," that would be the passive voice because the child is getting washed by someone other than himself. If we say, "The child washes himself," that would be the middle voice of the verb *to wash* because he performs the action on himself. With prophecies the passive voice of the verb is used. That means that Somebody is acting upon "prophecies" to cause them to cease and be abolished. That Somebody, of course, is God Himself.

The same verb and the same voice is used of *knowledge*. Paul says, "Whether there be knowledge, it shall vanish away." It is unfortunate that the same English word is not used. *Knowledge* here is not knowledge that can be acquired but that special understanding imparted by the Holy Spirit which enabled the early church to function before the completion of the New Testament canon. It could be acquired by apostolic instruction. It was revealed to the apostles and relayed through the prophets. Like "prophecies" this unique gift of knowledge, the ability to "know" supernaturally or by apostolic instruction, apart from a completed written revelation, would be abolished.

With "tongues," the situation would be quite different. Paul says, "Whether there be tongues, they shall cease." Tongues, of course, was the supernatural ability to speak in foreign languages. Paul says they would "cease." He uses a different verb and a different verb voice. He does this deliberately under direct, plenary verbal inspiration of the Holy Spirit. The word he uses is *pavō*. It means "to stop," or "to come to an end." This time the middle voice is used. Literally that means that tongues will make themselves to cease. They will come to an automatic end. God will not have to bring any force to bear upon them to cause them to stop. They will cease in and of themselves.

If we can decide when "prophecies" and "knowledge" will cease, when they will be stopped by God, we will know that tongues came to an end before that. Tongues served quite a different purpose than "prophecies" and "knowledge." These latter two have to do with the impartation of divine New Testament truth now incorporated in the canon of Scripture and available to the church. Tongues had to do with the unbelief of the Jewish people, especially the generation which rejected Christ and resisted the Spirit. Paul will have more to say about that in the next chapter. In any case, "tongues" was to be the first to cease. Paul reminds the Corinthians of this since they were making so much commotion over this gift. It was like a bucket of cold water being poured over them—tongues will simply peter out before God Himself puts an end to "prophecies" and "knowledge."[23]

Now comes *Paul's definitive explanation* (1 Cor. 13:9–12). First comes *a word of illumination* (13:9–12). There was the *problem of partial knowledge:* "For we know in part, and we prophesy in part" (13:9). The emphasis here is on *in part,* which is repeated four times in verses 9–12. At best, the early church had to get along with a partial revelation. The expression *ek merous* means "bit by bit." This "bit by bit" state of affairs would continue until the goal of these gifts of communication was reached. Until the New Testament canon was complete, nobody had access to the full and final revelation. That would have to wait until the end of the first century, when John wrote the book of Revelation and the Holy Spirit officially closed the Book (Rev. 22:18–19).

There was, however, *the promise of perfect knowledge* (1 Cor. 13:10). There was to be, first, *a total revelation of the truth:* "But when that which is perfect is come"; accompanied by *a total replacement of the temporary:* "then that which is in part shall be done away." Many conservative and careful scholars try to insert the second coming of Christ here. To say the least, that is quite inconsistent with the context. It introduces a topic quite out of keeping with the whole force and thrust of these three chapters. Paul has not been talking about the second coming of Christ. He has been talking about divine revelation and the various gifts of the Holy Spirit. He has majored on the comprehension gifts and the communication gifts. He has just plainly announced the impending cessation of these gifts. Evidently "that which is perfect," which was to come, has to be explained in the light of the immediate context in particular and the argument of the overall passage in general. The context and general argument has nothing whatever to do with the second coming of Christ. It has everything to do with the completion of the New Testament. There can be no doubt that the second coming of Christ will usher in a new and marvelous age of understanding and completion. Nobody denies that. The fact still remains that it is a subject foreign to the context of 1 Corinthians 13:10.

The word for *perfect* is *teleios.* It is derived from the word *telos (the end).* The Latin equivalent word is *finis*—"nothing beyond." Hence, the word means "perfect," that which is mature, whole, or complete. It means "to reach the goal"

---

23. W. E. Vine says, "The gift of tongues was about the first to be discontinued. All attempts to reintroduce it are either fraudulent or the outcome of deception; they are contrary to Scripture and are void of the actual operation of the Spirit of God" (*1 Corinthians,* 183).

(neuter gender). The goal of the communication gifts was the completion of the New Testament. With the completion of the New Testament we no longer need the gifts of inspired speaking (*prophecies*) and supernatural knowledge. With the completion of the New Testament and the passing of any need for supernatural phenomena, Christianity became mature. It was no longer adolescent. It was adult.

The Holy Spirit gave the various supernatural manifestations as they were required. The apostles needed gifts of wisdom and knowledge. They needed the sign gifts to give them credibility (Eph. 2:20; 2 Cor. 12:12). The prophets also needed the supernatural speaking gifts to enable them to retail revealed truth as, when, and where needed The apostles and prophets have gone. The evangelists, pastors, and teachers remain. The Bible stands supreme. The apostles completed their testimony. The New Testament canon was completed and closed. That which is perfect had come. The New Testament Scriptures, inspired and collected by the Holy Spirit into a single volume, are perfect.

Paul concludes his definitive explanation with *a word of illustration* (1 Cor. 13:11–12). He draws our attention to *the childish stage of things:* "When I was a child, I spake as a child, I understood as a child, I thought as a child: but when I became a man I put away childish things" (13:11). Speech arises out of understanding and understanding out of thought. The more a child matures, the more he thinks, the more intelligent his understanding and the more sensible and profitable his speech.

In choosing this illustration Paul has in mind the three gifts he specifically declared would come to an end as the church grew up to mature manhood in Christ. "I *spake* as a child" (that points to "tongues," for we speak with the tongue); "I *understood* as a child" (that points to "knowledge," for, normally, knowledge is the basis for understanding); "I *thought* as a child" (that points to "prophecy," because the Holy Spirit, in revealing truth, did not override the thought process of the prophet. On the contrary, He illuminated it so that the personality of the prophet would always be discernible in his utterings and writings. In time "prophecy" would be replaced by teaching, which would call for a more mature thought process).

The "speaking" in tongues, the "understanding" in knowledge, and the "thinking" in prophecy was still in its infancy so long as the speaking, understanding, and thinking had to be, to some considerable degree, directly and supernaturally controlled by the Holy Spirit. The goal of the Holy Spirit was to wean the church off this immature process as soon as possible. The church had almost arrived in "the knowledge of the Son of God, unto a perfect man, unto the measure of the stature of the fulness of Christ" by the time Paul wrote to the Ephesians (Eph. 4:11–13). By that time the church had no further need of the sign gifts and of the ecstatic gifts. They are not ever mentioned. The church had grown up. The gifts of the apostle and prophet were still extant because a half-dozen books still needed to be written and put into general circulation. But the church had "become a man" and had "put away childish things," that is, the things associated with the infancy and early days. Indeed, the notable absence of the transitional gifts in all the other Epistles shows how soon the church was able to dispense with them.

Paul's reference to being "a child" here really has nothing to do with the behavior of a child, but with how a child communicates. The Greek word for *child* is *nēpios,* which signifies a babe, a child not old enough to speak. Immaturity is always associated with this word in the New Testament. The Corinthians were smart enough to see that Paul was telling them to grow up. Nothing could be more unseemly, surely, than a man babbling like a babe. It was high time they put away the infantile communication process and began to think, understand, and speak like adults.

So much for the childish state of things. Paul points them on to *a changed state of things:* "For now we see through a glass, darkly; but then face to face: now I know in part; but then shall I know even as also I am known" (1 Cor. 13:12). Now no one denies that, by *application,* this statement can be made to refer to the second coming of Christ. But application is not interpretation, and it is interpretation which we are pursuing here. The interpretation of any passage is largely determined by its context. The context here is the revelation of truth and the communication of truth. In Paul's day mirrors were not made of glass but of polished metal. They gave a much dimmer and darker reflection than our modern mirrors. Until the New Testament was completed even the most enlightened believers could only grasp the tremendous truths, now being revealed, imperfectly. It was a time of partial vision. Much still remained dark, difficult to discern, and hard to understand.

We now have a completed revelation. God has told us all we need to know to get us from earth to glory. We have the completed Bible in our hands. It is all the difference between night and day, between seeing someone's image in a dull, metal mirror and seeing that person face to face. It is no longer "bit by bit" (i.e., "in part"); now it is "face to face!" I can also "know even as also I am known." Until the canon of Scripture was completed a believer could know only in part.

Now he has access to the whole truth. He can know the Father, the Son, and the Holy Spirit. He can know himself. He can know God's plans and purposes. He can know the mind of God concerning the nations, Israel, and the church.

Paul's statement here that "I shall know even as also I am known" obviously cannot mean that, one day, at the Rapture, we shall know as completely as God knows. Simply to state the idea is to see its error. God is omniscient, we aren't. God's knowledge is total, absolute, and infinite. Ours can never be. Paul is not stating that, at the second coming, we "shall be as gods, knowing good and evil." That was the Devil's original lie. Our knowledge will never be of the same kind or in the same degree as God's knowledge. What is meant is that our knowledge will be complete, within limits, even as God's knowledge is complete without limits.

There can be no doubt that our knowledge will be greatly enhanced at the second coming of Christ. But that is not the subject under discussion. The subject is not the coming of the Christ but the completion of the canon. The final completion, assembly, and circulation of the New Testament Scriptures has put in our hands the means to know the entire range of revealed truth. It enables us to know even as we are known. God knows us. Now we can know Him.

The book of Hebrews begins, "God, who at sundry times and in divers manners spake in time past unto the fathers by the prophets, hath in these last days spoken unto us by his Son" (Heb. 1:1–2). Throughout the Old Testament era, God spoke through men like Moses and Malachi, men like Job and Jonah and Jeremiah, men like David and Daniel. What was revealed was the truth: inspired, inerrant, and infallible truth. It was all so inadequate, however, so partial and incomplete. There was so much more to be said.

Then God sent His Son, and, in Him, gave full expression to the great, eternal thoughts of our hearts. The truth was clothed in flesh and blood. "The Word was made flesh." The Lord Jesus, however, did not stay here. He went back home. Before He went He promised to send His Holy Spirit. The things that He had said and done and embodied and revealed needed to be written down. In a series of statements He promised that the Holy Spirit would complete the written revelation so that we might be led into all truth.

The Holy Spirit came. He began the process of writing the New Testament and, until such time as the process was completed, and the full record and revelation given, He gave transitional gifts of comprehension and communication. The Book is now completed. The transitional gifts have served their purpose and have been withdrawn. The Bible is now complete and in our hands. We can now know, even as we are known. The Holy Spirit is still here to apply that truth to our minds and hearts, to our consciences and wills. God has no more to say.

So then, Paul has written about that which is passing. He concludes this great chapter by going back to his original theme—love. He rounds it all off by reminding us, one more time, of *that which is permanent:* "And now abideth faith, hope, and [love], these three: but the greatest of these is [love]" (1 Cor. 13:13). Prophecy, tongues, knowledge, these three! They will cease. Faith, hope, love, these three! They will abide. Faith looks back to Calvary. Hope looks on to the coming. Love is for now! Love is forever! Love is what God is! Love is the greatest thing of all.

      c. Comparison (14:1–40)
          (1) Reactions (14:1–20)
              (a) By way of introduction (14:1–6)
                  i. Prophecy is positively a preferred gift (14:1)
                      a. What should be done (14:1a)
                      b. What should be desired (14:1b)
                      c. What should be discerned (14:1c)
                 ii. Prophecy is patently a preferred gift (14:2–6)
                    In contrast with prophecy
                      a. Tongues do not enlighten the church as a whole (14:2–3)
                          1. A comment (14:2)
                              (i) The needless godward aspect of tongues (14:2a)
                                  (a) What he says is missed by most
                                  (b) What he says is mysterious to most
                          2. A contrast (14:3)
                              (i)   Prophecy is constructive (14:3a)
                              (ii)   Prophecy is convicting (14:3b)
                              (iii) Prophecy is consoling (14:3c)
                      b. Tongues do not edify the church as a whole (14:4)
                          1. Tongues is self-oriented (14:4a)
                          2. Prophecy is service-oriented (14:4b)
                        c. Tongues do not enrich the church as a whole (14:5–6)

        1. A confession (14:5a)

        2. A concession (14:5b–c)

           (i)   What Paul admonishes (14:5b)

           (ii)   What Paul admits (14:5c)

        3. A contention (14:6)

           (i)   Tongues are profitless (14:6a)

           (ii)   Preaching is peerless (14:6b–e)

               (a) Truth is unveiled (14:6b)

               (b) Truth is understood (14:6c)

               (c) Truth is unfolded (14:6d)

               (d) Truth is underlined (14:6e)

(b) By way of illustration (14:7–13)

    i. It is appropriate (14:7–8)

       a. Pipe and harp must give a distinctive musical sound to be of value (14:7)

       b. Trumpets must give a definite martial sound to be of value (14:8)

    ii. It is applied (14:9–13)

       a. Some blunt facts stated (14:9–11)

           1. The farce of speaking in tongues (14:9)

           2. The futility of speaking in tongues (14:10–11)

               Who wants to be

               (i)   Just a blaring voice (14:10)

               (ii) Just a barbarian voice (14:11)

       b. Some blunt facts stressed (14:12–13)

           1. Their zeal recognized (14:12)

           2. Their zeal redirected (14:13)

(c) By way of instruction (14:14–20)

    i. Paul's decision (14:14–17)

       a. His resolve (14:14–15)

           1. His assessment: tongues are lacking (14:14)

           2. His assertion: truth is logical (14:15)

               (i)   So I will pray intelligently (14:15a)

               (ii) So I will praise intelligently (14:15b)

       b. His reason (14:16–17)

           1. A gracious admonition (14:16)

        2. A grudging admission (14:17)
     ii. Paul's declaration (14:18–20)
        a. His possession of the gift (14:18)
        b. His practice of the gift (14:19–20)
           1. A bluntly stated choice (14:19)
           2. A bluntly stated challenge (14:20)

Paul returns now to the question of the gifts, especially the two gifts of prophecy and tongues. He has dealt at length with the subject *in terms of confusion* (1 Cor. 12:1–31), seeking to show the character and relative importance of the various gifts. He has dealt with the subject *in terms of correction* (13:1–13), seeking to show the absolute supremacy of love and the transient nature of tongues, knowledge, and prophecy. Now he deals with the subject *in terms of comparison* (14:1–40). Although both prophecy and tongues were temporary gifts, he argues, prophecy far surpassed tongues in terms of importance.

This new approach to the problem is in three parts—*reactions* (14:1–20), *reasons* (14:21–25), and *restrictions* (14:26–40). Paul turns first to *introduction* (14:1–6). First, *prophecy is positively a preferred gift* (14:1). We note what should be *done:* "Follow after charity"; and what should be *desired:* "and desire spiritual gifts"; and what should be *discerned:* "but rather that ye may prophesy." The word for *follow* is *diōkō,* which literally means "to chase" or "to pursue." The Corinthians were chasing after tongues. Paul does not say that there is anything wrong with setting one's heart on the gifts of the Spirit. He does say that the highest gift one could desire is the ability to speak the messages of God.

Moreover, *prophecy is patently a preferred gift* (14:2–6). That becomes evident when it is set alongside tongues, the other communications gift. For instance, *tongues do not enlighten the church as a whole* (14:2–3). Here is Paul's *comment:* "For he that speaketh in an unknown tongue speaketh not unto men, but unto God: for no man understandeth him; howbeit in the spirit he speaketh mysteries" (14:2). Unintelligible language benefits nobody. Apart from an interpreter, nobody understands a word the speaker says. Maybe he is speaking "mysteries" in the Spirit. What good does that do anyone? The whole process is silly. Suppose a person who normally speaks English suddenly starts to speak in Arabic, which neither he nor anyone else in the church can understand. Why not speak in English? Can't God understand and speak English as easily as Arabic? Speaking in tongues under such circumstances is foolish.

Now comes *Paul's contrast* (14:3). Prophecy is *constructive:* "But he that prophesieth speaketh unto men to edification"; it is *convicting:* "he . . . speaketh unto men to . . . exhortation"; it is *consoling:* "he . . . speaketh unto men to . . . comfort." That makes much more sense. The word for "edification" is *oikodomē,* used of building a house. Prophesying (or *preaching,* as it would be today) builds spiritual character and encourages spiritual growth both in the individual believer and in the local church. The word for *exhortation* is *paraklēsis.* The word primarily has to do with calling someone to one's side for aid. It carries the idea of an appeal and entreaty. The word for *comfort* is *paramuthia.* It refers primarily to speaking closely to a person, to consoling a person with a degree of tenderness. How much more productive prophecy is than a sterile speaking in tongues nobody understands.

Moreover, *tongues do not edify the church as a whole:* "He that speaketh in an unknown tongue edifieth himself: but he that prophesieth edifieth the church" (14:4). Supposing the "tongue" to be genuine, and under the various controls described in this chapter, and when the self-consciousness is not overwhelmed by the controlling spirit, the person employing the "tongue" might be built up in his own soul. The preacher or prophet, by contrast, benefits the whole church. What is done in the local church should benefit everybody.

Tongues do not enlighten the church, they do not edify the church. Furthermore, *tongues do not enrich the church as a whole* (14:5–6). First comes *a confession:* "I would that ye all spake with tongues, but rather that ye prophesied: for greater is he that prophesieth than he that speaketh with tongues" (14:5a). Paul does not deny that the gift of tongues existed in the early church, that it was a valid gift, that it had a definite reason for existing, and that it was a worthwhile gift. He goes even further. He voices the wish that they all had this gift. At least there was some enthusiasm among those who had it, some sign of spiritual life. There is a parallel here to an incident in the life of Moses. Two men, Eldad and Medad, had the Spirit of the Lord resting upon them and "they prophesied in the camp." The context reveals that they were, in actual fact, members of the group of seventy men to whom Moses delegated part of his administrative responsibilities. All the other members of this group were likewise prophesying. For some reason these two were not with the others. Their sudden inspiration seems to have startled the people who were present. One of those there, a young man, ran to Moses to tell him what was happening and Joshua urged Moses to put a stop to it. Moses replied, "Enviest thou for my sake? would God that all the LORD's people were prophets, and that the LORD would put his Spirit upon them" (Num. 11:24–30).

Like Moses, Paul was not perturbed because some people spoke in tongues. After all, it was still a valid gift when he wrote this letter and still operational in the church. It would be desirable for all God's people to be so gifted, he thought. That would certainly be an improvement over the present situation, where some had the gift and some didn't, and where those who had the gift scorned those who didn't, and where those who lacked the gift envied those who had it, and where those who did not have it were prepared to go to any lengths (if they were like the present-day, so-called charismatics) to get it.

Even while going so far as to admit that he would have welcomed the news that everyone at Corinth spoke with tongues, Paul immediately qualifies the admission. It would be far better, however, if they all prophesied. Prophecy was a greater gift than tongues, no matter how much the Corinthians and their heirs and successors might trumpet the lesser gift.

Paul does, however, make *a concession:* "Except he interpret, that the church may receive edifying" (1 Cor. 14:5b). There were evidently some cases where a person had both the gift of tongues and the gift of interpretation. In that case he could translate what he had just said so that those present, who did not understand the foreign language in which he had just spoken, could profit from the message. That, of course, would upgrade the "tongues" to prophecy. Some justification could be found for the tongues in such a case.

Now comes *a contention* (14:6). First, Paul says, *tongues* in and of themselves, are *profitless:* "Now, brethren, if I come unto you speaking with tongues, what shall I profit you?" (14:6a). The Corinthians spoke Greek. Doubtless many understood Latin and some, especially the Jewish believers, understood Aramaic and Hebrew. Possibly Paul spoke all those languages fluently himself. It is not at all unusual for Europeans today to speak three or four languages common to the continent. They grow up in a multilingual culture. It was probably equally likely that many people in the Roman world spoke several languages. But supposing, when Paul made his next visit to Corinth, he came speaking in tongues, speaking Chaldee or Celtic or German. Who would understand a word he said? It would be an exercise in futility. Paul had more sense than to even contemplate such a nonsensical enterprise. No indeed! He would come speaking the Greek of the marketplace, the lingua franca of the Roman world.

By contrast, *prophecy* (preaching) is *peerless* (14:6b–e). Paul elaborates upon this. If he comes he will come speaking "by revelation" (so that truth might be *unveiled*), "or by knowledge" (so that truth might be *understood*), "or by prophesying" (so that truth might be *unfolded*), "or by doctrine" (so that truth might be *underlined*). Any of these methods of communication would be advantageous and profitable to the church. So why speak in a foreign language, however eloquently and accurately? The whole thing made no sense at all.

Paul turns now to *illustration* (14:7–13). First, *Paul's illustration is appropriate* (14:7–8). He draws his illustration from the realm of music. He points out that pipe and harp must give *a distinctive musical sound* to be of value: "And even things without life giving sound, whether pipe or harp, except they give a distinction in the sounds, how shall it be known what is piped or harped?" (14:7). Each instrument, whether wind or stringed, must be distinguishable, otherwise all that is produced is a mere noise. Musical instruments are not played at random. There are laws that govern their use. The musician must know how to produce the various notes. He must know how to combine them into chords. If proper music is to result, he must observe such things as key and timing and volume. If various kinds of instruments are to play together there must be a score which tells each one when to sound and when to be silent. There has to be a conductor who rules over all. What kind of a tune would it be if each player went his own merry way, blowing into his pipe, striking at his harp, regardless of the laws of music and in defiance of the musical score and the conductor? Instead of having a symphony you would have a din. That was exactly what was happening at Corinth, especially with the "tongues" people.

Moreover, trumpets must give *a definite martial sound* to be of value: "For if the trumpet give an uncertain sound, who shall prepare himself to the battle?" (14:8). For many centuries, commands were relayed to the rank and file by means of trumpets. They sounded reveille to awaken the camp. They sounded the advance or the retreat. At the end of the day they sounded taps to send the soldiers to their quarters. Each command was associated with a set tune. What confusion there would be in the ranks, what an advantage, indeed, for the enemy, if the trumpeter simply sounded out a series of discords or played a tune that had no military meaning. Instead of an orderly movement of troops there would be utter confusion and, doubtless, a subsequent court-martial for the trumpeter. This was the very thing that was happening with the "tongues" people at Corinth.

Now *Paul's illustration is applied* (14:9–13). First, *some blunt facts are stated* (14:9–11). Paul underlines *the farce of speaking in tongues:* "So likewise ye, except ye utter by the tongue words easy to be understood, how shall it be known what is spoken? for ye shall speak into the air" (14:9). That's pretty blunt! One might just as well stand on a cliff overlooking the sea and speak into the teeth of a howling wind as get up in the local church and speak in a language, or use a vocabulary, nobody can understand. It would be an exercise in futility. This was what was happening at Corinth.

Paul underlines *the futility of speaking in tongues* (14:10–11). Who wants to be *a blaring voice* or *a barbarian voice?* He says, "There are, it may be, so many kinds of voices in the world, and none of them is without signification. Therefore if I know not the meaning of the voice, I shall be to him that speaketh a barbarian, and he that speaketh shall be a barbarian to me." The word for *voices* here signifies languages. Paul did not know how many languages there were. "Many kinds," he says. According to the Wycliffe Bible Translators' International Linguistic Center in Dallas, Texas, there are more than 5,000 known language groups in the world. These languages are all made up of various kinds of sounds, not one of which is unintelligible to those who speak them. But if these sounds mean nothing to us, then we are foreigners to those who make them and they are foreigners to us. To the Greeks anyone who did not speak Greek was a barbarian.

Nothing can be more exasperating than to be in a country where a foreign language is spoken. I have been in many such countries. The sense of isolation and insecurity it produces can be overwhelming. I was on a plane once flying from Denmark to Norway. Everyone else on the plane was a Scandinavian. All about me people were talking animatedly to each other. I couldn't understand a word that was said. Later I attended a service in a Norwegian church. I was handed a hymnbook in Norwegian. Nothing made any sense. On another occasion I took a trip down through a number of countries in Latin America. There I was inundated in a sea of Spanish and Portuguese. I could not read the announcements placarding the times of the planes. I could not understand even well-meaning comments directed to me. Fortunately on this trip I was traveling with a friend who spoke Spanish. But how much better it would have been, I thought, if I could only have spoken in tongues! *That* kind of tongues would make sense, but what was happening at Corinth, and what happens among the "tongues enthusiastics" today, makes no sense at all. They were babbling away in foreign languages, Greeks though most of them were, like so many "barbarians"— a term they often used with contempt.

But Paul is not yet finished. Now *some blunt facts are stressed* (14:12–13). First, *their zeal is recognized:* "Even so ye, forasmuch as ye are zealous of spiritual gifts, seek that ye may excel to the edifying of the church" (14:12). Paul could find no fault with their desire to exercise their spiritual gifts. Indeed, he had already twice encouraged them along these lines (12:31; 14:1). However, their motive in desiring the various gifts must be right. Paul keeps hammering away at the central point. All verbal ministry in the local church must be for the building up of the body. It must contribute to the real growth of the church.

So, *their zeal is redirected:* "Wherefore let him that speaketh in an unknown tongue pray that he may interpret" (14:13). That was just plain, practical common sense.

Paul turns now to *instruction* (14:14–20). Note, first, *Paul's decision* (14:14–17). We have *his resolve* (14:14–15). He gives us *his assessment—tongues are lacking:* "For if I pray in an unknown tongue, my spirit prayeth, but my understanding is unfruitful" (14:14); he gives us *his assertion—truth is logical:* "What is it then? I will pray with the spirit, and I will pray with the understanding also: I will sing with the spirit, and I will sing with the understanding also" (14:15). We must remind ourselves again that tongues was a valid gift in the church at the time. Paul himself had the gift. He has not yet told us why the gift was given—but he will do so within a few more verses. Its significance was very limited indeed. Before he gets around to explaining its true importance he continues to systematically devalue it and put curbs on it. So, he says, a person exercises his gift on tongues in prayer! To what end? His spirit (or whatever part of him it is which exercises this gift) prays—but his own reasoning faculty is by-passed. As a result even he himself does not understand what is said! There may indeed be some sense of religious exaltation which accompanies the experience (those who claim to speak in "tongues" today seem to derive some such ecstasy from it—something easily counterfeited by the flesh or by a deceiving spirit) but praying in tongues does not profit even the speaker's own mind, let alone being profitable to anyone else.

Paul lays down the rule. Praying and singing in "tongues" is unprofitable, even when valid. Here is his resolution—to pray with both the Spirit *and* the understanding also. If he is going to pray and if he is going to sing, he is going to make quite sure he is in the Spirit and that he employs his reason as part of the process. What sound common sense! After all, if a person who speaks only English prays, why pray in the Japanese tongue? Doesn't God understand English? Of course He does! So pray in English. Then both God, and the person praying, will understand what is being said.

We have not only Paul's resolve, we have also *Paul's reason:* "Else when thou shalt bless with the spirit, how shall he that occupieth the room of the unlearned say Amen at thy giving of thanks, seeing he understandeth not what thou sayest? For thou verily givest thanks well, but the other is not edified" (14:16–17). Paul keeps going over and over the same ground. He does not deny the ability of praying in tongues, for tongues had not yet ceased. He did not deny that a person praying in tongues might be saying some very fine things. But that does not help anyone at all. The others who did not understand the tongue being spoken would not be able to endorse the prayer with an intelligent "Amen!" Evidently the practice of thus audibly associating themselves with the prayer, praise, and preaching of the brother leading the church in worship was common. The "un-learned" here simply refers to those who were unable to understand the foreign language used by the person speaking in tongues.

Finally, we have *Paul's declaration* (14:18–20). We note *his possession of the gift:* "I thank my God, I speak with tongues more than ye all" (14:18); we note *his practice of the gift:* "Yet in the church I had rather speak five words with my understanding, that by my voice I might teach others also, than ten thousand words in an un-known tongue. Brethren, be not children in understanding: howbeit in malice be ye children, but in understanding be men" (14:19–20). Paul wanted the Corinthians to understand that he was not depreciating the gift of tongues because he did not possess the gift himself. Indeed, he was thankful to God that he did possess it, if for no other reason than to put an end to any such assertion. Indeed, he spoke with tongues more than they did. So then, if some kind of superiority attached to those who possessed the gift of tongues, something Paul has already emphatically denied (14:5) but which the Corinthians themselves seemed to imagine to be the case, well, they must rank Paul among the foremost.

What did he do with this gift? He deliberately refrained from using it in the church. To what extent? To the extent he would rather say five intelligible words everyone could understand than speak ten thousand words in a tongue nobody could under-stand. No greater disparagement could be imagined in the gift of tongues. It was immeasurably more important to teach others than it was to try to impress them with a display of a gift, especially a gift which was of only marginal importance.

Paul concludes all this part of the discussion by exhorting the Corinthians, once again, to be men, to grow up. Especially he urged them, if they had to be children, to be children in malice. The word translated *malice* is *kakia.* The word really has to do with depravity, with vicious disposition and desire. Paul urged the Corinthians, in other words, to be as innocent as babies as far as evil was concerned. They were being childish in the matter of "tongues." Let them rather be childish in regards to evil desire.

(2) Reasons (14:21–25)
      (a) The Scripture and its significance (14:21)
          i. The content of the quotation (14:21a)
          ii. The context of the quotation (14:21b)

(b) The signs and their significance (14:22)
  i. Tongues: a warning sign to the Jewish unbeliever (14:22a)
  ii. Prophecy: a welcome sound for the Christian believer (14:22b)
(c) The sinner and his significance (14:23–25)
  i. The reaction of the unsaved to hearing tongues (14:23)
  ii. The reaction of the unsaved to hearing prophecy (14:24–25)
    a. What he sees (14:24a)
    b. What he senses (14:24b–25b)
      1. Conviction (14:24b–25a)
      2. Conversion (14:25b)
    c. What he says (14:25c)
(3) Restrictions (14:26–40)
  (a) A simple rule (14:26)
    i. Various ministries may be valid in the church (14:26a)
    ii. Valid ministries must be valuable to the church (14:26b)
  (b) A silence rule (14:27–35)
    i. Silence, as regards the Word (14:27–33)
      a. When it comes to tongues and the matter of interpretation (14:27–28)
        1. What is permitted (14:27a)
        2. What is prohibited (14:27b–28)
      b. When it comes to truth and the matter of interruption (14:29–33)
        1. The rule (14:29–30)
          (i) Be content (14:29a)
          (ii) Be cautious (14:29b)
          (iii) Be courteous (14:30)
        2. The reasons (14:31–33)
          Ministry of the Word of God is to be
          (i) Permitted to all (14:31a)
          (ii) Profitable to all (14:31b–33)

> (a) It must be a help to the saints of
>   God (14:31b)
> (b) It must be in harmony with the
>   Spirit of God (14:32–33)
>   *(1)* A test (14:32)
>   *(2)* A truth (14:33)
>   ii. Silence as regards the women (14:34–35)
>   *a.* An absolute rule (14:34)
>   *1.* A blunt prohibition (14:34a)
>   *2.* A biblical precept (14:34b)
>   *b.* An absolving regulation (14:35a)
>   *c.* An abiding requirement (14:35b)
> (c) A sensible rule (14:36–40)
>   i. For the conceited man (14:36)
>   ii. For the confident man (14:37–38)
>   *a.* The man who is virtually unreachable (14:37)
>   *b.* The man who is virtually unteachable (14:38)
>   iii. For the concerned man (14:39–40)
>   *a.* Keep the best in view (14:39)
>   *b.* Keep this test in view (14:40)

Paul's reactions (1 Cor. 14:1–20) now give way to Paul's *reasons* (14:21–25).[24] What was the significance of tongues? Why was it given? Why did Paul so confidently assert that it would come to an end of its usefulness and die a natural death?

---

24. Again and again, throughout this long dissertation, Paul has been at pains to depreciate the gift of tongues. He seems to be writing it off. There was the obvious extremism associated with the gift. He does not actually ridicule the extremists by likening the whole body to a tongue! But he comes close enough by likening the whole body to an ear. There was the foolish *exaggeration* of those who imagined tongues to be high on the list of desirable gifts, whereas the Holy Spirit lists it at the bottom and bluntly states that the person who prophesies is greater than the person who speaks in tongues. There is the relative *excellence* of the gift, as something far inferior to love, that great fruit of the Spirit. There is the careful *examination* of the gift in the light of its obvious inferiority to prophecy and in the light of Paul's two, telling illustrations. There is the personal *experience* of the apostle, who exercised the gift more than anyone but who virtually refused to use it at all in a public meeting of the church. There is the anticipated *expiration* of the gift altogether and the fact it would come to an automatic end

Paul begins his explanation by referring us to *the Scripture and its significance:* "In the law it is written, With men of other tongues, and other lips will I speak unto this people; and yet for all that will they not hear Me, saith the Lord" (14:21). By *the law* here Paul means the Old Testament, for which it was a generic term. Here it includes Isaiah, just as in John 10:34, in 15:25 it includes the Psalms.

The actual quotation here is from Isaiah 28:11–12 and it is admirably suited to Paul's purpose in explaining the significance of tongues. In Isaiah's day the nations of Israel and Judah were riddled with apostasy. The deterioration in Judah was retarded somewhat by the two godly kings Hezekiah and Josiah. Just the same it proceeded apace toward inevitable judgment. The situation in Israel, however, was beyond all hope. The people had turned a deaf ear to the prophet's warnings (28:12). The leaders of the nation ridiculed his attempts to warn and teach them (28:9). They sneered at Isaiah because they thought he was treating them as though they were children (28:9). They scoffed at his attempts to spell out to them "precept upon precept; line upon line; here a little, and there a little," their wickedness and its inevitable consequences (28:10).

There could be only one outcome—judgment. Already Assyria was reaching for superpower status. Her armies were fast becoming the scourge of the Middle East. The day would soon come when they would descend upon Israel and put an end to Samaria and the Northern Kingdom. The Israelites were soon to be uprooted, deported, and scattered and *they would be forced to listen to people who spoke foreign languages.* "For with stammering lips and another tongue" was Isaiah's way of putting it. The word for *stammering* means "jabbering." For their refusal to listen when God spoke, simply, clearly, lovingly, truthfully, they could look forward to deportation and exile. All they would hear would be the "jabbering" of foreign languages. It was the judgment of God.

Now *that* is the very passage of Scripture which Paul uses to explain the gift of tongues. Doubtless "tongues" served a secondary, utilitarian purpose in that, from time to time, the tongue being spoken would be understood, as on the Day of Pentecost. But that was not the primary reason for the gift. In any case, most times

---

in and of itself. Finally there is the biblical *exegesis,* which Paul is now to set before us, which explains simply and categorically just why the gift of tongues was given. If it were as useful as the so-called charismatics claim, why do missionaries (even those who have the "gift") have to painstakingly learn foreign languages?

This entire depreciation of the tongues gift is blithely ignored by those who imagine "tongues" to be the very epitome of spiritual experience.

those present in the church, when tongues were being spoken, would not understand a word of what was said and would require the message to be translated.

"This people" (referred to in the quotation from Isaiah) are the *Jewish* people. The gift of tongues was a sign to them, and a judgment sign at that, for the situation of the Jews in Paul's day was exactly parallel with that of the Jews in Isaiah's day. The nation was apostate, so much so, indeed, that the Jerusalem Jews, who repented on the Day of Pentecost, actually had to be baptized *before* they could receive the remission of sins (Acts 2:37–38).[25]

The seriousness of the situation was graphically portrayed by the Lord Jesus. Just before the crucifixion He roundly cursed the Jewish leaders (Matt. 23:1–39) and pronounced a curse on the fig tree (24:32–36). That act was symbolic and full of menace because the fig tree was a well-known symbol of the nation of Israel.[26]

It was to confirm and reinforce the impending judgment on the Jews, pronounced by the Lord on the eve of Calvary, that the Holy Spirit gave the sign gift

---

25. This is the only instance in the New Testament where baptism was required as part of salvation. So great was the crime of Calvary, Jews who were convicted of their sin and who recognized Jesus as Messiah and Savior had to publicly separate themselves from the nation, its leaders, and its great sin by water baptism. Then they could receive remission of sins and the gift of the Holy Spirit.

26. The Lord's public ministry, as recorded by Matthew, began with eight beatitudes (Matt. 5:1–12) and it ended with eight woes directed against the nation and especially its leaders. Having openly cursed the nation of Israel, the Lord added the words "That upon you may come all the righteous blood shed upon the earth from the blood of righteous Abel unto the blood of Zacharias son of Barachias, whom ye slew between the temple and the altar" (Matt. 23:35). In the Jewish Bible the first and last martyrs were Abel and Zacharias. In other words, if God were to take all the innocent blood that was shed throughout the entire Old Testament period, and heap it on the heads of the Jews of His day, their guilt would be great—but not nearly so great as it actually was for planning the crime of Calvary. "All these things," He added, "shall come upon this generation" (Matt. 23:36). He then went on to describe the impending destruction of Jerusalem by the Romans. The judgment fell in A.D. 70. For another few decades the full outpouring of wrath lingered until after the Bar Kokba rebellion in A.D. 135, when the Romans put a full and final end to Jewish national life.

The Lord long foresaw what was coming. "Whereunto shall I liken this generation?" He demanded. "It is like children sitting in the markets, and calling to their fellows." They suggested playing weddings. No response! They suggested playing funerals. No response! "For John came neither eating and drinking, and they say, He hath a devil. The Son of man came eating and drinking, and they say, Behold a

of tongues to the early church. Tongues was a *sign*. It was a sign for the *Jews*. It was a *judgment sign* for Jews. Jews, confronted by this tongues phenomenon, were being reminded of both Isaiah's prophecy and the Lord's prophecy. The people of Isaiah's day were so hardened in their rejection of God's Word that nothing remained but judgment—deportation and being forced, generation after generation, to speak Gentile languages. Just so the Jews of Paul's day were equally hardened. They had rejected the Son of God and were now rejecting the Spirit of God. All that remained was judgment. The nation was again to be invaded, this time by the Romans. Jewish national life would again be terminated. Once more the Jews would be uprooted and scattered among the nations. For generation after generation they would be forced to speak Gentile languages.[27] When the Jews of Paul's day heard Christians speaking in tongues, the Holy Spirit was actually bearing witness to these Jews that their doom was upon them. When the judgment fell, tongues ceased. They were no longer relevant.

Now we can see why Paul so consistently depreciated tongues and elevated prophecy and preaching. Prophecy added to the Word of God, tongues added to the warnings of God. Prophecy was elevating, tongues were alarming. Prophecy was primarily for the church, tongues were for the Jews. That which would be produced by prophecy was eternal, that which was pronounced by tongues was temporal.

In all his explanation of the gifts, Paul appealed only once to the Bible. He referred the Corinthians (and us) to Isaiah 28:11–12. "There!" he says, "if you must have it spelled out, *that* is what 'tongues' are all about—judgment on the Jew."

Those who claim to have the gift of tongues today ignore the basic message and general thrust of 1 Corinthians 12:14. They seize instead on isolated texts

---

man gluttonous, and a winebibber, a friend of publicans and sinners" (Matt. 11:16–19). The term "this generation" occurs sixteen times (Matt. 11:16; 12:41, 42; 23:36; 24:24; Mark 8:12 (twice); 13:30; Luke 7:31; 11:30, 31, 32, 50, 51; 17:25; 21:32). It occurs also with descriptive epithets—"evil and adulterous" (Matt. 12:39, 45; 16:4; Mark 8:38; Luke 11:29); "faithless and perverse" (Matt. 17:17; Mark 9:19; Luke 9:41); "untoward" (Acts 2:40). All this was for one simple reason. This was the generation that rejected the Messiah. In the great prophecy on the Mount of Olives, just prior to going to Calvary, the Lord gave a graphic description of the sure and certain doom of the Jewish nation (Matt. 24:11–3; Luke 21:5–24).

27. When the Jewish State was reborn in May 1948, there were Jews in the country from no less than 112 different nations!

such as Paul's statement "I thank my God, I speak with tongues more than ye all" (14:18) or "forbid not to speak in tongues" (14:39) and, in both cases, ignore the context.[28]

Paul, then, talks about the Scripture and its significance. Now he turns to *the signs and their significance* (14:22). He says that *tongues were a warning sign to the Jewish unbeliever:* "Wherefore tongues are for a sign, not to them that believe, but to them that believe not'" (14:22a). It is astonishing how seldom tongues are mentioned in the New Testament. Apart from these three chapters in Corinthians, where the whole subject is doctrinally reviewed and put in its proper perspective, it is mentioned elsewhere only in the book of Acts and there only three times. Moreover, each time Jews and some form of Jewish unbelief were involved.

It is mentioned in Acts 2:4–13 in connection with the Day of Pentecost. On that occasion Peter confronted the Jewish nation, the Jews of the homeland and the Jews of the Diaspora, and charged them with the murder of the Son of God. About a dozen and a half different languages were known to have been represented in the Jewish crowd that was present on the occasion. The entire setting, sermon, and significance was Jewish. The horrendous guilt of the nation was in view.

---

28. They ignore also other equally pointed statements regarding tongues coming to an end in and of themselves and regarding women keeping silent in the church. They ignore Paul's warning about testing the spirits and John's even more potent warning. They ignore the Holy Spirit's teaching that the spirits of the prophets are subject to the prophets (14:32). They accept extrabiblical revelation and even prefer it to biblical revelation. They ignore sound doctrine and base belief on their "experience" instead. They encourage the uninitiated to babble as a preliminary step to getting "the gift." They ignore the clear introductory words of Paul that the Holy Spirit sovereignly dispenses the gifts and that not everyone has this or that gift—including tongues. They elevate "tongues" as some kind of superior gift, whereas Paul consistently marks it down as an inferior gift. They claim that speaking in tongues is evidence of the baptism of the Spirit and ignore the Holy Spirit's clear teaching that the baptism of the Spirit is enjoyed by all members of the body of Christ. They extend the right hand of fellowship to anyone and everyone who speaks in tongues regardless of their doctrinal beliefs. Thus a Roman Catholic can speak in tongues one moment and participate in the dark error of the Mass the next moment and be warmly embraced as a brother by a tongues-speaking Methodist, Baptist, or Presbyterian. Worst of all, they ignore the fact that lying and deceiving spirits are abroad looking for people, good people, Christian people, respected people, whom they can deceive. We might well ask where the modern "tongues" movement came from and by what spirit its practitioners produce the phenomenon which attracts so many people to it. In view of all the evidence, it is difficult to see how the Holy Spirit could be the Author of so much doctrinal confusion.

Tongues are mentioned again in connection with the conversion of Cornelius and the incorporation of Gentiles into the body of Christ (Acts 10:44–48). The church up to this time had been entirely Jewish in composition, with the recent addition of some Samaritans who had some (diluted) kinship with the Jews. Now Gentiles were added. Soon their numbers would completely eclipse that of the Jews. The Jews had deep-seated prejudices against the Gentiles, whom they regarded as unclean and called dogs. It was evident some sign would have to be given to convince the skeptics in Jerusalem that this new venture was of God. Indeed, when Peter arrived back in Jerusalem, he was put on the carpet by those "that were of the circumcision" and accused of breaking the religious taboos (Acts 11:1–3). Peter confronted this form of Jewish unbelief by pointing to the Pentecostal signs, including tongues, which had accompanied his preaching in the house of Cornelius (11:15–17). Even "the circumcision" were convinced.

The only other occasion when tongues are mentioned in the book of Acts was a number of years later. The incident took place near Ephesus on Paul's third missionary journey. There he met "certain disciples" who turned out to be disciples of John the Baptist and who were ignorant of much concerning Christ and the Holy Spirit. Paul enlightened them, they were baptized, he laid his hands on them, the Holy Spirit came upon them, and "they spake with tongues, and prophesied" (Acts 19:6). How many were there? Only twelve men. Again, the whole setting was Jewish.[29]

The New Testament has no more to say about tongues. As the church became increasingly Gentile, and as the Jewish nation settled down into a persistent rejection of both Christ and the Holy Spirit and became active in persecuting the church and maligning its apostles and prophets, so the clay of Jewish unbelief hardened. Tongues became increasingly irrelevant. Judgment now could not long be delayed. Most of the Epistles ignore tongues altogether. At Corinth, the

---

29. The incident itself is a mere footnote to the book of Acts. The form of Jewish unbelief involved was the skepticism of "the circumcision" regarding Paul's apostleship. Peter, it was claimed, was a far more important apostle than Paul. Indeed, they said, Paul's apostleship should be discounted altogether. Throughout the book of Acts, Luke constantly shows that everything Peter did, Paul also did. Once Peter gave the Holy Spirit by the laying on of hands (Acts 8:14–17). Once when Peter preached people spoke with tongues (10:44–46). So that it could never be said that, in these particulars, Peter was superior to Paul, the Holy Spirit records the incident of Acts 1:44–46. Again, persistent Jewish unbelief forms the background of the incident. See John Phillips, *Exploring Acts* (Grand Rapids: Kregel, 2001).

"tongues" thing was "much ado about nothing." Tongues were a sign, a judgment sign, a judgment sign to the Jew, a judgment sign to the unbelieving Jew.
And that was it.

By contrast, *prophecy was a welcome sound for the Christian believer:* "But prophesying serveth not for them that believe not, but for them which believe" (1 Cor.
14:22b). It is unbelief which keeps on asking for a sign. There is nothing particularly startling about proclaiming the Word of God. The ministry of the Word in
the local church might, perhaps, produce conviction in the occasional unbeliever
who happens to be present, as Paul hastens to declare (14:25), but that is not its
primary purpose. Its true function is to minister edification to the people of
God. No signs are needed for that.

Paul turns now, indeed, to *the sinner and his significance* (14:23–25). He speaks,
first, of *the reaction of the unsaved when they hear tongues:* "If therefore the whole
church be come together into one place, and all speak with tongues, and there
come in those that are unlearned, or unbelievers, will they not say ye are mad?"
(14:23). The whole church in one place! It seems evident that such church gatherings were common even then, way back in the early days of the church. Paul
does not contemplate or anticipate people staying home from such gatherings.

Now Paul envisions an extreme case—every believer present speaks in tongues!
At Corinth it seems to have been a universal craving. Paul imagines a meeting of
the church where everyone has his heart's desire, everyone has the coveted gift of
tongues, and everyone leaps to his feet to speak in tongues. He invites the
Corinthians to imagine the scene. What confusion! What a bedlam of noise!
What cacophony of din! What a roaring Niagara of meaningless sound! Every
believer is on his feet. All the women are on their feet. Each one is seized by a
compulsion to make his or her voice heard in a foreign language. It looks and
sounds like an insane asylum.

An unlearned person comes in! An unbeliever comes in! To the uninitiated
believer *(idiōtēs)* and to the rank outsider alike it is a scene of total and absolute
chaos. "They're mad!" would be the verdict of those trying to make sense of what
would seem to them as gibberish. They would walk out in confusion if not outright contempt. What a disgrace to the local testimony that would be.

By contrast, Paul directs attention to *the reaction of the unsaved when they hear*
prophecy (14:24–25). We note *what he sees:* "But if all prophesy, and there come
in one that believeth not, or one unlearned . . ." (14:24a). Here the scene evoked
is one of order. Paul now envisions a church meeting where everyone has the gift
of inspired preaching. Everywhere the visitor turns prophets are present. He listens

to this one and to that one. He sees people who have something to say. They are making sense.

We note, too, *what he senses:* "He is convinced of all," says Paul, "he is judged of all; and thus are the secrets of his heart made manifest" (14:24b–25a). He is *convicted* by the Holy Spirit. His soul is laid bare. It seems to him that those speaking read the very secrets of his innermost heart. No matter where he turns, no matter who speaks, no matter whom he hears, his soul is stripped naked. "And so falling down on his face he will worship God" (14:25b). He is *converted.* He falls on his face before God and rises to his feet a worshiper!

We note, furthermore, *what he says.* He declares, "God is in you of a truth!" (14:25c). Not content with that, he "reports" it. The word is *apangellō.* He makes the word known. He tells others. He becomes himself an evangel of the joyful message.

Thus, once again, Paul puts down tongues and exalts prophecy. He now turns from stating his reasons to stating *restrictions* (14:26–40). He introduces, under direct inspiration of the Holy Spirit, three basic rules governing the communication gifts. First there is *a simple rule:* "How is it, then, brethren? When ye come together every one of you hath a psalm, hath a doctrine, hath a tongue, hath a revelation, hath an interpretation. Let all things be done unto edifying" (14:26). That was both the privilege and the problem of "the open platform," or pulpit.

I was raised in a fellowship which did not believe in what it called "a one-man ministry." That is to say, no one man was the pastor or the preacher. Since all believers were priests, all could minister, especially at the Lord's Table, as the Holy Spirit led. Thus it often happened that one brother in the assembly could give out a hymn, another would lead in prayer, another would read a passage of Scripture, another would speak devotionally, another doctrinally, another would exhort. If all were truly led by the Spirit, the result was harmony of hymn and prayer and ministry. Often a discernible theme would emerge and all the believers would be edified and encouraged. More often than not, however, carnal brethren, or those who had really nothing to say, or those who simply liked to be heard, or those who had a favorite hymn or Scripture passage, regardless of whether or not it was suitable to the occasion, inflicted themselves on the believers, spoiling the Holy Spirit's orchestration of the service.

In Paul's day, such seems to have been the general arrangement when the church gathered for public worship. People came prepared and eager to exercise their various gifts. Moreover, it seems that each one was determined to be heard.

At Corinth each one came, conscious of his (or her) gift, and each one determined to be heard, even if it meant shouting down someone else. "Let all things be done unto edifying," Paul says. That was the simple rule. There was nothing very edifying about the carnal way the believers were pushing ahead of one another in their eagerness to hold the limelight.

Paul now introduces *a silence rule* (14:27–35). He covers two areas where silence is enjoined in the church. First, he speaks of *silence as regards the Word* (14:27–30). There are, indeed, times in the corporate life of the church when silence is golden. All too often the least gifted, the least spiritual, the least respected want to inflict themselves and their opinions on the church. This is especially so where the local church adheres to an egalitarian form of government or ministry.

Paul now lays down the law as to who can have the pulpit and when. He has a rule to be observed when it comes to *tongues and the matter of interpretation:* "If any man speak in an unknown tongue, let it be by two, or at the most by three, and that by course; and let one interpret. But if there be no interpreter, let him keep silence in the church; and let him speak to himself, and to God" (14:27–28). Instead of the discordant din of half a dozen people all striving to be heard at once, Paul introduces a rule of common sense. It is strange how many people think that the Holy Spirit overrules common courtesy and common sense. Not so; God is a God of superlative order and He insists on order throughout His universe and among His people (14:40). One of the gifts He has given to the church is "governments" (12:28), and that comes ahead of tongues. God wants there to be rule and law and order among His people. The "tongues" people were put under the restraint. Anyone with the gift had to first make sure someone was present who could interpret it before he even so much as exercised it. If there was no interpreter he was to remain quiet and be content with silent prayer and communion with the Lord. Even when interpreters were present, only three, at most, could participate audibly in any one service.

Paul has a rule, also, to be observed when it comes to *truth and the matter of interruption* (14:29–33). First, he states *the rule* (14:29–30). The rule is three-fold. *Be content!* Paul says: "Let the prophets speak, two or three" (14:29a). Paul puts prophesying (his favorite gift) under the same restraint as tongues (his least favorite gift). No more than two or three prophets (or preachers) are to participate in any service. When all was said and done this was simply plain common sense. Otherwise the meetings of the church would become interminable and become burdensome and wearisome to the Lord's people who might, consequently, be tempted to stay away.

Be cautious! Paul says, "And let the other judge" (14:29b). No one is to take any message at face value. All teaching, however seemingly inspired, must be subject to critical appraisal. Even Paul himself was not exempt from this rule. When his own teaching was tested by his hearers he commended them for their caution (Acts 17:10–11). It is the height of folly to accept teaching uncritically just because the preacher is prominent, personable, or popular.

This rule was particularly vital before the completion of the New Testament canon. All preaching and teaching must be tested by the Book and be in keeping with sound principles of hermeneutics. Now that the Book is complete we have no excuse for entertaining error. Any extrabiblical "revelation" (tongues, prophesying, the so-called word of wisdom or word of knowledge) is suspect. After all, if what is thus spoken is indeed by inspiration it is already in the Bible and we do not need it; if it is not in the Bible we don't want it. All extrabiblical revelations are cultic and need, as Paul says, to be "judged."

Be courteous! Paul adds, "If any thing be revealed to another that sitteth by, let the first hold his peace" (1 Cor. 14:30). In other words, no one was to monopolize the service. Each speaker must be ready to accept the fact that he was not the only gifted person present. If someone else present had a message, a speaker should bring his own message to a close and make room for him. All speakers must be willing to give way to others and listen quietly while someone else speaks. Trespassing on another brother's time is both discourteous and displeasing to the Holy Spirit.

Having stated the rules, Paul states *the reasons* (14:31–33). In the first place, the ministry of the Word of God is to be *permitted to all:* "For ye may all prophesy one by one" (14:31a). Nobody has a monopoly on truth. Room must be made for all those with a message to participate as the Lord leads. This does not mean that scope and opportunity must be given for the exercise of all available gifts at each and every service. Paul has already put a cap on that. On the other hand, gifts must not be stifled by some hierarchal structure in the church or by the domination of a forceful one or two.

Then, too, the ministry of the Word of God is to be *profitable to all* (14:31b–33). That is to say, it must be *a help to the saints of God:* "That all may learn, and all be comforted" (14:31b). The Holy Spirit did not distribute the various gifts in order to minister to pride, the flesh, or a natural love of showing off. On the contrary, the gifts are to be used in such a way that others can learn and be instructed in the truth of God and be "comforted." The word is *parakaleō*, which means "to call aside" or "to appeal to" (by way of exhortation, entreaty, comfort, or instruction). A succession of speakers would be more likely to achieve this variety of goals than would a single speaker. As led by the Holy Spirit, succeeding speakers might often build on what had gone before. Also, a variety of speakers would be more likely to touch the needs of an assortment of listeners, some of whom would be drawn to this speaker rather than that speaker.

Moreover, the ministry of the Word of God must be *in harmony with the Spirit of God* (14:32–33). Paul *proposes a test:* "And the spirits of the prophets are subject to the prophets" (14:32). A person under the control of a deceiving spirit will be under the compulsion of that spirit. The person who is in the grip of self-induced hypnosis and ecstatic hysteria loses all self-control. Not so a person speaking under the influence of the Holy Spirit.

I once attended a service in a church that practiced speaking in tongues. The preacher delivered a good message, well-reasoned and interesting. Toward the end, however, he launched out into "tongues." All of a sudden his face became contorted. The pitch of his voice went up so that it no longer sounded like him speaking. Words were forced out between his lips like bullets out of a machine gun. All over the building people began to give way to emotional excitement. Some went down to the basement of the church where a "tarrying meeting" was being held. Soon the sounds rising from the basement were like those of howling dogs. I did not wait to see the end of this display. It was quite evident to me that what was taking place was not of the Holy Spirit. The spirit of that preacher was no longer under the control of that preacher. He was under the control of a spirit of some kind. His facial contortions, the uncanny pitch of his voice, and the staccato verbalization of his words were indications that the Holy Spirit was not the one who was in control. One of the fruits of the Spirit, after all, is self-control (Gal. 5:23—"temperance," from *enkrateia,* "self-control"). That preacher had lost his self-control. He lost it the moment he abandoned his sermon for "tongues."

Paul now proffers *a truth:* "For God is not the author of confusion, but of peace, as in all the churches" (1 Cor. 14:33). Anything which produces disorder and confusion is not of God. Paul bluntly tells the Corinthians that other churches did not have the same kind of confusion which existed among them. The confusion at Corinth was the direct result of people speaking in tongues and prophesying simultaneously, each striving to be heard above the resulting uproar.

Silence as regards to the Word has been twice enjoined (14:28, 30). Now Paul speaks of *silence as regards the women* (14:34–35). There can be little doubt, so far as the modern "tongues" movement is concerned, that if the women were silenced the whole thing would either die a natural death or shrink to insignificant proportions. Paul sets before us here three things. First, there is *an absolute rule* (14:34). There is *a blunt prohibition:* "Let your women keep silence in the churches" (14:34a); there is *a biblical precept:* "for it is not permitted unto them to speak; but they are commanded to be under obedience, as also saith the law" (14:34b). The word for *silence* here is a strong one. It is *sigaō.* It means "absolute silence."

Some take this to mean that women are prohibited from speaking in the church under any circumstances whatsoever, but that runs contrary to the teaching of 1 Corinthians 11, where women are permitted to teach, if under the direct control and authority of the men, and if they put a covering on their heads, while so doing, as the visible token of their submission to that authority.

Others maintain that the command for women to keep silence is of a cultural nature and was confined to Corinth. That is at odds with Paul's opening statement to the Corinthians that this letter is addressed not only to them but to "all that in every place call upon the name of Jesus Christ our Lord" (1:2). Moreover, Paul bases his mandate on the Law, not just on a local situation. The "Law" is the Pentateuch (as in 9:8). The reference seems to be to Genesis 1:26–27; 2:21–24; and, perhaps, to Numbers 30:3–12.

How, then, are we to understand this command to women to maintain absolute silence in the church? Again, we look to the context for a clue. Paul has just finished telling the men in the church to be silent, as regards tongues-speaking, if there was no interpreter present (1 Cor. 14:27–28). He has also told them to be silent if someone else is called on to prophesy (14:30). Now he tells women to be absolutely silent. Evidently this absolute silence refers to the same two things. The same word, *sigaō,* is used in all three instances (14:14, 28, 30). With the women the Holy Spirit takes the ban further than with the men. He commands women in the church never to speak in tongues and never to interrupt a preacher. In addition to the strong word *sigaō,* Paul adds the statement "It is not permitted unto them to speak"—again, in the context of speaking in tongues and interrupting preachers.

This absolute rule is followed by *an absolving regulation:* "And if they will learn any thing, let them ask their husbands at home" (14:35a). This is a general rule and is not intended to discriminate against unmarried women who, doubtless, could ask questions through their married friends or of the elders of the church under appropriate conditions. Paul takes it for granted, too, that Christian husbands are well-taught believers and the spiritual leaders in their homes.

There is, finally, *an abiding requirement:* "For it is a shame for women to speak in the church" (14:35b). Paul is not about to back down. He is writing with apostolic authority and under the inspiration of the Holy Spirit. He is not displaying some kind of anti-women bias. He is declaring the commandments of the Lord. Women were not to speak in tongues. They were not to interrupt meetings of the church. They were to get answers to their questions at home. Disregard of these rules was shameful. A woman breaking these rules shames the God-ordained male leadership in the church and shames herself as well.

Finally, Paul states *a sensible rule* (14:36–40). He has a rule for *the conceited man:* "What? came the word of God out from you? or came it unto you only?" (14:36). Paul seems to have anticipated a storm of protest over these God-ordained restrictions. Echoes of such a protest can be heard to this day. Feminists regard Paul as a woman-hater.

So arrogant were the Corinthians that Paul had to direct some pointed questions to them. "Do you imagine that the Word of God originated in your church or that you have some kind of monopoly on God's truth?" he demands. Paul was the one who was writing Scripture, not them. Defiance of God's Word, as penned by Paul, was, and is, sheer arrogance. The Corinthians did not originate divine truth. It was brought to them—by Paul. Nor was it only to them that God's Word came. It was sheer conceit on their part that they knew better than the inspired apostle what was right and proper in the church.

Paul has a word also for *the confident man* (14:37–38). There is the man, for instance, who is *virtually unreachable:* "If any man think himself to be a prophet, or spiritual, let him acknowledge that the things that I write unto you are the commandments of the Lord" (14:37). Pauline prejudice? No, indeed! The very "commandments of the Lord." These rules and regulations are not optional. They are not put up for public debate and popular vote. They are not to be set aside as unworthy of a more enlightened age. These are Holy Ghost-inspired, divinely revealed, God-breathed edicts that carry as much force in the church as the commandments issued at Sinai carried for Israel. Paul has already equated them to the Law. Now he says they are the Law. Paul's ruling on these matters was not his own opinion. It was the Lord's wisdom that spoke these rules. He, in His omniscience, knew what was best for the church. So then, the true test of whether or not a man was a prophet, or spiritual, would be in his reaction to these rules. A true prophet, a truly spiritual person, would accept them and implement them. Only false prophets and carnal believers would quibble about them and quarrel with them. Then, and now. Such people, indeed, are virtually unreachable because they have already made up their minds and will tolerate no rules, however divinely inspired.

The confident man, the man who brushes aside God's Word in favor of his own opinions and "open-mindedness," is not only virtually unreachable, he is also *virtually unteachable:* "But if any man be ignorant, let him be ignorant" (14:38). As our English proverb puts it, "You can lead a horse to water, but you can't make it drink." There is not much that can be done about willful ignorance. We are reminded of the sad and solemn word of Hosea to his apostate people: "Ephraim is joined to his idols: let him alone" (Hos. 4:17). Nobody, not even an inspired Old Testament prophet, or an inspired New Testament apostle, can force someone to believe something he is determined not to believe. Such willful ignorance is culpable and cannot be pleaded as an excuse when the inevitable punishment comes. Broadmindedness is at the bottom of much of the "charismatic" disorder in the church, along with a deliberate rejection of these commandments of the Lord through Paul. It was broadmindedness which prompted Solomon to marry a host of foreign women. It was broadmindedness which allowed them to set up shrines in Jerusalem for their pagan gods. It was broadmindedness which tolerated their worship of these pagan and dreadful gods. It was broadmindedness which led Solomon, at last, to participate actively in that worship himself. It was broadmindedness which caused him to disregard portions of the Word of God he disliked. It was broadmindedness which brought down on his head the judgment of God (1 Kings 11:1–13). The church cannot afford such broadmindedness.

Finally, Paul has a rule for *the concerned man* (1 Cor. 14:39–40). He says that we should keep the *best* in view: "Wherefore. brethren, covet to prophesy, and forbid not to speak with tongues" (14:39). This is a favorite verse with those today who claim to have the gift of tongues. Every time the "tongues" issue comes up they fall back on this text: "Forbid not to speak with tongues." They tear the text from its context. They treat it as a talisman and they find this tactic very effective. It usually silences those who have never mastered the teaching of 1 Corinthians 12–14. Such a use of a text is cultic and dishonest. The Holy Spirit has fully stated why tongues were originally given to the church. He has depreciated the value of the gift repeatedly. He has put strict controls on its use. He has declared why and when the tongues phenomenon would cease. It would have been improper to forbid a person to speak with tongues at a time when the gift was still valid and in force. Even then, however, while tongues were permitted, prophecy was heartily endorsed. Once tongues ceased and prophecy was replaced by the canon, the words "forbid not to speak in tongues" became irrelevant.

During the past century "tongues" have been reintroduced into the church by the Irvingites and their heirs. The whole modern movement is extrabiblical, highly suspect, and accompanied by all kinds of deception and delusion. People claim to have the "sign" gifts. They crave and covet the gift of "tongues." Undoubtedly they do produce strange phenomena. Where it all comes from is another question. Since the modern "tongues" outbreak in the church coincided with a new interest in spiritism and the occult in the secular world, we are entitled to be highly skeptical and more than ordinarily cautious. The tongues movement is fraught with serious spiritual perils. The fact that many good, kind, sincere, zealous, and well-meaning people, believers many of them, are associated with it does not dispel the dark clouds of suspicion that hang over it.

For centuries the question of forbidding to speak with tongues was a dead issue. Nobody spoke with tongues. The great revivalists, evangelists and missionaries, and church leaders of the past and present have all been within the banks of historic Christianity. "Tongues" and the "charismatic" sign gifts were unknown to them.

Then came the Irvingites and a new move to reintroduce the apostolic gifts into the church. Those who investigated the movement soon began to warn about fraud, deception, and demonism.[30] Traditional Pentecostalism took root, but its appeal was mostly to the poor and the uneducated. Then the "tongues" movement crossed the tracks and became popular in Hollywood and among the rich and famous. It took on the established churches and leached away millions of believers discontented with the status quo. It offered excitement, thrills, new experiences, "miracles" of all sorts, and lots of hand-clapping, emotionalism, and applause. It developed very quickly. It displayed prejudice against sound doctrine and espoused a new way of "interpreting" the Bible, one which would accommodate the theological peculiarities of the movement. For instance, many in the movement think they are actually preparing the world for the millennium.

So then, should we forbid people to speak in tongues now? Probably not. If a person is determined to speak in "tongues," regardless of what the Holy Spirit has said about the friction, duration, and termination of the gift; and regardless of the way in which "the commandments of the Lord" are disregarded in the practice of "tongues"; and regardless of sound doctrine based on proper hermeneutical principles; and regardless of the danger of being deceived by end-time seducing spirits (1 Tim. 4:1; 2 Tim. 4:3); and regardless of all the trickery associated with the movement—what would be the use of forbidding a person to do it? However, the person who insists on speaking in tongues puts himself outside the pale of historic Christianity and the creedal confession of many a local church.

So far as the employment of the gifts is concerned, Paul has one last word. We

---

30. See Sir Robert Anderson, *Spirit Manifestations and the Gift of Tongues* (Neptune, N.J.: Loizeaux, 1935).

should keep this *test* in view: "Let all things be done decently and in order" (1 Cor. 14:40). The word for *decently* is *euschēmonōs*. It means "becomingly." It is translated "honestly" in Romans 13:13 in contrast with the shamefulness of Gentile social life. Honesty is essential in handling divine things. As for "order," God's order can be seen in the universe—from tiny atoms to giant galaxies. It is the basis on which all science builds. It breathes through the Bible from beginning to end. It is essential in His church—order, based on divine Law.

PART 5

Disbelief in the Church

1 Corinthians 15:1–58

A. The resurrection of Christ (15:1–19)
  1. An undeniable fact of history (15:1–11)
    a. Paul and his fruit in the gospel (15:1–2)
      (1) He reminds them of what he preached (15:1a)
      (2) He reminds them of what they professed (15:1b–2)
        (a) Their salvation (15:1b)
        (b) Their standing (15:2)
            i. The basis of profession of faith in Christ (15:2a)
           ii. The burden of proof of faith in Christ (15:2b)
    b. Paul and the facts of the gospel (15:3–8)
      (1) The facts stated (15:3–4)
        (a) Paul takes us to the cross (15:3)
            i. The reality for Christ's death (15:3a)
           ii. The reason for Christ's death (15:3b)
        (b) Paul takes us to the cemetery (15:4a)
        (c) Paul takes us to the calendar (15:4b–d)
            i. A deed to be remembered (15:4b)
           ii. A day to be remembered (15:4c)
          iii. A detail to be remembered (15:4d)
      (2) The facts substantiated (15:5–8)
        (a) Seen! By his friends (15:5)
            i. By the man who denied (15:5a)
           ii. By the men he discipled (15:5b)
        (b) Seen! By his flock (15:6)
        (c) Seen! By his family (15:7a)
        (d) Seen! By his followers (15:7b)
        (e) Seen! By his foe (15:8)
    c. Paul and his faith in the gospel (15:9–11)
      (1) His testimony (15:9)
      (2) His triumphs (15:10–11)
        (a) Transforming grace (15:10a)
        (b) Transcending grace (15:10b–11)
            i. His method (15:10b–c)
                a. To work with utter abandonment (15:10b)
                b. To work with utter abasement (15:10c)

           ii. His message (15:11)

                a. Apostolic (15:11a)

                b. Authentic (15:11b)

    2. An indispensable fact of theology (15:12–19)

        a. The lie recorded (15:12)

           (1) The truth as it was preached (15:12a)

           (2) The truth as it was perverted (15:12b)

        b. The lie refuted (15:13–19)

           (1) In terms of our faith (15:13–15)

                (a) Implication: the resurrection story is a myth (15:13a)

                (b) Application: the resurrected savior is a myth (15:13b)

                (c) Implication: our preaching of the Resurrection is foolish (15:14)

                (d) Application: our preaching of the Resurrection is false (15:15)

           (2) Terms of our forgiveness (15:16–17)

                (a) Implication: the Resurrection is a myth (15:16)

                (b) Application: our redemption is a myth (15:17)

           (3) In terms of our future (15:18)

                (a) Implication: the death of Christ is permanent (15:18a)

                (b) Application: the dead in Christ have perished (15:18b)

           (4) In terms of our feelings (15:19)

                (a) Implication: we have no eternal home (15:19a)

                (b) Application: we have no earthly hope (15:19b)

Paul pauses. He has dealt with *divisions* in the church (1 Cor. 1:10–4:21), with *discipline* in the church (5:1–6:20), and with *difficulties* in the church (7:1–14:40). Now he turns his attention to *disbelief in the church* (15:1–58). The subject matter of this section is twofold. Paul deals, first, with *the resurrection of Christ* (15:1–19), then with the *resurrection of Christians* (15:20–58).

We can almost be grateful to the Corinthians for all their quarrels and questions! At least they gave the great apostle an opportunity to deal with matters which, ever since, have been of great interest and importance to the church. How impoverished we should be, for instance, without Paul's full-length discussion of the gifts and without this magnificent treatise on the Resurrection.

Paul begins with *the resurrection of Christ*. He establishes it as *an undeniable fact of history* (15:1–11). At the heart of the Christian gospel is the resurrection of Christ. No other religion is based upon the historical fact of a bodily resurrection. This is unique to Christianity. It sets it apart. It stands or falls with that. Paul declares a fact the Corinthians could not *deny—his fruit in the gospel* (15:1). He reminds them *what he preached:* "Moreover, brethren, I declare unto you the gospel which I preached unto you" (15:1a). When he preached on Mars Hill in Athens, the intellectual Greeks gave him a fair hearing until he mentioned the resurrection of Christ. Then they laughed him out of court (Acts 17:22–32). It was the proclamation of the resurrection of Christ that separated between the living and the dead. Paul preached Christ crucified at Corinth (1 Cor. 2:2) but he never left Christ on the cross. He always went on to declare Him to be risen from the dead (15:4).

He reminds them *what they professed:* "which also ye received, and wherein ye stand: by which also ye are saved, if ye keep in memory what I preached unto you, unless ye have believed in vain" (15:2b–3). Their salvation rested on the death, burial, and resurrection of Christ. So did their standing before God. It was the very basis of their profession of faith. The expression "if ye keep in memory" ("if ye hold fast") records a condition ("if") followed by the indicative mood. In such cases the hypothesis is assumed to be the case, the condition being unfulfilled, but no doubt being thrown upon the supposition.[1] Paul lets them know, however, that a failure to hold on to what he taught them would be disastrous. Christ did rise from the dead. There was no room for doubting that fact. To deny it was to deny the truth. Indeed, if there was no resurrection, then the preaching of the gospel was wholly without any validity at all. A dead Christ simply meant a dead religion.

Paul turns now to *the facts of the gospel* (15:3–8). First, *the facts are stated* (15:3–4). First, *Paul takes us to the cross:* "For I delivered unto you first of all that which also I received, how that Christ died for our sins according to the scriptures" (15:3). There can be no doubt that Christ died. There were hundreds of witnesses to His death. He not only died but His dead body was pierced by a Roman spear to demonstrate once and for all that He was dead.

One weird theory, invented to explain away the bodily resurrection of Christ, is that Jesus did not really die on the cross. According to the theory, He swooned.

---

1. E. W. Bullinger, *The Companion Bible* (Grand Rapids: Kregel, 1990), app. 118.

He was put in the tomb. In the cool of the tomb He supposedly revived. He managed to escape from the tomb and elude the guards. He found a refuge nearby and, on the third day, showed Himself to be alive—thus giving rise to the story of His resurrection!

To believe all that calls for an enormous degree of gullibility. We are asked to believe that Jesus did not really die. In order to believe that, we have to believe that a Roman soldier, in charge of a public execution, left the scene before making quite sure the victim was really dead. We know that he did make sure. His last orders were to expedite the deaths of the three men being crucified, because of the approaching Jewish Sabbath, by breaking their legs. This was done to the two thieves. The soldiers were astonished when they came to Jesus to note that He was dead already, so "they brake not his legs: but one of the soldiers with a spear pierced his side, and forthwith came there out blood and water" (John 19:33–34). That was medical proof enough that Jesus was truly dead. John takes his oath that this is what happened (19:35). He adds a scriptural reason why it happened: "For these things were done that the scripture should be fulfilled, A bone of him shall not be broken" (19:36; Exod. 12:46; Num. 9:12; Ps. 34:20).

In order to believe the "swoon" theory we are also asked to believe that the Lord's enemies, the Sanhedrin, and its agents, who had plotted and schemed for weeks to bring about His death, would leave Calvary without making quite sure He was dead.

We also have to believe that the Lord's friends, Nicodemus, Joseph of Arimathea, and the faithful women, who took Him down from the cross and lovingly prepared His body for burial, would have embalmed a body in which life still lingered.

In addition to all this we have to believe that Jesus revived in the tomb, that He was able to escape from the enswathing bandages, carefully putting them back on the stone slab in such a way that it would look as though He had risen through them, that He accomplished this feat in total darkness, and that He managed, with every bone in His body out of joint, weak, and emaciated by exhaustion, pain, and loss of blood to roll away a massive stone, sealed as it was, elude the guard, and escape into the night. More, and most incredible of all, we have to believe that, on the first day of the week, He perpetrated a deliberate fraud by pretending to have been raised from the dead—contrary to everything we know about His character, integrity, and devastating honesty.

How much simpler to believe the bare statement of gospel truth: "Christ died";

and the immediate explanation: "for our sins according to the Scriptures." Every animal sacrificed in the Old Testament pointed forward to Calvary. The entire Jewish religion was predicated on Calvary. Psalms 22 and 69, Isaiah 53, and a host of other Scriptures pointed to Calvary. So Paul takes us to the cross.

Then he takes us to *the cemetery:* "And that he was buried," he says (1 Cor. 15:4a). Isaiah had long since foretold that He would have an honorable burial. He was to be "with the rich in his death" (Isa. 53:9). Two of the most influential men in the country, Joseph of Arimathea and Nicodemus, men of wealth and power, members of the Sanhedrin, joined forces to bury Him. The weight of spices alone, provided by Nicodemus, was worth a king's ransom (John 19:39), and Joseph contributed an exceedingly valuable tomb. He was buried. But His body was miraculously preserved from the corruption and decay which was always such a quick result of death in a tropical clime (Ps. 16:10; Acts 2:27; John 11:39).

Next, Paul takes us to *the calendar:* "and that he rose again the third day according to the Scriptures" (1 Cor. 15:4). We note that there was *a deed to be remembered:* "He rose again!" Well might we sing

> Vainly they seal the dead
>   Jesus my Savior;
> Vainly they watch His bed,
>   Jesus my Lord!
> Up from the grave He arose
> With a mighty triumph o'er His foes;
> He arose a Victor from the dark domain
> And He lives forever with His saints to reign;
> He arose! Hallelujah! Christ arose!

The resurrection of Christ is the best proved fact in history. There is more concrete evidence for the resurrection of Christ than there is for the conquest of Britain by Julius Caesar.

One day, Napoleon was master of Europe, putting down kings, controlling the lives of millions. But look now! He is a caged lion, an exile on a remote island, St. Helena, under constant surveillance, a prisoner of the British navy. Something must have happened. Something did—Waterloo! One day Jesus was nailed to a Roman cross, beaten, scourged to the bone, crowned with thorns, spit upon, and mocked. But look now! Within a few short years He is acknowledged to be God by millions and there is a church dedicated to His worship in every major city of the Roman Empire. Something must have happened. Something did—Resurrection!

Come back to Waterloo. The battle was fought on a Sunday morning in the year 1815. Across the channel, England watched and waited for some word about the outcome of that fight. The fate of Europe hung in the balance. Then word came. The semaphore began to flash the tidings to the eager watchers on the British shore. It was, however, a foggy day. The message was only partially received. It read, "Wellington . . . defeated. . . ." The country went into mourning. But then the weather cleared and the full message came through: "Wellington . . . defeated . . . Napoleon!"

Now come back to Calvary. The Lord of Glory was nailed to Calvary's tree. He was taken down dead and was buried. The rocks rent. The sun went out. The graves gaped wide. The message seemed all too clear: Jesus defeated! The tomb was closed upon Him. It was sealed and guarded. It was all over. Death had triumphed. The world spun on its way through space carrying the lifeless body of God incarnate. Three days later Jesus rose from the dead. The message came through loud and clear: Jesus defeated death!

And indeed He has. When John, on the isle of Patmos, saw Him, he saw One who could declare, "I am he that liveth, and was dead; and behold, I am alive for evermore, Amen; and have the keys of hell [hades] and of death" (Rev. 1:18).

There was, indeed, a deed to be remembered. There was also *a day to be remembered:* "He rose again the third day." That was what He had repeatedly told His disciples He would do (Matt. 27:63; John 2:19). They simply did not believe it. His enemies did. Once the crucifixion was an accomplished fact the chief priests and Pharisees approached Pilate. They said, "Sir, we remember that that deceiver said, while he was yet alive, After three days I will rise again. Command therefore that the sepulcher be made sure until the third day, lest his disciples come by night, and steal him away, and say unto the people, He is risen from the dead: so the last error shall be worse than the first" (Matt. 27:63–64).

When the Resurrection did, indeed, take place on the third day, the Sanhedrin paid the guard large sums of money to circulate a lie. We read that the Jewish elders took counsel and "gave large money unto the soldiers, saying, Say ye, His disciples came by night, and stole him away while we slept. And if this come to the governor's ears, we will persuade him, and secure you" (28:11–15). The guard took the money and the Sanhedrin's lie was accepted as true by the Jews.

What a silly lie it was! If it had been the truth the soldiers would have been the first to deny it, for it would have cost them their lives to admit they had been asleep on guard duty and had lost that which they were guarding. But consider the lie itself. "While we *slept* the disciples came and stole the body!" Suppose a witness were to appear in court, take the oath, and bear testimony that the events about which he was going to speak took place when he was sound asleep! The lie simply does not make sense. Yet such was the lie that was propagated by order of the Sanhedrin. Such was their extremity they had to resort to a lie which is palpably false.

"He rose again the third day!" says Paul. For years Paul (or Saul as he was in those days) was the Sanhedrin's chosen instrument to stamp out Christianity. Nobody since has ever had a tithe of Paul's opportunity to get at the truth. Every available theory was mastered by him, on the spot, within a year or two of the Resurrection. He chose not to believe in it—until he met the risen Christ personally on the Damascus road. Thereafter, absolutely convinced about the reality of Christ's resurrection, he flung himself unreservedly into His cause.

Paul points also to *a detail to be remembered:* "He rose again the third day, according to the Scriptures." The Lord Jesus Himself pointed to Jonah as a type of Himself: "For as Jonas was three days and three nights in the whale's belly, so shall the Son of man be three days and three nights in the heart of the earth" (Matt. 12:40).

Paul proceeds. *The facts are substantiated* (1 Cor. 15:5–8a). Paul lines up a number of eyewitnesses to the resurrection of Christ. "He was seen!" he says. He was *seen by His friends* (15:5). He was seen by *the man who denied:* "He was seen of Cephas" (15:5a). Peter had a private and personal interview with the risen Lord (Luke 24:34)—doubtless he told Paul about it when they were together in Jerusalem. It must have been a memorable meeting between broken Peter, so ashamed of himself for denying his Lord, after all his boasting. "I have prayed for you that your faith fail not," Jesus had told him. He needed those prayers.

He was seen of Peter, too, on the shore of the sea of Galilee when the Lord again challenged him and asked him if he really loved Him (John 21:1–22).

Something must have happened to make cowardly Peter brave. We see Peter one day, cursing and swearing and denying the Lord simply because a kitchen maid said he was one of the Lord's disciples. We see Peter a few weeks later, boldly charging the Jewish nation with the appalling guilt of having murdered their Messiah—"This Jesus hath God raised up," he said, "whereof we all are witnesses" (Acts 2:32). Then, too, a few days later he and John stood on trial before the Sanhedrin on the charge of having healed a lame man in the name of

Jesus. Peter boldly threw the truth in the faces of these powerful men: "Be it known unto you all, and to all the people of Israel, that by the name of Jesus Christ of Nazareth, whom ye crucified, whom God raised from the dead, even by him doth this man stand here before you whole" (4:10).

He was seen also by *the men He discipled:* "[then he was seen] of the twelve" (1 Cor. 15:5b). The expression "the twelve" had become a general term for the complete body of the apostles. Judas, of course, was not present when the Lord appeared to the disciples in the Upper Room—nor was Thomas, on the first occasion. It is debatable whether or not Matthias could be counted as one of the twelve (Acts 1:21–26).

Here, then, were a near dozen men who were drawn from various backgrounds and walks of life. It can be conceded that they were good and honest men. They were the kind of men we would expect to find on any jury. The number included some successful businessmen, one of whom had very high connections in the capital; a tax collector; a zealot once identified with a Palestinian freedom group; a confirmed skeptic; and a somewhat impulsive man God later used to launch Christianity on its way.

They seemed to be extraordinarily hard to convince, which adds to their credibility as witnesses. The resurrection day itself had been a day of strange rumors and reports, none of which the disciples were prepared to believe. That the tomb was empty, no one could deny. Peter and John had confirmed it (John 20:1–10). The story of Mary Magdalene, that she had seen the Lord, and of the other women, that they had seen angels, was discounted as unbelievable (Mark 16:9–11; Luke 24:13–16).

But then in the evening the Lord suddenly materialized in the Upper Room. They were still unconvinced, thinking it was an apparition they saw (Luke 24:36–40). The Lord set about convincing them that it was truly He, that the body in which He appeared was His body and that it was genuine. He showed them His hands and His side (John 20:19–20). He ate food. He invited them to come and touch Him (Luke 24:36–43). A week later He came back and convinced even the skeptical Thomas (John 20:24–29). He was seen by His friends.

He was *seen by His flock:* "After that, he was seen of above five hundred brethren at once; of whom the greater part remain unto this present, but some are fallen asleep" (1 Cor. 15:6). Matthew tells us that the disciples, soon afterward, went back to Galilee, where the Lord appeared to the eleven on a mountain (Matt. 28:16). Jesus had appointed to meet them in Galilee, away from the hostility of Jerusalem (26:32). It is not at all improbable that this was the occasion to which Paul refers. If so, He appeared to many more than the eleven on that occasion.

No wonder Paul could say to King Agrippa that these things were public knowledge (Acts 26:26). Paul had personal knowledge that a large number of contemporary witnesses, who had personally seen the risen Christ and who could independently corroborate one another's testimony, were still living when he wrote. If, as seems likely, Paul wrote this letter in A.D. 55, it was only a little over twenty years since all these marvelous things had happened. Five hundred witnesses ought to be enough to convince any but the most determined unbeliever. Some had "fallen asleep" indeed. The use of this metaphor for death refers to the body, not to the soul. It pictures for us a condition of rest and implies that the believer goes on living even when his body lies in the cemetery, and that, just as bodily sleep is a temporary condition, so is death itself. But the majority were still alive.

Then, too, the risen Lord was *seen by His family:* "After that he was seen of James" (1 Cor. 15:7a). According to Matthew 13:55, the Lord had four brothers (half-brothers, that is), James, Joses, Simon, and Judas. He had at least three sisters.[2] The Lord is called Mary's "first-born" (Matt. 1:25; Luke 2:7), leading to the natural inference that she had other children (Ps. 69:8). After the miracle at Cana, the Lord went to Capernaum accompanied by His mother, brethren, and disciples (John 2:12). Later on His brothers, accompanied by His mother, sought to hinder Him (Matt. 12:46–47; Mark 3:31–32; Luke 8:19–20). They manifested the same spirit of unbelief later and John bluntly states that to be so (John 7:3–10). We do not see them again until we find them all in the Upper Room, after His resurrection and ascension, waiting for the coming of the Holy Spirit (Acts 1:14). Their unbelief had vanished.

At some time between, Jesus had sought out James and made a believer out of him. One suspects that James, with his narrow, Pharisaical views, must have been a real trial to Jesus during the years they lived together in the Nazareth home. The Lord thoroughly convinced and converted James. He became "a servant of the Lord Jesus Christ" (James 1:1) and a pillar of the Jerusalem church (Acts 12:17; 15:13–21; 21:18; Gal. 1:19; 2:9, 12). He wrote one of the New Testament books, as did his brother Jude. The conversion of the Lord's immediate family members as a result of His resurrection makes them excellent witnesses.

Then, too, the risen Lord was seen by *His followers:* "then of all the apostles"

---

2. Note the expression: "And his sisters, are they not all with us?" Had there been two, it would read "both."

(1 Cor. 15:7b). This seems to be a larger company than "the twelve" of verse 5. It may be that James was counted as an honorary apostle.

Finally, the risen Lord was seen by *His foe:* "And last of all he was seen by me also, as one born out of due time" (15:8). The conversion of Saul of Tarsus was an event of the first magnitude. He had been the most bitter, energetic, and determined foe of Christianity. He traveled far and wide, seeking to stamp out what he considered to be a pernicious cult. He was on a mission of persecution when he met the risen Lord. The story of his conversion is of such significance that it is told three times in the book of Acts (9:1–22; 22:1–21; 26:1–23).

Years ago two men, Lord Lyttleton and Gilbert West, both confirmed skeptics, met in England to lay plans to demolish Christianity, once and for all. They agreed that Christianity rested on two major premises—the resurrection of Christ and the conversion of Saul of Tarsus. If they could undermine these two things, they thought, they could destroy the Christian religion. Gilbert West undertook to disprove the Resurrection, and Lord Lyttleton agreed to take on the conversion of Saul of Tarsus. They agreed to separate for a period of time, pursue their studies, assemble their arguments, and meet again later to review their progress. What happened is one of the romances of the faith. Both men were converted while looking for evidence to support their claims and both men wrote their books to prove the accuracy of the New Testament narrative. Gilbert West became the author of a book on the resurrection of Christ, a classic in its day, and Lord Lyttleton championed the conversion of Saul of Tarsus.

"Last of all he was seen of me!" says Paul. He was the last witness. In this chapter we shall also meet the last enemy (1 Cor. 15:26), the last Adam (15:45), and the last trump (15:52). Paul never ceased to be amazed at the grace of God which found him, an enemy, a persecutor, and an injurious man, and saved him, put him in the ministry (1 Tim. 1:12–13), and ordained him to be an apostle (1 Cor. 15:9).

He saw himself as "one born out of due time." The phrase expresses the word *extromā*—"an abortive offspring," only in Paul's case he was belatedly born, not prematurely born. He takes a self-depreciating view of himself, as compared with the other "twelve." They were disciples before they were apostles. They kept company with the Lord during His earthly ministry. They were witnesses of His resurrection. Paul was a persecutor of the church. It was something he was never able to forget. He had many detractors. Perhaps some of those who hated him called him "an abortion of an apostle." Paul simply bowed his head to their hateful words. He could not think badly enough, himself, of what he had once done to the church. The faces of those he had persecuted haunted him. The cries of the little children he had made fatherless lingered in his memory.

Just the same, although "one born out of due time," he was an apostle and the last eyewitness of Christ's resurrection.

Paul turns now to *his faith in the gospel* (15:9–11). We note *his testimony:* "For I am the least of the apostles, that am not meet to be called an apostle, because I persecuted the church" (15:9). It is hard for us to imagine Paul feeling inferior to anyone. He was a trained Jewish rabbi, a cosmopolitan Greek scholar, a Roman citizen, a fearless ambassador for Christ, and the church's foremost missionary and theologian. We can well believe the disciples were intimidated by him and that the Jerusalem church was both awed and alarmed by the scope, genius, and authority of Paul's gospel. Yet Paul himself felt keenly the advantage the "twelve" had over him. They had known Jesus intimately, lived with Him, seen His miracles, heard His teaching. Peter may have denied Him, Thomas may have doubted Him, but Paul had persecuted Him. He had the blood of Christian martyrs on his hands.

In testifying before King Agrippa, Paul said, "I verily thought with myself, that I ought to do many things contrary to the name of Jesus of Nazareth. Which thing I also did in Jerusalem: and many of the saints did I shut up in prison, having received authority from the chief priests; and when they were put to death, I gave my voice against them. And I punished them oft in every synagogue, and compelled them to blaspheme; and being exceedingly mad against them, I persecuted them even unto strange cities" (Acts 26:9–11). The Holy Spirit says that Saul was "breathing out threatenings and slaughter [*phonos,* "murder"] against the disciples of the Lord" (9:1). "I persecuted this way unto the death," Paul said, "binding and delivering into prisons both men and women" (22:4). Indeed, the death of Stephen seems to have inspired him with fresh hate. "He made havoc of the church," the Holy Spirit says. The word *havoc* is *lymainomai,* which means "to maltreat," "to outrage," "to lay waste." It is the word used of a wild boar uprooting saplings.

No wonder, although Paul ranked with the very chiefest of the apostles (2 Cor. 11:5), he spoke disparagingly of himself as the least and most unworthy of them all.

We note also *his triumphs* (1 Cor. 15:10–11). He recalls the *transforming grace:* "But by the grace of God I am what I am: and his grace which was bestowed upon me was not in vain" (15:10a). And what was he? He was the great apostle to the Gentiles. He was the man who wrote the greater part of the New Testament.

He was the man who made "full proof" of his ministry, as he urged others to do (2 Tim. 4:5). It was grace which found him, the Torquemada of the Sanhedrin, a religious bigot, a whirling human tornado of hate and rage. It was grace which caused the scales to fall from his eyes so that there, on the Damascus road, on a mission of terror, he might actually see the Lord of Glory. Grace! It became one of Paul's favorite words. It became, in his hands, the distinguishing descriptive word of this present age. It was grace which saved him. It was grace which transformed hate into love, pride into humility, the agent of the Sanhedrin into the great ambassador of Christ. "His grace which was bestowed upon me was not in vain," says Paul.

He recalls *transcending grace* (1 Cor. 15:10b–11) : "But I laboured more abundantly than they all: yet not I, but the grace of God which was with me. Therefore whether it were I or they, so we preach, and so ye believed." This was the man who, traveling at the rate of some seventeen to twenty miles a day, covered some 5,580 miles on foot and some 6,770 miles by sea to take the gospel to the untold millions of the world who were still untold. In the space of some twenty years or less, Paul evangelized along a line of some 1,500 miles all the way from Antioch to Illyricum. While the other apostles were still debating the Great Commission, Paul was evangelizing Tarsus and all that part of his native land. While they were still putting out tentative feelers as to the possible expansion of the church, within the hampering swaddling clothes of an obsolete Judaism, Paul was out conquering Asia Minor, Macedonia, and Greece.

"Yet not I," he says. It was "the grace of God" at work. Then, turning from this line of truth, he says, "No matter!" Whoever has done the work, I or they, it makes no difference! Grace (based on Calvary and the resurrection of Christ) has been the very foundation of your faith.

Paul turns now to his second great point. The resurrection of Christ is not only an undeniable fact of history, it is also *an indispensable fact of theology* (15:12–19). Truth concerning the resurrection of Christ was under attack at Corinth. So we have *the lie recorded* (15:12). Paul demands, "Now if Christ be preached that he rose from the dead, how say some among you that there is no resurrection of the dead?" Of course God raised His Son from the dead! Some people have "intellectual" problems with the whole concept, as did the Sadducees and the Greeks (Matt. 22:23–33; Acts 17:32). Paul, probably the greatest of all intellectuals, had no such problem. Even in his unconverted days it was not the possibility of resurrection which troubled him. He had been raised a Pharisee, and the Pharisees believed in resurrection (Acts 23:6). What Paul had denied had been the resurrection of Christ—and that intellectual problem had been swept away on the Damascus road by the incontrovertible evidence of a real and risen Christ (9:3–6).

Denial of the resurrection of the *dead* was a direct theological attack on the resurrection of *Christ*. Paul could understand an infidel denying this foundational truth of Christianity—but a *believer?* a professing Christian? Never! Paul's opening barrage is a snort of indignation.

The unbelief which crept into the church at Corinth has lingered in the church to this day, despite all the evidence, and is now firmly entrenched in liberal theology. One of its most outspoken advocates has been Harry Emerson Fosdick. He said that the idea of Jesus' risen life is "confused for us in narratives that contradict each other in every important detail."[3] The fact is that "in every important detail" the narratives are in total agreement and Dr. Fosdick's statement is a lie.[4]

Dr. Wilbur M. Smith wrote to twenty outstanding authorities in New Testament literature in the United States to ask them, in confidence, how they accounted for the empty tomb. One man with a Ph.D. degree in Germany, the author of nearly a dozen books on New Testament criticism, a professor for some forty years in one of our largest theological seminaries, said he could "no more explain how the tomb of Joseph of Arimathea had become empty on Easter morning than he could explain how Santa Claus comes down the chimney at Christmas time." Said Wilbur M. Smith, "My heart is heavy when I find a New Testament scholar, past the age of seventy, having to resort to the kindergarten fable of Santa Claus in trying to escape the evidence for the empty tomb of our Lord."[5]

In the Easter 1944 edition of *The Christian Century,* the editor wrote a lengthy article on "The Resurrection Fact," in which he did his best (or worst) to repudiate the resurrection fact. He made much play about the impossibility of harmonizing "the numerous difficulties and inconsistencies" of these New Testament records. According to him, they were "artificially enforced." He added, "They are convincing only to those whose liberalism treats the Scriptures as a sort of jigsaw puzzle enabling to connect this clause or statement with another clause or statement in a manner that will produce the result on which their fixation on the letter of Scripture requires."

---

3. Harry Emerson Fosdick, *A Guide to Understanding the Bible* (New York: Harper and Bros., 1938), 294.
4. Wilbur M. Smith, *Therefore, Stand* (Natick, Mass.: W. A. Wilde Co., 1959), 401–2.
5. Ibid., 384, 389.

Said Dr. Wilbur M. Smith: "I think that men, great giants of intellect, men whose works have been consulted by the scholars of many generations, men like Bengel, Schaff, Bishop Lightfoot, Bishop Westcott, Bishop Ellicot, Dr. A. T. Robertson, Professor James Orr, would justly resent as an insult the fact that they, in finding proof of the bodily resurrection in the New Testament, were only like a lot of children fitting together a jigsaw puzzle."[6]

One such intellectual giant was Thomas Arnold, for fourteen years the famous headmaster of Rugby, one of England's prestigious educational institutions, author of a famous three-volume *History of Rome,* and appointee to the chair of Modern History at Oxford. He declared, "I have been used for many years to study the histories of other times, and to examine and weigh the evidence of those who have written about them, and I know of no one fact in the history of mankind which is proved by better or fuller evidence of every sort, to the understanding of a fair enquirer, than the great sign which God hath given us that Christ died and rose again from the dead."[7]

Paul would have even less patience with the liberal theologians of today than he had with the skeptics at Corinth in his day. We now have *the lie refuted* (1 Cor. 15:13–19), the lie that Jesus did not really rise from the dead, and refuted by one who had firsthand information, by one who had personally met the risen and ascended Christ and who was instantly converted from rabid unbelief to absolute, unswerving conviction that Christ was alive, by one who had personally spoken to scores of credible eyewitnesses, by one, indeed, who was not likely to be taken in by "a lot of children fitting together a jigsaw puzzle." The lie is refuted by Paul himself.

He stacks up his arguments along three lines. He deals with the lie *in terms of our faith* (15:13–15). He advances two implications and two applications. Here is *the first implication: the resurrection story is a myth:* "But if there be no resurrection of the dead . . ." (15:13a). If it is impossible to believe that anyone, at any time, has risen from the dead, that resurrection itself is unscientific, incredible, and, indeed, impossible, what then? That, indeed, is the position taken by agnostics and liberals. The popular argument is paraded often enough—here is a man whose body was carried in fragments to different parts of the earth. How was he to recover his body after it had decayed, returned to dust, been mingled with the earth, grown again into plants, and become a part of other animals, age after age? Such an argument is possible only to a person who does not know God or whose

---

6. Ibid., 409–10.
7. Ibid., 425–26.

concept of God is too small. The God we know can take carbon and make a diamond or give it another body altogether. He can make of the same substance a piece of charcoal. All He has to do is arrange the particles differently to create one body, famous for its hardness and brilliance, or to create a different kind of body, one black and crumbly.

Then too, our omniscient and omnipotent God has not disclosed how much or how little of our present body goes into the composition of our resurrection body. A grain of corn is sown into the ground. It springs up straight and tall, a sheaf of corn. It is only a small part of the body that was sown which springs up out of the ground. The rest is left to rot. The evidence of the risen Christ in the Upper Room is that a resurrection body is the *same* body that died, it is a *changed* body, and it is a *new* body with new powers.

In any case, our bodies are constantly being dismantled and replaced. Each minute 3 billion cells die and are replaced by new ones, each cell a universe of incredible complexity. Over a period of some seven years each member of the body, the eyes, the ears, the hands, the heart, the liver, the blood, and the circulatory system are all dismantled and rebuilt. The body a man has is not the same body he had as a child. We have no information as to which of the various bodies we inhabit over the course of a lifetime God will use to make our new one. Not only so, our bodies are constantly being nourished and renewed by food which comes from far and wide, some items, indeed, from the far corners of the globe.

The body we now have is a marvelous tribute to the creative genius of our God. Here are just a few figures to consider. Each person has 12 ribs, 400 muscles for the spine, along with 1,000 ligaments. He has 2 million sweat glands for the skin. A piece of skin the size of a postage stamp has 3 million cells, 100 sweat glands, 15 oil glands, 25 nerve cells. He has 26 bones for the foot, along with 112 ligaments and 20 muscles. His wrist has 8 bones, his palm has 5 bones, and his fingers 14 bones. His ear contains 4,000 wax glands, 30,000 circuits for the auditory nerve, and 3 fluid canals for the inner ear to control his balance. He has tens of millions of electrical circuits for his eyes and 137 million light-sensitive receptors. He has something like a quadrillion cells in his body. He has 5 million red cells and between 5,000 and 10,000 white cells per cubic millimeter of blood along with 100,000 miles of blood vessels. Hemoglobin alone, just one molecule in his bloodstream, contains 9,520 atoms, which all have to be hooked up in proper sequence. His stomach contains 35 million glands to produce his gastric juices. He has 26 feet of intestine. His kidneys contain a million minute nephrons. All this, just for starters!

When we consider the awesome complexity of the human body we should stand in awe of the power and genius of the God who designed and made it. Indeed, when we come to think of it, it is no more remarkable that we should live *again* than it is that we should live *at all!* The God who can make a body once out of the dust of the earth can certainly make it again. He is omniscient. He tracks every speck of dust in cosmic space, knows the entire history of any such speck, and forgets no single detail of its history. *That* is omniscience. To poke fun at God's ability to do anything He wants to do is the very essence of man's love for darkness rather than light.

Here, again, is the first implication—the resurrection body is a myth. Here is *the first application: the resurrected Savior is a myth:* "Then is Christ not risen" (15:13b). How dark and dreadful a world this instantly becomes. A dead Christ! He was mistaken when He promised to rise from the dead. He only pretended to raise Jairus's daughter and the widow's son and Lazarus. He died a martyr's death, was buried, and remained dead. That is the word hell would like us to believe, that the liberals in the church would like us to believe. The resurrection of Christ is a myth—Christ is not risen. Christianity is a lie. Indeed, it is astounding that it ever got started at all.

Charles Maurice de Talleyrand-Perigord (1754–1838) knew better than that. He was a French bishop-statesman excommunicated by the pope in 1791 for his radical views. Later on he became prime minister of France. He was approached on one occasion by a M. Lepeaux who confided to Talleyrand his dilemma. He had tried to introduce a new religion which he regarded as an improvement on Christianity. He explained that, all his efforts notwithstanding, he seemed to be making no progress. What should he do? Talleyrand agreed it was not easy to start a new religion. He hardly knew what to suggest. He pondered the problem for a while. "There is one thing you might try," he said at length. "I should suggest you get yourself crucified and then rise again on the third day."

Without the bodily resurrection of Christ, Christianity's beginnings are as inexplicable as it would have been if M. Lepeaux's new religion had taken root and taken the world by storm. For on the resurrection morning itself, to all intents and purposes, the Sanhedrin had won. Jesus of Nazareth was dead and buried and His tomb sealed and guarded. One of the Twelve was dead and damned, easily bought for the price one would pay for a woman slave. Another had lied and cursed and was a wholly discredited fugitive. The other ten were huddled in terror in a room in town where they could be kept under surveillance and apprehended at leisure. There was no fear that these dispirited and demoralized men could start anything, let alone a movement which would defy the Jewish Sanhedrin and the Roman senate alike.[8] Almost to a man they were a collection of nonentities, fishermen, a tax collector, some women. None of them had mustered up enough courage to appear as a witness in their leader's defense when He was on trial for His life.

So then, here is what we have in Paul's first implication and application. No Resurrection? Then no risen Savior, Jesus is still dead. The tomb has triumphed. Christianity is a fraud and a farce. This brings us to *the further implication: our preaching of the Resurrection is foolish:* "And if Christ be not risen, then is our preaching vain, and your faith is also vain" (1 Cor. 15:14). That verse ought to be written in bold letters over the portals of every liberal church and seminary in the world. Those who deny the bodily resurrection of Christ have no message for a sin-cursed, dying world. All they have are lies and platitudes. Before the Spaniards discovered the new world, Spanish coins carried a picture of Hercules at the Straits of Gibraltar. They also carried the words *"Ne plus ultra"*—"There is nothing beyond." After the voyage of Columbus the inscription was changed to "plus ultra—something beyond." That is the message of the empty tomb! Pity the wretched liberal, for all his education, charm, and polish, for all his well-paid pulpits and professorships. Pity his congregation and his students. He points them to the tomb and denies the Resurrection and says, "There is nothing beyond!" He is nothing but a wolf in sheep's clothing. Nothing beyond, indeed!

A little boy was looking at a picture in an art store window, a painting of the Resurrection. A man also stopped to look. The boy said, "That's Jesus." The man made no reply. The boy continued, "Them's Roman soldiers," and, after a moment, continued, "They killed Him." The man asked, "Who told you that?" The boy said, "I learned it in Sunday school." The man turned and walked away. The boy called after him, "Say, Mister!" He ran and caught up with him. "Say, Mister," he continued, "I wanted to tell you, He didn't stay dead. He came back to life!" Paul would have said a hearty "Amen!" to that.

---

8. According to Eusebius, Pilate sent a report of the rumored resurrection of Jesus to the Emperor Tiberias at Rome. The emperor treated the matter with sufficient seriousness to refer it officially to the Roman senate, whose province it was, under the law, to consider all claims to deity in the empire. "For an ancient law prevailed that no one should be made a god by the Romans except by vote and decree of the Senate." The Senate rejected the Nazarene's claim to deity—presumably because they had not first examined the matter and given it the stamp of their approval. (*Eusebius Church History,* vol. 2; cited by D. L. Jamison, *Dawn,* 15 September 1927).

"If Christ be not risen, then is our preaching vain, and your faith is also vain." For that means the Son of the living God, the Creator of the universe, could be killed forever by a hammer and some nails and a rough-hewn cross of wood. That means He can be imprisoned forever in a grave and bound by an embalmer's cloth until time shall be no more. That means that a stone and a seal can imprison Him forever. That is the liberal's gospel! Thank God it is a lie.

I remember a memorable Sunday evening in a school auditorium in South Wales during the dark days of the Second World War. Our church used the school auditorium for its services. This particular Sunday we had an extraordinary speaker, a certain Pastor Schutez, who was a German refugee, a fugitive from the Gestapo and a wanted man. He had been a well-known German pastor, a man of whom the rising Nazi leaders had taken note. He told us how one day he had attended one of the giant rallies that Hitler and his henchmen were so skilled in staging. The speaker at the rostrum was waxing eloquent against the Jews. The audience was responding with mounting hysteria. Then the speaker had spotted Schutez in the crowd. He picked him out as the butt of his scorn. "Pastor Schutez," he said, "You are a fool! Fancy believing in a crucified, dead Jew!"

Pastor Schutez jumped to his feet and, in ringing tones which could be heard all across the auditorium, he replied, "Yes, sir! I should indeed be a fool if I believed in a crucified, dead Jew. But I believe in the risen, living Son of God!" Well said, Pastor Schutez! Our faith, after all, is not in vain.

Here, again, is that *further implication—if there is no Resurrection, we have nothing to preach and nothing to believe.* Here is *the further application: our preaching of the Resurrection is false:* "Yea, and we are found false witnesses of God; because we have testified of God that he raised up Christ: whom he raised not up, if so be that the dead rise not" (15:15). If the liberals are right, then all the apostles and prophets of the early church were liars and false witnesses. To get rid of that witness we have to tear the book of Acts right out of the Bible altogether. For the preaching of the apostles was simply the preaching of His resurrection and their primary purpose was to bear witness to the fact. In almost every instance, indeed, where the word "witness" occurs, it is related to the apostolic witness to the Resurrection.

It occurs first in Luke's account of the Great Commission. "It behoved Christ to suffer," Jesus told His disciples, "and to rise from the dead the third day: and that repentance and remission of sins should be preached in his name among all nations, beginning at Jerusalem. And ye are *witnesses* of these things" (Luke 24:46–48).

Even before Pentecost, while in the Upper Room awaiting the coming of the Holy Spirit, the disciples had a sense of their mission. When they looked for a successor for Judas they agreed that the man they would choose would need to be one who had kept company with them "all the time that the Lord Jesus went in and out among us, beginning from the baptism of John, unto the same day he was taken up from us," and that he must be "one ordained to be a *witness* with us of the resurrection" (Acts 1:21–22).

On the Day of Pentecost, when charging the Jews with their guilt, Peter boldly declared, "This Jesus hath God raised up, whereof we all are *witnesses*" (2:32).

When Peter healed the lame man at the gate of the temple and the crowd came running he again spoke boldly of the national guilt: "Ye denied the Holy One and the Just," he declared, "and desired a murderer to be granted unto you; and killed the Prince of life, whom God hath raised from the dead; whereof we are *witnesses*" (3:14–15).

After their supernatural escape from prison, the apostles were again arraigned before the Sanhedrin. The high priest accused them of still preaching, although he had forbidden them to do so, and of trying "to bring this man's blood upon us." Peter and the apostles replied, "We ought to obey God rather than men. The God of our fathers raised up Jesus, whom ye slew and hanged on a tree. Him hath God exalted with his right hand to be a Prince and a Saviour, for to give repentance to Israel, and forgiveness of sins. And we are *witnesses* of these things; and so is also the Holy Ghost" (5:29–32).

When he preached the gospel to Cornelius and the Gentiles he told them "how God anointed Jesus of Nazareth with the Holy Ghost and with power: who went about doing good, and healing all that were oppressed of the devil; for God was with him. And we are *witnesses* of all things which he did both in the land of the Jews, and in Jerusalem; whom they slew and hanged on a tree: him God raised up the third day, and shewed him openly" (10:38–40).

When the great apostle Paul preached to the Jews of Pisidian Antioch in their synagogue on the Sabbath day, he rehearsed the history and prophecies of the Old Testament, pointed them to Jesus as the One who fulfilled the promises, and then told them what the Jewish leaders had done to Him. "And though they found no cause of death in him, yet desired they Pilate that he should be slain. And when they had fulfilled all that was written of him, they took him down from the tree, and laid him in a sepulchre. But God raised him from the dead: and he was seen many days of them which came up with him from Galilee to Jerusalem, who are his *witnesses* unto the people" (Acts 13:28–31).

When on trial before King Agrippa, Paul told that last king of the Jews that, having met the risen Christ, he was commissioned thus by the Lord: "I have appeared unto thee for this purpose, to make thee a minister and a *witness* both of these things which thou hast seen, and of those things in the which I will appear unto thee" (Acts 26:16). Indeed, in all his trials, before Jewish and Gentile judges alike, Paul bore witness of the Resurrection—before the Sanhedrin (v. 5), before Felix (24:15), before Festus (25:9), and before Agrippa—of whom Paul asked the pointed question, "Why should it be thought a thing incredible with you, that God should raise the dead?" (26:8).

Indeed, if we were looking for a verse to summarize the entire book of Acts, we would scarcely do better than Acts 4:33: "And with great power gave the apostles *witness* of the resurrection of the Lord Jesus."

No wonder, then, that Paul told the Corinthians that he would be a false witness if he proclaimed Christ's resurrection when there was no Resurrection. Conversely, he would be a false witness if he were to proclaim that there was no Resurrection when there was a Resurrection, and that very Resurrection the very chief cornerstone of all apostolic witness. Those who stand in classroom and pulpit today and deny the resurrection of Christ are the false witnesses, not Paul.

Having refuted the lie in terms of our faith, Paul now refutes the lie *in terms of our forgiveness* (1 Cor. 15:16–17). Again he has an implication and an application. Here is *the implication: the Resurrection is a myth:* "For if the dead rise not, then is not Christ raised" (15:16), a proposition he has already twice inferred (15:13, 15). Here is *the application: Our redemption is a myth:* "And if Christ be not raised, your faith is vain; ye are yet in your sins" (15:17). Everything comes to a screeching halt at the door of a closed and sealed tomb wherein, although beautifully embalmed, lies the corpse of a very dead man. Christianity has nothing more to offer than Buddhism, Hinduism, or Islam except, perhaps, a nobler ethic and a higher moral code. From Abel on, blood flowed in an ever-deepening crimson tide. On Israel's altars countless sacrifices added their smoke to the pall. Burnt offerings and peace offerings, sin offerings and trespass offerings, Passover lambs and Atonement goats, sacrifices for a leper cleansed and for a Nazarite vow ended, offerings for a temple dedication and daily sacrifices throughout the day, and so it went on and on. Although not one sacrifice, or all the sacrifices together, could put away a single sin, there was hope. All pointed to Calvary, to that richer blood that would flow from nobler veins when God, at long, long last, would provide Himself to be the Lamb. A lamb for an individual in the days of Cain and Abel, a lamb for a family on Passover eve. A lamb for a nation, or rather, a goat on the Day of Atonement. And, finally, a Lamb for the world at Calvary. Everything pointed to the cross.

Day after day, month after month, year after year, the slaughter went on. Every day, five times a day, the official sacrifices were offered up. At six in the morning it was the time of the burnt offering. That was when the Romans came and took Him in the garden, when he declared Himself to be obedient unto death, even the death of the cross. Three hours later, at nine in the morning, the meal offering was presented by the priest of the day. That was the hour when Pilate confessed, "I find no fault in Him at all." Three hours later, at high noon, the peace offering was slain. It was then He was on the cross, about to enter into midday-midnight darkness, and make peace by the blood of His cross. Three hours later, at three in the afternoon, the sin offering was killed. That was when Jesus said, "It is finished," and bowed His head and died. Three hours later, at six in the evening, the trespass offering was killed, the offering which took care of sin against man. By then Jesus was in the tomb of His fellow man.

The darkness and silence of the tomb was complete. A body lay there, once wrapped in swaddling clothes, now wrapped in grave clothes. And that was the end of it all—"if Christ be not raised." It was all one vast hoax, a giant game of bluff, ending with a corpse in a tomb. The sacrifices would come to an end, not because they had been fulfilled, but because they were meaningless. That's the "gospel" of the liberal. Our faith is vain. Our sins and our iniquities cling to us still. Hell has triumphed! Satan won! The curse remains! Judgment looms! Faith is folly!

Blessed be God, it's a lie! Death was not the end! He arose! Hallelujah, Christ arose! As a result, all the great doctrines of New Testament faith ring out with a clear and clarion call—not only forgiveness but justification, not only redemption but regeneration, not only remission of sin but sonship, heirship, and glory by-and-by!

But Paul is not through yet. He has two more propositions to make. He refutes the lie *in terms of our future* (15:17a–18). *Here is the implication: the death of Christ is permanent:* "And if Christ be not raised" (15:17a; implied again here). Here is *the application: the dead in Christ have perished:* "Then they also which are fallen asleep in Christ are perished" (15:18). The unsaved have a platitude they pass on one to anther when trouble comes, when "the strong tides lift and the cables strain": "Everything's going to be all right," they say. It is mere wishful thinking, based on nothing but incurable optimism, a desperate hope contradicted by the law of sin and death. If Christ did not rise then Christianity is only an expanded version of the same vain hope, only couched in more elaborate terms. We stand by the coffin and follow the remains of the loved one to the cemetery. The minister reads some well-known passages—John 14:1–3; 1 Corinthians 15:39–58; 1 Thessalonians 4:15–18; a verse or two from Revelation 5 or 21–22. A word of prayer, a word of personal comfort to the bereaved—but it is all a sugar-coated lie—"If Christ be not raised . . . they also which are fallen asleep in Christ are perished." We smoothed their path to the tomb with sugar-coated lies. We told them their sins were forgiven when they weren't. We pointed them to an "empty" tomb, still tenanted by the body of a dead Christ. Who would want to be a liberal with such a "gospel" as that? Surely no one in his right mind. Better far to abandon the faith altogether, give up the well-paying pulpit or professorship, and become an honest atheist.

Paul has one more logical proposition. He refutes the lie *in terms of our feelings* (1 Cor. 15:19). Here is *the final implication: we have no eternal home:* "If in this life only we have hope in Christ" (15:19a). If it all ends at the grave, if it is all a pious and enchanting dream, if all horizons end in a tomb, what then? Paul gives us *the final application: we have no earthly hope:* "We are of all men the most miserable" (15:19b). To be a Christian in a hostile world can be a costly business. It can mean privation and persecution, suffering, hardship, and martyrdom, sometimes of the most horrible and painful kind. Believers, down through the centuries, have paid gladly the full cost of discipleship in the sure and certain hope of Resurrection and the glory that is to follow. But if it were all for nothing, if Christ did not rise, if the tomb triumphs after all, then, indeed, we are of all men most miserable. We might have settled for a life of ease and pleasure. We might have gone in for the good things of this life. Instead, we threw them all away to go in search of a mirage in the desert which proved to be an illusion after all.

So much, then, for the resurrection of Christ. It is an undeniable fact of history. It is an indispensable fact of theology. Everything hinges on the Resurrection.

    B.   The resurrection of Christians (15:20–58)
        1. A word about its truth (15:20–28)
            a. A resurrection principle (15:20–22)
                (1) An illustration from the commencement of the Hebrew harvest (15:20)
                (2) An illustration from the commencement of all human history (15:21–22)

    (a) An appropriate pattern (15:21)

    (b) An appropriate process (15:22)

  b. A resurrection prophecy (15:23–28)

    (1) The Rapture (15:23)

      (a) The token harvest—at the time of Christ's resurrection (15:23a)

      (b) The total harvest—at the time of Christ's return (15:23b)

    (2) The reign (15:24–28)

      (a) The earthly kingdom (15:24–27)

        i. The commencement of the reign (15:24a)

        ii. The completion of the reign (15:24b–c)

          a. The yielding of all power (15:24b)

          b. The wielding of all power (15:24c)

        iii. The compulsion of the reign (15:25a)

        iv. The consummation of the reign (15:25b–26)

          a. The Devil subdued (15:25b)

          b. Even death subdued (15:26)

        v. The commentary on the reign (15:27)

          a. A relevant notation (15:27a)

          b. A relevant quotation (15:27b)

      (b) Eternal kingdom (15:28)

        i. An appointed surrender (15:28a)

        ii. An absolute supremacy (15:28b)

Paul turns now to the second part of this great discussion—*the resurrection of Christians* (15:20–58). He has a great deal to say about it. Indeed, nowhere else in the Bible are we told more about it than here. He begins with *a word about its truth* (15:20–28) and concludes with *a word about its triumphs* (15:29–58). He begins this section with *a resurrection principle* (15:20–22). He has two illustrations. He begins with an illustration from *the commencement of the Hebrew harvest:* "But now is Christ risen from the dead, and become the firstfruits of them that slept" (15:20). The feast of firstfruits was the third of seven annual feasts celebrated by the Jews. It was associated with the Passover and the feast of unleavened bread. It was kept on the morrow after the Sabbath. In other words, it was associated with the first day of the week. The Lord Jesus was in the tomb on the Sabbath after Passover. He rose from the dead the next day, the day the priest took a sheaf of corn from the field and waved it over the whole field as a token that the whole harvest would eventually be reaped. Thus this feast pointed forward to the very day of the resurrection of the Lord Jesus (Lev. 23:9–14).

The reaping of the harvest, among the Hebrew people, was in three stages. The joyous occasion began with the firstfruits, it continued with the great harvest itself, and concluded with the gleanings. All three stages refer to what the Holy Spirit calls "the first resurrection" (Rev. 20:6) and which the Lord Jesus called "the resurrection of life" (John 5:28–29). The Lord's resurrection was the firstfruits, the general resurrection of the Lord's people at the Rapture (1 Thess. 4:13–18) is the harvest, the resurrection of those saved during the time of the Tribulation will be the gleanings.

It is important to note that the priest did not wave a single stalk of grain over the harvest field, but a whole sheaf. It is Matthew who, alone, shows how that was fulfilled at the time of Christ's resurrection. He says that when Christ died "the graves were opened; and many bodies of the saints which slept arose, and came out of the graves after his resurrection, and went into the holy city, and appeared unto many" (Matt. 27:52–53). Such was the wave sheaf. It is the guarantee that the whole resurrection harvest will take place when the time comes. "Afterward they that are Christ's, at his coming," Paul says (1 Cor. 15:23). That includes us!

Next, Paul gives an illustration from *the commencement of all human history* (15:21–22). He takes us back to Adam, the human father of the race. There is *an appropriate pattern:* "For since by one man came death, by man came also the resurrection of the dead" (15:21). Thus Paul links the Incarnation (another truth the liberals deny) with the Resurrection. The Lord Jesus became truly man. He was born in Bethlehem of the Virgin Mary, yet "conceived of the Holy Ghost." He became truly man without ceasing to be God. Had He not been truly man, in every sense of the word, He could not have died, been buried, and been raised again. Had He not been God, in every sense of the word, the life He laid down on the cross of Calvary would have been but a finite life and inadequate to atone for the sins of the entire human race. Paul clearly saw the connection between the ruin introduced into human history by Adam and the Resurrection assured for all the redeemed by another man, Jesus.

There is also *an appropriate process:* "For as in Adam all die, even so in Christ shall all be made alive" (15:22). Both Adam and Christ have a direct relationship to the human race. It was precisely because of that relationship that the Lord Jesus could play the part of a kinsman-redeemer (Lev. 25:25, 47; Deut. 19:6). That is why, as soon as Naomi heard that the name of the man who had befriended Ruth was Boaz, she exclaimed, "The man is near of kin unto us" (Ruth

2:20). The role of the kinsman-redeemer was *to purchase* (both the person and the property of the bride), *to propagate,* and *to protect.* In order to redeem, however, he had to fulfill three basic requirements. He had to have *the resources* to redeem, for redemption was a costly business—thus in the first reference to Boaz in the book of Ruth we are told that he was a "mighty man of wealth" (2:1). He also had to have *the resolve* to redeem, a resolve the other man in the story did not have. He was interested enough in the property but had no interest, except one of rejection, in the person, Ruth herself. Most of all he had to have *the right* to redeem. He had to be a near kinsman.

All of which points directly to Christ, of whom Boaz was a type and to whom the Mosaic legislation concerning a kinsman-redeemer pointed. For He is indeed our Kinsman-Redeemer by virtue of His having actually been born into the human family. God saw me in my father before I was born, He saw my father in his father before he was born. My grandfather was in my great-grandfather and he in his father—and so on, for each one of us, right back to Adam. Thus the whole human family was in Adam, theologically and biologically (the scientific term for it is "preformationism") when Adam sinned. Thus God was able to federate sin in Adam. In like manner, He has been able to federate salvation in Christ. Each believer is biblically viewed as being in Christ. This is the essential difference between the sin of a human being and the sin of Lucifer and the fallen angels. Each angel chose to sin; we were born in sin. There is no salvation for them, there is for us. By virtue of our birth we die, having inherited a sinful nature from Adam. By virtue of His birth we are made alive. God puts us "in Christ" as once we were inevitably "in Adam." So, by natural birth we are born subject to the curse, by new birth we are born again, born from above, born of the Spirit, born of God, born subject to new life in Christ.

Redemption, in the Old Testament, is set before us along two lines. There is redemption *by power* (the book of Exodus expounds that concept) and there is redemption *by purchase* (the book of Ruth expounds that concept). Our Kinsman-Redeemer redeemed us by purchase, on the cross of Calvary, and by power, when He arose from the dead having smitten the enemy with His deathblow. We were redeemed by purchase at His first coming; we shall be redeemed by power at His second coming. There would be small satisfaction in His having effected our purchase if He did not have the power to expel the enemy from our property, now His purchased possession. That is one reason why the millennial reign is essential. The Lord fully intends to take over the property He has purchased as well as the people He has purchased.

Which brings us, logically enough, to Paul's next point. Paul moves on from a discussion of a resurrection principle to a discussion of *a resurrection prophecy* (1 Cor. 15:23–28). He talks first about *the Rapture:* "But every man in his own order: Christ the firstfruits; afterward they that are Christ's at his coming" (15:23). We have already contemplated the Old Testament feast of firstfruits, but much more could be said. When the wave sheaf was symbolically waved over the harvest field it was not without sacrifice. A burnt offering, a meal offering, and a drink offering were part of the ritual of that day—but no sin offering. There was a burnt offering because that offering spoke of Christ offering Himself, in sinless, perfect obedience, wholly and altogether to God. That aspect of Calvary will be remembered when the dead in Christ rise. The meal offering symbolized the perfect, flawless, sinless life of the Lord Jesus, offered up to God. It was a life which brought forth the public approbation of God. That will be remembered. Had He not lived such a life He would have been unable to die for our sins. He would have died for His own, and that would have been the end of it. The drink offering speaks of Christ pouring out His soul unto death. That, too, will be remembered. His resurrection body still bore the marks of Calvary. But there was no sin offering connected with the feast of firstfruits because, by the time the wave sheaf was offered, on that glorious first day of the week, God could say: "Thy sins and iniquities will I remember no more." Calvary blotted them out forever!

We now await the great harvest day itself. The word here for Christ's *coming* is *parousia.* There are three words we associate with the second coming of Christ. The word *epiphany* (*the shining forth*) refers to the glory associated with the Lord's return (Matt. 24:27; 1 Tim. 6:14–16). For

> The beauty of the Savior
> Shall dazzle every eye,
> In the crowning day that's coming,
>   By and by.

The word *apocalypse* refers to the unveiling of the Lord Jesus in the eyes of this sin-cursed, Christ-rejecting world. The book of Revelation expounds all that will be involved in that. The word *parousia* has to do with the Lord's actual presence, into which we shall be ushered permanently when He comes again.

Paul has talked about the Rapture, now he talks also about the reign (1 Cor. 15:24–28), for Paul was no amillennialist but a firm believer in the actual reign of Christ upon this world, the scene of His rejection. Paul talks, first, about *the earthly kingdom* (15:24–27). He begins by pointing us to *the commencement of the reign:* "Then cometh the end" (15:24a)—the end, that is, of the climactic and cataclysmic events on earth which will follow the Rapture and precede the return and reign of Christ on earth. The word for *end* is *telos,* which signifies the very end. Many things have to happen, in the prophetic sequence of end-time events, before we arrive at the very end. Some of these are described in Matthew 24:1–14, where the nations are in view. The Lord envisioned the world being convulsed by deceivers, wars, famines, persecutions, pestilences, earthquakes, and such-like torments. Iniquity will abound. Moreover, He spoke of "the gospel of the kingdom" being preached in all the world "for a witness unto all nations." This gospel will be preached by the 144,000 Jewish evangelists who will speak for God after the Rapture of the church (Rev. 7). They will have enormous success. "Then shall the end *[telos]* come," Jesus said (Matt. 24:14). He then turned His attention to the Jewish world and foretold the setting up of "the abomination of desolation" in the Jewish temple and of the outbreak of an end-time holocaust of persecution, known as "the great tribulation" and without peer or parallel in all of history. He climaxed this section by describing the coming of the Lord in glory (24:15–29) and briefly described the vast convulsions of nature which will accompany that coming.

Paul passes over all this. However, he does point to the interval between the Rapture of the church and the Lord's actual return to the earth. "Then cometh the end," Paul said. The word for *then* is not *tote* (then, immediately) but *eita* (then, after an interval). The commencement of the Lord's actual reign on earth will await the fulfillment of the prophecies concerning the rise, reign, and ruin of the Antichrist. Some of these things Paul had already described in his second Thessalonian epistle.

Paul now leaps ahead to describe *the completion of the reign* (1 Cor. 15:24b–c). He describes *the yielding of all power,* speaking of the time when, at the conclusion of the millennial reign, the Lord Jesus "shall have delivered up the kingdom to God, even the Father" (15:24b). He describes also, going back to the duration of the millennial reign itself, *the wielding of all power:* "When he shall have put down all rule, and all authority and power" (15:24c). This happens twice, once at the beginning of the reign when He deposes the Antichrist and the False Prophet, and again at its close, when He casts Satan into the lake of fire.

When the Lord returns to earth, He will reign first of all in His "David" character and put down all His foes by might and power. Satan, the Beast, the

False Prophet, and all the Lord's foes, human, angelic, and demonic, will be summarily dealt with. Then the Lord will reign in His "Solomon" character as Prince of Peace. The world will at last know prosperity and order, under a reign of absolute righteousness, such as it has never experienced since the fall of Adam. The Lord will rule with a rod of iron (Ps. 2). The Sermon on the Mount will be the statute book. Countless millions will be regenerated, filled with the Spirit, anointed of God, able to live according to the sublime edicts of that Sermon. Satan will be incarcerated in the Abyss and will be unable to incite men to wickedness. Pilgrimages to Jerusalem will include a tour of the dread Valley of Hinnom, where they will see the terrible end of those who defy the Lord (Isa. 66:23–24).

Thus ten centuries will pass. The glowing Old Testament prophecies will come true. The desert will blossom as the rose. The harvests will be bountiful. The lion and the lamb will lie down together. A man will be but a youth at a hundred years of age. It will be the golden age. The Bible will be at the core of every curriculum. Spirit-filled and anointed men and women will teach the arts and the sciences. It will be an age of peace, prosperity, and progress.

It seems incredible people will grow tired of it. But, in the end, there will be a widespread revolt. Satan will be released and men by the million will flock to his standard. For as time goes on, more and more millions of people will be born who do not get born again. They grow up unregenerate. As children, who grow up in Christian homes sometimes become "gospel hardened," so people growing up in the millennial earth will become "glory hardened." In ever increasing numbers the unregenerate will begin to murmur against the inflexible laws of the kingdom. Memory of what the world was like when "sin reigned and death by sin" will fade. Millions, born during the Golden Age, will have no more memory of the miseries and horrors of premillennial times than children born today have of the First World War. People born, but not born again, will find themselves with passions they cannot express, with sin natures they cannot indulge. Increasingly a spirit of rebellion will smolder. The malcontents, afraid to express their lusts and longings openly, will begin to congregate at the far reaches of the planet, as far from the central Glory as possible. There they will nurse their growing hatred for holiness and godliness.

Then, Satan will be released from his prison (Rev. 20:7–10). The rebels will hail him as a savior, one who can emancipate them from the hated reign of righteousness. They will flock to his banners. They will mobilize and march on Jerusalem. Their swelling hordes are contemptuously labeled "Gog and Magog" by the Holy Spirit, perhaps to remind them of the most famous of all former anti-Semitic campaigns and its disastrous results (Ezekiel 38–39). Deluded by Satan, drunk with the wine of rebellion, determined to return the world to its former state, they will approach the Holy City. But their rebellion will come to a swift and inglorious end.

"Then cometh the end," Paul says, the very end indeed. Peter describes the detonation of the planet in the scorching flames of nuclear holocaust (2 Peter 3:10–13). Time shall be no more. The Lord, having wielded power on earth, will yield that power to God, even the Father, by delivering up the kingdom to Him. The kingdom of heaven will be absorbed into the kingdom of God.

Paul mentions, next, *the compulsion of the reign* (1 Cor. 15:25a). "For he *must* reign," he says. This is one of the divine imperatives. "He *must* needs go through Samaria," John said. He wanted to meet that woeful woman at that wayside well (John 4:4). "I *must* be about my Father's business," Jesus said, indicating that already, at the age of twelve, He knew who He was and why He was here (Luke 2:49). "Ye *must* be born again," He said to Nicodemus, to show him that religion was one thing, regeneration was something else (John 3:7). "Them also I *must* bring," He said concerning those "other sheep" which were not of the Hebrew fold (10:16). "The Son of man *must* be delivered into the hands of sinful men, and be crucified, and the third day rise again," the angels told the women at the empty tomb (Luke 24:7). "He *must* reign!"

The reference is evidently to the millennial reign for, in the eternal state, rule returns to the Father. This earth is the scene of man's rebellion. This earth witnessed the humiliation, suffering, shame, and death of God's beloved Son at the hands of sinful men. "He must reign" to demonstrate His deity and display His glory here, where all these things happened. "He must reign" to defeat Satan, finally, fully, and forever in the very world that Satan invaded and ruined. "He must reign" to fulfill scores of Old Testament prophecies which otherwise must be "spiritualized," contrary to sound hermeneutics, and explained away. That "He must reign" is one of the great compulsions of time.

Paul turns next to *the consummation of the reign* (1 Cor. 15:25b–26). First, *the Devil must be subdued*: "He must reign, till he hath put all enemies under his feet" (15:25b). For "God also hath highly exalted him, and given him a name which is above every name: that at the name of Jesus every knee should bow, of things in heaven, and things in earth, and things under the earth; and that every tongue should confess that Jesus Christ is Lord, to the glory of God the Father" (Phil. 2:9–11). The greatest of all His enemies is Satan, once known as Lucifer, son of the morning, the anointed cherub, the highest and greatest of all the creatures His hands had made. From some unknown point in a past before the worlds began, this powerful, finite, and fallen foe constituted himself the enemy of God the Son. Tirelessly, maliciously, fiendishly, resourcefully, increasingly, Satan has worked in the highest heaven, in the deepest hell, around our world, to overthrow the Son of God's love. He has had many allies and agents, human and angelic, to help him in his schemes. He has left a trail of defilement and desolation everywhere. He and all his minions must be put down. All of them, from the least to the greatest, must be put under the feet of the Lord Jesus. Moreover, God has chosen this planet to be the scene of battle and of Satan's final overthrow. The Lord will reign until the Devil is finally and absolutely subdued.

Then, too, *even death must be subdued:* "The last enemy that shall be destroyed is death" (1 Cor. 15:26). Death, after all, is our most feared foe. It dogs us all our days. It haunts our nightmares, gibbers at us out of the shadows, lies in wait in the form of accidents, illnesses, and old age. We dismiss it from our minds in the hurly-burly of life's busy days. We keep it at bay with a round of pleasure and activity, but ever and always it lurks in the shadows. It was the ghost which haunted Solomon all the way through the book of Ecclesiastes. Indeed, it got such a hold upon his mind and filled him with such horror that, increasingly, its dread name is written down, despairingly, on the pages of that sad book.

We know that Christ has conquered death and that He now has the keys of death and hades (Rev. 1:18). We have every assurance from God's Word that death simply ushers us into His presence. Yet still we dread it. It invades our homes and robs us of our loved ones. It appears to our imaginations as a grinning skeleton with a sharp scythe in its bony hands. It chills us when we gaze upon a lifeless corpse. We think of the nightmare horrors of the grave. We know that death has been defeated—but still we die. We believe in the Resurrection—but that we do not see, but we do see death, and it is ever present, horrible, hateful, and here. We know that we are going to die.

As we get older, death robs us of our friends, those we have known long since and loved. For, when all is said and done, and when all the glowing Scriptures regarding Resurrection and Rapture have been read, death simply grins back. It is an enemy. It is the *last* enemy. So, as best we can, let us heed Spurgeon's good advice: "If death is the last enemy," he said, "then leave him until last."

For there is such a thing as dying grace—and God gives dying grace for dying; not for living. When the time comes, God will be there and His grace sufficient.

It was part of the genius of John Bunyan that, when he brought Christian and Hopeful to the river of death, Hopeful had an easy crossing but Christian had a much more difficult time. When they came to the river, Bunyan tells us, "the pilgrims began to enquire if there was no other way to the gate." For the river was deep and there was no bridge. Beyond, the city of pure gold beckoned. Two men "in raiment that shone like gold, also their faces shone as the light," assured them they could not avoid the river. For when the pilgrims began to ask about another way, the shining cries told them that, although there was another way, "there hath not any, save two, Enoch and Elijah, been permitted to tread that path since the foundation of the world, nor shall until the last trump shall sound."

"You shall find it deeper or shallower as you believe in the King of the place," the pilgrims were told. "They then addressed themselves to the water," Bunyan says, "and, entering, Christian began to sink, and crying out to his good friend Hopeful, he said: 'I sink in deep waters; the billows go over my head; all his waves go over me.' Then said the other, 'Be of good cheer, my brother; I feel the bottom and it is good.'" Still Christian floundered and, at last, light broke through and he cried out to his fellow pilgrim: "Oh I see Him again, and He tells me 'When thou passest through the waters, I will be with thee; and through the rivers, they shall not overflow thee.'" It was not long after that before Christian "found ground to stand upon; and so it followed that the rest of the river was but shallow. Thus they got over."

Preachers of former generations used to tell great deathbed stories. They could tell of people whose closing hours were hours of torment as the pains of hell seized hold upon them. Voltaire died screaming out his terrors and so terrified his nurse that she said she would never attend the deathbed of another atheist so long as she lived. They told stories, too, of the deathbeds of God's saints, who rushed to meet eternity and called back to tell of "joy unspeakable and full of glory" opening up before them. D. L. Moody had such a death. He had an absolutely marvelous time of it, calling back to his son, Willy, that he could see his two grandchildren who had died in infancy, alive and glorious, on the other side. The reason we hear so little of such deathbed scenes nowadays probably lies in the fact that most terminal patients die in a hospital, heavily drugged.

Still, death remains an enemy. But even death itself is going to be destroyed, one of these days, by Jesus. The word for *destroyed* is *katargeō*. It means "brought to nought." It is translated "put down" in 1 Corinthians 15:24. It means "annulled" or "abolished." After the judgment of the wicked dead, at the great white throne, "death and hell were cast into the lake of fire," John saw (Rev. 20:14). It will be locked up with the Devil, the Beast, the False Prophet, and all Christ-rejecters to trouble and torment the world no more.

Paul turns finally to *the commentary on the reign* of Christ over the earthly kingdom: "For he hath put all things under his feet. But when he saith all things are put under him, it is manifest that he is excepted, which did put all things under him" (1 Cor. 15:27). This is a quotation from Psalm 8. One day God will proclaim that this three-thousand-year-old prophecy has been at last fulfilled. The one obvious exception to the subordination of everything to the Son is obviously the Father Himself. For just as the Holy Spirit is here to honor the Son, so the Son is here to honor the Father. That was His supreme object in life. It is His supreme object in eternity. The words spoken by David of man in general are now applied to the Man, Christ Jesus, the new federal Head of the human race.

In closing this interesting and informative section of his discussion, Paul draws attention to *the eternal kingdom:* "And when all things shall be subdued unto him, then shall the Son also himself be subject unto him that put all things under him" (15:28). This time the word for *then* is *tote,* which means "immediately." The vast cycle of sin and rebellion, the age-long "mystery of iniquity" in the universe, precipitated when Lucifer aspired to God's throne in heaven, has now come its complete circle. The Son, having all power at His disposal, gladly, willingly yields everything back to God. We shall be present on that coming occasion and will raise our hosannas and hallelujahs with all the heavenly hosts. Thus shall we awaken the echoes of the everlasting hills with ceaseless songs of praise. What will happen after that, it will take all eternity to unfold. There will be a new heaven and a new earth (2 Peter 3:13; Rev. 21:1–8). God will be "all in all," Paul concludes. The complete and absolute supremacy of God will be owned and acknowledged by all. Even the lost will have to own the sovereignty of God, even as in that marked-out segment of eternity which we call time, they are bound to acknowledge the Lordship of Christ (Rev. 5:13).

> 2. A word about its triumphs (15:29–58)
>   a. Challenges (15:29–34)
>   (1) A question of baptizing (15:29)
>   (a) What? Baptism is a futile ordinance if the dead rise not (15:29a)
>   (b) Why? Baptism is a foolish ordinance if the dead rise not (15:29b)
>   (2) Question of battling (15:30–32)
>   (a) If the Resurrection is a fact (15:30–32a)
>   i. It makes sense to face ever-present danger (15:30)

    ii. It makes sense to face ever-present death (15:31–32a)

        a. An exclamation (15:31)

        b. An example (15:32a)

  (b) If the Resurrection is a farce (15:32b–c)

    i. It makes sense to have fun today (15:32b)

    ii. It makes sense to just forget tomorrow (15:32c)

(3) A question of behaving (15:33–34)

  (a) A shoddy fellowship (15:33–34a)

    i. Beware of sinful company (15:33)

    ii. Beware of sinful compromise (15:34a)

  (b) A shameful fact (15:34b)

b. Changes (15:35–57)

  (1) A question asked (15:35)

    (a) By what means? (15:35a)

    (b) In what manner? (15:35b)

  (2) A question answered (15:36–57)

    (a) There will be a change of dimension (15:36–42a)

      i. Bodies terrestrial (15:36–39)

        a. God is a God of infinite vitality—witness the world of botany (15:36–38)

          1. The principle of life beyond death established (15:36)

          2. The principle of life with a difference established (15:37–38)

        b. God is a God of infinite variety—witness the world of biology (15:39)

      ii. Bodies celestial (15:40–42a)

        a. A contrast (15:40)

        b. A comparison (15:41)

        c. A conclusion (15:42a)

    (b) There will be a change of destiny (15:42b–c)

      i. A body destined for the grave (15:42b)

      ii. A body destined for the glory (15:42c)

    (c) There will be a change of dress (15:43a–b)

      i. A body clogged with lust (15:43a)

      ii. A body clothed in light (15:43b)

(d) There will be a change of disposition (15:43c–d)
    i. A feeble body (15:43c)
    ii. A flawless body (15:43d)
(e) There will be a change of dynamics (15:44)
    i. A human body: engineered for this world (15:44a)
    ii. A heavenly body: engineered for that world (15:44b)
(f) There will be a change of dynasty (15:45–52)
    i. The measure of the change (15:45–49)
        a. A radical change envisioned (15:45–46)
            1. A new orientation (15:45)
            2. A noted order (15:46)
        b. A racial change envisioned (15:47–49)
            1. A new Lord (15:47)
            2. A new life (15:48)
            3. A new likeness (15:49)
    ii. The mystery of the change (15:50–52)
        a. A great impossibility (15:50)
        b. A great imperative (15:51–52)
            1. Rapture for some (15:51a)
            2. Renewal for all (15:51b–52)
                (i) Note what (15:51b–52a)
                    (a) It will be sure (15:51b)
                    (b) It will be sudden (15:52a)
                (ii) Note when (15:52b–c)
                    (a) A word about the trumpet (15:52b)
                    (b) A word about the transformation (15:52c)
(g) There will be a change of durability (15:53)
    i. No more decay (15:53a)
    ii. No more death (15:53b)
(h) There will be a change of dominion (15:54–57)
    i. The fulfillment of Scripture (15:54–55)
        a. A wonderful saying (15:54)
        b. A wonderful song (15:55)
            1. The shout of those raptured (15:55a)

        2. The shout of those resurrected (15:55b)
     ii. The fact of sin (15:56)
        a. Its sting (15:56a)
        b. Its strength (15:56b)
    iii. The fullness of salvation (15:57)
        a. Giving thanks for our deliverance (15:57a)
        b. Giving thanks for our deliverer (15:57b)
  c. Choices (15:58)
    (1) A call to work—with an eye on the rules (15:58a)
    (2) A call to work—with an eye on the reward (15:58b)

Paul continues his discussion of *the resurrection of Christians* (15:20–58). He has given us a *word about its truth* (15:20–28). He now begins a lengthy section in which he gives *a word about its triumphs* (15:29–58). Everything about 1 Corinthians 15 (as with Romans 8 and Hebrews 11) is superlative. There is nothing like this passage anywhere else in the world. The worlds of philosophy, science, and comparative religion cannot match these verses. They shine light into the darkness of the tomb and dispel that darkness forever. Paul sets before us some *challenges* (15:29–34), some *changes* (15:35–57), and some *choices* (15:58).

He begins with some *challenges.* The first has to do with *a question of baptizing:* "Else what shall they do which are baptized for the dead, if the dead rise not at all? Why are they then baptized for the dead?" This is what is called, in books on hermeneutics, an obscure text. Certainly it is a difficult text. A wide variety of "interpretations" have been suggested to dilute it or avoid it. Some have suggested that "for the dead" means "those about to die." It is said to mean "over the sepulchers of the dead." Some have suggested "to supply the vacancies left by the dead." Those being "baptized" are supposedly going through a baptism of suffering.

When all is said and done, Paul appears to be referring to some form of vicarious baptism in vogue at Corinth (along with numerous other disorders) which Paul mentions, by way of argument, a practice he did not bother to refute but which he certainly did not endorse. The key is in the use of the personal pronouns— "what shall *they* do which are baptized for the dead if he dead rise not at all? Why are *they* then baptized for the dead?" He drops the third-person plural for the first person plural in the next verse, obviously to identify himself with that of which he did approve—"And why stand *we* in jeopardy . . . ?" He uses also the first-person singular and the second-person plural to continue his discussion. "*I* protest by *your* rejoicing which *I* have in Christ" (15:30–31). By using the third person in connection with baptism for the dead, Paul refers to it while disassociating himself from it, although he does not deem this to be either the time or the place to refute it.

It would seem that at Corinth, where some were questioning the doctrine of resurrection, others were actually being baptized by proxy for believers who had died before being baptized. Baptism for the dead is as unscriptural as praying for the dead. J. B. Phillips, in his paraphrase, makes no bones about it at all. He translates the verse, "Further, you should consider this, that if there is to be no resurrection, what is the point of some of you being baptized for the dead by proxy? Why should we be baptized for *dead bodies?*"

Historically, baptism for the dead was practiced by heretical cults such as the Cerinthians and Marcionites. Both Tertullian and Chrysostom mention the practice. Baptism for the unbelieving dead, a further stage in gross error, is one of the main dogmas of present-day Mormons, who make an enormous thing of it. Gordon H. Fraser, an expert on Mormonism, says that "the Mormons are constantly doing 'work for the dead' by compiling genealogies of their ancestors and other notables and then being baptized for them. The Mormons are very serious about all this. One Mormon admitted to me," he adds, "that he had been baptized over five thousand times for the dead."[9]

Baptism for the dead is a cultic practice. Believer's baptism is a Christian practice, one in which we proclaim to the world our death, burial, and resurrection with Christ. It, too, would be a meaningless ordinance if the dead rise not at all.

Now comes *a question of battling* (15:30–32). Paul considers two propositions. The first applies to one's attitude *if the resurrection is a fact* (15:30–32a). Then, two proposals make sense. It makes sense to *face ever-present danger:* "And why stand we in jeopardy every hour?" (15:30). Paul, in his second letter to the Corinthians, will describe at length some of the perils he faced for the cause of Christ (2 Cor. 11:23–33). What would be the point of it all if death wrote "The End!" over one's life? Within a few short years Nero would be on the rampage. Christianity would enter a new era of persecution that would last for some three hundred years. What nonsense to live in such constant jeopardy, when a pinch of salt on a pagan altar would buy immediate release. If Christianity ended at the grave, why go on enduring such untold and avoidable suffering? If the Resurrection, however, is a fact, it makes sense to face ever-present danger.

---

9. Gordon H. Fraser, *Is Mormonism Christian?* (Chicago: Moody, 1957), 113.

It also makes sense to *face ever-present death:* "I protest by your rejoicing which I have in Christ Jesus our Lord. I die daily. If after the manner of men I have fought with beasts at Ephesus, what advantageth it me, if the dead rise not?" (1 Cor. 15:31–32a). Paul constantly faced death in his ministry. Indeed, at Lystra he was stoned and left for dead (Acts 14:19–20). He lived in constant peril. The Jews in Jerusalem mobbed him in the temple and tried to murder him (21:31), they plotted to assassinate him (23:12–15), and when that failed also they tried twisting the arm of Festus, hoping he would send Paul back to Jerusalem from Caesarea so they could ambush him and kill him on the way (25:1–3). Paul told the Romans that believers were to regard themselves a being "killed all the day long . . . accounted as sheep for the slaughter" (Rom. 8:36). When Nero launched the first major round of persecution against the church, Christians were used as human torches to light up his gardens. He had them sewn up in animal skins and thrown to wild dogs. They were herded into the arena and thrown to the lions. Rome tolerated many religions, bowed the knee to countless gods and goddesses, but just to be known as a Christian was a sentence of death. Many notable Christians were martyred by the persecuting Caesars, including Ignatius, Justin, Blandina, Cyprian, Polycarp, and Origen. The holocaust continued under Caesar after Caesar until Constantine formally ended the persecution by the Edict of Milan in February 313.

Nor has the persecution abated with the passing of time. Christians were martyred by the thousands by the papacy during the Middle Ages. At one time, in the Soviet Union, 88 percent of all Russian Orthodox churches were closed and 400 leaders of unregistered Baptist churches were in prison. It has been estimated that of 66 million people killed between 1917 and 1953, half were Christians. Countless thousands were driven from their homes, imprisoned, or executed in China during the Cultural Revolution (1966–1976).

Paul says that he fought with wild beasts at Ephesus. This appears to refer to his sufferings at the hand of an infuriated mob—some time prior to the mob attack recorded in Acts 19. It is not considered likely that Paul was actually exposed in the arena, although even that is not impossible. Paul's Roman citizenship would, under normal circumstances, protect him from such an ordeal. As we know from what Paul suffered at Philippi, however, his Roman citizenship was no iron-clad guarantee when exposed to the passions of a mob. The phrase *after the manner of men* can be rendered "humanly speaking," which lends weight to the view that Paul was speaking figuratively here. Paul referred to Nero, as "the lion" (2 Tim. 4:17). The psalmist likened his enemies to wild beasts (Ps. 22:21).

If the Resurrection, then, is a fact, it makes sense to face ever-present danger and death for the cause of Christ. Paul, after all, was going in for a crown (2 Tim. 4:8), a crown of righteousness, but was not averse to having a martyr's crown (Rev. 2:10) given to him as well—although, of course, he had more sense than to deliberately court it.

On the other hand, *if the Resurrection is a farce* (1 Cor. 15:32b–c), then two other propositions make sense. It makes sense *to have fun today:* "What advantageth it me, if the dead rise not? Let us eat and drink" (15:32b); and it makes sense *to just forget tomorrow:* "for to morrow we die" (15:32c). This was the philosophy of the Epicurians—"Eat, drink, and be merry for tomorrow we die." It is the worldly man's view of life. Get all you can now because death ends all. Solomon, in his backsliding years, embraced a similar materialistic view (Eccl. 9:4–10). Paul seems, however, to be quoting directly from Isaiah 22:13. If death is, indeed, the end of it all, why not live to get as much enjoyment out of life as possible? That is the world's philosophy. However, it is a false and foolish philosophy because death is not the end. Beyond death is Resurrection and judgment for all, for believers at the judgment seat of Christ, and for unbelievers at the great white throne.

Now comes *a question of behaving* (1 Cor. 15:33–34). Since the Resurrection is indeed an inescapable fact, then we need to take good heed to our conduct and conversation. Belief always determines behavior. Paul warns about *a shoddy fellowship:* "Be not deceived: evil communications corrupt good manners. Awake to righteousness, and sin not" (15:33–34a). The word *communications* here is *homilia,* meaning "associations." The quotation has been rendered by F. F. Bruce, "Bad company ruins good morals." He identifies it as a quotation from Menander's comedy *Thais.* He thinks it had likely become an everyday proverb and that it could have been quoted as casually as people nowadays quote a witticism from Shakespeare. We would say today, "You get like the company you keep," or "Birds of a feather flock together." It does not necessarily follow that Paul himself was aware of the source of the proverb. Some have pointed out the unlikelihood of Paul quoting from the immoral play of a corrupt comedian like Menander in order to promote holiness among God's people. It is just as likely he could have quoted a well-known saying of his day, however, to reinforce his teaching.

It would seem that some of the Corinthians had not only embraced the teaching that there really was no Resurrection, but had fallen also into the lax moral lifestyle that such a denial would encourage. Paul warns them that they are being deceived. They need to sever connections with such shoddy fellowship. "Wake up," he says. "Wake to righteousness and sin not."

Beware of *a shameful fact*, he adds: "For some have not the knowledge of God: I speak this to your shame" (15:34b). The word used here is not *agnoia*, which would denote mere ignorance, but *agnōsia*, which suggests culpable ignorance. The only other place the word occurs is when the Holy Spirit tells us to "put to silence the ignorance *[agnōsia]* of foolish men" (1 Peter 2:15). The people who were denying the Resurrection, were refusing to see the obvious, bow to the evidence, learn through observation and experience. It is the same kind of ignorance displayed by those few cranks who still believe that the world is flat; or who deny that the Americans put a man on the moon, preferring to believe it was a propaganda stunt. This is not ignorance which can be corrected. It is stubborn ignorance. Martin Luther displayed it in the matter of the Real Presence in the wafer. Even after it had been proved to him that the Lord's words, "This is my body," employed a metaphor, and were not to be taken literally, he continued to stubbornly declare, "When He says 'This is my body' that is what He means, 'This is my body.'"

That such stubborn ignorance could prevail among the Corinthians over the matter of the Resurrection got to Paul. *"Agnōsia!"* he exploded, "willful ignorance, reprehensible ignorance, culpable ignorance. I speak this to your shame." Here they were, the whole Corinthian church, priding themselves on their wisdom and cleverness, yet falling for this error spread by deliberately ignorant men! "Shame on you!" he says.

Paul turns now to *some changes* (1 Cor. 15:35–57) that evidently must take place, so far as our present bodies are concerned, in the Resurrection. Undoubtedly this passage contains some of the most interesting and awesome revelations in the entire Bible. First, we have *some questions asked:* "But some man will say, How are the dead raised up? and with what body do they come?" (15:35). Doubtless these were the skeptical questions being asked by the Corinthian agnostics. When the Sadducees tried to trap the Lord Jesus with their agnosticism regarding the Resurrection, the Lord Jesus bluntly told them, "Ye do err, not knowing the scriptures, nor the power of God" (Matt. 22:29). Paul assumes that the Corinthians knew their Bibles (Job 19:25; Dan. 12:2–3) and he points them to illustrations from nature. For all around us, in the natural world, God has given abundant evidences that He knows how to raise the dead.

Now we have *some questions answered* (1 Cor. 15:36–57) in a series of statements and revelations that draw back the veil and show us great and marvelous facts about our resurrection bodies. There are to be no less than eight major changes.

First, there is to be *a change of dimension* (15:36–42). Terrestrial bodies are to be changed into celestial bodies. Paul begins by describing *bodies terrestrial,* bodies, that is to say, designed by God to allow us to live on "this terrestrial ball," upon the earth. Even with bodies framed and fashioned to cope with conditions of life on Earth, evidences of resurrection and illustrations of the resurrection principle abound. For instance, sleep is akin to death. We go to sleep often. We do not fear it. When tired, we crave it. A third of our natural lives is spent in suspended animation. Sleep is natural. We go to sleep fully expecting to awaken, in due time, refreshed, invigorated, and renewed. But the natural world has other and even more pointed illustrations.

First, we note, God is *a God of infinite vitality—witness the world of botany* (15:36–38). In the world of botany two principles are established which illustrate resurrection. There is, for instance, *the principle of life beyond death:* "Thou fool, that which thou sowest is not quickened, except it die" (15:36). But the exclamation and the explanation refer us back to the Lord Jesus. We have met this exclamation "Thou fool" before. The Lord used it, in the plural, when talking to His sad and skeptical disciples on the road to Emmaus as the day of Resurrection drew to a close. He had joined them. They had turned their backs on the city and all the stories of the day. They discounted all of them. He walked with them. He talked with them. He opened to them the Scriptures. Their hearts burned within them. However, when they first poured out into this Stranger's ears their doubts and disappointments and disbelief, He said to them, "O fools [O foolish ones], and slow of heart to believe all that the prophets have spoken" (Luke 24:25). The Lord, however, used a gentler word than Paul. He used the word *anoetōs,* which means "a dullard." The word points to a failure to perceive and understand, an unworthy lack of understanding resulting from a failure to reflect upon the facts. Paul uses the word *aphron,* which points, rather, to a "lack of common sense perception of the reality of things natural and spiritual."[10]

Paul was clearly almost out of patience with these Corinthian converts of his, so ready to embrace skepticism, so full of their own ideas and importance, so lacking even in plain common sense regarding the truth. Evidently some had dismissed the truth of Resurrection because they imagined that it meant the reanimation of the exact materials that comprise our present bodies. Those materials, buried or burned, lost at sea, or devoured by wild beasts, or cremated and thrown to the four winds, would certainly be difficult to reassemble—although, of course, a simple matter for an infinite, omniscient, and omnipotent God. If

---

10. Vine, *Expository Dictionary of New Testament Words,* 1:118.

that was the basis of their skepticism they were fools indeed. Paul points them to the everyday example of corn sown into the ground and the ears of grain that resulted.

This is an echo of the Lord's own words regarding His own impending death, burial, and resurrection. He said, "Verily, verily, I say unto you, Except a corn of wheat fall into the ground, and die, it abideth alone; but if it die, it bringeth forth much fruit" (John 12:24). His application was different but His illustration was the same. The corn had to be sown. It had to die. Then it emerged from the soil, changed almost beyond recognition. God has established the principle of life beyond death throughout the entire world of vegetation, from the humblest weed to the tallest tree and the most useful grain.

Not only is the principle of life beyond death established, but *the principle of life with a difference* is established: "And that which thou sowest, thou sowest not that body that shall be, but bare grain, it may chance of wheat, or of some other grain: but God giveth it a body as it hath pleased Him, and to every seed his own body" (1 Cor. 15:37–38). A change of dimension indeed! Note well the phrase "not that body that shall be." That remark alone should put to silence those who imagine that a resurrected body consists of all the scattered particles of dust into which the original body dissolves.

In discussing this entire subject of resurrection, Paul avoids two pitfalls. He does not teach that the body raised is the exact corpse that was buried—although identity survives. The disciples recognized the Lord's resurrection body by the nail prints in His hands and the wound in His side. Paul avoids the other pitfall, for he does not say that the resurrection body is a different body altogether. There is a mysterious blending of the old and the new. We shall recognize and know each other—we shall be that much the same; but we shall be clothed in dazzling splendor and be able to do things of which now we only dream—we shall be that much different. Christ's resurrection body is the prototype of ours. John says, "Beloved, now are we the sons of God, and it doth not yet appear what we shall be: but we know that, when he shall appear, we shall be like him; for we shall see him as he is" (1 John 3:2). Paul is even more revealing. He says that the Lord will "change our vile body" (the word is *tapeinōsis*—our body of humiliation) "that it may be fashioned like unto his glorious body, according to the working *[energeia]* whereby he is able even to subdue all things unto himself" (Phil. 3:21).

What happens when we plant a seed or a bulb in our garden? It dissolves. The outward husk, the material wrappings, fall prey to the action of the sun and the soil. Yet something survives, something no biologist's scalpel or microscope has ever been able to reveal—the life-germ. The outward body perishes, the life-germ, the essence of what the plant is, survives. It is virtually indestructible (corn found in Egyptian tombs, known to have lain there for thousands of years, has been known to germinate and grow when planted). The seed or bulb remains buried. The forces of nature begin the process of disintegration and decay. But, wonder of wonders, the seed, or bulb, begins to push new, living roots downward and a shoot upward. It rises, irresistible through the stubborn soil. And, behold! it is startlingly different from the dry seed and unlovely bulb that was sown. The husk does not rise; the life-germ does not die. The life-germ emerges from the ground in a new body, infinitely more astonishing, complete with leaves, calyx, and corolla, a thing of beauty.

This is true of all plant life. The giant oak grows from an acorn. The mighty cedar grows from a seed as unpretentious as that of the humblest wayside weed. The daffodil is the very bulb that was sown in the fall of the year but its brown dullness is replaced by green and gold. The lovely plant is composed of entirely new particles. "The breathing leaves," says D. M. Panton, "and waxen petals live in the sunshine and the wind, in another world from that of the bulb."[11]

Changed! Yes, indeed, but still identified with what was sown or planted. Wheat, buried in the ground, does not become barley; daffodils do not become tulips. Wheat comes up wheat. You will still be you. I shall still be me. What the seed is when it is sown, that is what it is when it springs up in new life. Yet how vastly different! All winter long the bulb lies dead and dormant, an unattractive thing, hidden in the earth. Then up it springs when the warm sun of springtime kisses its tomb. "Them that sleep in the dust of the earth shall awake!" Daniel said (12:2). Significantly throughout this amazing chapter, written to those doubting Corinthians so very long ago, Paul does not say we are *buried;* he says we are *sown.* I can bury an old boot—and that's an end of it. It will rot and eventually disintegrate. It will never spring up transformed from its tomb. Nobody would think of sowing a boot! We are sown! Planted!

So then, God is a God of infinite vitality. He is also *a God of infinite variety— witness the world of biology:* "All flesh is not the same flesh: but there is one kind of flesh of men, another flesh of beasts, another of fishes, and another of birds" (1 Cor. 15:39). Paul is giving further proof of the creative genius of God. That life should exist in a single form, even that of the humblest amoeba, is a miracle. No biologist can explain it. The modern science of genetics has done much to

---

11. D. M. Panton, *Dawn,* 15 August 1929, n.p.

explain how life operates. It does nothing to explain how it originates. Indeed, all it has done is expose the mind-boggling complexity of even the humblest form of life. We can tinker with the genetic code but, apart from God, we cannot explain where it came from, in all its complexity. The gulf between the inanimate creation and the animate creation is as vast as ever it was. But life exists on this planet, not in just one form but in a bewildering variety of forms. Each creature has its own genetic code. It has its own specialized lifestyle, function, and purpose. Paul lists the more obvious biological categories. He does not start with fishes and ascend through the birds and beasts to man—he would have little patience with Darwin and his disciples. He begins with man, a separate order of creation, as different from the animals as animals are from pine trees or as grass is from limestone.

God, who can fashion thousands of different kinds of bodies, who can create hundreds of thousands of kinds of plants and insects and countless kinds of animals, fishes, and birds; who can create these bodies of ours, engineering marvels; who can fashion bodies for the angels and the cherubim, will have no difficulty at all in making us anew in Resurrection.

Paul moves on from bodies terrestrial to *bodies celestial* (15:40–42a). He sets before us *a contrast:* "There are also celestial bodies, and bodies terrestrial: but the glory of the celestial is one, and the glory of the terrestrial is another" (v. 40). He sets before us *a comparison:* "There is one glory of the sun, and another glory of the moon, and another glory of the stars: for one star differeth from another star in glory" (15:41). He sets before us *a conclusion:* "So also is the resurrection of the dead" (15:42a). The word *celestial* is *epouranios.* It is normally translated "heavenly," but its meaning must be determined by its context. It is used of God the Father (Matt. 18:35), of the place where the Lord Jesus now sits enthroned (Eph. 1:20), of the sphere where all our blessings and battles are (Eph. 1:3; 2:6; 3:10). It is used of the resurrection bodies of believers (1 Cor. 15:49), and here (15:40) of the sun, moon, and stars of space. No doubt we are going to have "heavenly" bodies, the kind of bodies that belong to heavenly beings. The context here, however, contrasts our present "terrestrial" bodies with "celestial" bodies.

The point is that, as soon as Paul gets down to the business of describing what our resurrection bodies are like, he ransacks the terrestrial world for illustrations and then takes us to the celestial world, where sun, moon, and stars, which, indeed, we happily call "heavenly bodies," roam through vast empires, the fringes of which modern astronomy has only begun to explore.

To help us understand what our resurrection bodies will be like, he takes us to a realm where all our concepts of time and space are changed. He intimates that we now have terrestrial bodies, bodies that enable us to live on this one planet. One day we are going to have celestial (heavenly) bodies, bodies that will enable us to roam the vast universe of God. We must always remember that our resurrection body is going to be like that of our risen, ascended Lord.

Paul directs our thoughts, then, to what we now call "outer space" to give us a concept of what a revolutionary change in dimension he has in mind. When astronomers at last found themselves in possession of tools which would allow them to realistically explore the distances between the galaxies, weigh the stars, analyze their composition, track their paths, and measure their speeds, it was very quickly realized that a new yardstick was required to define distances in space. Their new measuring-rod was a light-year—the distance light travels in a single year. Light travels at about 186,000 miles a second, which works out to a round figure of about 6 trillion miles a year. That is just the unit of measure. We really cannot comprehend the measurements about which astronomers talk. Our own galaxy is said to measure 100,000 light-years from rim to rim. That is to say that traveling at 6 trillion miles a year it would still take 100,000 years to cross the galaxy—an empire of some 600 billion billion miles of stars. That is just our own galaxy. There are a hundred billion galaxies in known space besides our own.

Our resurrection bodies will be able to dissolve distance. Traveling at the speed of light, which astronomers say is the fastest entity in the universe, it would still take us 8 years to reach the star Sirius, 26 years to reach Vega, 680 years to reach Polaris, 900 years to reach Rigel in the constellation of Orion. But these stars are in our own backyard, so to speak. Traveling at the speed of light it would take billions of years to reach some of the remote stars.

However, the speed of light, is *not* the fastest thing in the universe. There is something infinitely faster than that—the speed of thought! I had that brought home to me many years ago. When I was a young man I was stationed as a soldier in Palestine and had the opportunity on one occasion to go into the church of the Holy Sepulcher in Jerusalem. A priest was swaying an incense burner, and for the first time in my life I smelled that particularly pungent and penetrating fragrance. A number of years later, at Christmas time, I was walking down State Street in Chicago and went into a Woolworth's store. They were selling manger scenes and, along with them, small incense burners. They had one of them lit, and the moment I entered that store I smelled incense for the second time in my life. *Instantly* I was back in the church of the Holy Sepulcher in Jerusalem in mind, imagination, and thought!

The speed of thought is the fastest thing in the universe. When we get our resurrection bodies we shall be able to travel around the universe at the speed of thought, taking our bodies with us. We shall not need mechanical means of transportation. We shall be able to do it because our resurrection bodies, while physical, will be controlled by the spiritual. There are several examples of this in the New Testament.

John tells how, after the feeding of the five thousand, Jesus sent the disciples across the lake by boat to Capernaum. He Himself stayed behind. Then came the threatening storm, followed by the apparition walking toward them on the wind-driven waves. They had gone "about five and twenty or thirty furlongs," says John, who knew the lake like the back of his hand. This is to say, they were about halfway across. They were afraid. However, Jesus hailed them: "It is I," He said, "be not afraid." John adds this: "Then they willingly received him into the ship: and *immediately* the ship was at the land whither they went" (John 6:21). One moment they were in the middle of the lake. The next moment they were pulling the boat on shore. Jesus had annihilated the distance in between.

While the Samaritan revival was still in force, the evangelist Philip was detached from it by the Holy Spirit and sent to meet a man from Ethiopia to lead him to Christ. Soon afterward, spying an oasis in the desert, the Ethiopian requested baptism. Shortly afterward Philip and the man descended into the water and the man was baptized. Then an astounding thing happened. The man turned to say something to Philip, but Philip was no longer there. We can well imagine that the Ethiopian questioned his servants and searched high and low for his new friend. He simply wasn't there. Luke tells us what happened: "The Spirit of the Lord caught away Philip, that the eunuch saw him no more: and he went on his way rejoicing. But Philip was found at Azotus." He was many miles away at the old Philistine town of Ashdod on the Palestine coastland. One moment he was way south of Gaza. The next he was at Ashdod heading north to the Roman capital of Caesarea (Acts 8:39–40). Incidentally, the word translated "caught away" is *harpazō*. It is used of Paul being caught up to paradise (2 Cor. 12:2, 4). It is used of the Rapture of the saints (1 Thess. 4:17), and of the catching up to heaven of the Man Child (Rev. 12:5). The verb contains the idea of force suddenly being applied.

So, then, our resurrection bodies will experience a change of dimension. They will cease to be limited by the terrestrial bodies we now have, limited by time, matter, and space. Our bodies will be transformed into celestial bodies able to defy gravity and distance.

Next, there will be *a change of destiny:* "It is sown in corruption; it is raised in incorruption" (1 Cor. 15:42b). Right now we have bodies *destined for the grave.* The word for *corruption* is *phthora.* Paul uses it to describe the coming millennial dawn, when creation itself "shall be delivered from the bondage of corruption" (Rom. 8:21). Peter uses the word to describe the corruption of latter-day apostates (2 Peter 2:12). Paul uses the word here to describe the destruction of our bodies by corruption in the grave.

By contrast, in the Resurrection we are going to have bodies *destined for the glory.* We are going to be raised in incorruption. Our resurrection bodies will be absolutely and eternally incorruptible. The Lord's body in Joseph's tomb was thus miraculously preserved in fulfillment of prophecy (Ps. 16:10; Acts 2:27). Our bodies will be miraculously restored, no longer subject to earthly conditions, but made fit to dwell in that "light unapproachable" (1 Tim. 6:16), where God sits enthroned. Our new bodies will be destined for glory!

Paul knew something of that. In his later epistle he tells the Corinthians that he had once been caught up into Paradise. He did not know whether he was in or out of the body. What he experienced was so real he could well have been in the body. He was fully alert to his senses. He could see and smell and taste and touch. On the other hand, his experiences were so extraordinary, so "extra-terrestrial," he could well have been "out of the body" altogether. His experiences were untranslatable (2 Cor. 12:1–4).

When he wrote later to the Philippians he told them that he was "in a strait betwixt two, having a desire to depart, and be with Christ; which is far better" (Phil. 1:23). The word for *desire* is *epithumai,* which is translated "lust" some thirty-one times. In other words, Paul had experienced such a taste of glory that he was now lusting to go to heaven! The word for *depart* is *analuo.* It means "to unloose." It signifies a departure and is used here as a metaphor based on a ship loosing from its moorings. It also carries the idea of returning. So, then, Paul, who knew what the Glory Land was like, lusted to weigh anchor, set sail for that other shore, but also to come back again. Musing on what it was like on the other side he says that it is "far better." Scholars tell us that it would be far better to translate *that* as "far, far better!" Indeed, so great was Paul's desire to thus depart and be with Christ in the Glory Land, God had to give him a thorn in the flesh to keep him in balance. Otherwise he might have become "so heavenly minded as to be of no earthly use" (2 Cor. 12:7).

One day we are going to receive bodies destined for Glory, never to be touched and tainted by corruption ever again.

Then, too, there will be *a change of dress* (1 Cor. 15:43a–b). Right now we have a body *clogged with lust:* "It is sown in dishonour" (15:43a). One day we shall have a body *clothed in light:* "It is raised in power [glory]" (15:43b). The word for dishonor is *atimia.* It carries the ideas of ignominy and disgrace (Rom. 1:26). It is translated "vile" passions (Rom. 9:21), that is, passions of dishonor. By contrast, our resurrection body will be characterized by "power [glory]." The word is *doxa,* which is of frequent and varied use in the New Testament. Paul has just used it to describe the glory of the stars (1 Cor. 15:41). Peter used the word in describing the glory of Christ in His transfiguration (2 Peter 1:17). The word is used to describe the supernatural pouring out from God (Luke 2:9; Acts 22:11) as, for instance, in the Shekinah glory in the pillar of cloud and in the Holy of Holies.[12] All these ideas cluster around our resurrection bodies, to be raised, thus, in splendor.

Again, the natural world provides us with an illustration. Here, for instance, is a caterpillar. It lives out its life as an earthbound, circumscribed grub, crawling in the dust. We can see it as it lifts its little head and stares at the vast expanse of the sky. We know exactly what the little fellow is thinking. It says to itself, "Oh! If only I could fly! If only I had wings! If only I could soar upward to the sky! If only I could catch the rising air currents and wing my way from tree to tree. But I'm only a wretched grub with a lot of legs, crawling up and down the trunks of trees."

Then comes the change. Something akin to death, more akin to death than sleep, overtakes the caterpillar. It feels it coming. It makes a coffin for itself, crawls inside, and dies to the only life it ever knew, the life of a caterpillar. Time passes and still the coffin hangs where it was placed with what was once a caterpillar inside. But then, suddenly, comes a mysterious call. Only the caterpillar hears it. It bursts out of its coffin. But it has been changed! It entered a caterpillar; it comes out a butterfly, changed beyond all recognition.

For the egg laid by a butterfly does not hatch a baby butterfly but a larva, different from a butterfly in the absence of wings, in the shape of its body, in the structure of its mouth, in the length of its antennae, in its internal structure, and in its lifestyle. In the case of the caterpillar, when the larva is fully fed, it becomes a passive pupa. Within the pupa case the organs break down and are reconstructed to form those of the adult. There is, indeed, a complete metamorphosis, marked off by a period of complete quiescence which intervenes between the larval stage and the butterfly stage of life. The caterpillar, then, sets before us our

---

12. Vine, *Expository Dictionary of New Testament Words,* 1:153.

earth-bound life. The chrysalis pictures our period of rest in death. The reconstructed butterfly mirrors our resurrection body.[13]

Remember, it is exactly the same creature that comes out of that little coffin that goes into it—but it has been changed. It has had a change of dress. It was sown a caterpillar, it was raised a butterfly. It is sown in dishonor, it is raised in glory! It spreads its gorgeous wings and soars upward to the sky in a blaze of beauty and color. So also is the resurrection of the dead. We shall be arrayed in light. Our very garments will become white and glistening as did the Lord's on the Mount of Transfiguration (Matt. 17:2; Luke 9:29).

There will also be *a change of disposition* (1 Cor. 15:43c–d). Our body will be sown a feeble body: "it is sown in weakness"; it will be raised a flawless body: "it is raised in power." Not only do our bodies get old and frail and sick, but much of the temptation to which we succumb comes by way of the body. The body itself is not evil, as the gnostics believed. The human body is a tribute to the genius of the Creator. However, it does often enough make itself the willing ally of sin, just as it can become the temple and instrument of the Holy Spirit.

The medieval church encouraged extraordinary measures to put the body down. Men retired into monasteries and women into nunneries to escape the temptations of the world, only to discover they took their lusts with them behind the cloister walls. They beat themselves, starved themselves, flogged themselves with chains, and wore irritating hair shirts next to their skin.[14]

God has a much better way than that to deal with these weak bodies of ours. He cleanses us in the precious blood of Christ. He regenerates us. He makes our bodies the temple of His Holy Spirit and calls us to present them as a living sacrifice and as instruments of service.

---

13. D. M. Panton, *Dawn,* n.p.
14. The most extraordinary example of the extremes to which people would go to mortify the body is the case of Simon Styles, an ascetic who lived in the fourth century. His feats of fasting, alone, were almost beyond belief. On one occasion he had himself walled up in a monastery for the entire period of Lent. He devised all kinds of fiendish means of self-torture. He ended up on a pillar. He moved to a hillside, not far from the monastery, and sat chained to a pillar, six feet high, with a heavy iron collar around his neck. As time went on, he increased the height of his pillar until it was dozens of feet high. There he perched. His disciples had to climb a ladder to take him what scraps of food he would condescend to eat. Throughout the bitter frosts of thirty Syrian winters and the scorching heat of thirty Syrian summers he sat upon his perch, disdaining any shelter from the elements.

Even so, all too often we stumble and fall and the agent of our downfall is our weak body. The Lord's ultimate answer is to give us a new body altogether.

The classic example is that of Peter, James, and John in the Garden of Gethsemane. The Lord had told them that He was overwhelmed with sorrow and that He was going yonder to pray. He asked them to watch and pray with Him. Before the sun set on the morrow He would be dead and buried. In between lay Gabbatha and Golgotha. Would they watch and pray? Of course they would! But we know what happened. They fell asleep. Their bodies let them down. They were exhausted and overwhelmed with sorrow themselves (Luke 22:45). They were unable to beat the thought that their Beloved was going to leave them and go back home to heaven. He woke them up. They fell asleep again. He understood. He said, "The spirit indeed is willing, but the flesh is weak" (Matt. 26:41).

One of these days we are going to have a body of power! It will never get tired, never grow old, never stumble, never fall, never get ill, never wear out, never yield to sin. Instead, it will be an invincible fortress, an incredible force at the disposal of the Lord for the development of all His future plans for the universe.

When the Lord's work at Calvary and in the underworld of hades was finished, He did not abandon His body in the tomb. It was now, forever, a part of Him. It was an instrument of power, of infinite worth. When His sojourn in hades was complete, He came marching out of those nether regions bearing with Him the keys of that place. And, on the way, He stopped by the tomb to pick up His body. He took it back to heaven with Him and there He sits, enthroned at the right hand of the Majesty on high, sitting on God's throne in a human body, wonder of wonders! and with every right to be there because He is God over all, blessed forevermore!

Battle-scarred it is, indeed, but it is a body of power. On the evening of the resurrection day the Lord visited the disciples in the Upper Room. There is a touch of humor in what He did. He did not go up the stairs and knock on the door. That would have scared the poor fellows out of their wits! Besides, Peter would have moved all the furniture against the door by now as protection against the temple police. No, indeed! He simply came in through the wall!

How He did that we don't know—yet. Our high school physics lessons tell us that all matter is composed of atoms, and atoms, consisting of energy, motion, and phenomena, are mostly empty space. We do not know how the Lord took the empty space of the atoms, or their equivalent, which comprised His resurrection body, and passed them through the empty space of the atoms which made up that wall. We only know He did it. He knows how it's done—not surprising, since He invented matter in the first place.

Once inside the Upper Room the Lord calmed His terrified disciples, assuring them that it was He Himself. He invited them to come and touch Him and examine His wounds. Then, to prove that His body was real, solid, and substantial, He ate a meal before them. Then, just as they were beginning to get used to His being there, He vanished. He did similar things on other occasions. As Luke put it, "He showed himself alive after his passion by many infallible proofs, being seen of them forty days" (Acts 1:3).

One day we are going to have a body with the same extraordinary powers, a body "like unto his glorious body." It is, of course, impossible for the angels of God, who inhabit those realms of light, ever to be jealous. That is not in their nature. But suppose for a moment it were possible for an angel to be jealous. I know what they'd be jealous of. There you go, down Hallelujah Avenue on your way to your ivory palace on Beulah Boulevard. You walk past Michael and Gabriel. You give them a friendly hail. As soon as you have gone on, Gabriel turns to Michael and says, "I say, Mike, I wish I had a body like *his*. It's just like HIS!"

Next there will be *a change of dynamics* (1 Cor. 15:44), because right now we have bodies *engineered for this world:* "it is sown a natural body" (15:44a). One day, however, we shall have bodies engineered for *that world:* "it is raised a spiritual body." Paul adds, "There is a natural body, and there is a spiritual body" (15:44b).

This raises some interesting issues. For many years I was puzzled by the statement concerning the Lord Jesus that He is "the first begotten of the dead" (Rev. 1:5; Col. 1:18). There were at least three people raised from the dead in the Old Testament and He Himself raised Jairus's daughter, the widow of Nain's son, and Lazarus. So then, Elijah raised one, Elisha raised two, and Jesus raised three. That means that there were six people raised from the dead before He was. If we count Jonah who, some believe, actually died in the whale's belly and was raised again, then the Lord Jesus was number 8.[15]

---

15. The spiritual significance of the number eight in the Bible is interesting. It has to do with resurrection and with a new beginning. In the octave the number 8 is significant. The eighth note is the same as the first note only raised high on the scale. In music, in color, and in the days of the week the eighth is a new beginning. Jesus rose on the eighth day. By Gematria (substituting Greek letters in a word for their numerical equivalent) the name "Jesus" yields the number 888. Thus in His human, saving name, the Lord Jesus is marked by resurrection. "I am the resurrection," He told Martha (John 11:25).

How could number 8 be number 1? The problem perplexed me until I studied this verse (1 Cor. 15:44). The whole point is that all the others were sown a natural body and raised a natural body. Therefore, they died again. Lazarus had to be loosed from his grave clothes. Jesus rose right through His! With all the others, the call to resurrection came from the outside. Jesus rose of His own volition (John 10:17–18). By virtue of our identification with Him, His resurrection becomes our resurrection (Rom. 6:3–5). We shall be sown a natural body and raised a spiritual body. Our present bodies are subject to everyday natural laws, our spiritual bodies are subject to higher spiritual laws as, for instance, are the bodies of the angels. They can appear and disappear at will. They can appear as angels or as men. The same angels appeared to Abraham as men and to Lot as angels (Gen. 18:1–2; 19:1, 15). At the same time they appeared to be men to the Sodomites (19:5). Their appearance can dazzle and strike fear. These are some of the known properties of a spiritual body. Doubtless there are many more. For one thing, angels can miraculously open prison doors (Acts 12:5–10) and they can control the ordinary forces of nature (Rev. 7:1).

What other potentials will be ours, when we receive spiritual bodies, can only be surmised. It is said that nobody has ever used more than 2 percent of his total mental capacity, not even Einstein, Beethoven, or Shakespeare. What is the other 98 percent for? If Adam had not sinned, doubtless he would have used all his mental capacity—naming all the animals was, in itself, an extraordinary feat (just try renaming them!). If he had not sinned, doubtless he would have begun by ruling the garden, gone on to rule the globe, and, possibly, ended up by ruling the galaxy. When we receive our resurrection bodies we shall be able to use all the vast, unsuspected resources, as yet untapped, which God built into the human brain when He fashioned it, with omniscient genius, from the dust of the earth. Who can tell what limits there will be to our achievements throughout the endless ages of eternity?

Next, there is to be *a change of dynasty* (1 Cor. 15:45–52). Paul discusses, first, *the measure of this change* (15:45–49) and then *the miracle of this change* (15:50–52). We begin with *a radical change* (15:45–46). There is to be a *new orientation:* "And so it is written, The first man Adam was made a living soul: the last Adam was made a quickening spirit" (15:45). The quotation comes from Genesis 2:7 (the exact expression is found in the Septuagint). The "last Adam" refers to the Lord Jesus, the Federal Head of a new human race.

We need to go back, here, to the very beginning of the human race. When God made man He did something unique, something He did not do with the animal creation. In the first place, He personally fashioned Adam's body with His own hands (Gen. 2:7—the word *formed* indicates the work of a potter as illustrated in Isa. 64:8). Then He breathed into his nostrils the breath of life so that Adam became "a living soul."

When God created the animals He simply spoke them into existence. Each animal became a living body with a soulish capacity and thus separated from the plant world as a higher order of life. Then to each animal He gave a governing principle to control its behavior. We call that governing principle instinct. An animal does what it does because it is what it is. Each kind of animal is locked into a particular behavior pattern. If it is a bee, it builds a hive, gathers nectar, and makes honey. If it is a salmon, it returns to the stream where it was born to spawn and die. Animals do these things by instinct. Each species follows the blueprint that governs its behavior. In the domesticated animals the hand and authority of man can raise them even higher.

When God created Man, He gave him higher mental powers than was ever given to an animal. No animal admires a sunset or writes a symphony. When God breathed into Adam's body the breath of life, he became "a living soul," but a soul with something no animal has, a soul with a spiritual capacity, an ability to know, love, and worship God and to be like God. For, instead of locking man into a behavior pattern, as He did the animals, God gave man instead a *spirit*. He did not want puppets but people, not just super-animals, but men, made in His own image and after His own likeness.

The soul of man included intellect, emotions, and will, so that man could think and feel and decide. After the Fall, God added conscience to monitor his behavior. The soul is the real person, who inhabits the body. The soul is deathless. It is the soul which leaves the body at death. It is the seat of our self-consciousness and personality. At the Resurrection the soul is reunited with the body, for better or for worse, for all eternity.

It was God's intention that the human spirit be indwelt and energized by the Holy Spirit. Before the Fall, Adam was man as God intended man to be, man inhabited by God. When sin entered, the Holy Spirit vacated the human spirit. Man in sin no longer has the governing principle of an indwelling Holy Spirit to govern his behavior. As a result, he is described as "lost." Neither the intellect, emotions, will, conscience, nor senses are adequate substitutes for ruling and guiding man. That is why Jesus told Nicodemus he needed to be born again (John 3:3) and explains why the new birth is so vitally necessary (3:12–13). When we accept Christ we are cleansed with His blood and our spirit is again indwelt by the Holy Spirit. He comes back into the *human* spirit to provide the guidance and government we lack by natural birth as descendants of fallen Adam. We can now begin to live as God intended us to live. There is one flaw in this process—we do not yet have our resurrection bodies (Rom. 8:22–23). Once we receive them the process will be perfected forever. We shall, indeed, be like Jesus.

The Lord Jesus, in contrast with all this, "was made a quickening spirit." He had a perfect body, fashioned by the Holy Spirit in the virgin's womb (Luke 1:35–37), a true human body like ours, but untainted by sin and free from His mother's blood. He had a soul, too, which was truly human while at the same time truly divine. He was "God manifest in flesh." His spirit was not only inhabited by the Holy Spirit, He was "made a quickening spirit." His center of being was not the soul but the spirit. His whole being was totally taken up into the life of the Spirit. He was, indeed, man inhabited by God. He was also God inhabiting man. As Paul puts it elsewhere, "[He], being in the form of God, thought it not robbery to be equal with God: but made himself of no reputation . . . and was made in the likeness of men" (Phil. 2:6–7). Or, as John put it, "In the beginning was the Word, and the Word was with God, and the Word was God . . . and the Word was made flesh, and dwelt among us" (John 1:1, 14). He was, in other words, "the last Adam" and "the second man" (1 Cor. 15:47).

In the resurrection we shall know this new orientation for ourselves. Instead of being soul-oriented, as we are now, we shall be spirit-oriented. Our present, fledgling attempts to "walk in the Spirit" (Rom. 8:9) will become an uninterrupted way of life. We, too, shall be taken up into the life of the Spirit. Our nature, person, and personality, our intellect, emotions, and will, our physical frame and vital senses will be under the control of the Spirit of God. The life-giving Holy Spirit already inhabits the believer's spirit. The full potential of all this, however, awaits the day when we receive our resurrection bodies.

There is not only a new orientation, there is also *a noted order:* "Howbeit that was not first which is spiritual, but that which is natural; and afterward that which is spiritual" (1 Cor. 15:46). That is the order of experience in a sin-cursed world, for children of Adam's ruined race. We begin life in Adam under the control of the natural. We have a natural birth. We obey natural laws. We are occupied with natural things. We have natural desires, aspirations, and ambitions. As natural beings we know little of the supernatural and nothing of the spiritual (2:14). Our lives tend toward evil because the natural man is born a sinner.

When we came under the convicting work of the Holy Spirit we learned that there was another world, another way of life—the spiritual. When we responded to the claims of Christ we were born again (1 Peter 1:23; John 3:6). That was the order—first the natural, then the spiritual. Obviously we have to be born before we can be born again. The new supersedes the old.

There is not only a radical change, there is also *a racial change* (1 Cor. 15:47–49). Paul enumerates three new things which should characterize the regenerated life of the believer now in anticipation of the resurrected life of the believer in a day yet to come.

There is *a new Lord:* "The first man is of the earth, earthy: the second man is the Lord from heaven" (15:47). Adam was made of clay, he was "earthy" (Gen. 2:7). He came out of the earth, proved himself to be earthy, and went back to the earth. That was the first man! The second man was from heaven. He came down from heaven, proved Himself to be heavenly, the grave could not hurt Him or hold Him, and He went back to heaven. His essential link with heaven marked His path on earth. He spoke of His Father as being in heaven (Matt. 6:9). At His baptism the heavens were opened to acknowledge Him (3:16). He talked to Nicodemus about "heavenly things" (John 3:12). John commented, "No man hath ascended up to heaven, but he that came down from heaven, even the Son of man which is in heaven" (3:13).

A new Lord! Some want to discard the title from this verse. Let it stand! It was as "the Lord from heaven" that Paul knew Him. The other apostles knew Him as "Jesus of Nazareth." So far as we know, Paul never knew Jesus "according to the flesh." He certainly never knew the human Jesus intimately as did the Twelve. He first knew Him as the risen, ascended Lord. As such he acknowledged Him (Acts 9:5–6). All his subsequent life and ministry was colored by his unique view of Jesus as "the Lord from heaven."

There is also *a new life:* "As is the earthy, such are they also that are earthy: and as is the heavenly, such are they also that are heavenly" (1 Cor. 15:48). Paul is pursuing for a moment, the practical implications of resurrection truth. We once shared in Adam's life, the life of fallen man. Its rags still cling to us. Adam was made in the image and likeness of God. His descendants, born after the Fall, were made in the image and likeness of Adam (Gen. 5:1–3). We inherited a sin nature from Adam (Ps. 51:5). "As is the earthy, such are they also that are earthy." We were sinners by birth, sinners by choice, and sinners by practice.

"As is the heavenly, such are they also that are heavenly." Where once we shared Adam's life, now we share the life of Christ. We are actually seated with Christ "in heavenly places" (Eph. 2:6). Our citizenship is in heaven (Phil. 3:20). Our home is in heaven. Our Beloved is in heaven. A new life, indeed!

Furthermore, there is *a new likeness:* "And as we have borne the image of the earthy, we shall also bear the image of the heavenly" (1 Cor. 15:49). Right now, even though we have new life in Christ, we still bear the image of our father Adam. Man was created to be "the image and glory of God," as Paul has already reminded his readers (11:7). He was to be a visible representation of God. He was intended to correspond to the Divine Original. Thanks to Adam's fall the image *(eikon)* of God in man is sadly defaced. However, vestiges of it still remain. Man, even in his fallen state, can be very noble and very brave. He can often display creative genius. He can show love of goodness and beauty. Just the same the marks of the Fall are very deep. Our thoughts, words, and deeds all bear the marks of spiritual blindness and moral decay.

The Lord Jesus, by contrast, was man as God intended man to be. He was a perfect man. There was not a single flaw in His character. He was a perfect, visible representation of God. He perfectly corresponded to the original. Jesus could say, "He that hath seen me hath seen the Father" (John 14:9). There was not one particle of difference. What the Father was, He was; what the Father said, He said; what the Father did, He did. As we have borne the image of the fallen man, so we shall bear the image of the perfect man. In our resurrection bodies, free from sin, we shall reflect the image and glory of God throughout the universe while the eternal ages roll. Such is the measure of the change.

Paul turns now to *the mystery of the change* (1 Cor. 15:50–52). There is, first of all, *a great impossibility:* "Now this I say, brethren, that flesh and blood cannot inherit the kingdom of God; neither doth corruption inherit incorruption" (15:50). The Lord Jesus, in His incarnation, assumed a body of flesh and blood. The blood that poured through His veins was poured out for our sins at Calvary (1 Peter 1:7). The Holy Spirit tells us that the Lord Jesus "by his own blood . . . entered . . . into the holy place, having obtained eternal redemption for us" (Heb. 9:12). Just as the blood of the sacrificial goat was taken by the high priest into the Holy of Holies and sprinkled upon the mercy seat to show that the sacrifice had been accomplished, so the Lord Jesus has presented His most precious blood in the true Holy of Holies and placed it upon the Mercy Seat in heaven. When He appeared in the Upper Room, after His resurrection, He described His body as being a body of "flesh and bones" (Luke 24:39), not flesh and blood. The inference is that a resurrection body, operating according to different laws from a natural body, has no more need for blood. In a natural body "the life of the flesh is in the blood" (Lev. 17:11).

The expression "flesh and blood" has passed into our language as synonymous with one's kinfolk. We say, "He's our own flesh and blood."[16] We use it to speak of our natural being as when we say, for instance, "It's more than flesh and blood can stand." The Lord used the expression in this way when, after Peter's great confession, Jesus said to him, "Blessed art thou, Simon Bar-jona, for flesh and blood hath not revealed it unto thee" (Matt. 16:17).

So far as we are concerned, the expression "flesh and blood" points to our physical, moral, and natural relationship to Adam. It speaks of our mortal bodies and our perishable nature. Nothing of that kind can inherit the kingdom of God, a sphere which is spiritual, immortal, and eternal. We need a new nature and a new body if we are to live where Jesus now lives. That is why Jesus set the great impossibility before Nicodemus—"Except a man be born again, he cannot see the kingdom of God" (John 3:3).

Now comes *a great imperative* (1 Cor. 15:51–52). There is, first of all, *Rapture for some:* "Behold, I shew you a mystery; we shall not all sleep" (15:51a). That is a reasonable inference, raised to the status of an absolute certainty by divine revelation. It stands to reason that if the resurrection of the dead is to take place at some specific point in time, there will be many living believers on earth when it happens. The question is, what will happen to them? Will they first have to die so that they too can be raised in their turn? That hardly seems likely. The whole point of Resurrection is to deal decisively with death. What will happen to them, then? Not Resurrection, but Rapture. They will not sleep. God will make some provision for them. It sounds good enough, but it lacks the ring of absolute certainty. That certainty can come only by divine revelation. Paul says little more about it here because he has already written about it fully elsewhere: "This we say unto you by the word of the Lord, that we which are alive and remain unto the coming of the Lord," he says, "shall not prevent [precede] them which are asleep. For the Lord himself shall descend from heaven with a shout, with the voice of the archangel, and with the trump of God: and the dead in Christ shall rise first: then we which are alive and remain shall be caught up together with them in the clouds, to meet the Lord in the air: and so shall we ever be with the Lord. Wherefore comfort one another with these words" (1 Thess. 4:15–18). That settles it! Rapture for some.

---

16. It is significant in this connection, however, that when God presented Eve to Adam he did not call her his own flesh and blood. Interestingly enough, he called her his own flesh and bones (Gen. 2:25). Perhaps this prefigures the bride of Christ and pictures our future bodies being like His resurrection body in this regard.

And *renewal for all* (1 Cor. 15:51b–52). We are to *note what* (15:51b–52a). The Lord's coming will be both sure and sudden: "But we shall all be changed, in a moment, in the twinkling of an eye." A friend of mine was preaching on this text some years ago, before the advent of tape recorders. A lady in the audience took down his message in shorthand and then typed it up and mailed copies to various friends. A copy eventually came his way and he was both annoyed and amused to see that she had made a ludicrous typing mistake. In the sentence "We shall all be changed," she had, unfortunately, left out the letter *c,* so it read "We shall all be hanged!" We can be thankful God has something very much better than that in store for us.

Changed! As the caterpillar is changed! It takes time, however, to change a caterpillar into a butterfly. At the coming of Christ the change for all those who love the Lord, whether living or dead, whether resurrected or raptured, will be instantaneous. In the early dawn of time, this same omnipotent Lord simply had to speak two words— *"Light be!"* and light was! And to this very day no one can tell us what light is. It is one of the most mysterious entities in the universe. We do not know what it is, whether it is particles or waves, although we know a great deal about what it does. It travels at an inconceivable velocity. It can pass unsullied through a grimy window. It is essential to life and growth in living things. Its speed is always constant. When passed through water it bends. When passed through a prism it reveals itself to be comprised of seven beautiful colors. It is related to the very essence of things—the equation $E = MC^2$ (energy equals mass multiplied by the speed of light squared) ushered in the nuclear age. All this and more as a result of two words from an omnipotent, omniscient God!

All He will have to say, on the resurrection morn, will be *"Life be!"* Instantly "we shall all be changed!" Paul can hardly wait to go on telling us how. Just another half verse and he'll continue listing the dramatic and dynamic changes we can anticipate with eager expectation.

"In a moment!" says Paul. The word is *atomos,* from which we get our English word *atom.* The word literally means "that which cannot be divided." It is derived from the negative (*a*) joined to *temnō,* "to cut." For centuries the atom was not only considered to be the smallest particle of matter, it was believed to be indivisible. Nobody had every dreamed of splitting one, or comprehended what enormous power an atom contained, until very recent times. The transformation and transfiguration of believers, living and dead, will take place in an atom of time. In a moment! It will take place "in the twinkling of an eye." The word for *twinkling* is *rhipē* (cognate to *rhiptō,* which means "to hurl"—a javelin, for instance). The word denotes rapid movement. The transformation of our bodies, living or dead, will take place in the split second it takes for an eye to gleam.

We are to *note when* (15:52b–c), pondering both *the trumpet:* "At the last trump, for the trumpet shall sound"; and *the transformation:* "and the dead shall be raised incorruptible, and we shall be changed." Note the drumbeat of certainty—shall! shall! shall! There is no power in earth or hell which can stop it.

Trumpets figured prominently in the national life of Israel. A loud trumpet heralded the year of jubilee (Lev. 25:9). There was a feast of trumpets. This celebrated Israel's new (civil) year and sounded the coming of the penitential day of atonement (Lev. 23:27; Ezek. 45:20). A trumpet was sounded by God at the giving of the Law at Sinai (Heb. 12:18–21).

The final ingathering of the Jewish exiles to the land of Israel will be accompanied by angelic activity and with "a great sound of a trumpet" (Matt. 24:31). Trumpets figure prominently, indeed, in connection with the last days. The Rapture of the church is accompanied not only by the Lord's shout and the voice of the archangel but also by the trump of God.

In the Apocalypse, the second series of judgments are heralded by trumpet-blowing angels. As each one sounds, another disaster overtakes the earth. These trumpets are blown by angels and are not synonymous with the trump of God of 1 Thessalonians 4:16. The last of these seven angelic trumpets warns the world of the rapidly approaching consummation of things and of the long-delayed outpouring of the wrath of God upon this planet (Rev. 11:15–19). We cannot be sure as to why Paul calls the resurrection-rapture trump "the last trump." Perhaps it is so called because the rapture of the church clears the way for end-time events to take place.

"The trumpet shall sound and the dead shall be raised incorruptible, and we shall be changed." Paul sometimes identifies himself with those who are in the grave when Christ comes, and sometimes with those who are alive and remain, as here (1 Cor. 6:14; 2 Cor. 2:14; 5:1–10; Phil. 1:21–24; 3:20). We must never lose sight of "the blessed hope" (Titus 2:13), but, at the same time, we must be prepared to die. Either way our future is assured.

Paul now comes back to the changes that will take place in our bodies at the Resurrection. There will be *a change of durability:* "For this corruptible must put on incorruption, and this mortal must put on immortality" (1 Cor. 15:53). There will be no more decay and no more death. We are going to live forever.

Away back, in the early dawn of time, men lived like the gods of Olympus. Methuselah lived to be 969 years of age. Jared, Enoch's father, lived to be 962.

Adam lived to be 930. Mahalaleel, Enoch's grandfather, was a mere youngster, dying at only 895 years of age! We can only surmise why people lived so long in those days. Perhaps, the human race being so young, men still retained some lingering vestige of the immortality for which the human body was originally engineered. Or perhaps climatic conditions on earth were quite different before the Flood. But, live as long as they did, in the end death hunted them down. After the Flood, human longevity was drastically curtailed until, by the time of Moses, the rule was "the days of our years are threescore years and ten; and if by reason of strength they be fourscore years, yet is their strength labour and sorrow; for it is soon cut off, and we fly away" (Ps. 90:10).

But we are going to live forever—in a land of fadeless day, in a city where they pave their streets with gold and build their walls with jasper and where they count not time by years. We are going to live on and on. We shall outlast all the suns and stars of space. We shall live beyond the reach of sin and death in a tumult of "joy indescribable, unspeakable, and full of glory!"

Finally, there will be *a change of dominion* (1 Cor. 15:54–57). In drawing this amazing discussion to a close, Paul points to three things. First, *the fulfillment of Scripture* (15:54–55). Look at *this wonderful saying:* "So when this corruptible shall have put on incorruption, and this mortal shall have put on immortality, then shall be brought to pass the saying that is written, Death is swallowed up in victory" (15:54). The quotation is from Isaiah 25:8. The old dynasty of sin and death is now no more.

Paul reminded the Romans about this old dynasty under which we were born and subject to which we lived as hopeless slaves until we met Christ. "Sin hath reigned unto death," he told them. Worse still, "death reigned" (Rom. 5:21, 14, 17). It was a hopeless picture, one for which no religion had the answer. There was new light, however, brought into the darkness of this dreadful regime by Christ. Sin and death ganged up on Him—in vain! "Christ being raised from the dead dieth no more; death hath no more dominion over him" (6:9). Because of the believer's identification with Christ, we can have a taste of victory even now. Paul could write, "Let not sin therefore reign in your mortal body . . . sin shall not have dominion over you" (6:12, 14). The old monarch has now been deposed. Victory is possible in Christ. All of which is very encouraging, or very depressing, to the believer in the measure in which he lives in Romans 8 or Romans 7. Most of us have known what a checkered thing victory so often turns out to be.

However, the best is yet ahead. The present state of affairs continues because we have not yet received our resurrection bodies. Corruption is to be replaced by incorruption, mortality by immortality, death by victory! Victory at last! Victory indeed! Victory forever! Isaiah's words anticipate the millennium, when death will be swallowed up by victory. Paul's quotation anticipated eternity.

We are invited, moreover, to look at *this wonderful song:* "O death, where is thy sting? O grave, where is thy victory?" (1 Cor. 15:55). The quotation is from Hosea 13:14. Death is seen here as a poisonous serpent, but having had its fangs removed, threatening, perhaps, but harmless to the believer. Hosea's prophecy was given against the background of the dissolution of the northern kingdom of Israel. There had been a rash of dynastic murders in Samaria. Zachariah was murdered by Shallum, he was murdered by Menahem. Pekahiah was murdered by Pekah and Pekah by Hoshea, who was thereafter a prisoner in Assyria. The death of the nation was imminent. "I will ransom them from the power of the grave; I will redeem them from death," was Jehovah's promise, even as He was preparing to put an end to the northern kingdom and send its people into exile. There are two concepts of redemption in the Old Testament—redemption by power and redemption by purchase, both of which are present in this verse, to give the promise exceptional emphasis. The word for *ransom* is *pādāh,* "to redeem by power—in the strength of legal right." The word for *redeem* is *ga'al,* "to redeem by purchase by virtue of kinship right." Then comes the rest of the promise: "O death, I will be thy plagues: O grave, I will be thy destruction." Again, Paul lifts the promise from the millennial to the eternal.

The way the prophecy is introduced by Paul it is a song of triumph to ring out across the universe on the resurrection morn. It is a duet. As "those who are alive and remain" leap toward the sky, they will shout, "O death, where is thy sting?" Death will gnash at them in vain. Then, as all those who, down through the long ages longed for the Lord's return in vain, come bounding from their graves, they will sing, "O grave, where is thy victory?"

Paul has about finished this magnificent passage. He has a few closing remarks of a practical nature to add before putting down his pen. He has a word about *the fact of sin:* "The sting of death is sin; and the strength of sin is the law" (1 Cor. 15:56). Death! Sin! The law! A terrible trio for the unregenerate man. The law activates sin, and sin activates death. Resurrection does away with all three! That Law activates sin is obvious upon a moment's reflection. Paul saw it clearly enough. He said, "For I was alive without the law once: but when the commandment came, sin revived, and I died" (Rom. 7:9). He says, "I had not known sin, but by the law: for I had not known lust, except the law had said, Thou shalt not covet"

(7:7).[17] Law stirs into active life man's inbred rebellion. A sign says, "Keep off the grass." Up until we saw that sign we had not the slightest interest in the grass, but the moment we see the sign we experience an urge to plant at least one foot on it. A sign says, "Do not touch," and at once we want to touch. All the things God says we are not to do suddenly become all the things we want to do. Law activates sin. It also exposes it. Paul could run his eye down the Ten Commandments in his unregenerate days and pride himself that he had kept them all—until he came to the tenth one, the one which said, "Thou shalt have no evil desire." That one got him. It branded him a sinner. Sin had always been immoral. The Law also made it illegal and grounds for criminal prosecution at the bar of God, truly a terrifying prospect.

The Law activates sin. Sin, in turn, activates death, for "the wages of sin is death" (Rom. 6:23). Had there been no sin there would have been no death. As it is, we are all subject to what he calls "the law of sin and death" (8:2), and only in Christ can deliverance be found from the tyranny of this law. The law of sin and death is the one great law of human behavior, which explains why people do what they do. Any system of psychology that ignores the working of this law cannot be reliable. Resurrection activates that full and final deliverance from this law, deliverance purchased for us at Calvary and guaranteed by the resurrection of Christ.

No wonder Paul mentions next *the fullness of salvation:* "But thanks be to God, which giveth us the victory through our Lord, Jesus Christ" (1 Cor. 15:57). For it is all well and good to stake our all on the certainty of Resurrection at the coming again of Christ. Ours, however, is also a present-tense salvation. The word *giveth* indicates a continuing process. The Lord's victory over sin and death can be made good in our everyday Christian lives by the Holy Spirit (Rom. 8:2).

Challenges! Changes! And now, in closing, *choices* (1 Cor. 15:58). Belief always impacts behavior. Paul militates against any attitude on our part that would make belief in the second coming of Christ an excuse for sitting back and doing nothing to further the cause of Christ in this world (1 Thess. 4:11). "Occupy till I come" is the Lord's own express command (Luke 19:13).

So Paul issues a call to *work—with an eye on the rules:* "Therefore, my beloved brethren, be ye steadfast, unmoveable, always abounding in the work of the Lord" (1 Cor. 15:58a). The second coming of Christ and all its attendant wonders ought to be spur enough for us to dig in our heels. The word *steadfast* is *hedraios.* It means to be seated. It suggests that you have settled your own personal convic-

---

17. See John Phillips, *Exploring Romans.*

tions about these great truths. Nobody is going to change them. You are not going to be lured away from them by some wile of the Devil. The word *unmovable* is *ametakinetōs*. It means to be firm. Having settled what we believe, the thing is to get going for God—"always abounding in the work of the Lord." With such glorious prospects before us, we should redouble our efforts to serve the Lord.

We are to *work*, moreover, *with an eye on the reward:* "Forasmuch as ye know that your labour is not in vain in the Lord" (15:58b). Some think that working for reward is an unworthy motive. Paul does not think so. He himself was eager to receive the crowns God offers for commitment to the cause of Christ. There's work enough for everyone.

What a chapter! One day not only to be with Jesus, but to be like Him forever. Well might we sing with John Nelson Darby,

> And is it so, I shall be like Thy Son?
> Is this the grace that He for me hath won?
> Father of glory, thought beyond all thought—
> In glory to His own blest likeness wrought.
>
> Yes it must be—Thy love had not its rest
> Were Thy redeemed not with Thee fully blessed,
> That love that gives not as the world, but shares
> All it possesses with its loved co-heirs.

So, then, Paul has dealt with divisions in the church, with discipline in the church, with difficulties in the church, and with disbelief in the church. He now has a few closing comments.

PART 6

Conclusion

1 Corinthians 16:1–24

A. Needs (16:1–9)
  1. Paul—his common sense about collections (16:1–4)
    a. The rule (16:1–2)
      (1) A similar pattern (16:1)
      (2) A systematic pattern (16:2)
        (a) Not haphazard (16:2a)
        (b) Not high-pressure (16:2b)
    b. The resolve (16:3–4)
      (1) They should suggest the men who should take the love gift to Jerusalem (16:3a)
      (2) He would send the men who would take the love gift to Jerusalem (16:3b–4)
        (a) He would positively accredit them (16:3b)
        (b) He would perhaps accompany them (16:4)
  2. Paul—his coming soon to Corinth (16:5–9)
    a. His impending plans (16:5–6)
      (1) When he would like to arrive (16:5)
      (2) What he would like to arrange (16:6)
    b. His immediate plans (16:7–9)
      (1) To postpone his visit to Europe (16:7)
      (2) To prolong his visit in Ephesus (16:8–9)
        (a) His plan (16:8)
        (b) His place (16:9)
            i. The great opportunities there (16:9a)
            ii. The great opposition there (16:9b)
B. News (16:10–12)
  1. A word about his beloved Timothy (16:10–11)
    a. He was a timid man (16:10)
      (1) Paul accepts his weakness (16:10a)
      (2) Paul acknowledges his work (16:10b)
    b. He was a true man (16:11)
      (1) A caution (16:11a)
      (2) A command (16:11b)
      (3) A comment (16:11c)
  2. A word about his brother Apollos (16:12)
    a. What Paul sought (16:12a)

b. What Paul saw (16:12b–c)
   (1) The present will of Apollos (16:12b)
   (2) The promised willingness of Apollos (16:12c)
C. Notes (16:13–24)
  1. Some practical comments (16:13–14)
  2. Some personal comments (16:15–18)
    a. The house of Stephanus applauded (16:15–16)
      (1) Their conversion (16:15a)
      (2) Their consecration (16:15b)
      (3) Their confirmation (16:16)
        (a) Paul endorsed their excellence (16:16a)
        (b) Paul endorsed their example (16:16b)
    b. The help of Stephanus applauded (16:17–18)
      (1) The coming of Stephanus and his group (16:17a)
      (2) The conduct of Stephanus and his group (16:17b–18a)
      (3) The commendation of Stephanus and his group (16:18b)
  3. Some parting comments (16:19–24)
    a. A word of greeting (16:19–21)
      (1) From the area (16:19–20)
        (a) From the churches (16:19)
        (b) From the Christians (16:20)
      (2) From the apostle (16:21)
    b. A word of guidance (16:22)
      (1) The Lord's curse (16:22a)
      (2) The Lord's coming (16:22b)
    c. A word of grace (16:23–24)
      (1) Paul's Lord (16:23)
      (2) Paul's love (16:24)

And so we come to *the conclusion* (1 Cor. 16:1–24), two dozen verses concerning needs, news, and notes from here and there down here. It seems a tame ending. We could wish that the Holy Spirit had left us at the end of chapter 15, with our heads still in the clouds. What a climax that would have been! We would have been looking for a sequel to tell us more about things to come. But no! We must come down from the mount, just as Peter, James, and John had to come down from the snowy heights of Hermon to face the trials and troubles of the world below. Yet we feel a sudden sympathy for Peter, who wanted to build some tabernacles and camp indefinitely within sight and sound of Glory!

One moment Paul is giving us a guided tour of some of the breath-taking mysteries of the universe, showing us marvels of which we had never even dreamed. The next moment he is talking about taking up a collection and of his future missionary plans, and the wonders of things to come suddenly seem far, far away. We need the balance.

If we had been writing this letter we would not have thrown away the thrilling climax of Rapture and Resurrection. We would put down our pens right there to leave the reader longing for more. If the mundane matters of chapter 16 had to be addressed, we would have found room for them somewhere else. The Holy Spirit has no need for such literary tricks. On the contrary, to Him, taking care of some impoverished believers in a far away land is as important and as interesting as electrifying truths about the world to come.

Paul begins his concluding chapter with *needs* (16:1–9). We note *his common sense about collections* (16:1–4). First, there is *the rule* (16:1–2). He writes, "Now concerning the collection for the saints, as I have given order to the churches of Galatia, even so do ye. Upon the first day of the week let every one of you lay by him in store, as God hath prospered him, that there be no gatherings when I come." Paul has in mind a collection of money for the impoverished believers at Jerusalem, which he was promoting throughout the various Gentile churches he had planted. These poor saints were ever on his mind. In his unconverted days, as a rabid persecutor of the church, he had made many of them poor. Now their faces haunted him. He longed to make amends. The collection of money for them occupies many a verse in Acts and in Paul's Epistles (Acts 11:29–30; 24:17; 1 Cor. 16:1–4; 2 Cor. 8:4; 9:1, 12; Gal. 2:10; Rom. 15:26). Paul saw this collection as one way the Gentiles in the church could repay part of their spiritual debt to the Jerusalem church. Moreover, he had promised the apostles at Jerusalem he would remember the poor (Gal. 2:10), and he was gladly discharging his pledge.

We do not know when Paul had given directions to the Galatian churches about giving. His orders seem to have been uniform throughout his churches and based on sound principles. To the Corinthians he cites the example of the Galatians, to the Macedonians he cites the example of the Corinthians, and to the Romans he cites the example of both the Macedonians and the Corinthians.

Two general rules emerge. There was to be nothing *haphazard* about their giving. It was to be done in a methodical and systematic way. They were to put something aside *par heautō* ,"at home," and store it there. Sunday by Sunday each member would make his contribution to the fund. No amount of percentage is stated. Each was to be guided by his income, circumstances, and personal exercise before the Lord.

Moreover there was to be no *high pressure* connected with their giving. "That there be no gatherings when I come." Paul did not want his commanding presence, persuasiveness, and personality to influence their giving. We can be sure that Paul had enough "sob stories" out of his own experience and enough skill in making an appeal as would have guaranteed a very large offering indeed. People would have been moved and swayed. They would have given impetuously and impulsively—and perhaps, afterward, regretted it. A great deal of modern "evangelism" uses high-pressure tactics to ensure extremely generous offerings. This kind of thing brings the Lord's work into disrepute and it displeases the Lord Himself. All giving, especially for special causes, should be done, not in the heat of the moment, but after careful and prayerful consideration of all the issues involved, in the calm atmosphere of our own homes.

Paul turns next to *the resolve* (1 Cor. 16:3–4). In the first place, *they should suggest* the men who should take their love gift to Jerusalem: "And when I come, whosoever ye shall approve by your letters" (16:3a). Some uncertainty seems to raise its head here as to exactly who would write these letters. Probably the Corinthians would choose the men they wanted to entrust with this mission of bounty and benevolence to Jerusalem, and Paul would himself add his own written accreditation and commendation. It is typical of Paul that he involves others as much as possible in the Lord's work. He was no dictator. He was the most autocratic of men when it came to matters of faith and morals. He knew when and where to draw the line. He was, however, the most democratic of men when it came to other matters of preference and procedure. After all, why shouldn't those who donated the money for the poor saints at Jerusalem have the say as to who should deliver it?

They should suggest the men. However, *he would send the men*. Indeed, he would not only *accredit* them but, possibly, he would *accompany* them: "Them will I send to bring your liberality unto Jerusalem. And if it be meet that I go also, they shall go with me" (16:3b–4). What a learning experience that would be. Imagine the prayer meetings and the Bible classes on board the boat. What an opportunity, not only to have Paul open the Scriptures day after day, but to ask him questions and learn of his plans and policies in the Lord's work. And, besides all that, to meet Christians and churches all along the way and learn more of the great heart of Paul for God's people everywhere. Nor would such a long journey be without opportunities for evangelism and soul-winning. Such a trip with such a teacher would be more valuable than six years in a seminary.

So much, then, for Paul's common sense about collections. We turn now to Paul and *his coming soon to Corinth* (16:5–9). He mentions, first, *his impending plans* (16:5–6). He tells them *when he would like to arrive:* "Now I will come unto you, when I shall pass through Macedonia: for I do pass through Macedonia" (16:5); and he tells them *what he would like to arrange:* "And it may be that I will abide, yea, and winter with you, that ye may bring me on my journey whithersoever I go" (16:6). At this point it seems that Paul planned to remain in Ephesus, where a revival was taking place, for a little longer at least. Then he would cross over into Macedonia, doubtless to visit and encourage the churches he had planted there at Philippi, Thessalonica, and Berea. From there he would come on to Corinth.

We learn from 2 Corinthians 1:15 that these plans were changed. Paul decided to visit Corinth twice. He would take a different route and visit Corinth, once on his way to Macedonia and again on his way back. Eventually that plan, too, was changed because of the explosive situation which developed in Ephesus. All this is most instructive as to how the Lord leads and guides in the life of a believer. Not even with a great apostle is everything cut and dried. God often uses our changing circumstances to indicate a change of plans and direction. Indeed, it is often easier to see how the Lord has led, looking back, than it is to discern how He is leading in the midst of life's pressures and problems. We must learn to acknowledge the Lord in all our ways and then rest confident in His sovereign overruling of circumstances to direct our paths (Prov. 3:6).

At this point, then, Paul hoped to come to Corinth and spend the winter, when any kind of travel was especially hazardous, with the Corinthians. These were his impending plans.

He mentions also *his immediate plans* (1 Cor. 16:7–9). For the time being he intended *to postpone his visit to Europe:* "For I will not see you now, by the way; but I trust to tarry a while with you, if the Lord permit" (16:7). Paul did not want to make his visit to Corinth just a flying visit. He very much wanted to spend some quality time with the Corinthian church. Letters, although they certainly serve important functions, and can be useful for putting things in writing so that there can be no mistake as to what was said, also have their drawbacks. They lack the stimulus of a face-to-face encounter. For now, a letter would have to do, however. Still, they could count on him coming as the Lord opened the door.

In the meantime, he intended *to prolong his visit in Ephesus* (16:9). It was *a place of great opportunities:* "For a great door and effectual is opened unto me" (16:9a); and *a place of great opposition:* "and there are many adversaries" (16:9b). Satan throws every obstacle he can in the way of effective Christian service. Never, since his conquest of Adam and Eve in the garden of Eden, has Satan feared and dreaded anything like he fears and dreads Christianity, Christ, and the church. He dare not relax. He cannot afford to neglect a single opportunity for hindering the onward march of the church. Well he knows it is "rooted in eternity, spread out through all time and space, and terrible as an army with banners."[18] In the church, Satan recognizes the most formidable obstacle to his plans ever mounted on this planet and one, moreover (since the church is seated with Christ in the heavenlies and energized and directed by the Holy Spirit Himself, the third Member of the Godhead), which has cosmic as well as global significance. It has been well said that "Satan trembles when he sees the weakest saint upon his knees." How much more must he have trembled at the apostleship, anointing, boldness, and determination of Paul. Lock the man up in prison and he converts his jailers and half of Nero's Praetorian guard; set him free and he evangelizes whole continents; persecute him and he draws still closer to the Lord; subvert his churches and he writes God-breathed letters that inspire and inform countless generations of Christians; kill him and you simply make a martyr and promote him to glory!

"A great door and effectual!" That was Paul's summary of the opportunities he was seizing at Ephesus. He had seen Holy Ghost revivals before, but nothing compared to what was happening there and of which Acts 19 records only the barest details. Not only the strategic city of Ephesus but all the surrounding hinterland was being reached. Churches were springing up far and wide. Places like Colossae, and Hierapolis, Smyrna, Pergamos, Thyatira, Sardis, Philadelphia, Laodicea, and Troas were all being taken by storm. Satan's kingdom was being shaken to its very foundations. Paul knew he had many adversaries and that he could expect a massive satanic counterattack before long. In the meantime the door of opportunity was still wide open and, much as he yearned to come to Corinth to comfort, correct, and confront, now was evidently not the time. For now the Corinthians would have to make do with this letter. Needs! It was a question of balancing one set of them against another and trusting the Holy Spirit, the true Lord of the harvest, to keep the Devil at bay and lead and direct His servant in His own infallible way.

---

18. See Lewis, *Screwtape Letters.*

Paul turns now to *news* (1 Cor. 16:10–12). First, Paul mentions a word about *his beloved Timothy* (16:10–11). Paul, it seems, had already dispatched Timothy and Erastus from Ephesus to Corinth. Erastus was an important convert. He was "the chamberlain of the city" (Corinth), that is, he was the city treasurer and, as such, a civil servant of great dignity and importance (Rom. 16:23; Acts 19:22). Doubtless Paul hoped that he would add considerable weight to young Timothy's presence when they arrived.

In any case, Paul paves the way for Timothy. Timothy was *a timid man*. Paul says, "Now if Timotheus come, see that he may be with you without fear: for he doeth the work of the Lord as I also do" (1 Cor. 16:10). Timothy and Erastus had taken the overland route to Corinth via Macedonia (Acts 19:22). Paul seems to have had some question in his mind as to whether he would make it all the way to Corinth. Since he was now writing the last two or three paragraphs of this letter, it was very likely it would arrive before Timothy did. The bearers of this letter would likely take ship to Corinth and could be expected to get there before Timothy in any case. Hence Paul's words here about his young ambassador. Doubtless Timothy, who was of a somewhat retiring disposition, felt keenly his personal inadequacy to confront the Corinthian intellectuals. Paul, however, was not counting on cleverness, he was counting on God.

Still, he smoothes Timothy's way as best he can. They were not to try to intimidate him. He might be a young man, but he and the great apostle were partners. In his own way young Timothy was as much the Lord's servant as was Paul. "Put him at ease!" Paul says, "Don't look down on him." Evidently, much as Paul appreciated Timothy's sterling worth, he was a bit afraid that the sophisticated Corinthians might try to bully him. The Corinthians, of course, knew Timothy. He had joined Paul there at the time Paul evangelized the city, having discharged a commission for Paul at Thessalonica.

For, if Timothy was a timid man, he was also *a true man* (1 Cor. 16:11). In this regard Paul has *a caution:* "Let no man therefore despise him"; and *a command:* "conduct him forth in peace"; and *a comment:* "that he may come unto me: for I look for him with the brethren." Just because a brother is young or inexperienced does not give anyone the right to despise him. The word for *despise* is *exoutheneō,* "to belittle," or "to treat with contempt." Paul wrote to Timothy along the same line. "Let no man despise thy youth; but be thou an example," he said (1 Tim. 4:12). The word is frequently translated "set at nought." It is found in the famous statement "This is the stone which was set at nought of you builders, which is become the head of the corner" (Acts 4:11). If carnal and worldly men so treated God's incarnate Son, it is not surprising that they sometimes treat God's servants the same way. It is very foolish to judge by outward appearances and to so lightly discount a humble, Spirit-filled believer, because of his age, because he has some impediment, because of his personal appearance or retiring disposition.

We can imagine what Timothy would be up against at Corinth. The church boasted an extraordinary number of very gifted and able men, howbeit carnal. Timothy would have to confront the intellectuals with their gnostic tendencies and sophisticated ideas. He would be up against the Cephas party, the legalists with all their rigid, pharisaical, and ritualistic tendencies and all their boast in the Law. There were those there who were impatient of anything short of sheer eloquence in the pulpit or private debate. There were those who were infatuated with the gift of tongues and who would be scornful of Paul's depreciation of the whole thing, not to mention the feminists who would be angry at Paul's instructions about the role of women in the church. So, one way or another, Timothy might well have been apprehensive of his ability to cope with the Corinthians.

"Hands off Timothy!" Paul warns them. "Don't forget I'm expecting him back here when he has discharged his commission over there. You'll have me to reckon with if you take out your resentments on him." "I look for him with the brethren," he adds. We cannot be sure which brethren he meant. Probably the reference is to the ones who conveyed this letter to Corinth. Paul seems to have expected that Timothy would meet up with them at Corinth or else meet them on their return journey somewhere in Macedonia. One of these brethren was Titus (2 Cor. 2:13; 7:6–7).

Paul now has a word about *his brother Apollos* (1 Cor. 16:12). We note *what Paul sought:* "As touching our brother Apollos, I greatly desired him to come unto you with the brethren" (16:12a). That is to say, he wanted him to be one of the party which took this letter to Corinth. Paul's relations with Apollos were friendly and quite free from jealousy. Evidently the Corinthians wanted Apollos to come. There were many of them who greatly admired his gift and eloquence. They doubtless suspected that Paul had refused their request because he was jealous of him or because he did not endorse all of his views. Paul was far too big and spiritual a man to be swayed by such considerations. On the contrary, Paul "greatly desired" Apollos to go. "I besought him much." The word for *desired* is *parakateō*, which means "to call aside," "to appeal to by way of exhortation." It would seem that Paul urged Apollos to go. He had every confidence in him.

Doubtless he had shared the contents of this letter with him. He could think of no better man to persuade the Corinthians to come to their senses.

We note, too, *what Paul saw:* "But his will was not at all to come at this time, but he will come when he shall have a convenient time" (16:12b). This was Apollos's own decision. Doubtless Apollos felt very keenly that his name had been abused by some of the Corinthians. He wanted no part of that party spirit in Corinth which was using his name to promote an alien cause. He decided it would be just as well if he stayed away from Corinth for now. Perhaps when Paul's letter had been read, digested, and had time to effect some changes he would go to Corinth. In the meantime it was his decision, not Paul's, which kept him away. This was all the more commendable in Apollos when it is remembered that he and Titus (one of the bearers of this letter) seem to have been close friends (Titus 3:13).

The letter closes with various *notes* (1 Cor. 16:13–24). First, Paul has *some practical comments:* "Watch ye, stand fast in the faith, quit you like men. Be strong. Let all things be done with charity" (16:13–14). The scene is a battlefield. The commander-in-chief is exhorting his troops on the brink of a decisive engagement. The lookouts and sentries are to keep a sharp lookout, the foe is very crafty and wholly unprincipled. When the assault comes, no ground must be yielded. The enemy will be swift to seize, occupy, and exploit any retreat. Bravery and courage must be the watchword. They must be men! And they must be strong. There is no room for weakness now.

The Zulu warlord Chaka was one of the greatest warriors of all time, and the military organization he evolved was one of the most efficient the world has ever seen. It was Chaka who invented it and directed it. At the commencement of the nineteenth century he was the ruler of a very small tribe. When he fell beneath the assegais of his brothers Umhlangana and Dingaan, all southeastern Africa was at his feet, and more than a million people were dead.

In the first volume of his trilogy on the Zulus, Sir Henry Rider Haggard tells how it was the Zulu warriors became so invincible. He has Mopo, the king's head witchdoctor, tell the tale.

"Never may I forget the first fight I stood by the side of Chaka. It was just after the king had built his great kraal on the south bank of the Umhlatuze. Then it was that the chief Zwide attacked his rival Chaka for the third time and Chaka moved out to meet him with ten full regiments (about 30,000 men), now for the first time armed with the short stabbing spear."

Mopo describes the lie of the land and the preparations for the coming battle.

He describes the spears "numberless as the stars," and the rising of the sun and how it dyed the spears red.

"Suddenly Chaka was seen stalking through the ranks, followed by his captains, his indunas, and by me. He walked along like a great buck, death was in his eyes, and, like a buck, he sniffed the air, scenting the air of slaughter. He lifted up his assegai, and a silence fell, only the sound of chanting still rolled along the hills.

"'Where are the children of Zwide?' he shouted, and his voice was like the voice of a bull.

"'Yonder, father,' answered the regiments. And every spear pointed across the valley.

"'They do not come,' he shouted again. 'Shall we then sit here till we grow old?'

"'No, father,' they answered, 'Begin! Begin!'

"'Let the Umkhandhlu regiment come forward,' he shouted a third time, and as he spoke the black shields of the Umkhandhlu leaped from the ranks of the impi.

"'Go, my children!' cried Chaka. 'There is the foe. Go and return no more!'

"'We hear you, father!' they answered with one voice, and moved down the slope like a countless herd of game with horns of steel.

"Now they crossed the stream, and now Zwide awoke. A murmur went through his companies; lines of light played above his spears.

"*Ou!* they are coming! *Ou!* they have met! Hearken to the thunder of the shields! Hearken to the song of battle!

"To and fro they swing. The Umkhandhlu gives way—it flies! They pour back across the stream—half of them; the rest are dead. A howl of rage goes up from the host, only Chaka smiles.

"'Open up! open up!' he cries. 'Make room for the Umkhandhlu *girls!*' And with hanging heads they pass behind us."

Mopo describes the remainder of the battle. He describes how the outcome of the battle swung in the balance. He describes the final victory over the host of Zwide.

"The host of Zwide was no more. Ten regiments had looked upon the morning sun; three regiments saw the sun sink; the rest had gone where no suns shine.

"Such were our battles in the days of Chaka.

"You ask of the Umkhandhlu regiment which fled. I will tell you. When we reached our kraal once more, Chaka summoned that regiment and mustered it. He spoke to them gently, gently. He thanked them for their service. He said it was natural that 'girls' should faint at the sight of blood and turn to seek their kraals. Yet he had bid them come back no more and they had come back! What then was there now left for him to do? And he covered his face with his blanket. Then the soldiers killed them all, nearly two thousand of them—killed them with taunts and jeers.

"That is how we dealt with cowards in those days. After that, one Zulu was a match for five of any other tribe."[19]

"Quit ye like men!" says Paul. "Watch! Stand! Be men! Be strong!" If men can be men in a human cause, surely they can be so in a heavenly cause. If wild African kaffirs can be men, not "girls," surely we can quit ourselves like *men* in the cause of Christ. Men in understanding (1 Cor. 1:20) and men in undertaking, too. The trouble with the Corinthians was that, for all their great gifts and potential, they were children (13:11). Paul reminds them again that love is the ultimate measure of the man.

Now come *some personal comments* (16:15–18). First, *the house of Stephanas is applauded* (16:15–16). Paul mentions *their conversion:* "I beseech you, brethren, (ye know the house of Stephanas, that it is the firstfruits of Achaia)" (16:15a). Stephanas was a Corinthian and among the very first of Paul's converts in the Greek peninsula. He was one of the few people Paul personally baptized (1:16). This should have given him status in the Corinthian church. There may have been some smoldering resentment among the Corinthian believers who may have thought that Stephanas had been telling Paul tales about them.

Paul mentions also *their consecration:* "They have addicted themselves to the ministry of the saints" (16:15b). What a blessed addiction! The word *tassō* means to be under authority (Luke 7:8). They were not "ordained" for this ministry by Paul or anyone else. They were appointed to it by the Holy Spirit. They had made up their minds to devote their lives to looking after the Lord's people. That is the idea behind Paul's words.

Paul mentions also *their confirmation.* He himself thoroughly endorsed their commitment to the cause of Christ: "[I beseech you, brethren,] that ye submit yourselves unto such, and to everyone that helpeth with us, and laboureth" (1 Cor. 16:16). Such men, regardless of their worldly status, were ranked among the aristocracy of the Christian faith. All such ministers, helpers, and workers ought to be heeded and helped by the church. Paul was always eager to endorse and encourage those who were active in the Lord's work.

---

19. H. Rider Haggard, *Nada the Lily* (London: MacDonald, 1958), 48–52.

Then, too, *the help of Stephanas is applauded:* "I am glad of the coming of Stephanas and Fortunatus and Achaicus: for that which was lacking on your part they have supplied. For they have refreshed my spirit and yours: therefore acknowledge ye them that are such" (16:17–18). Paul's love had no room for evil thoughts (13:5). On the contrary, the financial gift given to him by these three brethren met a real need in his life. This had not only greatly cheered him, he was sure the Corinthians would be glad to know that. No rebuke, open or veiled, is intended by Paul's words. He was not reproaching the Corinthians for failing to support him in the Lord's work. Paul was not like that. He had long since learned to look to God, not to man, for his financial needs. The words *that which was lacking on your part* can be rendered "the void caused by your absence," or "they have made up for my not seeing you." Fortunatus and Achaicus were colleagues of Stephanas. Fortunatus, if we can judge by his name, was a Roman. All three carried this epistle to Corinth. All three refreshed Paul's spirit by bringing him news (not all bad, surely) of the Corinthians. They would refresh the spirit of the Corinthians, too, by being the means of bringing this letter to them.

Paul now has *some parting comments* as he draws this lengthy letter to a close (16:19–24). First, there is *a word of greeting* (16:19–21). There is a word of greeting *from the area* (16:19–20)—*from the churches:* "The churches of Asia salute you. Aquila and Priscilla salute you much in the Lord, with the church that is in their house" (16:19). The *Asia* to which Paul refers here was the Roman province of which Ephesus was the capital and most important city. Paul had wanted to evangelize this whole, strategic area on his second missionary journey.

We can imagine how his whole soul was kindled at the prospect. He had come to Troas and could go no farther. Before him lay the Aegean Sea. Only four miles away was the Plain of Troy, and Paul was scholar enough to have heard, from Homer's immortal song, and from his history books, how Europe and Asia had battled there. Not far off the Persian king Xerxes had sat on a marble throne to review the 3 million men he had brought from far-off lands in the hope of conquering Greece. Beyond the Aegean lay Greece and Rome, from whence culture and imperial might emanated and held the world in thrall.

Paul longed to bring Asia Minor under the sway of the gospel. Instead, God had sent him to Europe. Now he was back in Asia, and churches were springing up everywhere. These churches sent brotherly greetings to the church at Corinth.

One of the Asian churches met in the home of Aquila and Priscilla. This godly Jewish couple had played no small part in the founding of the churches both in Corinth and in Ephesus. The mention of their names would evoke many a memory of Paul's evangelistic efforts in Corinth, for he had stayed with them and had worked alongside them at his tent-making trade (Acts 18:1–2). When his work at Corinth was finished this faithful couple accompanied Paul as far as Ephesus. They remained there, while Paul went on to Galatia and Antioch, to prepare the ground for his promised return (18:18–28). They must have had many friends in the Corinthian church. By evoking their names and sending their many greetings, Paul was doubtless hoping to revive memories of those earlier and happier days when the Corinthians themselves were still in the first bloom of their new life in Christ.

There were also greetings to be conveyed *from the Christians:* "All the brethren greet you. Greet ye one another with a holy kiss" (1 Cor. 16:20). "A hearty handshake all around, please!" is the way one translator paraphrases that. That, in itself, might be useful in breaking down rapidly rising barriers between the various factions. An embrace was a common form of greeting in Paul's day, as it is even today in some countries. To guard against abuse, Paul called for "a holy kiss," *(hagios),* a kiss free from anything inconsistent with being a Christian.

There is not only a word of greeting from the area, there is a word of greeting *from the apostle:* "The salutation of me Paul with mine own hand" (16:21). With the exception of Galatians, Paul's letters seem to have been dictated, and transcribed by an amanuensis, a secretary (Rom. 16:22; Gal. 6:11; Col. 4:18). It is widely believed that Paul's "thorn in the flesh" (2 Cor. 12:7) was a form of ophthalmia, resulting from the blinding light he had seen on the Damascus road, and the resulting blindness (Acts 9:3, 9, 12–17). Hence his need to use secretaries. However, he usually signed the letters himself and sometimes added a parting comment. There were forgeries abroad, which led Paul to tell the Thessalonians that henceforth he intended to personally sign all his letters to authenticate them (2 Thess. 2:2; 3:17). It was especially important, in the case of this letter, that he sign it. There must be no possible ground for his detractors at Corinth to deny that he had written this critically important letter.

The word of greeting is now followed by *a word of guidance* (1 Cor. 16:22). The Corinthians are reminded of the Lord's *curse* and of the Lord's *coming:* "If any man love not the Lord Jesus Christ, let him be Anathema, Maranatha!" Paul has already used that word *anathema* in this letter. "No man speaking by the Spirit of God calleth Jesus *accursed*" (12:3). The word for *love* here is *phileō,* used only here by Paul. He normally uses the higher word *agapaō.* It is a serious thing not to love the Lord. Paul surely is not invoking a curse in this life on the Christ rejecter. But if a man does not love the Lord, there is no hope for him at last. This is not an imprecation, but a sad and solemn statement of fact.

Anathema is a Greek word. Paul drops it at once and, to emphasize the contrast, breaks into Aramaic. "Maranatha!" he exclaimed. "The Lord cometh!" That was the thought with which he wanted to leave them. In view of all their divisions and disorders and doubts, what better way could he have closed this letter? Let them go back to the beginning. Let them read it again, chapter by chapter, verse by verse, line by line. Let them read it with this thought uppermost in their minds, as they ponder each paragraph and weigh each God-breathed word— "The Lord cometh."

And last, *a word of grace* (16:23–24). Paul closes with *a word about his Lord:* "The grace of our Lord Jesus Christ be with you" (16:23). Thus Paul closes all his letters. Paul begins and ends his letters with this word. He would leave them with thoughts of the Savior as Master, as Man, and as Messiah. He would leave them with thoughts of His grace.

He leaves them with *a word about his love:* "My love be with you all in Christ Jesus. Amen" (16:24). Yes, he had found it necessary to scold them and to correct them. Now let them go back and read again the thirteenth chapters of this letter. That is what he means when he tells them he loves them in Christ.

Appendix

The historical background of Paul's two surviving letters to the Corinthians is one of great interest; it is also one of considerable controversy. The letters themselves contain references to correspondence and to visits, actual and proposed. It is no easy matter to keep them sorted out in one's mind. Here is a suggested sequence of events:

1. Paul arrived in Corinth from Athens while on his second missionary journey. He had been scourged at Philippi, chased out of Thessalonica and Berea, and laughed out of court at Athens. When he arrived in Corinth he was alone, and under considerable stress. He had sent his colleagues Silas and Timothy back to Macedonia to strengthen and encourage the fledgling Macedonian churches he had just planted there. Nevertheless, he saw the immense importance of Corinth and began, right away, to evangelize this city.

2. Paul stayed in Corinth for eighteen months (A.D. 50–51), and his ministry was crowned with success.[1] Although the bulk of his converts came from the lower classes, he did win a number of notable citizens to Christ as well. His ministry at Corinth appears to have overflowed to the nearby seaport of Cenchrea, where a church was started, and possibly to other places in the area as well.

3. On July 1, A.D. 51, Gallio, a noble Roman with high contacts, arrived in Corinth to be the proconsul of the Roman province of Achaia. The leading Jews of Corinth, infuriated by Paul's successes, tried to prosecute Paul

---

1. Authorities differ as to the actual date suggested in this summary.

before Gallio on the charge of propagating an illegal religion. Gallio contemptuously threw the case out of court and turned a blind eye to some consequent anti-Semitic mob violence. Gallio's court ruling was in keeping with the general attitude of fair play shown by Roman officials in the empire's earliest contacts with Christianity.

4. Paul left Corinth, from the port of Cenchrea, probably in the spring of A.D. 52. While at Cenchrea, he appears to have become ill and Phoebe seems to have had a share in nursing him at this time (Rom. 16:1–2). About this time, too, Paul made a vow, perhaps in connection with his illness, which involved shaving his head (Acts 18:18).

5. The church Paul left behind at Corinth soon fell into disarray. Rivalries and squabbles broke out. A Judaizing cult took root. Pride, lawsuits, confusion, abuse of spiritual gifts, and immorality all raised their heads.

6. Meanwhile Paul was on his way to Jerusalem. He stopped briefly at Ephesus on his way and, sensing a receptive spirit in the synagogue, he left his colleagues Aquila and Priscilla there to prepare the ground against the time of his return. While he was away, Apollos visited Ephesus, was well received, and was encouraged to go on to Corinth, which he did.

7. Paul arrived at Jerusalem on this, his fourth visit to the city, and was coldly received. Jerusalem seemed to draw him as a magnet, despite the fact that he was mistrusted there by the Jewish believers and hated by the religious authorities.

8. He left Jerusalem and returned to Antioch to make preparations for his third missionary journey. He was now about fifty-two years of age. Only eight years later he could describe himself as "Paul the aged." Hardship, sickness, and persecution were already leaving their indelible mark.

9. Paul now made for Ephesus, where he remained for three years (Acts 20:1, 31) and where he had remarkable success.

10. Some time during his ministry at Ephesus he received disturbing news from Corinth. Some of the believers there had not made a complete break with immorality, a lifestyle taken as the norm in that pagan city.

11. Paul wrote the Corinthian church a letter (1 Cor. 5:9–11), of which no trace now remains. In it he warned the Christians to have no fellowship with fornicators. For the sake of convenience we can call this "the lost letter." It would not have been difficult for Paul either to have received this news or to have responded to it since communication between Corinth and Ephesus was easy and frequent enough both by land and sea.

12. This lost letter seems to have prompted a reply. Either by means of a letter or else as a result, perhaps, of a visit to Paul by some members of Chloe's household (perhaps a house-church), questions were raised.

13. Paul responded by commencing to write the epistle we now call 1 Corinthians. To distinguish it from other Corinthian correspondence we can call this letter "the long letter"—indeed, it is the longest of Paul's letters. It seems to have been written in stages. It begins with a reproach for their shortcomings and with a promise that he would visit them soon. In the meantime, he would send Timothy—indeed, Timothy may already have left.

14. By the time Paul had written chapters 1–4, he received another communication from Corinth in the form of a letter, seemingly brought by Stephanus, Fortunatus, and Achaicus (1 Cor. 16:17). In this letter the Corinthians assured Paul that they remembered his teaching and were going to do as he said. They also raised a number of further questions about marriage, about meat offered to idols, about spiritual gifts, and about the collection Paul was raising for the impoverished Jerusalem church.

15. If Paul found grounds for anxiety in this letter, they were nothing compared with the story his visitors had to tell. There were things hypocritically passed over in silence by the Corinthians in their letter. The church was rent by schisms. Worse still, there were grave scandals, severe disorders, and, above all, flagrant disregard of even the most common standards of decency and morality. So Paul added more chapters to his letter. He dealt with the verbal reports he had received about their moral and monetary disorders (chaps. 5–6), and finally answered their questions one by one (chaps. 7–16). When it was finished the letter was taken to Corinth, probably by Stephanus and his associates.

16. This long letter, dictated in stages, probably took several weeks to complete. It was finished sometime before Pentecost (1 Cor. 16:8) during Paul's last year in Ephesus (probably A.D. 55).

17. It seems that Paul planned to remain in Ephesus for a little while longer, probably until Pentecost. Then he envisioned a trip to Macedonia. He would remain there during the summer and fall months and go on from there to Corinth, where he would possibly spend the winter of A.D. 55–56 (1 Cor. 16:5–9).

18. But then he changed his mind. He would visit Corinth twice. He would

visit there on his way to Macedonia and he would return there on his way back from Macedonia. Then he would embark for Judea (2 Cor. 1:15). He hoped that by then the collection for the Judean churches would be complete and that he could take it with him when he went to Jerusalem.

19. Then there was still another change of plans. A fresh crisis had raised its head in Corinth. The long letter to the Corinthians had not accomplished its purpose and Timothy, who was no Paul, unable to quell the growing revolt, probably returned to Paul about this time, full of bad news.

20. Paul seems to have made a flying visit to Corinth (the second visit referred to in 2 Cor. 13:2). It proved to be a stormy one, painful for both Paul and his converts. The incipient rebellion against Paul and his authority appears to have come to a head. It seems to have been led by one man in particular. With remarkable restraint (for the power vested in an apostle was awesome, as Simon Magus and Elymas the sorcerer both learned) Paul appears simply to have left, for the time being leaving the situation still unresolved.

21. However, the Corinthians had by no means heard the last of him. When he arrived back at Ephesus he wrote them another letter, also missing from our New Testament.[2] This latest letter was sharp and threatening but drenched with tears (2 Cor. 2:3; 7:12). Since he seems to have regretted sending it the moment it was on its way, we can call this letter "the lamented letter."

22. The bearer of this letter seems to have been Titus, a colleague of Paul of tougher fiber than Timothy. Judging from hints dropped here and there in our canonical 2 Corinthians, Paul almost seems to have wished he had not written it. His deep and sincere expressions of love for the Corinthians were mingled with dire warnings, directed primarily against the man who led the opposition to him. It would seem, too, that before dispatching Titus with this fiery letter he had told his young friend that the gold of the Corinthians' love for him was genuine enough. Now that the letter was gone beyond recall, he seems to have had second thoughts, even about that. A severe depression came over the apostle.

23. As though this were not enough, Paul now found himself in terrible danger. He was belabored by fears within and fightings without. Indeed, the

---

2. Indeed there must be a voluminous Pauline correspondence of which no trace remains, just as the book of Acts gives us but the barest details of Paul's travels, sermons, sufferings, successes, and miracles.

threatening outward circumstances were so severe that Paul seems to have despaired of his very life (2 Cor. 1:8–9). More, his escape was so remarkable he saw it as a veritable resurrection from the dead (vv. 9–10).

24. From Ephesus, Paul went to Troas, evidently hoping Titus would show up with news from Corinth. He saw great opportunities for evangelism in that strategic city, and it says much for his state of mind that he was too unsettled to take advantage of them. Instead he appears to have waited at Troas, straining his eyes for a ship from across the Aegean to bring Titus and news. The onset of winter made it certain Titus would not come that way, so Paul headed north, taking the land route toward Macedonia.

25. Then Titus came! And had good news, too! The offending brother had been dealt with, so much so, indeed, he was in danger of being overwhelmed.

26. Paul seized his pen again, this time to write the epistle we call 2 Corinthians, and which, for the sake of clarity, we can call "the last letter." He began to pour out his heart.

27. But then the full story came out. It seems there was another side to the picture. Paul still had enemies. His change of plans over visiting Corinth was still being held against him as proof of his fickleness and cowardice. Disparaging remarks were being made about his lack of eloquence, his personal appearance, and the fact that he had no letter of commendation from the mother church in Jerusalem. He was wily, dishonest, inferior. It was even being said by some that he was mad.

28. Paul put down his pen. He seized it again. The startling difference in tone, beginning with chapter 10, has been noticed by all. Varied are the explanations. Some have even suggested that chapters 10–13 constitute yet another and a later letter, or, perhaps, a surviving fragment of Paul's earlier lamented letter.

29. There is a better explanation. The more Titus talked, the more evident it became that there were two factions still at Corinth. There was the majority party and the minority party. The majority were on Paul's side and were full of goodwill toward him. The minority party was made up of the Judaizers and their adherents. Chapters 1–9 appear to have the majority in mind. They are buoyant and conciliatory. Chapters 10–13 seem to have the minority in mind. They are sad and severe. Indeed, these chapters may well have been written after a pause in composition, after Paul had allowed himself sufficient time to digest the additional information leaked out by Titus.

30. When the letter was finally finished it was taken to Corinth, probably early in A.D. 56, by Titus and two other of Paul's colleagues, of whom one seems to have been Luke (2 Cor. 8:6, 16–19, 22–23).

31. In the meantime, Paul seems to have visited Illyricum (Rom. 15:19). Luke barely mentions this in Acts, simply saying that Paul "came into Greece." Paul then went back to Corinth, where he stayed for about three months as the guest of Gaius (16:23).

32. Things seem to have calmed down by this time, for Paul was able to compose his mind and write his monumental epistle to the Romans. Perhaps Paul was able to sense that his missionary days were drawing to a close and that it was high time for him to commit his gospel preaching to writing. When it was finished, Paul entrusted this priceless manuscript to Phoebe, his friend, a deaconess of the church at Anchrea, to take to Rome for him.

33. Meanwhile, Paul's presence in Corinth was not overlooked by his old synagogue foes. Gallio had rebuffed them on the occasion of Paul's first visit. They would get him this time. Somehow they received word that Paul was planning to be a passenger on a ship (possibly a pilgrim ship) bound from Cenchrea for Palestine. They hatched a plot. Paul would either be murdered at Cenchrea or, if he succeeded on embarking on the boat, at a convenient time he would be thrown overboard. Evidently Paul learned of the scheme because he changed his plans. Instead of sailing from Cenchrea, he took the overland northern route by way of Philippi (Acts 20:3). Another "change of mind" for the Corinthians to think about indeed!

Paul never lost sight of the fact that the Corinthian Christians were his own children in the faith, and he never stopped loving them. Read, for instance, Paul's great poem on love (1 Cor. 13). That was how he viewed the Corinthians. Many were carnal when they should have been spiritual;, many were worldly when they should have been heavenly; many had listened to lies, but they were still his children. He loved them with a love only rivaled by the love of Christ Himself.

Explore the

BIBLE

in greater depth with the
John Phillips
Commentary Series!